ALEXANDER DOVZHENKO

A LIFE IN SOVIET FILM

GEORGE O. LIBER

 Publishing

For Deborah and Jessica

First published in 2002 by the
British Film Institute
21 Stephen Street, London W1T 1LN

The British Film Institute is the UK national agency with
responsibility for encouraging the arts of film and television
and conserving them in the national interest.

© George O. Liber 2002

Cover images: (front, clockwise) Alexander Dovzhenko (*c*. 1921–3); Dovzhenko and father (late
1930s); *Earth* (Alexander Dovzhenko, 1930); *The Diplomatic Pouch* (Alexander Dovzhenko, 1927);
Earth: (back, clockwise) *Shchors* (Alexander Dovzhenko, 1939); *Arsenal* (Alexander Dovzhenko, 1928);
Earth; Dovzhenko and amateur theatre troupe (1912). Images courtesy of the Central State Archive of
Film, Photo and Phonographic Documents of Ukraine, Kiev.

Set by Fakenham Photosetting, Norfolk
Printed in the UK by St Edmundsbury Press, Suffolk

British Library Cataloguing-in-Publication Data
A catalogue record for this book is available from the British Library

ISBN 0–85170–927–3 (hbk)

Contents

Acknowledgments

This project began in the spring of 1994, when I taught a course entitled 'Soviet Film and Society' at the University of Alabama at Birmingham (UAB). I developed the course chronologically and showed ten of the most important Soviet films produced from 1925 to 1946 available on video. In a telephone conversation with Dominique Arel, I mentioned that I had enjoyed watching Alexander Dovzhenko's *Zvenyhora*, *Arsenal* and *Earth*, and how these films differed radically from those of Eisenstein, Vertov and Pudovkin. Dominique then suggested that I write a biography of Dovzhenko, using him to focus on the dilemmas of the Soviet and Soviet Ukrainian intelligentsia in the first half of the twentieth century. I accepted his suggestion with great enthusiasm. Even though this project has taken various twists and turns over the past seven years, I am still grateful to Dominique and to Maria Salomon Arel for their support and encouragement.

In the summer of 1994, I met Vance Kepley, Jr., the author of the superb *In the Service of the State: The Cinema of Alexander Dovzhenko* (Madison: University of Wisconsin Press, 1986). He has been very supportive of my project from the start and has been very generous with his advice and comments. Unlike Kepley's monograph, mine analyses Dovzhenko's life rather than his films. Readers seeking more in-depth evaluations of Dovzhenko's cinematography than the one that appears in this text should consult Kepley's work, as well as dissertations by Bohdan Nebesio and Ray Uzwyshyn.

In addition to Vance, Paul Goble, Mark L. Von Hagen, Liah Greenfeld and Paul A. Bushkovitch generously wrote letters of recommendation on my behalf to various funding agencies and organisations. Thanks to them and to Jerry F. Hough, I received internal and external funding at critical stages in the book's evolution. The Duke University Center on East–West Trade, Investment, and Communications, together with Jerry, sent me in the summer of 1991 on a two-month trip to Moscow and Kiev, where I gained access to archives and specialised collections which had previously been unavailable to me. Most importantly, the contacts that I made in 1991 proved critical in my starting and completing this project.

The International Research and Exchanges Board (IREX) funded my and my family's eleven-month stay in Moscow and Kiev during the 1995–6 academic year. UAB gave me a year-long sabbatical during the 1996–7 academic year, when I wrote the first rough draft of this book. The American Council of Teachers of Russian

(ACTR) paid for a ten-week stay in Moscow and Kiev in the summer of 1998. In December 1998, I spent three weeks at the Kennan Institute for Advanced Russian Studies in Washington DC on a short-term grant. I am very grateful to these institutions for their generous financial support.

At UAB, thanks to the efforts of my chair in 1994–5, James L. Penick, Jr., the Dean of the School of Social and Behavioral Sciences, Tennant S. McWilliams, granted me approval to take a leave of absence to accept the IREX grant for the 1995–6 academic year and to enjoy my first sabbatical the following year. Despite their initial misgivings, I am very grateful to them. Debbie Givens, the administrative associate of the History Department, skilfully negotiated UAB's bureaucratic mazes to provide me with funding for those two years. There are no bureaucratic fortresses she cannot storm successfully. Most importantly, when I taught she assigned me afternoon and evening classes, which freed up my mornings for writing. My current chair, Raymond A. Mohl, generously approved a line in the History Department's meagre budget to cover the costs of touching up a set of thirty-five photographs and the burning of two CD-ROMS with camera-ready photographs. He also generously relieved me from teaching one course during the autumn 2000 quarter.

This work builds on the books, articles and dissertations prepared by Ivan Koshelivets, Roman Korohodsky, Mykola Kutsenko, Vance Kepley, Jr., Marco Carynnyk, Bohdan Nebesio and Raymond John Uzwyshyn (see Bibliography). Without their efforts, often under adverse political circumstances, this book would not have seen the light of day. I am very grateful to them, especially for Korohodsky's insights, Kutsenko's chronology (however incomplete due to censorship regulations) of Dovzhenko's life and Nebesio's bibliography. The insights and reference tools paved my way. Although I have attempted to uncover all of the blank spots in Dovzhenko's life and political career as a film-maker, I am still unable to answer all of the questions posed by Marco Carynnyk ('Na pozharyshchakh velykoi materi vdovytsi', *Novyny kinoekranu*, no. 9 [1990] and no. 10 [1990]) and Ivan Koshelivets ('Pro zatemneni mistia v biohrafii Oleksandra Dovzhenka', *Dnipro*, nos 9–10 [1994]).

In the course of this monograph's long march from first draft to final product, I have incurred large intellectual and collegial debts, which I hope to repay in the future. I wish to express my gratitude to everyone who took precious time from their own work to advise me and to provide me with constructive criticisms. Mark Baker, Lance Gunnin, Ken Holmsley, Elena Zheltova, Roman Korohodsky and Taras Dudko (Dovzhenko's nephew) read my first (1997) draft. Josephine Woll, David Brandenberger, Vance Kepley, Jr., Hiroaki Kuromiya, Yuri Tsivian, Serhy Yekelchyk and Raymond John Uzwyshyn read the 2000 drafts; David Saunders, Richard Taylor, Serhii Zhuk, Yuri Tsivian, Michael Selivatchov and Dawn Charlton read the 2001 drafts.

In addition to the above-mentioned, I am grateful to R. N. Iurenev, M. P. Vlasov, Yuri Shapoval, Natalia Chernysh, Emily D. Johnson, Wendy Z. Goldman, Tatiana Derevianko (the director of the Dovzhenko Film Studios Museum), Natalie Kononenko, Julie Locher, Elena Kravchuk, Angela Cannon, Walter Brandner MD and Jean-Richard Bodon for reading sections of the book and/or answering specific questions. Vitaly and Larissa Charny kindly translated my ACTR application into Russian. I would like to thank M. N. Guboglo and Irina Zheltova for acting as my hosts in Moscow. Orest Pelech, the Slavic Bibliographer at Duke University's Perkins Library cheerfully responded to my many questions bibliographic and otherwise. Liz Papazian made me rethink socialist realism and helped me to translate Kozintsev's quote at the beginning of the book into idiomatic English. Irina Grashchenkova gave me copies of Dovzhenko's letters to Elena Chernova and copies of the film-maker's drawings (which appear in Chapter 5).

In Kiev, Natalia Viatkina and Lesia Atamaniuk of ACTR/ACCELS helped explain the current intellectual trends in Ukraine, as did Svitlana Kasianova, a fellow Dovzhenko scholar. I am very grateful to Lesya and her family for acting as my hosts in Zhytomyr.

In addition to the archives listed in the bibliography, I worked at the Russian State Library (the former Lenin Library) and the Russian Historical Library in Moscow; at the Museum of the Dovzhenko Film Studios and the Vernadsky Library of the Ukrainian Academy of Sciences in Kiev; and at the Dovzhenko Museum in Sosnytsia, Chernihiv Province. In the United States, I worked at the Library of Congress and the Regenstein Library at the University of Chicago. I am grateful to the staffs of all of these libraries for their patience and persistence.

UAB's Sterne Library has been my home for fourteen years. In addition to Bonnie Ledbetter, the Social Sciences librarian, who has always cheerfully procured the books I ordered and who has always been very helpful, I am also grateful to Eddie Luster and to Rebecca Narramore of the Interlibrary Loan Department. Without these three colleagues, my ambassadors to the intellectual world outside Birmingham, I would have been unable to fill in my monograph's blanks.

Mike Bennighof ruthlessly edited the 1999 drafts and Amy Shields meticulously edited those produced in 2000 and 2001. Mike and Amy played critical roles in shaping this book. They patiently listened to my monologues and plans, encouraged the best from me, and deleted the worst. Both, in their own unique way, facilitated my intellectual development over the course of this project. Both also served as my psychotherapists. Wendy Gunther-Canada, my intellectual sounding board over the past seven years, always provided excellent, well-measured advice.

Last but certainly not least important, Michelle Devins miraculously (and efficiently!) transformed my WordPerfect 5.1 text into MS Word and reformatted it according to BFI specifications at the midnight hour. I am very grateful for her professionalism and good humour. She patiently taught me how to master Word. Bill Bradley and Suzanne Scivley provided technical support at a very critical period.

If the number of those I consulted competes with the cast of a Cecil B. DeMille movie, so be it. I have learned much from everyone and this book is the better for it. Notwithstanding these long lists of friends, colleagues and advisers, I must add that I alone am responsible for the opinions and interpretations expressed in this monograph.

Parts of this book have previously appeared as articles in *Harvard Ukrainian Studies*, *KINEMA*, *Europe-Asia Studies* and *Australian Slavic and East European Studies*, and as sections from my first monograph, *Soviet Nationality Policy, Urban Growth, and Identity Change in the Ukrainian SSR, 1923–1934*. I am grateful to the editors of these journals and to Cambridge University Press for permission to use this published material.

I would also like to express thanks to the Ukrainian Archival Administration and to its deputy director, Volodymyr Lozytsky, for allowing me the right to publish the majority of the photographs and to the Russian State Archive of Cinema and Photography at Krasnogorsk to publish the photo of Dovzhenko and Khrushchev.

I extend my appreciation to the Canadian Institute of Ukrainian Studies and to the *Journal of Ukrainian Studies* for permission to cite passages from Marco Carynnyk's translation of Dovzhenko's 1939 autobiography (*Journal of Ukrainian Studies*, 19, no. 1 [1994]); to the MIT Press for permission to cite passages from Marco Carynnyk's edition of *Alexander Dovzhenko: The Poet as Filmmaker: Selected Writings* (Cambridge, MA: MIT Press, 1973); and to Yale University Press to cite an English translation of a diary passage from William Taubman, Sergei Khrushchev and Abbott Gleason, eds, *Nikita Khrushchev* (New Haven: Yale University Press, 2000).

I am grateful to Deborah Gardner Liber and to Jessica Hope Gardner Liber for accompanying me to Dovzhenko's homeland and for their constant love and support over the past seven years. They have patiently waited for the end of this project. Although this book is their book, I still owe them a trip to the Bahamas.

In the course of this project many wonderful people offered me help and encouragement, but did not live to see its completion. I would like to remember my father, Miroslav Liber, Marta Hladun, Nicholas Hnatyk, Inna Pustelnyk, Olena Korohodska, Irina Grashchenkova, Sulamif Tsybulnyk, Tom Renehan, Susan Renda and Voytek Zubek. May they rest in peace.

Birmingham, Alabama
15 September 2001

Note on Transliteration

Transliteration from the Cyrillic to the Roman alphabet presents a serious dilemma for all writers dealing with East Slavic topics. Writers must balance the two principal requirements of transliteration. On the one hand, they need to convey to the reader who does not speak Russian or Ukrainian a reasonable approximation of the original pronunciations. On the other hand, they should render an accurate representation of the original Russian or Ukrainian spelling for the specialist. Inasmuch as some of the Russian and Ukrainian names have a non-Russian origin or an accepted English spelling that does not follow the above-mentioned requirements (such as Eisenstein), this situation prevents the adoption of a completely consistent system of transliteration.

In dealing with these problems, I have opted for a dual system. In the text I have transliterated in a way that will make, I hope, Russian and Ukrainian names and terms more accessible to the non-specialist. In the notes and bibliography, however, I have adhered to a more accurate and consistent system for the specialist.

I have followed a modified version of the Library of Congress system for Russian and Ukrainian in transliterating Slavic words and proper names, but I have eliminated the soft sign in the text (but not in the notes and bibliography). I have used accepted English spellings of Russian and Ukrainian names wherever possible (such as Trotsky, Eisenstein and Hrushevsky, instead of Trotskii, Eizenshtein and Hrushevs'kyi). When transliterating personal names, I replaced the 'Ie' and 'Iu' vowels with 'Ye' and 'Yu' when they appeared as the first letter of a person's name; I replaced the 'ii' (Russian) and 'yi' (Ukrainian) endings with a 'y' ending. In order to remain accessible to a broader audience, I used Alexander (not Oleksandr), Julia (not Iuliia) and Barbara (not Varvara) for Dovzhenko and his wives.

In transliterating geographic designations in the Ukrainian Soviet Socialist Republic, I have followed closely the usage standardised in *Map and Gazetteer of Ukraine* (Toronto, 1985), compiled by Volodymyr Kubijovyč and Arkady Zhukovsky. In order to avoid confusing non-specialists, I have made only three exceptions to Kubijovyč and Zhukovsky's conventions: Kiev (not Kyiv), Odessa (not Odesa) and the Dnieper (not the Dnipro) River.

Abbreviations

D – Viacheslav Popyk, ed. 'Pid sofitamy VChK-DPU-NKVS-NKDB-KDB', *Dnipro*, no. 9–10 (1995), pp. 21–60.

DAMK – State Archive of the City of Kiev (Derzhavnyi arkhiv mista Kyieva), Kiev.

DIS – S. Plachynda, ed. *Dovzhenko i svit. Tvorchist' O. P. Dovzhenka v kontektsi svitovoi kul'tury* (Kiev, 1984).

DMM – *Dovzhenko Museum Memoirs* (Museum of the Dovzhenko Film Studios, Kiev).

DVVS – L. I. Pazhitnikova and Iu. I. Solntseva, eds. *Dovzhenko v vospominaniiakh sovremennikov* (Moscow, 1982).

FPARF – Historical-Documentary Department of the Ministry of Foreign Affairs of the Russian Federation (Istoriko-dokumental'nyi departament Ministerstva inostrannykh del RF), Moscow.

Hospody – Oleksandr Dovzhenko. *'Hospody, poshly meni syly': Kinopovisti, opovidannia, shchodennyk*, edited by Roman Korohodsky (Kharkiv, 1994).

KZ – *Kinovedcheskie zapiski* (Moscow).

MDFS – Museum of the Dovzhenko Film Studios (Muzei kinostudii im. O. P. Dovzhenka), Kiev.

'1939 Autobiography' – Marco Carynnyk, ed., 'Alexander Dovzhenko's 1939 Autobiography', *Journal of Ukrainian Studies*, 19, no. 1 (1994), pp. 5–27.

PF – Alexander Dovzhenko. *The Poet as Film-maker: Selected Writings*, edited and translated by Marco Carynnyk (Cambridge, MA, 1973).

PZh – Iu. I. Solntseva and L. M. Novychenko, eds. *Polum'iane zhyttia: Spohady pro Oleksandra Dovzhenka* (Kiev, 1973).

RGALI – Russian State Archive of Literature and Art (Rossiiskii Gosudarstvennyi arkhiv literatury i iskusstva), Moscow.

RGASPI – Russian State Archive of Socio-Political History (Rossiiskii gosudarstvennyi arkhiv sotsial'no-politicheskoi istorii), Moscow.

SDM – O. P. Dovzhenko Literary-Memorial Museum (Literaturno-memorial'nyi myzei O. P. Dovzhenka), Sosnytsia, Chernyhiv Oblast, Ukraine.

Service – Vance Kepley, Jr. *In the Service of the State: The Cinema of Alexander Dovzhenko* (Madison, WI, 1986).

Storinky – M. V. Kutsenko. *Storinky zhyttia i tvorchosti O. P. Dovzhenka* (Kiev, 1975).

TsDAHOU – Central State Archive of Civic Organisations of Ukraine (Tsentral'nyi Derzhavnyi arkhiv hromads'kykh ob'iednan' Ukrainy), Kiev.

TsDA-MLMU – Central State Archive-Museum of Literature and Art of Ukraine (Tsentral'nyi Derzhavnyi arkhiv-muzei literatury i mystetstva Ukrainy), Kiev.

TsDAVOVUU – Central State Archive of the Leading Organs of Government and Administration of Ukraine (Tsentral'nyi Derzhavnyi arkhiv vyshchykh orhaniv vlady ta upravlinnia Ukrainy), Kiev.

UVOKShch – Oleksandr Dovzhenko. *Ukraina v ohni: Kinopovist', shchodennyk*, edited by O. M. Pidsukha (Kiev, 1990).

ZA – Viacheslav Popyk, ed. 'Pid sofitamy sekretnykh sluzhb', *Z arkhiviv VUChK-HPU-NKVD-KHB*, no. 1–2 (1995), pp. 235–80.

ZBK – 'Pervoe Vsesoiuznoe soveshchanie tvorcheskikh rabotnikov sovetskoi kinematografii', in E. Zil'ber, ed., *Za bol'shoe kinoiskusstvo* (Moscow, 1935).

ZDUVOShch – Oleksandr Dovzhenko. *Zacharovana Desna/Ukraina v ohni/Shchodennyk* (Kiev, 1995).

Do I contradict myself?
Very well, I contradict myself.
I am large. I contain multitudes.

Walt Whitman (1855)

'Living with wolves, one howls like a wolf.'
Under no circumstances!
With all of your strength, preserve the human voice.

Grigory Kozintsev (1968)

Introduction

On 15 October 1956, Henri Langlois, the executive director of the *Cinémathèque française*, issued an invitation for the Soviet Ukrainian film-maker Alexander Dovzhenko and his wife, Julia Solntseva, to take part in a ceremony that December commemorating the living founders of world cinema. Other honorees included Charlie Chaplin, Erich von Stroheim, Luis Buñuel, René Clair and Roberto Rossellini. Langlois assured Dovzhenko that French film critics considered him one of 'the greatest masters of our time', an integral member of this pantheon. With the deaths of Soviet film directors Sergei Eisenstein (in 1948), Vsevolod Pudovkin (1953) and Dziga Vertov (1954), Dovzhenko remained the greatest living representative of the first generation of Soviet film-makers.[1]

This invitation represented the highest honour any organisation bestowed on Dovzhenko in his lifetime. It surpassed his sixtieth birthday celebrations in Moscow in January 1955 and all the state honours he received in the Soviet Union, especially from his native Ukraine.[2] Dovzhenko, who had always wanted to meet Chaplin and who had not travelled abroad in over twenty-five years, enthusiastically agreed to take part in the *Cinémathèque*'s ceremony.[3]

Sadly, he never reached Paris. During the night of 25 November 1956, he died of a heart attack, ten weeks after his sixty-second birthday and just six days before the beginning of the *Cinémathèque*'s salute at the Sorbonne.

Some time on Friday, 23 November, or the next day, Dovzhenko and Solntseva left for their *dacha* at the writers' colony in Peredelkino, a Moscow suburb. Dovzhenko visited his friends and neighbours, talking about his ideas and plans. As usual, when Dovzhenko spoke, no one could interrupt him.

One of his neighbours, the writer Kornely Zelinsky, protested vociferously when the film-maker told him of his plans to leave Peredelkino for Moscow that Sunday evening. He told Dovzhenko, 'Stay here . . . Take care of yourself. In the evening I'll come over and we'll continue our discussion about the meaning of life.' Dovzhenko laughed. 'Its meaning is incomprehensible,' he replied, 'and that is why I should go soon.'[4]

Zelinsky felt that Dovzhenko needlessly strained himself, but working hard comprised an integral part of the film director's personality. 'I often told Dovzhenko to stay in his rustic pine building, in his cosy nook [at Peredelkino], in order to take care of his heart,' Zelinsky wrote. 'It was the same on 25 November 1956.'[5]

That evening Dovzhenko and Solntseva returned to their Moscow apartment, located near the Kiev railway station. They found the elevator out of commission and had to walk up several flights of stairs. The climb exhausted him, and he lay down on the sofa. Solntseva called for a doctor.

The first doctor could not stop Dovzhenko's worsening condition. She called her supervisor, but he refused to come. Solntseva then phoned the couple's private physician, who agreed to attend Dovzhenko. Solntseva then summoned an ambulance.

Dovzhenko closed his eyes and passed away on the sofa at 11 p.m.[6] In his creative work, he presented an idealised type of death, as exemplified by that of the grandfather in his film *Earth* (1930). Contrasting strongly with the agonies of victims of wars and other tragedies, the idealised version celebrated the end of an old man's long and productive life. Surrounded by friends and family, the grandfather relinquishes his life, in harmony with nature's cyclical rhythms. Dovzhenko, however, did not die in this manner, as he wished.[7] The night before he planned to start shooting his next film, his first since Stalin's death, Dovzhenko met his untimely end a frustrated man. Although he died in the presence of his wife, he never completed the films he wanted to produce. Stalin and his allies had thwarted his vocation as a film-maker.

One hour after his final release, Solntseva telephoned Mykola Bazhan, the Deputy Prime Minister of the Ukrainian SSR, a poet and Dovzhenko's former flatmate from the 1920s. Dovzhenko had expressed his desire to be buried in Ukraine, and she believed Bazhan could help. But Bazhan was not at home. Although Solntseva explained the reason for her call to Bazhan's wife, he never called back.

Solntseva claimed to have phoned other officials in Kiev, but to no avail. 'Ukraine refused to bury Dovzhenko in Kiev,' she asserted.[8] She then buried her husband, one of the most prominent Ukrainian intellectuals of the twentieth century, in Moscow, perpetuating his exile for eternity.

Dovzhenko's memorial service took place on 28 November 1956 at the Central House of Literature. Reflecting Dovzhenko's troubled relationship with the Ukrainian cultural and political elites, very few highly placed Ukrainians attended. Only R. Babiichuk, the Ukrainian Minister of Culture, the writers Vasyl Minko and Oleksandr Pidsukha, and the Moscow-based opera singer Ivan Kozlovsky came. No one represented the Kiev Film Studio, which Dovzhenko had helped found in 1928.

Despite the absence of the Ukrainian elites, the memorial service and funeral included many Ukrainian symbols. Dovzhenko lay in a casket on an old decorative Ukrainian cloth, dressed in the peasant manner in an embroidered Ukrainian shirt. Fruit and flowers covered the coffin, and two tall sheaves of Ukrainian wheat stood tied in bands at his feet. Minko and Pidsukha brought some soil from Ukraine, a sheaf of rye, a red guelder rose and apples (supposedly picked from the orchard the film-maker planted in the Kiev Film Studio's grounds) and placed them at Dovzhenko's feet. The fruit, plants, and soil, according to Ukrainian folklore, represented fertility. They would guide the soul to rebirth in the next world. The native soil would prevent the deceased from becoming one of the unquiet dead.[9]

At the funeral service, Kozlovsky, a soloist with the Bolshoi Theatre in Moscow and a good friend of Dovzhenko's, sang two of the film-maker's favourite Ukrainian songs. The violinist Leonid Kogan played a selection from one of Beethoven's adagios.[10]

Representatives from the Union of Writers, the Moscow Film Studios (Mosfilm), the Soviet Army and the All-Union State Institute of Cinematography (VGIK) in Moscow spoke briefly. N. A. Mikhailov, the Minister of Culture of the USSR and his Ukrainian counterpart, Babiichuk, also eulogised the Soviet Union's most famous film-maker.

At the service at Novodevichy Cemetery, as a band played the Soviet national anthem, Dovzhenko's friends and colleagues lowered him into his grave. His Ukrainian friends then threw handfuls of Ukrainian soil into the open grave and bade the film-maker farewell.[11]

Only after his death did the Communist Party of Ukraine acknowledge Dovzhenko's achievements. On 15 March 1957, the Presidium of its Central Committee approved a decree in his honour. Recognition took several forms: publication of the film-maker's collected works and the renaming in his honour of the Kiev Film Studio, the middle school in the town of Sosnytsia (which the film-maker attended) and a newly constructed steamboat to sail the Kiev–Chernihiv route on the Desna River.[12]

Only in death did the film-maker receive the honours he longed for and so richly deserved. The Soviet authorities, especially those in Ukraine, found it easier and safer to deal with him after his death.

Alexander Dovzhenko remains one of the central icons of Ukrainian and Soviet film. Following in the footsteps of Eisenstein, Pudovkin and Vertov, Dovzhenko's movie-making brought his films international acclaim.[13] Best known for directing *Zvenyhora* (1927), *Arsenal* (1928) and *Earth*, he remained an important Soviet director until his death.

Unlike Pudovkin, Vertov and Eisenstein, Dovzhenko did not leave a comprehensive body of theoretical writings on film.[14] Instead, he communicated his ideas on film-making in public talks and in private conversations with his friends and colleagues. As a man who created spontaneously, he best displayed his ideas in his films.

Combining elements of history and folklore, stark realism, visual poetry, propaganda and subtle satire, Dovzhenko's films portray conflicts between the old and the new, life and death, love and hate, and over man's relationship to the land. His cinematic focus on the countryside and on peasants differs from the urban environments that dominated films by Eisenstein, Pudovkin and Vertov. Decades after their release, Dovzhenko's three great films shock the viewer with their visual imagination, wildness, striking idiosyncrasy of images and daring compositions. Although Dovzhenko's work shows collisions, his presentation of images on the screen creates a seamless whole, overshadowing his narrative. His early films stand as philosophical-lyrical poems glorifying nature and the inevitability of life, death and rebirth. Although he attempted to present the party line on screen, his images of the power of nature transcended his films' political messages. Defining himself through his Ukrainian peasant roots, he attempted to negotiate a compromise between his Ukrainian and Soviet identities.

From the late 1920s until 1956, Dovzhenko's survival and creative instincts constantly clashed. His public pronouncements did not necessarily reflect his private visions. To bare his soul, even to his closest friends, became very dangerous. Nevertheless, Dovzhenko often expressed his frustrations in public outbursts.

But to what extent did the film-maker's private world differ from his public one? To what extent did Dovzhenko accept the new Stalinist conventions?

Clear answers to these questions may never emerge. As the Canadian critic Marco Carynnyk has pointed out,

> We still know little about the man behind the myth and cannot view his films or read his writings in the form in which he left them. His major films have been cut; his minor films lie buried in archives; some of his most cherished projects never made it to the screen; his film scripts have been censored; his correspondence, diaries, and notebooks continue to be published in bowdlerized versions.[15]

Dovzhenko himself contributed to our limited understanding of his life by his own rewriting of his past in conformity with Stalinist orthodoxy. To protect himself, he wrapped himself under layers of disguises. Thus, both political censorship and Dovzhenko's own self-representations, as well as the inevitably biased views offered by his wives, friends and enemies, have complicated our view of him and his legacy.

In his memoirs, Eisenstein asserted that Dovzhenko remained a man of 'impassioned eloquence'.[16] Among his closest friends and colleagues, Dovzhenko used his passionate charisma to express his messsages. 'Don't compromise!' and 'Be yourself!' he demanded.[17] In their accounts of the film-maker, his friends, colleagues and students remember how he spoke these words with great fervour. One memoirist quotes him:

> . . . if you are an artist, do not create with a view of pleasing someone. The only groups which the artist should please, 'the only ones standing tall', consist of our society, the

party, and the people, as well as the great truth of Communism. Do not write a line in order to gain someone's approval, do not smile without sincerity to those you are dependent on, do not compromise yourself, or else your creativity will be crooked, even harmful. On your journey you will often meet petty, superficial, and vindictive people. Why should you change your thoughts and beliefs to suit their tastes? Will you extricate yourself by changing over to an Aesopian language? Do not laugh with them, and do not flatter them – fight with them. To create by pleasing someone means that you are unsure of your own sincerity and maturity, that you are not ready to converse with the people, with your spectators. The Soviet artist is sincere and is responsible to the party. In order to be an artist, you must have iron courage.[18]

In the context of Dovzhenko's own creative life and political survival, the irony of his advice becomes shockingly apparent. His vision and his obligations to the party and the Soviet state often diverged.

In order to survive the Stalinist purges, Dovzhenko became politically agile. According to one of his junior colleagues, he 'thought one thing, said another, filmed a third and wrote a fourth'.[19] Even with his agility, however, he had no guarantees that he would survive the capriciousness of the 1930s. Dovzhenko did outlast Stalin, but only partly because of his chameleon-like talents. His survival came at great personal cost.

In response to the conflict between his internal desires and external pressures, he became a man of paradoxes. A 'workaholic' and perfectionist, he never expressed any satisfaction with his work. He came from the peasantry and claimed to work on behalf of the common people, but as a first-generation intellectual, he lived among the cultural and the ruling elite. Although purged from the Communist Party in 1923, he asserted his loyalty to Communist ideals throughout his life. His Communist beliefs, as reflected in his private diaries at the end of his life, remained at odds with their official implementation.

Most importantly, Dovzhenko attempted to reconcile his Communist internationalism with his Ukrainian identity. The film-maker proudly identified himself as a Ukrainian, but served a regime hostile to anyone probing the limits of the official Soviet Ukrainian identity. Although Dovzhenko predicted a radiant Communist future for mankind, he often expressed his fears for the future of Ukrainian culture. The Soviet security organs soon recognised him as the 'political barometer of the Ukrainian intelligentsia' and assigned him the code name 'the Zaporozhian Cossack' (*Zaporozhets*).[20] Constantly recalibrating his identity, seeking official praise and approval, and fearing public condemnation and criticism, he lived in a 'golden cage'. He had the privilege to create, but owing to Stalin's influence, the review process, censorship and his own self-censorship, he could not create the films he envisaged. As a result of his compromises, Dovzhenko personified a twentieth-century Faust of sorts.

He stood out as one of the most visible intellectuals of the Soviet period. His

Dovzhenko during the filming of *Michurin* (1948)

compromises reflected the concessions made by other prominent Soviet intellectuals and film-makers who served the Soviet state. In addition, Dovzhenko carried
another source of tension, his Ukrainian identity. As one of the major sources of his
creativity, his national identity also called his political loyalties into question,
especially in the 1930s and 40s when the Stalinist order closely identified itself with
Russian national interests.

As a contradictory and paradoxical figure, Dovzhenko often showed surprising inconsistencies in his responses to the dilemmas he confronted. His public voice did not always reflect his internal vision, what he claimed and what he imagined he stood for.

This study will attempt to probe this conflict and investigate the shifting boundaries between Dovzhenko's public and private worlds. In order to do so, this biography will emphasise the role of Ukrainian culture in shaping his creative vision.

Notes

Please note: The Russian archival citations of *fond/opis'/delo* and the Ukranian equivalents, *fond/opys/sprava*, appear in the form 000/000/000.

1. See the copy of Langlois's letter to Dovzhenko at the Museum of the Dovzhenko Film Studios in Kiev (MDFS).
2. Dovzhenko became a Distinguished Artist of the Ukrainian SSR in 1932 and a People's Artist of the Russian Soviet Federated Socialist Republic in 1950. He received the Order of Lenin on the occasion of the fifteenth anniversary of Soviet cinematography in 1935; the Stalin Prize, First Class, in 1941; and the Stalin Prize, Second Class, in 1949. In 1943 he accepted the Order of the Red Banner for his work during the war. On the occasion of his sixtieth birthday, the Supreme Soviet of the USSR awarded him another Order of the Red Banner. But he never won the highest Soviet honour: People's Artist of the USSR.
3. *Storinky*, p. 324.
4. K. Zelinskii, 'Liudyna – maibutne', *PZh*, p. 677.
5. Zelinskii, p. 676.
6. Julia Solntseva, 'S tribuny veka', Tatiana Timofeevna Derev'ianko Archive, pp. 5–8, 12–13; 'Poslednyi den' Aleksandra Dovzhenko', *Dnipro*, no. 9–10 (1994), p. 79.
7. According to S. A. Svashenko, one of Dovzhenko's most famous actors, the film-maker expressed this desire while working on his film *Michurin* between 1946 and 1948. See Svashenko's 'O blizkom, dorogom cheloveke', RGALI, 2081/1/1184, pp. 11–12.
8. Solntseva, pp. 10–11. According to Serhii Trymbach, who was on good terms with Solntseva, she asked the Ukrainian authorities several times about the possibility of burying Dovzhenko in Kiev, as he desired, but she did not receive any response. Serhii Trymbach, 'Dovzhenko: Chervone i chorne', *Kul'tura i zhyttia*, no. 36–7 (11 September 1993), p. 5.
9. I am grateful to Natalie Kononenko for explaining the significance of these symbols.

10. Kozlovsky sang 'Meni odnakovo, chy budu ia zhyty v Ukraini, chy ni' and 'Chuesh, brate mii'.
11. Liubov Zabashta, 'Rozpovid' pro Dovzhenka', *PZh*, p. 415; 'Spisok vystupavshykh na grazhdanskoi panakhide A. P. Dovzhenko v Tsentral'nom dome literatorov i na Novodevich'em kladbishche (28 November 1956)', RGALI, 2081/1/1222, pp. 1–2; Solntseva, 'S tribuny veka', p. 11; Lev Arnshtam, 'Liudyna, shcho prozhyla 1000 zhyttiv', *PZh*, p. 474; A. I. Serdiuk, 'Vospominaniia ob A. P. Dovzhenko', RGALI, 2081/1/1185, pp. 9–12; Zelinskii, pp. 676–7; and 'Pokhorony A. P. Dovzhenko', *Sovetskaia kul'tura*, 29 November 1956.
12. TsDAHOU, 1/6/2609, pp. 115, 135.
13. *New York Times*, 27 November 1956, p. 38.
14. According to Ray Uzwyshyn, Dovzhenko did leave a body of written statements on aesthetics and film theory, but they remain untranslated, largely uncompiled and subsequently unanalysed in the West. These works include: A. P. Dovzhenko, *Lektsii na stsenarnom fakul'tete* (Moscow, 1963) and O. P. Dovzhenko, *Pro krasu*, compiled by Oleh Babyshkin (Kiev, 1968). The film-maker's most important work remains: 'Do problemy obrazotvorchoho mystetstva', *VAPLITE*, no. 1 (1926), pp. 25–36 (reprinted in an abridged form in Iurii Lavrinenko, *Rozstriliane vidrodzhennia* [Paris, 1959], pp. 867–76).
15. '1939 Autobiography', p. 5.
16. Sergei Mikhailovich Eisenstein, *Memuary* (Moscow, 1997), vol. 1, p. 152; S. M. Eisenstein, *Selected Works, vol. 4: Beyond the Stars: The Memoirs of Sergei Eisenstein* (London and Bloomington, IN, 1995), p. 191.
17. 'Don't compromise!': Oleksii Mishyrin, 'Polumiane serdtse', in M. Kovalenko and O. Mishyrin, *Syn zacharovanoi Desny* (Kiev, 1984), p. 141; Dzh. Firsova, 'Slovo ob uchitelia', *DMM*, Folder 6; A. P. Dovzhenko, 'Kratkaia avtobiografiia', RGALI, 2081/1/350; *Les lettres françaises*, 11–17 May 1961, p. 7; N. Mashchenko, 'Zabyt' ego nel'zia', *DVVS*, p. 254; Aleksei Svachko, 'V kino prikhodit Dovzhenko', *DVVS*, p. 70. 'Be yourself': Khristo Santov, 'Vin khvyliuvavsia zavzhdy', in *DIS*, pp. 91–2.
18. Viktor Ivanov, 'Sadivnychyi', *PZh*, p. 404.
19. Author's interview with Mykola Pavlovych Mashchenko, the director of the Dovzhenko Film Studios, Kiev, 25 April 1996.
20. *ZA*, p. 272. Colonel Popyk, a former press officer for the Ukrainian security organs, coined this phrase ('political barometer'). The designation, 'the Zaporozhian Cossack', appears in *D*, pp. 23, 44; *ZA*, p. 278.

1

Becoming a Teacher

The conflicts Alexander Dovzhenko presented in his films sprang not solely from his imagination, but drew from the experiences of his childhood and youth. His family's encounters with death, poverty, illiteracy, class inequality, religion and national identity left lasting impressions on his life and career.

Dovzhenko was born on 29 August 1894 ([old style]; 10 September 1894 [new style]), a few weeks before Louis and Auguste Lumière, the French 'fathers' of cinema, developed their famous *cinématographe*, which revolutionised the film world. He lived with his parents, Petro Symonovych Dovzhenko and Odarka Yermylivna Nekrasov-Dovzhenko, in Viunyshche, a small village adjoining the town of Sosnytsia in Chernihiv Province of the Russian Empire.[1] Sosnytsia is located on the banks of the Ubed River, a tributary of the Desna River, seven kilometres from a steamboat wharf and twenty-two kilometres from a railway station.[2] In 1897, Sosnytsia's inhabitants totalled only 7,087, mostly Ukrainian-speaking peasants.[3] The town's demographic and cultural isolation exercised a profound influence on the young Alexander.

Parents and Early Years

The Dovzhenkos were peasants, descendants of Cossacks who, in the eighteenth century, had migrated to Sosnytsia from the neighbouring Poltava region.[4] Alexander was the seventh of their fourteen children, but due to multiple deaths in the family, he became the oldest child by the time he turned eleven.[5]

Misfortune and sorrow dogged the Dovzhenkos. Four of Alexander's older brothers, Ivan, Serhii, Vasyl and Lavrin, died during a scarlet fever epidemic in 1895. Avram, the oldest brother, met his end after contracting typhus in 1905 while working as a stevedore in Rostov.[6] Five siblings passed away in childhood. His younger sister Anna died in childbirth in 1920. Alexander's youngest brother, Andrii, died in 1926.[7] Of Petro and Odarka's fourteen children, only Alexander and Polina survived into adulthood.

The deaths of his brothers and sisters led Dovzhenko to construct an internal coping mechanism long before the Soviet regime and evoked a creative response in his life and work. The 'questions of life and death affected my imagination when I was

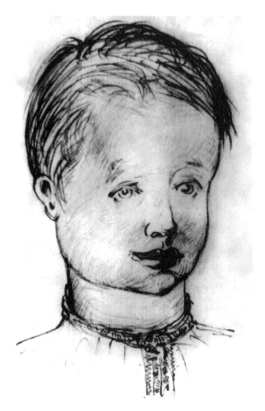

Self-portrait of Dovzhenko as a
young boy. Drawn when
completing *The Enchanted Desna*
(1950s)

still a child so strongly that they left an imprint on all my work', he acknowledged.[8] In response to the tragedies in his family, the nature of death in his films varied. The villains in his films died 'grotesquely', but his heroes experienced 'beautiful deaths, without suffering'.[9] The film-maker considered some deaths – such as those of victims of war or of individuals 'isolated from life' – as more horrible than others.[10] He regarded most of the deaths he encountered as 'senseless', but for Dovzhenko, death never represented the 'final conclusion'. As exemplified by the grandfather's death scene in *Earth*, death constituted an integral component of the great chain of life.[11]

Dovzhenko's parents, however, found it difficult to adhere to this view of life. In order to master their pain, they expressed their mourning in different ways. His mother sought solace in increased religious expression. In the course of her life, twelve of her fourteen children passed away, four in a single day. Although many families in that time and place suffered similar painful losses, these deaths sapped her emotionally and physically. Her hair turned grey before her thirtieth birthday.[12] She cried often and experienced disabling depression for long periods of time. She could not do the 'woman's work' around the house assigned by custom and tra-dition. Still, her faith remained. She often prayed for Alexander's safety: 'O God, leave me Sashko [Alexander's diminutive]; protect him from bad people. Give him strength. Give him happiness, so that people will love him as I love him.'[13]

In conformity to her Orthodox Christian beliefs, she – like many peasants – also believed in evil spirits, which often appeared in her dreams. She feared 'everything: the dark night, an angry dog, horses, bulls, a drunken person. But she especially feared thunder and lightning. When she heard thunder in the distance, she crossed herself and started to look for places to hide.'[14] Her religious fervour and her superstitious nature both grew out of her natural responses to the deaths of her children.

Petro reacted in a different manner. Although he prayed and crossed himself at meals, he went to church only occasionally, never fasted, and held a low opinion of the church and its servants. The model for Opanas Trubenko, the bereaved father in Dovzhenko's *Earth*, Petro considered priests 'deceivers'.[15] He responded to the deaths of his children by working harder. He directed all of his pain and sorrow into his cultivation of the soil, which according to the film-maker's 1939 autobiography, never adequately supported the family. In emphasising his 'humble roots', Dovzhenko exaggerated his family's economic difficulties.

The majority of the peasants in the Ukrainian countryside confronted a stark reality of poverty and death. After the emancipation of the serfs in 1861, the peasant population exploded. Ninety-four per cent attempted to survive on thirteen acres (five desiatins) or less of land per family. Although the Dovzhenko family

The Dovzhenko house in Sosnytsia in the 1940s

possessed between twenty and twenty-five acres and two horses, they could barely survive. Dovzhenko's father and grandfather, Symon Tarasevych, had to supplement the family's income by working outside the family farm.[16]

Family members and neighbours remembered them as 'always busy'.[17] Petro Symonovych worked 'day and night', not just to feed his family, but to give his children an education. Before his marriage, he worked as a servant in the province of Tavria, a region touching the Black Sea and including the Crimea. Even after establishing his family, he journeyed frequently to distant markets, sold tar and transported people and materials in his large boat. He travelled to the neighbouring Poltava Province and to Kherson Province to the south.[18] When his wife became ill, Petro took over a number of her responsibilities, such as milking the cow, feeding the pigs and chickens, working the garden and selling its beets, carrots, onions, cabbage and potatoes at the market.[19]

Becoming the oldest child in 1905, Alexander took on commensurate responsibilities. He helped his mother with the household duties by sweeping floors, washing dishes and clothes, and making the beds. He brought water from the well and wood for the stove, and even baked bread while watching over his little brothers and sisters. Alexander also helped his father plow, mow and harvest the fields. Survival demanded self-discipline and hard, often back-breaking work, which encouraged his perfectionism, not only in physical labour, but in intellectual labour as well.[20] Attending school and learning to read and write opened new opportunities for him, especially in a region where the overwhelming majority of men and women remained illiterate.

Poverty, isolation and mandatory Russian-language instruction all hampered the spread of literacy in Ukraine. After the emancipation of the serfs, many villages in the Russian Empire, especially those under the *obrok* (payment in cash) system, established long-term relationships with neighbouring cities, and such contacts encouraged literacy.[21] Emancipation did not free the peasants in the Ukrainian provinces (which included the provinces of Kiev, Podilia, Poltava, Volyn, Kharkiv, Chernihiv, Katerynoslav, Kherson and Tavria) from their bondage to the soil. On the contrary; because they did not receive enough land for subsistence, those bonds became a noose. In the Ukrainian provinces, the *barshchina* (payment in labour) system permanently tied the peasants to the land. Literacy emerged only when the peasants had to deal with the more complex world outside their villages.

In 1897, only 19 per cent of the total population in the nine Ukrainian provinces could read and write.[22] Among ethnic Ukrainians the literate portion of the population dropped to a mere 13 per cent. Many of these literates, however, did not necessarily read or write Ukrainian. Russians and Jews in the Ukrainian provinces displayed respectively double and triple the literacy rates of ethnic Ukrainians. Among Jewish males the literacy rate rose to nearly 100 per cent. In rural areas, 95 per cent of the peasants, the overwhelming majority of whom spoke Ukrainian, remained illiterate.[23]

Mandatory instruction in Russian maintained a stranglehold on the expansion of literacy. Ukrainian children often could not understand their teachers or their lessons, and many children who did learn to read in Russian quickly forgot it.[24]

As a result, Ukrainian peasants could not understand the significance of learning to read and write. Education seemed impractical, if not irrelevant, to most peasants. At the same time, Ukrainian-speaking peasants quickly learned that their non-standardised language with its competing dialects remained inferior to the highly developed Russian language used in school and in government offices. The peasants' linguistic inferiority mirrored their social inequality and political impotence.

Two hundred and fifty years of tsarist policies laid the groundwork for these inequities. The tsarist government never expanded literacy on a mass scale. Committed to an autocratic political and rigid social order, tsarist officials believed that introducing literacy to members of the lowest caste would undermine the status quo. Tolerating the teaching of reading and writing in the peasants' own language represented even greater risks.

Tsarism oppressed Poles, Finns and Georgians but did not challenge their status as distinct and separate nations. The 22,400,000 Ukrainians who lived in the Russian Empire in 1897 did not enjoy similar national recognition. They constituted the second largest national group within the Empire, as well as the largest non-dominant ethnic group in Europe, yet tsarist ideologists viewed the Ukrainians as simply the Little Russian branch of the Great Russian nation.[25] Inasmuch as peasants did not possess the means to organise, the government feared that the Ukrainian national movement, however small, might influence the peasant masses, who as yet thought more in local than in national terms. In order to quarantine the potential influence of the Ukrainian national movement on the peasant masses, the government sought to repress all individuals with a distinct Ukrainian identity 'in the political or cultural sphere' who tried to establish contacts with the masses.[26] Despite the government's best efforts, it did not always succeed in repressing the Ukrainian intelligentsia's activities.

In the nineteenth century, the tsarist government institutionalised these repressions. In July 1863, Petr Valuev, Russia's Minister of Internal Affairs, banned all scholarly, religious and educational publications in the Ukrainian language. Only fictional literature could appear in the 'Little Russian dialect'. Valuev declared that the Ukrainian language 'never existed, does not exist, and shall never exist'. With the Ems Decree of 1876, Tsar Alexander II further restricted the publication and importation of Ukrainian books. He prohibited the use of Ukrainian on stage, and forbade Ukrainian-language teaching of any subject in the elementary schools.[27] The government abolished these measures in 1905 but reinstated them at the beginning of the World War I.

With the exception of Dovzhenko's grandfather, Symon, no other adult in the family learned to read. Dovzhenko's father, Petro, never forgave his own father for not sending him to school.[28] Although Petro could not read or write, he evinced curiosity about the world around him. He 'loved to talk about political matters, and about war, freedom, land, and the wealth of Ukraine'.[29]

Although most peasants perceived education as a minor issue, Dovzhenko's father viewed his illiteracy as a life-long handicap. He consequently encouraged and pushed his children to learn to read and to pursue an education. When Alexander studied at the Teachers' Institute in Hlukhiv, his father often brought him food.[30] When his son desperately needed money for tuition and living expenses at the Institute, his father 'sold a *desiatyna* of land'. According to Alexander, 'he cut it off from his heart'.[31]

Petro's perspective differed from most of his peasant neighbours'. By selling one-seventh of his land, he demonstrated a serious commitment to his son, who struggled at the Institute. For someone highly dependent on the land and its produce, selling even a small portion created great financial strain in the short term. Petro made this sacrifice as an investment in his son's future. Through education, he began the process of 'de-peasantising' his children.

Petro's wife, Odarka, reluctantly agreed with his plan. She desired the best for her children. But as the matriarch of the family, she felt ambivalence, fearing that literacy would take Alexander far away from home and lead him, as it had her first-born, Avram, to an early death.[32]

Although they recognised the difficulties, members of Alexander's family supported his schooling. They supplemented his education with tales that had moral values and interpretations. The future film-maker came from a family of wonderful storytellers. The patriarch of the family, Symon Tarasevych, excelled as a narrator. Young Alexander, his favourite grandchild, loved to listen to his enchanted accounts of caravans crossing the steppes with their wares, and about the moon, the rivers and lakes they encountered on their journey.[33] Alexander's father, Petro Symonovych, also wove riveting tales about travellers, driving their teams of animals on expeditions and of the heroic adventures of their ancestors, the Zaporozhian Cossacks.[34] Dovzhenko's mother recounted the origins and development of old customs and traditions, especially the complex Ukrainian wedding ceremony.[35]

Despite these shared traits and values, the Dovzhenkos often experienced bitter family conflicts. A tense, often explosive, relationship existed between Symon and Petro.[36] Shouting matches often broke out between the two. Although Petro drank infrequently, when he did, Symon would yell at him: 'You only want to get drunk!'[37] With this accusation, Symon implicitly branded Petro as lazy, a thoroughly unfounded criticism.

The issue of property and its legal inheritance divided them. Petro wanted to administer his own land without paternal interference, but he could not do so as long as Symon lived. To take full possession of the land, Petro needed his father to die, but Symon kept on living.[38]

This discord undoubtedly distressed Alexander because he deeply loved both father and grandfather. In his films, he drew upon both of these strong personalities when portraying such characters.

His mother felt no such love for her father-in-law. Her hatred of Symon escalated over the course of time. Property issues apart, he came to represent something more than an obstacle. Odarka considered him an evil magician. She persuaded herself that Symon, who regularly read the Psalter on Sundays, had cursed her. She believed this curse struck her with illness for three consecutive years. Her blind hatred even led her to burn the Psalter in question.[39] She often attacked him verbally, argued with him, or embarrassed him. Alexander disapproved of her actions, but according to one memoirist, he always expressed his criticism with a smile and with humour.[40] The lingering image of his mother, a woman 'who spent her whole life crying and saying goodbye', overshadowed the other women in his films.[41]

The film-maker's grandfather,
Symon Tarasevych Dovzhenko
(early twentieth century)

Perhaps as an escape from the deaths and conflicts in the family, young Alexander became a dreamer. He created an imaginary world and often withdrew into it. Dovzhenko wrote: 'My dreams and imagination were so strong that at times I lived on two levels – the real and the imaginary – which struggled with each other and yet seemed reconcilable.'[42] At the same time he, like his father, exhibited a curiosity about the world surrounding him. He became a precocious child. Friends from his childhood claimed 'to remember' his sophisticated questions: 'Why do sunflowers turn toward the sun? Why do common people bow before the rich and stupid people? Why do city people consider my mother an ignorant peasant woman when she speaks the native language of her forefathers?'[43]

Alexander's curiosity aroused in him a great enthusiasm for learning and for school. In 1902 he began his studies at the primary school in Sosnytsia, which like most schools in the Russian Empire, taught the Bible and Orthodox Christian precepts, Old Church Slavonic, Russian, writing, arithmetic and singing.[44] He finished in 1906 and continued at the town's three-grade (later four-grade) higher elementary school.[45]

Alexander excelled at the primary school.[46] Ivan Trofymovych Tyshyna, who sat next to him in class in 1904, remembered the ten-year-old as 'quiet, sensible, and well-mannered'. Alexander became the top pupil in his class, arithmetic his best subject. Whenever a classmate gave the wrong answer, the maths teacher called on Alexander. His teachers loved him, and long after he left the Sosnytsia elementary schools, they cited him as the 'good student' all pupils should emulate.

At the Sosnytsia elementary school, Alexander learned to read and write, radically transforming the young boy's view of the world. Reading offered more than utilitarian benefits. With stories about exotic places and new ideas, books introduced Alexander to a wider realm, far beyond Sosnytsia, the Ukrainian provinces, and even the Russian Empire itself.

Alexander loved to read. He became one of the most active patrons of the town's library. *Uncle Tom's Cabin* and *Robinson Crusoe* provided him with an introduction to literature.[47] Later he began to read the Russian classics, Ukrainian literature, songs, stories and proverbs. Taras Shevchenko and Nikolai Gogol became Alexander's best-loved authors, Gogol's *Taras Bulba* his favourite book.[48] He also enjoyed the amateur theatre in Sosnytsia and often attended its performances.[49]

After he graduated from Sosnytsia's higher elementary school in the spring of 1911, Alexander had to think about his future. He later claimed that after flirting with the ideas of becoming a sailor, an artist, an architect and a writer, he settled on teaching.[50] In truth, circumstances more than personal choice determined Dovzhenko's career in education. As the son of peasants and the graduate of a higher elementary school, no university or any other institution of higher learning

Alexander (top row, third from left) as a member of the amateur theatre troupe in
Sosnytsia (Summer, 1912)

would have accepted him as a student. Only by taking the entrance examinations
to a teachers' institute could he further his education and strive to become a 'gentle-
man', as his parents hoped.[51]

Becoming an Educator

In the autumn of 1911, Alexander took the entrance examinations to the Teachers'
Institute in Hlukhiv, a city 100 kilometres from Sosnytsia and the eighteenth-
century capital of the semi-autonomous Cossack state. Providing teachers with a
'more advanced educational training' and ensuring their political reliability, this
teacher's institute constituted one of only twelve to fourteen throughout the entire
Russian Empire.[52] Dovzhenko wrote: 'I had chosen this school because I had the
right to take the entrance exam for it and because it granted scholarships of 120
rubles a year. The pursuit of a scholarship, that is, of the opportunity to study
brought me to the college.'[53]

The institute maintained rigorous standards for admission. Between 200 and 250
candidates competed for the twenty-five seats in the entering class. The candidates
ranged from those who had taught for five to ten years in the primary schools to those
who had only recently graduated from the higher elementary schools. The latter,
which included Alexander, rarely passed the entrance examinations on their first try.[54]

The examinations tested the candidates in all the elementary school subjects. One question quoted an aphorism from Gogol and asked the candidates to comment on it: 'Setting out on life's long journey, carry with you the best from your youth.'[55] Dovzhenko later implied that he produced a very long essay, but in fact, as one of his biographers claimed, he simply replied: 'I have not completed my journey and cannot tell what is necessary to preserve from youth or how to carry it through life.' Although Dovzhenko gave the shortest response of the candidates, the examiner awarded him a five, the highest grade.[56]

Alexander won a place at the Institute. Turning seventeen in September 1911, he became one of the youngest students in his class. Few memoirs describe his experiences in Hlukhiv. According to surviving accounts, Alexander hated the school. In contrast to his elementary school days, when he had excelled as a student, his grades averaged only four on a scale of five.[57] Contrary to his hopes, the Institute did not provide him with a scholarship. For the first two years he had to tutor and his father had to make sacrifices of his own just to make ends meet. In addition to his poverty and to his academic difficulties, the school's political orientation alienated him. Its teachers and administration proudly identified with the conservative tsarist order and produced (according to Dovzhenko) 'well-behaved, politically illiterate, and naive teachers for the advanced primary schools'.[58]

In order to achieve these aims, the Teachers' Institute attempted to insulate the students from urban vices, including gambling, prostitution and radical politics. The Ministry of Education established a rigid schedule within which the students enjoyed very little free time. Because almost all of the students boarded at the institutes, 'this type of control was fairly easy to implement. Each hour of the day was accounted for ... In addition to the constant surveillance by the faculty, an elaborate system of student monitors reported unauthorized activities of other students.'[59]

The instructors at the Teachers' Institute exacerbated this oppressive environment. Few of the teachers provided him with the encouragement he had received during his elementary school days. His poverty, moreover, made him long for home.

Despite these hardships, Dovzhenko graduated from the Teachers' Institute in June 1914. He became a member of a very select group, the educated elite. In 1897, only 1 per cent of the total population of the Ukrainian provinces had completed secondary school or attended an institution of higher learning.[60] Only 47,000 ethnic Ukrainians did so, representing less than 0.3 per cent of the Ukrainian population. In contrast, 143,000 ethnic Russians completed a similar education; they comprised 5 per cent of the Russian population in the Ukrainian provinces.[61] Although Ukrainians constituted 80 per cent of the population of the Ukrainian provinces, Russians dominated their intellectual life. The situation had not materially altered seventeen years later.

Alexander as a student at the
Hlukhiv Teachers' Institute
(*c.* 1911–14)

In the summer of 1914, Dovzhenko accepted a position as a teacher at the Second Mixed Higher Elementary School in Zhytomyr, a city of nearly 70,000 in Volyn
Province. He taught physics, biology, geography, history and physical education at
the school, which contained six grades and attracted 204 boys and girls during the
1914–15 academic year.[62]

One colleague from the school remembers Dovzhenko as a 'young, talented,
energetic and sharp man'.[63] His pupils loved him and his lectures. Instead of sitting
isolated behind the teacher's desk (a common practice among teachers in the Russian Empire), he would sometimes stand near the window and dreamily look out into
the distance. Because he was almost as young as his students, he did not distance
himself from them.

At the Zhytomyr elementary school, Alexander met Barbara Krylova in the
autumn of 1916, when she began to teach science classes there. As the youngest of
the teachers, their seriousness, energy and enthusiasm distinguished Dovzhenko
and Krylova from their older colleagues and drew them together. Their working
together turned to friendship, then to love. They married in July 1923.[64]

Employing the storytelling abilities honed at his family's dinner table,

Dovzhenko delivered charismatic lectures.[65] If one accepts the accounts of his former students, he had found his vocation. His charm and youth, his curiosity and love of learning, his skills as a raconteur and his commitment to hard work made him an excellent teacher. According to his account, however, Dovzhenko began during this time to dream of becoming an artist: 'I drew at home and took private drawing lessons with the hope of going to the Academy of Fine Arts, at least as an auditor.'[66] As his sister Polina recalled in the 1960s, he had begun to draw as a child in Sosnytsia. Although he did not have much free time at the Teachers' Institute in Hlukhiv, he did not abandon his interest in art. After beginning his first teaching position in Zhytomyr, where he taught drawing in addition to his other subjects, he sketched in his free time and produced caricatures of his colleagues.[67]

Politics

Although Dovzhenko received his training in a conservative environment, he did not become an uncritical supporter of the tsarist order. In their memoirs, his friends and colleagues did not dwell much on his social or political views before the tsarist political order collapsed in March 1917. When Julia Solntseva began to solicit these memoirs in the late 1950s and early 60s, depictions of Dovzhenko's political views had to adhere to the official Soviet interpretation of the film-maker as an uncompromising opponent of the tsarist order.

According to one classmate, when Dovzhenko attended the Sosnytsia town school, he smuggled in a book that satirised Russian princes and tsars in verse form.[68] With the outbreak of the 1905 revolution, Alexander and his young friends acted as lookouts for clandestine meetings held by the town's young people, who gathered in the woods to read proclamations, listen to speeches, sing revolutionary songs and compose leaflets, which he later helped to distribute.[69] Another friend recalled how Alexander, in the summer of 1913, had developed 'social views'. What specifically these views entailed, Alexander's friend did not reveal.[70] Another memoirist remembered how Alexander, at the age of twenty, visited his parents during the summer, and told stories, some of which featured a poor man fighting the rich and emerging victorious, to the younger boys.[71]

Krylova claimed that Dovzhenko often criticised the tsarist order and spoke about the common interests of workers and peasants in their struggle against social injustice. He introduced her to the slogans of the French Revolution, 'liberty, equality and fraternity', a phrase as revolutionary in twentieth-century Russia as it had been in eighteenth-century Western Europe. Prior to the revolutions of 1917, he often spoke about living on behalf of the working people. 'I will devote my life to truth and justice!' she quoted him as declaring.[72]

These accounts of dubious veracity tell us very little of substance about Dovzhenko's political sympathies or loyalties. His political views developed in a fam-

Alexander (top row, second from left) and his colleagues at the Second Mixed Higher Elementary School in Zhytomyr (1914–15)

Alexander with two of his colleagues at the Second Mixed Higher Elementary School. Barbara Krylova (his future wife) stands next to him (1916–17)

ily that broke the mould. Although his parents worked the land, the soil did not anchor their vision of the future. Not only did his parents provide him with a primary school education, they also encouraged him and his siblings to seek a higher education and backed that encouragement with hard-won financial support. By educating their children, they accepted more risks than their peasant neighbours. At the kitchen table, Alexander learned the value of assessing his environment, calculating his options and taking chances. His family's hard work and efforts might not have overcome their social, political, or economic handicaps, but he learned that he need not accept an inferior station in life.[73]

Rejecting inequality inevitably led to political awareness. The Teachers' Institute intellectually enhanced Dovzhenko's views of politics. Here, he read political tracts, discussed politics with his classmates and some of his teachers, and developed his own interpretation of the world. At that time, however, Dovzhenko did not embrace fully formed or consistent views. Like most subjects of the Russian Empire, Dovzhenko enthusiastically greeted the outbreak of the Great War. In his 1939 autobiography, he admitted: 'I welcomed the First World War like a philistine, uncritically, and when the first war-wounded flooded the town of Zhytomyr, my pupils and colleagues and I stunned them with shouts of hurrah and strewed them with flowers.'[74]

Although Dovzhenko may have volunteered for the army when the war broke out, as a teacher in a higher elementary school, he received an exemption from military service. On 16 June 1917, the Zhytomyr county bureau – in accordance with the new regulations issued in November 1915 – classified him as 'unfit for military service'.[75] Shortly after this evaluation, Dovzhenko underwent a heart operation.[76]

Dovzhenko's political inconsistency paralleled his uncertainty regarding his Ukrainian identity. His parents possessed a vague idea of their national identity. They lived in their own self-contained community and interacted with people like themselves. Nevertheless, they recognised that they differed radically from the Poles and Jews, and somewhat from the 'Russians' as well. The exact differences between the Ukrainians and Russians, however, remained difficult both to define and measure.

Shared Orthodox faith blurred the differences between Ukrainians and Russians. Thus, Petro and Odarka gave their son the Christian name 'Alexander' in honour of the Russian prince Alexander Nevsky's nameday, 30 August, the day their priest baptised their child.[77]

Many of the Dovzhenko family's activities differed from those prevalent in the Russian environment. Like three-quarters of their neighbours in Sosnytsia, they spoke Ukrainian at home.[78] They shared a deep pleasure in Ukrainian folk music. When his mother felt well enough, she sang Ukrainian folk songs and Alexander loved to listen to her. When she sang, she was happy and – temporarily, at least –

Dovzhenko's parents, Petro Symonovych Dovzhenko and Odarka Yermylivna Dovzhenko, and sister, Polina Petrivna (before 1917)

healthy. In addition to his mother's wide repertoire, Alexander transcribed Ukrainian folk songs at the local market from *kobzars*, the blind minstrels who travelled from village to village.[79] Living separately from Russian villagers and honouring their own distinct traditions did not necessarily prove, however, that the Dovzhenko family possessed a coherent understanding of their 'Ukrainianness'.

What did a Ukrainian identity mean? This question begged an answer after Alexander started school, where his teachers delivered their lectures in Russian, a language foreign to young Alexander. He could speak in Ukrainian at recess, but the use of Russian at school in preference to his native language divided his universe into two systems. The first included all who could speak and use the 'higher' language; the second included those who could only employ the everyday language.

Alexander must have learned to read Russian and Old Church Slavonic before Ukrainian. He probably learned to read his native language only at the Teachers' Institute.[80] Alexander's literacy in Russian and Ukrainian may have helped form his Ukrainian identity.[81]

If the dichotomy between the Russian and Ukrainian worlds in Alexander's elementary school jarred him, then his experiences at the Teachers' Institute produced an even greater shock. Hlukhiv possessed a population twice as large as Sosnytsia's;

it contained more non-Ukrainians, especially Jews. Although the majority of the city's residents identified themselves as Ukrainians, Hlukhiv – like most of the cities of its size in Ukraine – was a Russian-speaking city.[82] Although the majority of the students came from the Ukrainian provinces, the Institute's administration forbade them 'to speak Ukrainian', even outside class. According to Dovzhenko, the Institute's administrators 'were making us into Russifiers of the country. In the Kiev, Podilia, and Volyn Provinces, we even received extra pay, eighteen rubles a month, I think, for Russifying the countryside.'[83]

Even though the school had a mission to promote the autocracy, the Orthodox faith and Russian nationality, a number of Alexander's classmates and teachers subverted this mission. At the Teachers' Institute, Alexander not only read works by the Russian revolutionaries Nikolai Chernyshevsky and Alexander Herzen, but also encountered Ukrainian-language books, journals and newspapers for the first time.[84] He could read current legal and illegal Russian- and Ukrainian-language political literature. Mentored by some of his liberal teachers and schoolmates, he sharpened his political consciousness and later asserted that at the Institute he stopped believing in God.[85]

Dovzhenko continued his political journey in Zhytomyr, where he often met with students from the elementary and higher schools at their homes. According to one memoirist, he often brought a copy of the Ukrainian bard Taras Shevchenko's *Kobzar* and books written by 'progressive' writers. During these visits he often sang Ukrainian songs with them.[86] Although this memoirist does not provide details, a close reading of the text suggests that Dovzhenko's activities represented Ukrainian national activities prohibited by the tsarist authorities during the war.

Conclusion

As a result of his literacy and higher education, Alexander Dovzhenko achieved status as a member of the intelligentsia, an educated man with a political conscience and a commitment to political action. Most of all, he felt a sense of social responsibility, an obligation that paralleled his family responsibilities. From an early age, he took on the duties of his dead brothers and sisters; as an *intelligent*, he felt accountable for making life better for the poor and for the nationally oppressed. He developed an image of himself as a servant of the people. Most of all, he wanted to make a difference, at first as a teacher, a profession he understood as 'very necessary, responsible, and honorable'.[87]

Dovzhenko saw teaching as the vocation that would allow him to do the greatest good for the greatest number. He wanted to teach children, introduce them to new ideas and attempt to make them independent thinkers. Beyond teaching subjects such as physics, mathematics and art, Dovzhenko hoped to impress upon his pupils that hard work, self-improvement and critical thinking could lead to positive social changes. He imagined that as a teacher he would fight social, political and national oppression with his subtle, quiet and charismatic mien, his most effective weapons.

Becoming a teacher meant not only responsibility, but respectability as well. Young Alexander eagerly strove to please his parents and teachers, hoping to gain approval from figures of authority, and he succeeded in this aim. His polite, obedient and self-effacing attitudes encouraged adults to view him as a grown-up in a young person's body. Although he occasionally challenged authority, he did so behind the scenes. He never presented himself as a rebel. His efforts to reconcile his critical thinking abilities with the approval of authorities inevitably led to self-censorship and preference falsification, long before the establishment of the Soviet order.

The desire for outward respectability frequently conflicted with his goals of promoting social justice and the Ukrainian national identity, however he defined it. This clash between inner voice and outer image represented a theme that would haunt Dovzhenko to the end of his life.

Even after he left the teaching profession, he remained a teacher, attempting to balance responsibility and respectability. His film-making became a war against ignorance by other means.

Notes

1. Until 1949 Dovzhenko claimed to have been born on 30 August/ 12 September 1894. Drawing on baptismal records, Dovzhenko's biographer Mykola Kutsenko discovered that he was born on 29 August 1894 and baptised on 30 August. *Storinky*, p. 7 (29 August 1894 [old style] equals 10 September 1894 [new style]). See Professor I. S. Astapovich's 'Spravka' from 25 March 1970, Auxiliary Materials, Sosnytsia Dovzhenko Museum (cited hereafter as SDM). Also see DAMK, 153/5/2508.

2. Iu. S. Vynohrads'kyi, 'Deshcho pro batkivshchynu O. P. Dovzhenka', RGALI, 2081/1/1113, p. 39 (back).

3. N. A. Troinitskii, ed., *Pervaia Vseobschaia perepis' naseleniia Rossiiskoi imperii, 1897 g.*, vol. 48 (St Petersburg, 1904–5), pp. 112–15.

4. For a very brief history of the Dovzhenko family in Sosnytsia, see Iurii Vynohrads'kyi, 'Rid Oleksandra Dovzhenka', *PZh*, pp. 122–3.

5. Iakiv Nazarenko, in his 'Dorohy dytynstva ta iunosti', in *PZh*, p. 128, asserted that Alexander was the seventh child in his family. In Nazarenko's 'Ego shkol'nye gody', *Raduga*, no. 9 (1964), p. 141, he claimed that Alexander was the ninth child. Nazarenko claims that the Dovzhenko family had fourteen children, as does Alexander Dovzhenko. '1939 Autobiography', p. 7. But in his diary entry of 11 December 1943, the film-maker claims that he had

twelve siblings. *UVOKShch*, p. 241; *Hospody*, p. 215; and *ZDUVOShch*, p. 338.

6. Vitalii Pryhorovs'kyi, 'Tarasovychka: Pro matir O. P. Dovzhenko', *Desnians'ka pravda*, 19 July 1994, p. 3.

7. P. P. Dovzhenko-Dudko, 'Pro brata', *PZh*, p. 115.

8. '1939 Autobiography', p. 8.

9. Amanhal Bartelemi, 'Svit novoi liudyny', in *DIS*, p. 126.

10. Bartelemi, p. 126.

11. Heorhii Stoianov-Bihor, 'Velykyi mystets', polumianyi propahandyst', in *DIS*, p. 184.

12. Dovzhenko-Dudko, 'Pro brata', p. 115.

13. Quoted in V. Pryhorovs'kyi, 'Tarasovychka', p. 3.

14. Hanna Pylypivna Senchenko, RGALI, 2081/1/1212, p. 39.

15. Senchenko, p. 39.

16. In his '1939 Autobiography', Dovzhenko claimed that his family possessed between seven to seven-and-a-half *desiatinas* of land (a *desiatina* [*desiatyna* in Ukrainian] equals 2.7 acres). See '1939 Autobiography', p. 7. Vasyl' Artemovych Kopyl', a neighbour of the Dovzhenkos, asserted that the family possessed approximately ten hectares (a hectare equals 2.47 acres). V. A. Kopyl', RGALI, 2081/1/1212, p. 8. Also see Ivan Koshelivets', *Oleksandr Dovzhenko: Sproba tvorchoi biohrafii* (Munich, 1980), pp. 18–21; Bohdan Nebesio, 'The Silent Films of Alexander Dovzhenko: A Historical Poetics' (unpublished PhD dissertation, University of Alberta, Edmonton, 1996), pp. 28–9. Both Koshelivets' and Nebesio claim that Dovzhenko's family lived better than their neighbours.

17. See the memoirs by Symon's niece, Olena Samiilivna Khakalo, RGALI, 2081/1/1212, p. 48; and by Petro Symonovych Dovzhenko's neighbours: RGALI, 2081/1/1212, pp. 8, 25, 41–2, 50; Nadia Kolomiiets', 'Dorohi sertsiu liudy', *PZh*, pp. 126–7; and Vitalii Pryhorovs'kyi, '"Zahynuv vid holody": Z notatok pro bat'ka O. P. Dovzhenka', *Ukraina moloda*, 9 September 1994.

18. Ivan Ivanovych Lytavchyk, RGALI, 2081/1/1212, p. 24.

19. Kolomiiets', 'Dorohi sertsiu liudy', pp. 126–7 and Stepan Alekseevych Lytovchyk, RGALI, 2081/1/1212, p. 25.

20. Ia. P. Stepanenko, RGALI, 2081/1/1212, p. 42; and V. A. Kopyl', RGALI, 2081/1/1212, p. 8.

21. Jeffrey Brooks, *When Russia Learned to Read: Literacy and Popular Literature, 1861–1917* (Princeton, NJ, 1985), p. 12.

22. Calculated from Troinitskii, vols 8, 13, 16, 32, 33, 41, 46, 47, 48.

23. Bohdan Krawchenko, *Social Change and National Consciousness in Twentieth Century Ukraine* (New York, 1985), p. 14.

24. Ben Eklof, *Russian Peasant Schools: Officialdom, Village Culture, and Popular Pedagogy, 1861–1914* (Berkeley, CA, and London, 1986), p. 445.

25. Andreas Kappeler, 'The Ukrainians of the Russian Empire, 1860–1914', in A. Kappeler, ed., *The Formation of National Elites: Comparative Studies on Governments and Non-Dominant Ethnic Groups in Europe, 1850–1940* (Aldershot and New York, 1992), vol. 6, p. 106.

26. Krawchenko, p. 31.

27. See Fedir Savčenko, *The Suppression of Ukrainian Activities in 1876* (Munich, 1970). This monograph first appeared in 1930.

28. Nazarenko, 'Dorohy dytynstva ta iunosti', p. 129.

29. I. I. Lytavchyk, RGALI, 2081/1/1212, p. 24.

30. A. P. Iakovets', RGALI, 2081/1/1212.

31. '1939 Autobiography', p. 9.

32. Pryhorovs'kyi, 'Tarasovychka', p. 3.

33. Vira Makarenko, 'Nezabutnie dytyn'stvo', *DMM*, File 5, p. 1. On young Alexander as his grandfather's favourite, see O. S. Khakalo, in RGALI, 2081/1/1212, p. 49.

34. The travellers (with their teams of animals) were a distinct social group within Ukrainian society. They created their own folklore.

35. Nazarenko, 'Dorohy dytynstva ta iunosti', p. 135.

36. I. I. Lytavchyk, RGALI, 2081/1/1212, pp. 23–4. Also see Dovzhenko's diary entries for 15 and 16 December 1943; and 11 January 1944. *UVOKShch*, pp. 242, 243, 253–4; *Hospody*, pp. 216–17, 230–1; *ZDUVOShch*, pp. 340, 341, 354–5.

37. Lytavchyk, p. 24.

38. Lytavchyk, pp. 23–4.

39. Pryhorovs'kyi, 'Tarasovychka', p. 3.

40. V. A. Kopyl, RGALI, 2081/1/1212, p. 9.

41. '1939 Autobiography', p. 8.

42. '1939 Autobiography', p. 9.

43. S. Samsonenko, 'Dovzhenkove iunist'', *DMM*, File 2, p. 1.

44. Eklof, pp. 483–7.

45. V. M. Pryhorovs'kyi, '"Unykaty riznochytan" (Deiaki utochnennia do biohrafii O. P. Dovzhenka)', *Ukrains'ka mova i literatura v shkoli*, no. 8 (1979), p. 76.

46. H. P. Senchenko, in RGALI, 2081/1/1212, p. 40.

47. I. T. Tyshyna, RGALI, 2081/1/1212, p. 46.

48. I. Ie. Nekonechnyi, RGALI, 2081/1/1212, p. 34; Tyshyna, RGALI, 2081/1/1212, p. 46; Jerzy Plazewski, 'Poslednii iz troitsy', RGALI, 2081/1/1169, p. 1; Vira Makarenko, 'Nezabutnie dytynstvo', *DMM*, File 5, p. 2; Ivan Soroka, 'Hohol' u Sosnytsi', *Dnipro*, no. 5 (1964), p. 130; Iukhym

Martych, 'Kukhol' Dovzhenka', in his *Zustrichi bez proshchan': Biohrafichni rozpovidi* (Kiev, 1970), p. 165; and Ia. Nazarenko, 'Ego shkol'nye gody', p. 152.

49. Tyshyna, RGALI, 2081/1/1212, p. 46.

50. Nazarenko, 'Dorohy dytynstva ta iunosti', p. 37; '1939 Autobiography', p. 9.

51. Koshelivets', p. 31.

52. Christine Ruane, *Gender, Class, and the Professionalization of Russian City Teachers, 1860–1914* (Pittsburgh, 1994), p. 36.

53. '1939 Autobiography', p. 9.

54. M. I. Maltsev, 'Iz vospominanii odnoklassnika A. P. Dovzhenko', RGALI, 2081/1/1154, p. 7. Ia. Nazarenko claimed that 300 took the entrance exams, but the Teachers' Institute accepted only thirty. Ia. Nazarenko, 'K sol'ntsu, k schast'iu!', *Znamia*, no. 7 (1965), p. 133.

55. Cited in G. A. Mariagin, 'Legendy k biografii Dovzhenko', RGALI, 2081/1/1158, p. 14.

56. Samsonenko, 'Dovzhenkova iunist'', File 2, p. 9, cites Dovzhenko's claim; Mariagin, 'Legendy k biografii Dovzhenko', p. 14.

57. See Dovzhenko's certificate from the Ministry of Higher Education, DAMK, 153/5/2508, pp. 3, 10.

58. '1939 Autobiography', p. 9. Ivan Majstrenko graduated from the same type of institution on the eve of the March 1917 revolution and described it as a hotbed of socialism and Ukrainian nationalism. Dovzhenko may be hiding something here. See Ivan Majstrenko, *Istoriia moho pokolinnia: Spohady uchasnyka revoliutsiinykh podii v Ukraini* (Edmonton, Alberta, 1985), especially pp. 13–32. I am grateful to Serhy Yekelchyk for reminding me of this source.

59. Ruane, pp. 36, 37.

60. Calculated from Troinitskii, vols 8, 13, 16, 32, 33, 41, 46, 47, 48.

61. Kappeler, p. 115.

62. T. Baimut, 'Novye materialy k biografii A. P. Dovzhenko', *Iskusstvo kino*, no. 10 (1959), p. 149.

63. According to Ivan Ivanovich Afanas'ev (Dovzhenko's colleague who worked at the school from 1911 through 1918), as cited in Baimut, p. 149.

64. V. S. Dovzhenko, 'Moi vospominaniia ob Aleksandre Petroviche Dovzhenko', RGALI, 2081/1/1123, p. 1; and Varvara Dovzhenko, 'Naidorozhche, vichne', *PZh*, p. 141. Krylova's biographer claimed that she and Dovzhenko secretly married in the first part of 1917 (see Mykola Kutsenko, 'Spovid' pro trahichne kokhannia', *Vitchyzna*, no. 4 [1991], p. 183), but this is not the case. In the spring of 1917 they began to live together, but did not necessarily marry.

65. Baimut, p. 149.
66. '1939 Autobiography', p. 10.
67. Gennadii Konovalov, 'Dovzhenko nachinalsia tak …', in B. N. Tarasenko and G. M. Kapel'gorodskaia, eds, *Uroki Aleksandra Dovzhenko: Sbornik statei* (Kiev, 1982), pp. 123–4.
68. I. Ie. Nakonechnyi, RGALI, 2081/1/1212, p. 34.
69. Ia. Nazarenko, 'Ego shkol'nye gody', pp. 144, 145.
70. P. A. Moiseenko, RGALI, 2081/1/1212, p. 32a.
71. N. V. Kolenko, RGALI, 2081/1/1212, p. 14.
72. V. S. Dovzhenko, RGALI, 2081/1/1123, pp. 2, 3; and Varvara Dovzhenko, 'Naidorozhche, vichne', p. 142.
73. Nazarenko quoted Dovzhenko saying at the Teachers' Institute: 'One needs not only to know how to restrain oneself, but also how to act; not only to endure suffering, but most importantly to fight for happiness.' Nazarenko, 'K sol'ntsu', p. 134.
74. '1939 Autobiography', p. 10.
75. Tat'iana Kyrylenko-Baturenko, 'Dobryi den', Uvazhemaia Tat'iana Timofeevna (9 April 1988)', Folder 7, *DMM*, p. 1 (b), makes this assertion; on Dovzhenko's physical evaluation, see RGALI, 2081/2/184.
76. *PZh*, p. 143.
77. Dovzhenko claims that this is the case and that he was born on 30 August 1894. See Oleksandr Hryshchenko, *Z berehiv zacharovanoi Desny* (Kiev, 1964), p. 15.
78. Troinitskii, vol. 48, pp. 112–15.
79. Mykhailo Kovalenko, 'Z Dovzhenkovoi krynytsi', in M. Kovalenko and Oleksii Mishurin, *Syn zacharovanoi Desny* (Kiev, 1984), pp. 24–5. For a history of the Kobzars, see Natalie O. Kononenko, *Ukranian Minstrels: 'and the Blind Shall Sing'* (Armonk, NY, 1998).
80. '1939 Autobiography', p. 10.
81. A number of scholars have argued that literacy is a key ingredient in the formation of a national consciousness and that, in general, illiterates have difficulties in developing a sense of national awareness. See Ernest Gellner, *Thought and Change* (Chicago, 1965), chapter 7; Gale Stokes, 'Cognition and the Function of Nationalism', *Journal of Interdisciplinary History*, 4, no. 4 (1974), pp. 543–70; Ernest Gellner, *Nations and Nationalism* (Ithaca, NY, 1983); Benedict Anderson, *Imagined Communities: Reflections on the Origin and Spread of Nationalism* (London, 1983); and Roman Szporluk, *Communism and Nationalism: Karl Marx versus Friedrich List* (New York and Oxford, 1988), especially chapter 6.
82. Troinitskii, vol. 48, pp. 112–15.

83. '1939 Autobiography', p. 10.

84. '1939 Autobiography', p. 10; and Kovalenko, 'Z Dovzhenkovoi krynytsi', p. 26.

85. '1939 Autobiography', p. 10.

86. P. Kosmins'kyi, 'Donos sviatoho ottsia', *Molod' Ukrainy*, 7 September 1983, p. 2.

87. 'Spohady Marii Tymofiivny Nyrkovskoi', SDM, A-228.

2

Revolution and Civil War

The records left by Dovzhenko, his family and friends leave gaps as to his precise whereabouts and political allegiances during the course of the Revolution and the Civil War. The omission of this information stems from a good reason: his political trajectory between 1917 and 1920 did not follow a pro-Bolshevik course. He started the Revolution as a Ukrainian nationalist; only in April 1920 did he join the Communist Party (Bolshevik) of Ukraine.

In the various versions of his autobiography, he emphasised his own political backwardness, omitting details about his activities between 1917 and 1920.[1] Accounts written by his family and friends after Stalin's death attempted to fit Dovzhenko and his politics into the proper political slots. Barbara Krylova-Dovzhenko, for example, recounted in the late 1950s how her then fiancé greeted the tsar's abdication in the spring of 1917 in Zhytomyr:

> I saw him on the street, happy and excited. He was running somewhere, and without stopping, he waved and enthusiastically yelled out: 'It's started!' ...
>
> A demonstration was organized. Everyone was happy. But Alexander Petrovych was not among us. I searched for him with my eyes ... And suddenly I felt as if an electrical spark penetrated my heart. He was standing on the platform, his face inspired and pale ... the wind ruffled his hair ... he held a crumpled cap in his hand, and his expansive gestures with this hand made him seem stronger and more courageous. His voice sounded excited and passionate ... He spoke about a single will, a single goal, and how the recently awakened people came together, about their formidable strength.[2]

Her account conspicuously omits the words Dovzhenko spoke and the political viewpoint he asserted. She preferred vague generalities: 'His heart burned with hatred and contempt toward the enemies of our Fatherland, the various occupiers and nationalists; he mercilessly ridiculed them.' She asserted that in late 1917 or early 1918, he established contact with the advancing Red divisions then approaching Kiev and helped pave the way for them.[3] For obvious political reasons, she completely fabricated the assertion that Dovzhenko worked on behalf of the Bolsheviks.

One of Dovzhenko's neighbours from Sosnytsia provided a more accurate account of Dovzhenko's views. He remembered a conversation he had with the young teacher in the summer of 1917, while he was recuperating from a heart operation that left him with complications for the rest of his life.[4] In this dialogue, Dovzhenko expressed support for the Bolshevik Party, but because 'he passionately loved his Ukrainian people and their language and their traditions', he did not approve of this party's leaders speaking before the crowds in Russian.[5]

While Dovzhenko may have agreed with the Bolshevik social and political programme, as an *intelligent* who identified himself with the Ukrainian people, he viewed the Bolshevik Party as a Russian-speaking party, a party alien to the Ukrainian-speaking provinces. In 1917 he interpreted the world primarily through the lens of national, not class, divisions. In his 1939 autobiography, he admitted as much in recounting his reaction to the tsar's overthrow:

> I called out slogans at meetings and was happy as a dog that had broken its chain, sincerely believing that now all men were brothers, that everything was completely clear; that the peasants had the land, the workers had the factories, the teachers had the schools, the doctors had the hospitals, the Ukrainians had Ukraine, the Russians had Russia; that the next day the whole world would find out about this and, struck with our vision, would do likewise. I was particularly pleased that Tsar Nicholas II was a Russian, not a Ukrainian, indeed that his entire family was not Ukrainian. To my way of thinking this proved the complete noncomplicity of Ukrainians with the despicable, overthrown regime. This was nationalism.
>
> At that time all Ukrainians seemed to me to be especially nice people. It was easy to complain about the years (three hundred!) we had suffered from the damned Russians. We had even forgotten Ukrainian and spoke a broken Ukrainian-Russian [creole]. This language made me think of all Ukrainians as peasants, or at least descended from peasants, not gentlemen. After all, the gentlemen spoke Russian and wouldn't even dream of speaking Ukrainian. Hence, we had no gentlemen. Hence, everything was all right. It seemed to me then that the Ukrainian bourgeois separatist movement was the most revolutionary movement, the farthest to the left, and therefore the best ... I knew nothing about Communism ...[6]

Although teachers at the Institute at Hlukhiv had introduced Dovzhenko to Chernyshevsky and Herzen, perhaps even to Marxist literature, Dovzhenko depicted himself as politically naive during the revolutionary period. He wrote the preceding account of his political views in 1939, when he applied for readmission to the Communist Party, which dropped him from its rolls in the summer of 1923. In filling out the membership form, he had to admit his sympathies in 1917, which filled thick files at the headquarters of the Ukrainian People's Commissariat of Internal Affairs (NKVD) by the end of the 1930s.[7]

In seeking readmittance to the party, Dovzhenko had to reveal his nationalist past, but at the same time he had to downplay, justify and excuse these activities. He claimed that he had joined the pro-peasant Ukrainian Communist Party (Borotbist), which had splintered off from the Ukrainian Socialist Revolutionary Party (UPSR) in February 1918 and which united with the left wing of the Ukrainian Social Democratic Workers' Party in August 1919.[8] When this reorganised Borotbist Party dissolved itself and merged with the Communist Party in April 1920, Dovzhenko joined the Communists.[9]

He started the Revolution as a member of the UPSR and as a supporter of the Ukrainian Central Council (*Ukrains'ka Tsentral'na Rada*), which became the coordinating body for most Ukrainian groups attempting to win wide-scale political, social and cultural rights for Ukrainians from the Provisional Government in Petrograd. The *Rada* claimed authority over all political activities in the nine Ukrainian provinces.[10]

V. V. Bobienko, a former archdeacon of the independent Ukrainian Autocephalous Orthodox Church, who was arrested in the 1930s, claimed at a session with his NKVD interrogator to have heard Dovzhenko speak at the Sosnytsia meeting hall in the summer of 1917. At that time, 'he appeared on behalf of the Ukrainian Socialist Revolutionary Party, he stood for the independence of Ukraine, and agitated on behalf of the Central *Rada*'.[11] Although it is unclear how the NKVD extracted this testimony from Bobienko, in light of Dovzhenko's background and his Ukrainian identity, Bobienko's assertion, the only available document of the young teacher's political affiliation in 1917, sounds plausible.

The UPSR supported the idea of a democratic federal Russian republic with national-territorial autonomy for the Ukrainian provinces and the free development of the Ukrainian language in all governmental institutions. Most importantly, it sought radical agrarian reform with state ownership of the large estates. Eventually self-governing bodies within local communities would supervise the redistribution of these estates among the peasants. The Ukrainian Socialist Revolutionaries (SRs) derived their support from the poor and middle peasants and partly from the rural proletariat. Like the Russian Socialist Revolutionaries, the Ukrainian party gained great influence in the countryside but not in the cities. They constituted the most important political base for the Central *Rada*.

At the beginning of 1918, Alexander visited Sosnytsia, perhaps for the Christmas holidays.[12] Rumours had spread that the leaders of the local land administration conspired to re-establish the 'bourgeois' and tsarist order in Sosnytsia and in the surrounding region. At a meeting where poor peasants, artisans, workers and civil servants spoke loudly against such an action, Dovzhenko jumped on stage and pushed the speaker aside, demanding the land administration's dispersal. 'Let's fight for soviet power!' he shouted.[13] The neighbour recounting this event, unfortunately, did not mention which soviet power or whose soviet power Dovzhenko supported, but his interpretation of soviet power most likely differed from that of the Bolsheviks. From his point of view, it did not mean Bolshevik control of the soviets. For him, soviet power probably meant local control. Since the overwhelming majority of the countryside spoke Ukrainian, local control meant Ukrainian control.[14]

Improving the plight of the Ukrainian peasantry lay at the heart of Dovzhenko's political beliefs. His sister Polina recounted how, in the summer of 1918, large numbers of peasants visited him at home in Sosnytsia. They sat up talking until the early morning hours. Dovzhenko's mother could not understand what her educated son had in common with these country bumpkins. Alexander explained: 'These grandfathers, Mother, represent history.'[15] Although a teacher living in the large city of Kiev, he did not divorce himself from his peasant past or from the revolution in the Ukrainian countryside.

Thus, Dovzhenko began the revolution in 1917 as a member of the UPSR, the largest, most powerful and most pro-peasant political party within the Central *Rada*'s coalition. His support of the peasantry and their interests formed the cornerstone of his Ukrainian socialism. The peasants' illiteracy, lack of discipline and political apathy, however, caused this cornerstone to wobble.

By the end of 1917, the *Rada* had failed to gain control over the chaotic situation in the Ukrainian provinces that followed the collapse of the Provisional Government. Despite the overwhelming victory of the Ukrainian political parties at the elections to the Constituent Assembly in November, their success proved ephemeral. Ukrainian-speaking peasants may have voted enthusiastically for the UPSR, but they did not necessarily support a Ukrainian government claiming control over them. Only the issue of land confiscation and redistribution excited the peasants. With little support in the cities and with mass confusion in the countryside, an organised Ukrainian nationalist movement disintegrated in late 1917 and early 1918. Bolshevik-led invasions accelerated this process.

After the Bolsheviks won power in Russia's largest cities in November and December 1917, they invaded Ukraine in January 1918. In response the *Rada* declared the independence of the Ukrainian National Republic. Mykhailo Hrushevsky assumed the mantle of leadership as the country's first president. By signing a separate peace treaty with the Central Powers at Brest-Litovsk in February, he sought to stabilise the Ukrainian provinces. In exchange for diplomatic recognition and military support, the *Rada* agreed to give a specific amount of grain to Germany and to Austria-Hungary. In return 400,000 German and Austro-Hungarian soldiers entered Ukraine, drove off the Bolshevik armies and restored order to the countryside.

Although the *Rada* returned in triumph in March 1918, it could not reignite peasant enthusiasm. The land question led to increasing division. Because the Germans and the Austrians coveted the Ukrainian harvest for the purpose of feeding their starving populations, they wanted the large estates to remain intact, while the peasants wished to see them broken up and the land apportioned among themselves. The *Rada* found itself in a classic dilemma. On the one hand, it could not alienate the peasantry, its largest constituency, by abandoning land reforms. On the other hand, the *Rada* desperately needed German arms in order to survive.

Desperate for wheat, German officials began to interfere in Ukrainian affairs. In early April, the commander-in-chief of the German occupation army, Field Marshal Hermann von Eichhorn, ordered the peasants as well as the large landowners to sow all arable land. Finally, on 29 April 1918, German commanders in Ukraine supported General Pavlo Skoropadsky's coup against the *Rada*. Although Skoropadsky identified himself as a Ukrainian and had supported the Ukrainianisation of military units under his command in 1917, he quickly alienated the Ukrainian nationalists and the peasants by surrounding himself with conservative figures, many of them Russian and apparently hostile to the Ukrainian state and to land reform. Many of these individuals gravitated towards the re-establishment of a Russia 'one and indivisible' and a return to the pre-revolutionary social order. With their support, Skoropadsky reintroduced a landlord-oriented agrarian policy and supported reprisals against peasants who divided the landlords' estates.[16]

Dovzhenko spent the last four months of 1917 and most of 1918 in Kiev. He became a teacher at the Seventh Higher Primary School in Kiev in September 1917 and audited courses at the Kiev Commercial Institute (later the Institute for the National Economy) and at the newly founded Academy of Arts, where he sought to learn artistic techniques and to become a professional artist.[17] Here, he may have met Vasyl H. Krychevsky, the academy's director, who became his set designer for *Zvenyhora*, and his son, Vasyl V. Krychevsky, who became the set designer for *Earth*.[18]

In Kiev Dovzhenko lived through the pivotal events of 1918: the Central *Rada*'s proclamation of Ukrainian independence on 22 January; Matvei Muraviev's Red Army troops' occupation of the city on 8 February; the subsequent execution of thousands of Ukrainians for supporting the *Rada*; the 3 March entry of Germans into the city; and Skoropadsky's ascension as Hetman of Ukraine. In early 1918 Kiev's streets ran red with blood.

During his three semesters (autumn 1917 and spring and autumn 1918) at the Commercial Institute, Dovzhenko most likely met Alexander Shumsky and Vasyl Blakytny, fellow-students who later became the leaders of the Borotbist Party. At the Institute, Dovzhenko chaired the Student Union and organised a large citywide meeting against Skoropadsky. Held in the autumn of 1918, this demonstration was in protest at the Hetman's draft of students into his army. As the students left this demonstration, Skoropadsky's troops shot into the crowd, killing twenty students and wounding nearly one hundred.[19] Despite this tragedy, Dovzhenko's organising abilities probably impressed Shumsky and Blakytny, who went on to pave his way into the Communist Party. Until the mid-1920s, they remained Dovzhenko's major patrons and mentors.

With the collapse of Austria-Hungary in October 1918, the revolution in Germany and the armistice on the Western front on 11 November, German and Austrian troops sought to return home as quickly as possible. Since by that time no regime could survive without the support of a strong foreign army, Skoropadsky's rule came to an end. After a mass peasant and nationalist uprising in November and December led by the Directory, he abdicated and fled with the retreating Germans.

After Skoropadsky, the Directory – the Ukrainian nationalist successor to the Central *Rada* – came to power in December, only to lose its support quickly. Many peasant detachments, which had joined the Directory's army in order to oust Skoropadsky, now abandoned Symon Petliura, its commander. The uneasy alliance between the urban-centred Ukrainian nationalists and the peasants came to an end. Chaos reigned.

The Soviet Russian government's second and third invasions, mass peasant uprisings in the spring of 1919, the emergence of anarchist bands, the White and Allied interventions, pogroms against the Jews and the Polish-Soviet War of 1920 all transformed Ukraine into a confusing carousel of death and destruction.[20] According to historian Richard Pipes, in 1919, 'no fewer than nine different governments attempted to assert their authority over the land. None succeeded.'[21]

This chaos reinforced peasant desires to withdraw from all active political involvement. The invasions, interventions and occupations by the Bolsheviks, Whites, Germans, Poles and others dislocated existing social and political relationships, inaugurated antagonisms between groups and radically sharpened existing tensions.[22] These migrations into the Ukrainian provinces fuelled the bitter struggle between the food-producing 'natives' (the Ukrainians) and the food-consuming 'outsiders' (the Russians, Jews, Germans, Poles and Bolsheviks), further differentiating those who worked the soil from those who came from the cities, demanded grain, initiated mass conscriptions and disrupted the peasant way of life.

As the Red Army advanced, the Directory abandoned Kiev in early February 1919. It barely survived, controlling only small areas of territory for short periods of time. Over the next two years, this geographic area constantly shifted, as did its provisional seat of government.

Dovzhenko lived in Kiev after the first Bolshevik occupation in January 1918, but he did not reside there during the second Bolshevik occupation from 5 February 1919 to the end of August 1919. This seven-month span remains the most undocumented period in his life.

In order to defend the Ukrainian revolution, Dovzhenko left Kiev with Petliura's forces in February. By the summer of 1919, Petliura's army controlled only a small sliver of territory and declared Kamianets-Podilsk, located 300 kilometres southwest of Kiev, its temporary capital. It served this function from July to November 1919. At Kamianets-Podilsk Dovzhenko met the humourist Ostap Vyshnia, the poet Volodymyr Sosiura and the artist Anatol Petrytsky, who also retreated with the Directory.[23] They became his closest friends for life.

Two more documents confirm Dovzhenko's role as a Ukrainian nationalist soldier: a neighbour's claim to have seen a photograph of him in a Ukrainian nationalist uniform in 1918 or 1919, and Dovzhenko's admission that he served in the army of the Ukrainian National Republic in 1919 after the uprising against Hetman Pavlo Skoropadsky.[24] This admission never appeared in his autobiographical statement, which he attached to the party application form in 1939.[25] Most importantly, he claimed that he never participated in any battles against the Red Army.[26]

At least one man (the aforementioned Bobienko, the former archdeacon from Sosnytsia) contradicted Dovzhenko, asserting that during the Red Army's advance on Kiev in February 1919, he fired on the Bolshevik troops from Vladimir's Hill. 'I heard', he claimed, 'that when A. P. Dovzhenko retreated with Petliura's army he participated in Jewish pogroms in Fastov and Kazatyn.'[27]

Bobienko's statement leaves some room for doubt since this witness provided his 'confession' to the NKVD, well known for its use of threats and torture. In the 1930s, members of the security organs began to collect information on Dovzhenko, in the event orders came to build a case against him. Although the secret police built a 'paper trail' on the film-maker composed of contradictory statements and coerced confessions, he did actively fight against the Red Army.

On 19 September 1919, the Red Army overran Zhytomyr, and the Cheka captured Dovzhenko with 'arms in his hands' shortly afterwards.[28] In his 1939 application to the Communist Party, he claimed that the Cheka released him after an investigation, implying that the secret police could not find any evidence against him.[29] According to documents recently published in Ukraine, a revolutionary court on 27 December 1919 ascertained that he voluntarily joined Petliura's army and returned to the areas controlled by the Red Army. The court considered Dovzhenko an enemy of the newly founded Bolshevik order and sentenced him to imprisonment in a concentration camp until the end of the Civil War. Because prominent Borotbists intervened on his behalf with the Russian Communist Party's provincial committee, the Cheka court did not carry out Dovzhenko's sentence.[30]

The Cheka imprisoned Dovzhenko during the last four months of 1919. In his 1939 autobiography, he alluded – albeit vaguely – to these months of isolation, pain, doubt and uncertainty: 'I paid for the mistakes of my raw mind and passionate heart with months of suffering and serious reflection.'[31] He did not include any details.

After his release, Dovzhenko hid what had happened to him; he then rewrote some parts of his past. He told some of his friends that he had voluntarily left the Ukrainian nationalists and joined the Bolshevik cause. With the exception of his closest friends, such as Vyshnia, Sosiura and Petrytsky, who joined him as comrades-in-arms in the nationalist camp, few knew of Dovzhenko's actual activities during the Revolution. No one recorded them.

Maksym Vovchenko, a friend from Zhytomyr and the Commercial Institute, met Dovzhenko in Kiev in 1920 and heard Dovzhenko's revised account, another reinvention of himself. According to Vovchenko, his friend explained how he became bitterly disappointed with the nationalist cause:

> 'I left this camp in disgrace and went over to the side of the Red armies, became a Bolshevik, and became a member of the party,' he concluded. 'You were right in not coming with me, you would have died. How many of our good young men sacrificed themselves for this absurd idea!' he said. 'I want to write a novel about all this and I'll call it *Knights of the Absurd*'.[32]

In his 1939 autobiographical statement, Dovzhenko expressed his disillusionment with Ukrainian nationalism even more explicitly:

> The world had proved to be much more complex than I had imagined. Ukraine proved to be more complex too. It had plenty of its own and foreign masters, who spoke excellent Ukrainian, and the [princelings] with whom I associated in my search for truth turned out to be a sorry lot of ignoramuses, charlatans, and traitors. I fled from them with a profound feeling of disgust and bitterness. This memory is the most oppressive one I have.[33]

Whatever the veracity of his disillusionment with the Ukrainian nationalists, Dovzhenko's remarks sought to rationalise his acceptance of the Communist cause – to himself, if not to others. He did so with the help of the Borotbists. After the successful third Bolshevik invasion of Ukraine in late 1919, the leaders of the Borotbists decided to dissolve their party and join the Communist Party (Bolshevik) of Ukraine (CP[b]U), hoping to Ukrainianise it from within. In late March 1920, the Fourth Congress of the CP(b)U voted to admit into its ranks approximately 4,000 Borotbists, including such leaders as Blakytny, Shumsky, Grigory Grinko (Hryhory Hrynko), Panas Liubchenko and others.[34]

The Communist Party accepted these former Borotbists with great caution. On 25 March 1920, at a meeting of the Provisional Bureau of the Central Committee of the CP(b)U, the party's leaders ordered Communist organisations in the provinces to accept, first of all, former Borotbists who had joined the party before

General Anton Denikin's White Army invasion in August 1919, and, secondly, those who had joined the anti-Denikin underground afterwards.[35]

Dovzhenko did not fit either category. As a member of the Directory's armed forces, he may have fought against Denikin's forces, but no evidence proves that he ever became a Borotbist.[36] Although the Borotbists emerged from the UPSR, the political party that first attracted Dovzhenko in 1917, the Borotbists broke with the Directory in late 1918.[37] In 1919, Dovzhenko and the Borotbists fought on opposite sides.

Given his alliance with the Ukrainian SRs between 1917 and 1919, Dovzhenko could not have become a member of the Communist Party in 1920 without joining under the Borotbist umbrella.[38] He came under this umbrella because Blakytny and Shumsky, who occupied important positions in the CP(b)U after the merger, must have pulled strings on his behalf.[39]

In the course of the Revolution and Civil War, very similar people, as Andrea Graziosi points out, 'sharing often identical backgrounds, could evolve in diverging ways'.[40] Different choices often led people in opposite directions, but these paths also intersected. Blakytny, Shumsky and Dovzhenko emerged from the same cloth, but the first two chose the Borotbists, then the Communists, while Dovzhenko elected to become a Ukrainian Socialist Revolutionary.

Although these choices generated much brutality in battle, the Borotbists and the Ukrainian SRs differed only slightly in terms of ideology. Both claimed to fight on behalf of the toiling people in the countryside, for local control, for Ukraine and for a free world.[41] Both political parties demanded the radical redistribution of land in the countryside to the poorest peasants. The major issue that divided the two groups focused on their relationship with and attitude towards the Bolsheviks. The Borotbists sought to ally themselves with this predominantly Russian political party, while the Ukrainian SRs opposed them. The choice between alliance with the first party or the second often hinged on arbitrary decisions, contingent on circumstances beyond the control of any individual.

Blakytny and Shumsky realised the tragedy of the situation. They, especially Blakytny, reacted fondly to Dovzhenko.[42] They recognised his organisational abilities. By gaining his release from the Cheka and by pulling him into the Borotbist ranks on the eve of its merger with the Communist Party, they saved him from an uncertain fate.

Conclusion

In 1918 Dovzhenko read one of his short stories, 'A Person Tied up in a Sack', to Maksym Vovchenko. Although Vovchenko forgot the story's contents, he vividly remembered its central image fifty years later. 'Even now I see on the sidewalk a sack . . ., in which a person, not having the possibility or the strength to climb out of it, contorts and throws himself to the left and right.' Vovchenko then concluded: 'I thought that Dovzhenko was the person in the sack.'[43]

The sack became a metaphor for Dovzhenko's politics after 1917. When the Revolution broke out, all tsarist restrictions evaporated. Dovzhenko could publicly express his views, participate in mass meetings and demonstrations, and even join political parties. The Revolution set his heart and mind on fire. He became intoxicated: the new revolutionaries would sweep away the injustices and inequalities of the past. Men and women around the world would soon enjoy liberty, equality and fraternity. He could now celebrate his Ukrainian identity without fear of political reprisal.

To Dovzhenko, as to many others, the course of the Ukrainian Revolution brought great disappointment. Ukrainian intellectuals with socialist sympathies in the cities sought to create an independent Ukrainian National Republic, but they could not permanently bind the peasantry to their cause, nor could the Ukrainian National Republic withstand Bolshevik attack. Joining Petliura's army, Dovzhenko fled Kiev and spent nearly eight months on the run. Defeat followed defeat, exacerbating peoples' differences, generating squabbles and creating a sense of impending doom in the ever-shifting camps. He undoubtedly imagined that he had joined a great cause. This belief brought him great exhilaration in 1917 and 1918, but great despair in 1919.

Falling into the hands of the Cheka in September 1919, the trauma of imprisonment caused Dovzhenko to re-evaluate his revolutionary enthusiasms and his loss of innocence. In his cell, he had much time to himself. He could reflect on his world turned upside down. The Ukrainian Revolution had collapsed. Ukrainian peasants, his own flesh and blood, had betrayed his hopes and aspirations.

He may well have concluded that his efforts to establish an independent Ukrainian state were 'absurd' and brought him nothing but deprivation, suffering and brushes with death. At perhaps his darkest and most depressing moment, the Borotbists in Zhytomyr gained his release and offered him an opportunity to redeem himself. After regaining his freedom, Dovzhenko took every chance to transform himself.

His political journey between 1917 and 1920 lacked a coherent logic, but this inconsistency emerged from the chaos unleashed by revolution, invasion and civil war. He took calculated risks and made every effort to eke sense out of his confusing surroundings. When his circumstances changed, he did what many did during this turbulent period – he switched sides. He survived as best he could in an incredibly violent, volatile and difficult period.

Dovzhenko's political choices between 1917 and 1919 left a sword of Damocles hanging over his head for the rest of his life.[44] Although the Stalinist national security state began to emerge only a decade later, Soviet security organs had already flagged Dovzhenko. His nationalist allegiances and his arrest became powerful incentives to conform publicly, especially during the purges of the 1930s. His experiences as a Cheka prisoner in 1919 may have permanently wounded him emotionally, if not physically. Although he became a 'person tied up in a sack', vestiges of his earlier 'knighthood of the absurd' remained an integral part of his life.

Notes

1. Between 1928 and 1954, Dovzhenko wrote at least ten different autobiographical statements. The 1939 autobiography remains his most complete. Dovzhenko's autobiographies are held in RGALI, 2081/1/350, 2081/1/381 and 2081/1/944.
2. Varvara Dovzhenko, 'Naidorozhche, vichne', *PZh*, pp. 142–3.
3. RGALI, 2081/1/1123, p. 4; and Varvara Dovzhenko, 'Naidorozhche, vichne', p. 143.
4. *PZh*, p. 132; Bohdan Nebesio, 'The Silent Films of Alexander Dovzhenko: A Historical Poetics' (unpublished Ph.D. dissertation, University of Alberta, Edmonton, 1996), p. 30.
5. Panteleimon Antonovych Moiseenko, RGALI, 2081/1/1212, pp. 32a and 32b. Citation appears on p. 32b.
6. '1939 Autobiography', pp. 11–12.
7. Some of these files are in TsDA-MLMU, 1196/2/6–14. By examining the handwritten numbering on the upper right-hand corner of the documents, one can see that this is not a complete set. Viacheslav Popyk published excerpts from the Cheka/OGPU/GPU/NKVD/KGB archives in *D*, pp. 21–60; and *ZA*, pp. 235–80. Most of the secret police files on Dovzhenko, however, remain under lock and key in Moscow and Kiev.
8. '1939 Autobiography', p. 13.
9. '1939 Autobiography', p. 13.
10. The most useful studies of the Ukrainian Revolution include: John S. Reshetar, Jr., *The Ukrainian Revolution, 1917–1920: A Study in Nationalism* (Princeton, NJ, 1952); Arthur E. Adams, *Bolsheviks in the Ukraine: The Second Campaign, 1918–1919* (New Haven, CT, 1963); Petr A. Arshinov, *History of the Makhnovist Movement, 1918–1921* (Detroit, 1974); Taras Hunczak, ed., *The Ukraine, 1917–1921: A Study in Revolution* (Cambridge, MA, 1977); Jurij Borys, *The Sovietization of Ukraine, 1917–1923: The Communist Doctrine and Practice of National Self-Determination* (2nd ed., Edmonton, Alberta, 1980); and Steven L. Guthier, 'The Roots of Popular Ukrainian Nationalism: A Demographic, Social, and Political Study of the Ukrainian Nationality to 1917' (unpublished PhD dissertation, University of Michigan, Ann Arbor, 1990).

11. Cited in *ZA*, p. 238.

12. In the Orthodox calendar, Christmas occurs on 7 January.

13. P. M. Nyrkovskii, 'Vospominaniia ob A. P. Dovzhenko', RGALI, 2081/2/213, pp. 9–9a (citation on p. 9a). Another account of this incident, which the unknown author placed in September 1917, appeared in 'Vospominanie ob A. P. Dovzhenko', *DMM*, File 1, pp. 1–2.

14. John L. H. Keep, *The Russian Revolution: A Study in Mass Mobilization* (New York, 1976); Andrea Graziosi, *The Great Soviet Peasant War: Bolsheviks and Peasants, 1917–1933* (Cambridge, MA, 1996); and Andrea Graziosi, *Bol'sheviki i krest'iane na Ukraine, 1918–1919 gody* (Moscow, 1997) explore this peasant understanding of 'soviet power'.

15. Cited in R. Korohods'kyi, 'Zadushenyi holos', *Slovo*, no. 12 (June 1991), p. 5.

16. For an analysis of Skoropadsky's rule, see Taras Hunczak, 'The Ukraine Under Hetman Pavlo Skoropadsky', in Hunczak, ed., *The Ukraine, 1917–1921*, pp. 61–81; and Oleh S. Fedyshyn, *Germany's Drive to the East and the Ukrainian Revolution, 1917–1918* (New Brunswick, NJ, 1971), especially pp. 60–183.

17. DAMK, 153/5/2508, p. 16 (over), contains Dovzhenko's third (Autumn 1918) semester transcript from the Commercial Institute; also Mykhailo Kovalenko and Oleksii Mishurin, *Syn zacharovanoi Desny* (Kiev, 1984), p. 110.

18. Nebesio, 'The Silent Films of Alexander Dovzhenko', p. 48.

19. '1939 Autobiography', pp. 12-13; Mykhailo Kovalenko, 'Z Dovzhenkovoi krynytsi', in Kovalenko and Mishurin, *Syn zacharovanoi Desny*, p. 27. Maksym Vovchenko, a friend in Kiev, claimed that when Skoropadsky's troops opened fire, all the students 'fell to the pavement, only Dovzhenko remained standing, waving his hands and yelling something to the officers'. M. Vovchenko, 'Iakym ia znav O. Dovzhenka', *DMM*, File 8, p. 18. Perhaps this event occurred. Most likely, Vovchenko embellished Dovzhenko's actions. According to *Ukraine: A Concise Encyclopedia* (Toronto, 1963), vol. 1, p. 752, Skoropadsky's Council of Ministers declared a general military conscription and reorganised the armed forces on 24 July 1918.

20. Different sources estimate the total number of victims of pogroms to be between 50,000 and 200,000. See Elias Heifetz, *The Slaughter of the Jews in the Ukraine in 1919* (New York, 1921); I. Cherikover, *Antisemitizm i pogromy na Ukraine, 1917–1918* (Berlin, 1923); Leo Motzkin, ed., *The Pogroms in the Ukraine under the Ukrainian Governments, 1917–1920* (London, 1927); and Richard Pipes, *Russia under the Bolshevik Regime* (New York, 1994), pp. 110–12. Also see Henry Abramson's *A Prayer for the Government: Jews and Ukrainians in Revolutionary Times* (Cambridge, MA, 1999).

21. Richard Pipes, *The Formation of the Soviet Union: Communism and Nationalism, 1917–1923*, rev. ed. (Cambridge, MA, 1997), p. 148.

22. Geoff Eley, 'Remapping the Nation: War, Revolutionary Upheaval, and State Formation in Eastern Europe, 1914–1923', in Peter J. Potichnyj and Howard Aster, eds, *Ukrainian-Jewish Relations in Historical Perspective* (Edmonton, Alberta, 1988), pp. 205–46.

23. Varvara Oleksiivna Hubenko-Masliuchenko and Larysa Mykolaivna Petrytska, the widows of Ostap Vyshnia and Anatol Petrytsky, respectively, told this to Roman Korohodsky in the early 1960s. Korohods'kyi, 'Zadushenyi holos', p. 5. In his autobiographical novel, *Tretia rota: roman*, 2nd ed. (Kiev, 1997), the poet Volodymyr Sosiura (1898–1965) does not mention Dovzhenko's participation in Petliura's forces. He most likely sought to protect Dovzhenko's (as well as his own) 'communist' reputation.

24. On this alleged photograph, see *D*, p. 22; *ZA*, p. 241. For Dovzhenko's admission, see 'Anketa vstupaiushchego kandidatom v chleny VKP(b), zapolnennia A. P. Dovzhenko (20 November 1939)', RGALI, 2081/1/944, p. 2.

25. '1939 Autobiography', pp. 12–13.

26. RGALI, 2081/1/944, p. 2.

27. Cited in *ZA*, p. 238.

28. 'Zakliuchenie po delu No. 112 na Dovzhenko Aleksandra Petrovicha, 25 let', in *D*, p. 22.

29. 'Anketa', RGALI, 2081/1/944, p. 2.

30. 'Zakliuchenie po delu No. 112', p. 22. This document, unfortunately, does not reveal which Borotbists helped Dovzhenko. Also see *Hospody*, pp. 642–3 and TsDA-MLMU, 1196/2/13.

31. '1939 Autobiography', p. 12.

32. Vovchenko, pp. 19–20.

33. '1939 Autobiography', p. 12.

34. *Ukraine: A Concise Encyclopedia*, vol. 1, p. 803.

35. 'Protokol No. 1, Zasedaniia komissii po likvidatsii i vlianii byvshei partii kommunistov borot'bistov v partiiu kommunistov-bol'shevikov Ukrainu ot 3-go aprelia 1920-go goda', TsDAHOU, 39/4/237, p. 102.

36. I examined TsDAHOU 43/1/3, 6, 10, 13, 19, 35, 40, 41, 43, 44, 46, 47, 50, 51, 54, 56, 77, 82, 85, 88, 96, and could not find any trace of Dovzhenko as a Borotbist.

37. TsDAHOU, 43/1/3, pp. 1a–1b; and 43/1/44, pp. 9–11.

38. Dovzhenko's 31 July 1922 letter to the CP(b)U's Central Committee, where he reveals his Communist Party card number as 172255, provides evidence, however limited, that he became a member of this political party. The original document remains in TsDAHOU, 1/6/37, p. 26. Roman Korohodsky published this short document in his *Dovzhenko v poloni: Rozvidky ta esei pro Maistra* (Kiev, 2000), p. 58.

39. As a member of the Central Committee of the Ukrainian Communist Party (Borotbist), Shumsky led the struggle against Skoropadsky and the Directory in the Zhytomyr and Kiev provinces in 1918 and 1919. See 'Dovidkova karta, Aleksandr Iakovlevich Shumskii', TsDAHOU, 39/4/237, pp. 1 and 5.

40. Graziosi, *The Great Soviet Peasant War*, p. 76.

41. Graziosi, *The Great Soviet Peasant War*, pp. 76–7.

42. See Lidiia Vovchyk-Blakytna, 'Tov. Vasyl' i Sashko', *Vitchyzna*, no. 1 (1984), p. 164.

43. Vovchenko, pp. 4–5.

44. Korohods'kyi, 'Zadyshenyi holos', p. 5.

3

Warsaw, Berlin and Revolutionary Diplomacy

Due to social and political chaos as well as intentional obfuscation, many details of Dovzhenko's activities between 1919 and 1923 remain undocumented. In their place, many legends and myths emerged.

Between December 1919 and April 1920, according to official accounts presented during the late Soviet period, Dovzhenko served in Zhytomyr Province's War Commissariat, then worked as a literacy instructor on the staff of the Soviet Ukrainian 44th Rifle Division. By April he headed the Zhytomyr Party School. With Poland's invasion of Ukraine in April 1920, he left Zhytomyr for Kiev, where he worked in the Communist underground until Soviet troops recaptured the city on 12 June 1920.[1]

Inasmuch as there is no archival evidence to support these official accounts, this reconstruction of Dovzhenko's past between December 1919 and June 1920 is most likely not true. We are on firmer ground after June 1920, when Dovzhenko worked as secretary of the social education administration in the newly Sovietised department of education in Kiev Province. On 21 July Dovzhenko's superiors promoted him to membership at the bureau's executive committee (*Kollegium*), where he became the secretary of the entire department.[2] In this capacity, he oversaw the arts, among other things. His other responsibilities included supervising the First Ukrainian State Theatre (the Shevchenko Theatre), working with a committee organising teachers, and establishing local Soviet governments in the villages of the province.[3]

Dovzhenko worked in the Kiev provincial administration for almost a year. He inventoried the schools, theatres and art institutes under his jurisdiction, coordinated food procurement and food rationing for his employees, and closed the numerous religious schools in the city and province.[4] In addition, in April 1921 he accepted a promotion to deputy head of the *Kollegium*. According to Dovzhenko, 'this was a period of very hard work for me. I was very young and healthy and could work without ever becoming tired.'[5]

On 16 April 1921, Grigory Grinko, the Ukrainian Commissar of Education and a former Borotbist, sent a telegram to L. Levitsky, the head of the Kiev provincial department of education and Dovzhenko's supervisor. He ordered Levitsky to send

Dovzhenko, during his years abroad
(*c.* 1921–3)

Dovzhenko to Kharkiv immediately 'for temporary work abroad with Comrade Shumsky'.[6] Nine days later Grinko sent another telegram, repeating his demand that Dovzhenko come to Kharkiv as soon as possible.[7]

Assuming that Dovzhenko arrived in Kharkiv by the end of April, no records attest to his activities in the period between April and late July 1921, when the Ukrainian Commissariat of Foreign Affairs appointed him the head of the general department of the Soviet Ukrainian Republic's Embassy in Poland. He arrived in Poland in mid-September 1921 and worked there until February 1922, when the Commissariat of Foreign Affairs transferred him to Berlin. After the Ukrainian Politburo recalled him on 30 July 1922, he received its permission to stay in Germany in order to study art. After a year's study, Dovzhenko returned to Ukraine in July 1923.[8]

Dovzhenko's diplomatic career in Warsaw and then in Berlin was short and undistinguished. Even the most 'official' version of his life, his 1939 autobiography, hints that he encountered serious problems in carrying out his responsibilities abroad:

> I worked in Warsaw for about a year, first with the Russian-Ukrainian-Polish
> Commission on [the] Exchange of POWs and then as chargé d'affaires at the embassy.
> In the conditions of 1921 this desk job was so unpleasant and tedious that I had to stay

inside the embassy building for weeks at a time ... in the spring of 1922 [when] I was transferred to Berlin to the lower post of secretary of the consulate of the Ukrainian SSR in Germany ... After three or four months of work there I was relieved of my duties and, having been granted, on orders from [Christian] Rakovsky, who was on his way to the Genoa Conference, a scholarship of 40 dollars a month by the People's Commissariat of Education, [I] entered a private art school with the intention of transferring to the Academy of Arts in Berlin or Paris in the fall.

In the summer of 1923 I returned to Kharkiv and did not go back to Berlin. Events in Hamburg [an allusion to strikes] prevented this. The People's Commissariat of Foreign Affairs, to which I was still assigned, offered to send me as a diplomatic courier to Kabul in Afghanistan. I was all set to leave when family affairs kept me from doing so. Instead, I got a job on the staff of the Kharkiv newspaper *Visti VUTsVK* as an illustrator.[9]

After this dramatic series of events abroad, Dovzhenko returned to Kharkiv and received the shocking news that the Communist Party had banished him from its ranks:

I had been expelled while still abroad for failing to send in my papers for clearance. Actually, I had sent in my papers. They were lost at the Central Committee and accidentally found under a bookcase several years later, as I learned from Vasyl Blakytny, the newspaper editor and Central Committee member, the day before he died. I took the expulsion from the party very badly.[10]

Dovzhenko desperately wanted to return to Berlin in the autumn of 1923, but circumstances beyond his control prevented him from doing so. His explanation ('events in Hamburg prevented this') placed the cart before the horse. His oblique reference alludes to the German Weimar government's suppression of the Communist-led strike in Hamburg in October 1923 and the subsequent expulsion of Soviet diplomats from the country. These events took place some two and a half months *after* Dovzhenko left Germany. By the beginning of August 1923, he had begun his new career as an illustrator for *Visti*, the official news organ of the Soviet Ukrainian government.[11] The German 'October' could not have prevented him from returning to Berlin in August or September. As for his expulsion from the Communist Party, Dovzhenko's claim about 'lost' party documents carries no weight at all. Once again, a close examination reveals Dovzhenko's desire to gloss over distressing episodes in his life and present a more palatable version of the past.

Over the years, especially after Dovzhenko's death and promotion to the Soviet cultural pantheon, his accounts of the past came to constitute the core of his 'official' biography. But even the official myth provides clues that Dovzhenko's mission abroad failed to garner official approval. Misfortune plagued his mission.

It seems incredible that the Ukrainian Commissariat of Foreign Affairs would choose Dovzhenko, a man with a 'counter-revolutionary' political past and no diplomatic experience, to represent the newly established republic abroad, even granting the patronage of Shumsky and Blakytny. Although he may have studied German privately in elementary school, and German, French and English at the Commercial Institute, his foreign language proficiency remains uncertain.[12] Until 1921 he had never travelled beyond the boundaries of the Ukrainian provinces. On the surface, the Commissariat made a surprising, even foolish choice, when it co-opted him, a very minor Soviet official, for such an important assignment. The new Commissariat, however, had few educated Ukrainians in its ranks and its leaders hoped to present a 'Ukrainian' face to the world. He fit the bill.

Dovzhenko, moreover, became a part of the Borotbist network. He began his post-Civil War career in the Commissariat of Education, which Borotbists had headed since 1919. In his work in the Kiev Province's department of education in 1920, Dovzhenko indirectly reported to Panas Liubchenko, a former Borotbist and the head of the Kiev Province CP(b)U committee.[13]

In addition to his Borotbist affiliations, he possessed a number of personal and political assets. He was an excellent speaker and a charismatic individual. Born into a peasant family, he identified himself as a Ukrainian and spoke the language. Although many Communist veterans of the Revolution and Civil War disdained Dovzhenko as a 'Ukrainian nationalist' and 'counter-revolutionary', in the context of the new post-revolutionary realities he could play a useful role. Given the political fragility of the Soviet Union, Poland and Germany, Dovzhenko's career abroad would encompass more than just diplomacy.

Dovzhenko's Real Story

Dovzhenko became a revolutionary diplomat, dedicated to undermining the political and social order in Poland and Germany, after Soviet Russia signed the Treaty of Riga with Poland on 8 March 1921, which concluded the Polish–Soviet War. Revolutionary diplomacy joined two new institutions, the Communist International (the Comintern) and the Foreign Department (INO) of the Cheka (Soviet Russia's first secret police organisation), in seeking to overturn the postwar political order.[14] Unlike traditional diplomacy, revolutionary diplomacy sought to ignite a worldwide revolution by using diplomatic privileges and immunities.

On 27 July 1921, Dovzhenko's name appeared on the Embassy's payroll for the first time.[15] Officially, he served as one of the two billeting officers for the newly established Soviet Ukrainian Embassy in Warsaw.[16] His initial assignment was to find appropriate office space as well as living quarters for its staff, which proved no easy task.

Dovzhenko and his partner, Ivan Smalets, found a building, Hotel Victoria, in downtown Warsaw. Centrally located, with sufficient room and a restaurant on the premises, the hotel met their requirements.[17] They found this building in mid-September, just before the majority of the Ukrainian diplomatic mission was due to arrive.[18] Despite promises, the Poles had not completed the necessary repairs and reconstruction when the delegation turned up in Warsaw on 4 October. The workers had only completed the first floor. In response, the Ukrainian delegation refused to occupy it and spent at least a week living in the train in which they had come.[19]

Nevertheless, the Soviet Ukrainian Embassy opened its doors on 5 October 1921, and became fully operational on 24 October, after the Polish government accepted Shumsky's credentials as Soviet Ukraine's first ambassador to Poland.[20] The Embassy soon employed 201 men and women,[21] a surprisingly large number for a state that exercised little control over its own foreign policy.[22] The Embassy's inner circle consisted of former Borotbists. In addition to Shumsky and Dovzhenko, the Embassy staff included Lidia Evhenivna Vovchyk (the code clerk and Blakytny's wife), Ivan Siak, the second secretary, and Karlo Maksymovych, an important official within the Communist Party of Western Ukraine (initially known as the Communist Party of Eastern Galicia), which operated in the Ukrainian territories controlled by Poland.

Approved by the CP(b)U's Organisational Bureau and by Soviet Ukraine's Commissariat of Foreign Affairs, this group and other members of the Embassy staff shared a common mission: to penetrate and undermine independent Poland. The former Borotbists solicited Western aid for the victims of the famine raging in Ukraine, monitored political trends in Poland, especially Poland's relationship with its national minorities, kept track of Ukrainian émigrés in Europe and supervised the Communist Party of Western Ukraine.

The Ukrainian Embassy also coordinated the repatriation and exchange of the 11,000 Ukrainian soldiers held in three Polish internment camps.[23] On 2 October 1921, Dovzhenko and his friend Dmytro Kapka (Dmytro Leontiiovych Kapkunov) began their work on this commission.[24]

When visiting the internment camps, which contained adherents of the Ukrainian National Republic, of the anarchist Nestor Makhno and of the former Hetman Pavlo Skoropadsky, Dovzhenko often addressed the prisoners. He urged them to take advantage of the amnesty offered by the Soviet Ukrainian government in February 1921 and return to Ukraine.[25]

The Soviet Ukrainian government wanted these refugees repatriated for two reasons. First of all, it needed young and skilled hands to rebuild its ruined mines, factories, transportation system and agriculture after seven years of turmoil.[26] Second, the Soviet Ukrainian government did not want these refugees to remain in Europe, where they would continue to embarrass the new Soviet order politically, if not militarily.

In violation of the Treaty of Riga, the Polish government tolerated military exercises in the internment camps. Led by generals allied with Petliura and the Ukrainian National Republic, volunteers from these camps often participated in incursions into Soviet Ukraine.[27] Agitators such as Dovzhenko worked to convince them of the futility of their opposition to the new Soviet order and the invincibility of the newly established Soviet Ukrainian Republic. However many interned soldiers Dovzhenko may have persuaded to return to Ukraine, his mission became more difficult, if not impossible, after the massacre at Bazar.

In late October 1921, one of Petliura's lieutenants, General Yury Tiutiunnyk, mobilised over 1,000 Ukrainian volunteers from the camps and slipped across the border into Soviet Ukraine.[28] Shumsky learned of this planned attack (the last major Ukrainian nationalist military campaign against the Bolsheviks until 1941) six weeks before it started; he passed word to the appropriate Soviet authorities.[29]

Forewarned, on 17 November 1921, Soviet General Grigory Kotovsky's troops surprised and defeated this group near the village of Bazar in the Zhytomyr Province. The Red Army killed 250 insurgents in the battle and captured almost 500.[30] On 21 November 1921, the Soviet captors asked their prisoners to join the Red Army. Three hundred and fifty-nine refused. The Red Army immediately executed them in cold blood.[31]

News of this blood-bath spread beyond Soviet Ukraine.[32] Not only did this repulse the thousands of Ukrainian soldiers still interned in Poland, but it outraged anti-Communist groups throughout Europe. Moreover, it possibly alienated the former Borotbists in the Communist ranks. These executions, in effect, undermined Shumsky's mission to reach out to the Ukrainian nationalist community in Western Europe.

On 30 November 1921, Shumsky sent a coded message to the Ukrainian Commissariat of Foreign Affairs in Kharkiv. He suggested that the government should have put on a large show trial, similar to previous trials of the Socialist Revolutionaries and Mensheviks, in order to discredit their opponents, rather than executing those captured.[33]

In a subtle manner, Shumsky's letter expressed feelings of betrayal. Shumsky's forewarning about Tiutiunnyk's planned invasion demonstrated his loyalty, as well as that of his former Borotbist colleagues, to the Communist Party. He did not articulate any concern for the murdered Ukrainians; instead, he emphasised how this massacre created a 'negative impression' abroad.

Despite its careful wording, Shumsky's letter isolated him not only from the Commissariat of Foreign Affairs, but also from the Ukrainian Politburo. Communist hardliners, who had already engaged in a slow but steady undermining of the Borotbists, stepped up their campaign after Shumsky's protest. With Shumsky's memorandum, Communist patience with the Borotbists came to an end.[34]

Although Dovzhenko did not record his reaction to Bazar, speculation suggests that images of the slaughter may well have haunted Dovzhenko's imagination, creating deep feelings of regret, even guilt, about his activities and raised the question of what cause he served. The massacre may also have undermined his belief in the Borotbist–Communist alliance. Finally, after Bazar, Ukrainians who heard Dovzhenko talk in the internment camps would have greeted his political pitch with skepticism and hostility.

Most importantly, Dovzhenko – as a member of Shumsky's staff and a former Borotbist – worked in Shumsky's shadow. When the Ambassador became vulnerable in 1922, so did those he protected: Dovzhenko, Vovchyk, Siak and Maksymovych. Shortly after Shumsky sent his message, almost all of Dovzhenko's former Borotbist colleagues left the Warsaw Embassy, some to other diplomatic postings, others back to Ukraine.

On 2 February 1922, the Ukrainian Commissariat of Foreign Affairs transferred Dovzhenko to the Ukrainian Trade Representative's Office in Berlin, at a lower rank.[35] He later became the secretary of the consulate of the Ukrainian SSR in Germany.[36] Despite his demotion, Dovzhenko may not have considered his transfer a downgrading. For Dovzhenko, a budding artist, Berlin in 1922 represented a Mecca for art, a world of possibilities.[37] Hence, when the Ukrainian Politburo officially relieved him of his duties on 30 July 1922, Dovzhenko expressed a desire to remain in the city.[38]

While still a diplomat, he met Ukrainian students at the Academy of Arts and visited them often.[39] He became enamoured with the art world. With the demise of his diplomatic career, Dovzhenko saw an opportunity to explore his vocation as an artist. On 31 July, he wrote a letter to the Central Committee of the CP(b)U, asking for permission to remain in the city as an art student. He wanted to learn 'graphics, composition, metal sculpting and journal illustration'. He promised that when he returned to Ukraine he would be a 'useful comrade'.[40]

On 21 August 1922, the Politburo granted Dovzhenko's request.[41] He would study in Germany with a grant from the Commissariat of Education.[42]

Dovzhenko remained in Berlin for nearly a year and enthusiastically entered the world of art, first through his friendships with Ukrainian artists, then through his meetings with Germans. Mykola Hlushchenko, a Ukrainian artist residing in Berlin, met Dovzhenko in 1922 and remembered his sophisticated conversations with the young diplomat about art in general and about his own technique specifically. Dovzhenko, he asserted, demanded sharp, critical comments about his work.[43] The work of French artists, Van Gogh and Georg Grosz profoundly influenced him (Hlushchenko, unfortunately, did not specify how).[44]

Dovzhenko and his Ukrainian friends greeted the art world of the early Weimar period with awe, fascination and enthusiasm. Although Expressionism in art and literature, Bauhaus architecture, the physics of relativity, psychoanalysis and psychology, the sociology of knowledge and atonal music originated before the war, they entered into the popular consciousness and began to influence people's attitudes about themselves and their world only in the 1920s.[45] This revolutionary art stimulated Dovzhenko's imagination, inspiring him with new ideas and new forms. To Dovzhenko, who had not yet reached the age of thirty, everything seemed possible.

In Berlin he audited courses at the Higher State School of Representative Arts, actively participated in the discussions of the 'Kunstlerhilfe' group, attended private viewings and visited art exhibitions and museums. He also met Kathe Kollwitz, Georg Grosz and other prominent German artists. He first exhibited his drawings here, at student art shows. Impressed with his works, Gerhard Janensch, one of Dovzhenko's professors at the Higher State School, recommended that his student hold an exhibition at the Galerie Casper on Kurfurstendamm Boulevard, located several doors from Dovzhenko's Berlin apartment. Janensch then introduced Dovzhenko to Willy Jaeckel, a well-known Expressionist painter, who gave him private art lessons.[46]

After his successful exhibition, Dovzhenko began to draw for four to five hours every day. Beyond painting, Dovzhenko studied the work of prominent German caricaturists.[47] In Warsaw, he had drawn distorted images of the Embassy staff and of current political events.[48] During his Berlin period, he published his first political cartoons in *Molot* (*The Hammer*), a journal of humour and satire edited by Ukrainian Communists in New York City.[49] Income from these caricatures supplemented his meagre government stipend.

For Dovzhenko, Berlin became the centre of the universe, and he wanted to prolong his stay in paradise. On 12 June 1923, Dovzhenko wrote a letter to Volodymyr Zatonsky, the new Soviet Ukrainian Commissar of Education, asking for an eighteen-month extension of his scholarship. He wanted, he wrote, to prepare for serious art, such as art on 'walls in clubs, in village buildings, in children's halls and in orphanages'. In the meantime, he needed to maintain his scholarship for another six weeks, until the end of the school year, 15 July. Shortly after returning to Ukraine in July 1923, Dovzhenko promised to show Zatonsky, or his designated deputy, his art work. Ia. P. Riappo, Zatonsky's deputy at the Commissariat of Education, renewed Dovzhenko's scholarship, but only for the extra six weeks.[50] In effect, this move denied his request for an eighteen-month extension. Dovzhenko had to return home.

Conclusion

The lapses in Dovzhenko's biography, especially his 1921 'disappearance', have led one scholar, Roman Korohodsky, to assert that he secretly worked at that time for the Cheka's Foreign Section (INO) or the Comintern.[51] This fascinating but as yet unproved theory does hold some possibility. Dovzhenko's diplomatic responsibilities allowed him to travel freely in Poland and in Germany, where he made contacts and met people who could have provided him with 'special' information. Three of the films he made, *The Diplomatic Pouch* (1927), *Aerograd* (1935) and *Goodbye, America* (1951), attest to an interest in and knowledge of the world of espionage.

Dovzhenko's positions, activities and films, however, do not prove that he worked as an intelligence officer. Although he undoubtedly cooperated with the INO and the Comintern and although his activities complemented the work of these organisations, his collection of information comprised an integral part of his duties as a 'revolutionary' diplomat.

Dovzhenko's 'black hole' in 1921 may be explained by his preparations to accompany Shumsky abroad, especially language training. To fulfil his responsibilities he had to learn Polish. His command of Russian and Ukrainian would have proved useful in the context of his duties, but he had to confront the radical differences between Polish and the two East Slavic languages, especially when speaking with Poles.

German would have presented even greater difficulties for Dovzhenko. When posted to Germany in February 1922, he certainly took intensive German language lessons. Although he may have learned some German in elementary school and at the Commercial Institute in 1917 and 1918, he would have needed greater competence in German to understand the lectures in art, art technique and art history that he attended in Berlin.

The most important consequence of Dovzhenko's years abroad focused not on his 'membership' in the Cheka or the Comintern, but in the shadow of Bazar. Learning of the executions there, Dovzhenko may have recalled his own experiences in a Cheka cell in 1919 and thought about his own vulnerability and the arbitrariness of life and death. Given his feelings about his native Ukraine and his dread of 'senseless deaths', Bazar probably marked him not only internally, but externally as well.[52]

Although Dovzhenko did not write a critical memorandum, as did Shumsky, his association with Shumsky placed him under the scrutiny of the security organs. His political reliability and loyalty came into question for the second time in two years. He experienced one demotion after another, culminating in the loss of his party membership. By 1923 the Communist Party began to punish high-ranking members who criticised its line. The party also disciplined those, such as Dovzhenko, suspected of harbouring dissenting thoughts. Dovzhenko's ties to Shumsky and the shadow of Bazar would haunt him and colour many of his subsequent actions.

Notes

1. *Storinky*, pp. 19–20.
2. TsDAVOVUU, 166/1/941, pp. 12–12a, 26–38.

3. Dmytro Kapka, 'Zvela mene dolia z Dovzhenkom', *PZh,* p. 156; and '1939 Autobiography', pp. 13–14.

4. Roman Korohods'kyi, 'Dovzhenko v poloni: natsional'na porazka i bil'shovyts'ka "Nauka peremahaty"', *Kur'ier kryvbasu,* no. 67–8 (1996), p. 74.

5. '1939 Autobiography', p. 13.

6. TsDAVOVUU, 166/1/74, p. 79.

7. TsDAVOVUU, 166/1/74, p. 88.

8. *Storinky,* pp. 19–27.

9. '1939 Autobiography', pp. 14–15. At this time Rakovsky was the head of the Soviet Ukrainian government.

10. '1939 Autobiography', pp. 15–16.

11. Compare *Storinky,* p. 27, and the history of the strike in Richard A. Comfort, *Revolutionary Hamburg: Labor Politics in the Early Weimar Republic* (Stanford, CA, 1966), pp. 120–30.

12. On Dovzhenko's learning German in elementary school, see Ia. Nazarenko, 'Ego shkol'nye gody', *Raduga,* no. 9 (1964), p. 149; on his learning these other languages, see his Commercial Institute transcripts, DAMK, 153/5/2508, p. 4, 5, 16 (over).

13. Ivan Koshelivets', *Oleksandr Dovzhenko: Sproba tvorchoi biohrafii* (Munich, 1980), p. 51.

14. Roman Korohods'kyi (Korohodsky), a Ukrainian archivist and scholar, believes that during Dovzhenko's imprisonment in the autumn of 1919 he willingly or unwillingly joined the security organs to save himself. Korohods'kyi's argument is plausible, but not verifiable. See Korohods'kyi, pp. 74–83.

15. TsDAVOVUU, 4/2/82, pp. 60, 62, 75, 93.

16. See the documents issued by the Russian Federation's Archive of Foreign Relations at SDM, A-393.

17. FPARF, f. People's Commissariat of Foreign Affairs of Ukraine, op. 5, papka 7, d. 24, p. 16.

18. For a list of these individuals, see TsDAVOVUU, 4/1/667, p. 107.

19. FPARF, f. People's Commissariat of Foreign Affairs of Ukraine, op. 5, papka 24, d. 7, pp. 11, 12; and Polish Dept., op. 4, papka 18, d. 189.

20. Korohods'kyi, p. 81; and FPARF, f. Polish Dept., op. 4, papka 18, d. 189, p. 80.

21. Korohods'kyi, p. 81.

22. Between 1920 and 1922, thirty countries recognised the Ukrainian Soviet Socialist Republic and Austria, Italy, Latvia, Lithuania, Germany, Poland, Turkey and Czechoslovakia established diplomatic relations with it in this period. See Nina Koval'ska, 'Do istorii dyplomatychnykh vidnosyn URSR',

Vsesvit, no. 5 (1988), p. 161. Nevertheless, Soviet Ukrainian foreign policy did not operate independently of that in Soviet Russia.

23. FPARF, Embassy of the RSFSR in Poland, op. 2, papka 6, d. 5, pp. 4–5, provides a figure of 11,500 interned Ukrainian soldiers; pp. 12–13 provides a figure of 10,400. *Dokumenty i materialy do historii stosunkow polsko-radzieckich* (Warsaw, 1965), vol. 4, p. 104 (cited in Vasyl' Veryha, *Lystopadovyi reid* [Kiev, 1995], p. 18) claims 10,000.

24. Kapka, p. 157.

25. Shumsky makes a reference to this amnesty decree in his 8 February 1922 protest letter to the Polish Minister of Foreign Affairs, FPARF, op. 2, papka 6, d. 5, p. 2.

26. Heorhii Zhurov, 'Oleksandr Dovzhenko – dyplomat', *Vsesvit*, no. 5 (1988), p. 159.

27. See Shumsky's protest letter to the Polish Foreign Minister, FPARF, op. 2, papka 6, d. 5, p. 1.

28. See Shumsky's protest to the Polish Foreign Minister about Poland's support of this incursion. FPARF, RSFSR Embassy in Poland, op. 1, papka 2, d. 3, pp. 22–5.

29. Korohods'kyi, p. 79.

30. *Radians'ka entsyklopediia istorii Ukrainy* (Kiev, 1969), p. 100; cited in Korohods'kyi, p. 79.

31. Korohods'kyi, p. 79; and I. Z. Pidkova and R. M. Shust, *Dovidnyk z istorii Ukrainy* (Kiev, 1993), vol. 1, pp. 42, 217. The best accounts of this massacre are: Veryha, *Lystopadovyi reid* and *Druhyi zumovyi pokhid: Lystopadovyi reid/Bazar* (Kiev, 1995). Both Veryha (pp. 167–75) and *Druhyi zumovyi pokhid* (pp. 189–200) provide a list of the 359 executed.

32. 'An extraordinary Committee of Inquiry, appointed by the Soviet to investigate the recent incursion of General Petliura's troops into the Ukraine, has, it is reported, adopted a resolution that the 360 men captured by the Red Army be shot.' 'Imperial and Foreign New Items', *The Times* (London), 23 December 1921, p. 7g.

33. TsDAVOVUU, f. 4, op. 1, d. 569, pp. 171–2 (over); cited in Korohods'kyi, p. 80.

34. Korohods'kyi, p. 80.

35. Korohods'kyi, p. 82.

36. See '1939 Autobiography', pp. 14–15.

37. Between 1900 and 1918, Berlin became a Mecca for artists, especially for film actors and actresses, from Eastern Europe. Edward Zajička, ed., *Encyklopedia kultury polskiej XX wieku: Film/kinematografia* (Warsaw, 1994), p. 304.

38. Korohods'kyi, p. 82.

39. Mykola Hlushchenko, 'Slovo pro druha', *PZh*, p. 165.
40. TsDAHOU, 1/6/36, p. 26; and Korohods'kyi, pp. 80–1.
41. SDM, A-393, p. 13; and Korohods'kyi, p. 82.
42. TsDAHOU, 1/6/37, p. 53; cited in Korohods'kyi, p. 81; M. B. Pohrebins'kyi, 'Do naukovoho zhyttiepysu O. Dovzhenka', *Radians'ke literaturoznavstvo*, no. 8 (1971), p. 77–8; and SDM, A-393, pp. 2, 13.
43. Hlushchenko, p. 165.
44. G. Konovalov, 'Dovzhenko nachinalsia tak ...' in B. N. Tarasenko and G. M. Kapel'gorodskaia, eds, *Uroki Aleksandra Dovzhenko: Sbornik statei* (Kiev, 1982), p. 125.
45. Gordon A. Craig, *Germany, 1866–1945* (New York, 1978), p. 470.
46. Hans-Joachim Schlegel, 'Berlin i Germaniia Aleksandra Dovzhenko', *KZ*, no. 31 (1996), p. 143. Willy Jaeckel (1888–1944) was a prominent German painter, print-maker, and a member of the Prussian Academy of Arts. See E. Bénézit, *Dictionnaire critique et documentaire des peintres, sculpteurs, dessinateurs et graveurs* (Paris, 1999), vol. 7, p. 444; Jane Turner, ed., *The Dictionary of Art* (London and New York, 1996), vol. 16, p. 862.
47. Konovalov, p. 125.
48. For a description of these caricatures, see Mykhailo Hnatiuk, 'Narodzhennia khudozhnyka', *PZh*, pp. 161–4.
49. Mykola Tarnovs'kyi, 'Syla khudozhnyka', *PZh*, p. 170.
50. RGALI, 2081/2/186, pp. 1–2; and TsDAVOVUU, 166/3/47, pp. 93, 94–5.
51. Korohods'kyi, pp. 67–83. Nearly two decades later, Prokhorenko, a Ukrainian NKVD officer, assessed Dovzhenko in the following manner: 'He is a man, in my opinion, who says everything he thinks and is not capable of engaging in clandestine activities.' *ZA*, p. 277. In a diary entry from 30 June 1945, Dovzhenko asserted that he 'did not like to keep secrets'. *UVOKShch*, p. 270; *Hospody*, p. 251; *ZDUVOShch*, p. 375.
52. Korohods'kyi, pp. 67–83.

4

First Frames

On 20 June 1926 Dovzhenko abandoned the art world for the film world. In his 1939 autobiography, he recorded how he became a director:

> ... I sat up all night at my studio, assessed my thirty-two unsuccessful years of life, and in the morning left the house, never to return. I went to Odessa and got a job at the film studio as a director. Thus in the thirty-third year of my life I had to start learning all over again: I had not been an actor or stage director, did not go to see films very often, and was not familiar with all the theoretical intricacies of film as a synthetic art.[1]

After his death, this statement became an integral part of the officially sponsored mythology of Dovzhenko's life: one of the most popular political cartoonists in Ukraine effortlessly and almost immediately moved from one career to another. In reality, however, this shift in careers, Dovzhenko's fourth such change, involved far more complex transitions.

His decision to enter the film world seems abrupt, even irrational. Perhaps the Soviet Ukrainian government's denial of Dovzhenko's request for further study in Berlin led him to see his career as a political cartoonist as a depressing compromise with the realities of life. He may have preferred to abandon the graphic arts altogether rather than remain a pseudo-artist drawing political caricatures. In light of his interests in theatre, literature, painting and political caricature, Dovzhenko's shift from political cartoons to the moving image represents an expansion of his artistic abilities rather than an abandonment of one set of artistic media for the other. His wife's illness and their separation forced him to re-evaluate and reinvent his life. His longstanding interest in film contributed to his conversion into a film director.

Krylova-Dovzhenko's Illness

Shortly before he left Berlin for Ukraine on 17 July 1923, Dovzhenko married Barbara Krylova in a civil ceremony at the Soviet Embassy.[2] Within hours of exchanging their vows, they began their return trip home by train, with a stop in Warsaw. On 18 July they reached Ukraine.

Dovzhenko and Barbara Krylova in
Berlin (1922)

After their return, the newlyweds visited the Dovzhenko family in Sosnytsia.
Dovzhenko helped his father with household chores and rested on the banks of his
beloved Desna River. From Sosnytsia he travelled to Kharkiv and found a position
as staff cartoonist for *Visti*, the main Soviet Ukrainian governmental organ.[3] He
would never try to revive his diplomatic career.

He and Krylova-Dovzhenko moved to Kharkiv, a city of 417,000, the third-largest
city in Ukraine after Kiev and Odessa. They lived here for the next year and a half.[4]
As the capital of the newly founded Soviet Ukrainian Republic, Kharkiv attracted
not only a new and large group of bureaucrats, but also many intellectuals who
hoped to find employment in the new Ukrainian cultural institutions and participate
in the creation of a new Soviet Ukrainian culture.

Despite formal Soviet recognition of the right of the non-Russian nationalities to
use their languages in the party and government, the exact position of the Ukrainian language in the Ukrainian Soviet Socialist Republic (SSR) remained uncertain
until August 1923, when its government issued its most decisive decree on Ukrainianisation. It claimed that despite the formal equality of the Ukrainian and Russian

languages, the Russian language remained the dominant one. In order to overcome this inequality, the Soviet Ukrainian government would adopt a number of measures that would guarantee 'a place for the Ukrainian language corresponding to the numerical superiority of the Ukrainian people on the territory of the Ukrainian SSR'.[5]

The decree obliged all public officials to learn Ukrainian; it also provided for the gradual transition of the language of all official documents and correspondence from Russian to Ukrainian, although Russian and other minority languages could be used at the local level. Subsequent resolutions ordered all state institutions, newspapers and state-owned trade and industrial organisations to abandon Russian as a working language and adopt Ukrainian. Within a year, all official business in the Council of People's Commissars, in central and local institutions and in the commissariats was to be conducted in Ukrainian. Replies to individual requests in all central and regional organisations should be in the language of the original request. The Ukrainian and Russian languages were to be employed in all central and provincial-level courts, the Ukrainian language in regional-level courts. The decree allowed an exception for the inhabitants of regions in which the non-Ukrainian minorities spoke another language. From now on, no one who did not speak both Russian and Ukrainian would be hired for any position in any state institution. Those who were already in the civil service and who did not know the two most widely used languages in Ukraine had to learn them in the course of a year. Those who did not would be dismissed.[6]

There were now two official languages in the Ukrainian SSR – Ukrainian and Russian – which enjoyed a special administrative status. The numerical superiority of the Ukrainians and the official promotion of that language created the possibility of the Ukrainian language becoming the most important language in the republic.

Visti led the struggle on behalf of Ukrainianisation, and its charismatic editor, Vasyl Blakytny, drew pilgrims from the provinces to his offices. Hundreds, like Dovzhenko, began their careers here. At *Visti*, Dovzhenko (who employed the name 'Sashko') produced satirical drawings commenting on important Soviet and international events. His political caricatures lampooned prominent foreign leaders (such as Benito Mussolini; the British Home Secretary, William Joynson Hicks; Germany's Chancellor Gustav Streseman; and Field Marshal Paul von Hindenburg), Ukrainian bourgeois nationalists, clergymen and religious believers and corrupt Soviet bureaucrats.[7] He also drew humorous sketches of his friends. In addition to drawing caricatures for *Visti*, he created them for other Ukrainian newspapers and journals headquartered in Kharkiv. Despite his success in this endeavour, Dovzhenko also aspired to master other forms of art, such as book and journal illustration. In what little spare time he enjoyed, he worked on his paintings at his apartment.

Dovzhenko and the editorial board of the newspaper *Visti*. Sitting (from left to right):
V. Koriak, F. Taran, Vasyl Blakytny, Radysh and Dovzhenko (1924)

He rarely enjoyed any leisure time at home. He often attended meetings with like-minded friends and colleagues. Encouraged and subsidised by the Soviet state, members of the new Ukrainian intelligentsia acquired a decisive voice in developing a new Ukrainian cultural universe, national in form but socialist in content. Influenced by the Ukrainian and Bolshevik revolutions, young artists (such as Heorhy Narbut, Vasyl Krychevsky, Anatol Petrytsky and Mykhailo Boichuk), poets (such as Pavlo Tychyna and Maksym Rylsky), writers (Mykola Khvylovy), playwrights (Mykola Kulish) and theatre directors (Les Kurbas) became the leading innovators of the Ukrainian cultural renaissance of the 1920s.

Members of this 'generation of 1917' constantly argued over the ends and means of the Soviet-sponsored Ukrainian cultural development. How should it evolve? What kind of culture should it be? What models should it follow? These men and the organisations they founded constituted the 'heart and the brain trust' of the Ukrainian renaissance of the 1920s, which the Stalinists decimated in the 30s.

Although Dovzhenko participated in these discussions and debates about the future of Ukrainian culture in the Soviet multinational state, he did not play a leading part in them. He joined two literary organisations, *Hart* and *VAPLITE*. Although Dovzhenko did not consider himself a writer, these organisations accepted artists 'working in different media who shared the organization's views'.[8]

Hart was an organisation of proletarian writers with Borotbist backgrounds that emerged after January 1923. Using the Ukrainian language as a means of artistic expression, its members sought to create 'one international, Communist culture' and fight against all 'petit-bourgeois propertied ideology'.[9] Although *Hart*'s platform envisioned the triumph of world revolution on the Bolshevik model, its members foresaw the success of national-liberation movements as its precondition.[10]

In November 1925, Dovzhenko became a founding member of *VAPLITE* (The Free Academy of Proletarian Literature). Like *Hart*, this new organisation voiced the aspirations of the Ukrainian intelligentsia for a fully developed national culture. Seeking to implement the slogan of 'national self-determination', this group of writers dreamed of creating a new urban Ukrainian culture equal to that of the Russian. Inasmuch as Russian writers considered their work second-rate simply because they wrote in a language that lacked international prestige, these Ukrainian writers denied their intellectual marginality vociferously.[11]

In addition to their emphasis on national and cultural rights, *VAPLITE*'s members demanded individual freedom of thought and expression. In their creative work and also in their literary criticism, they aspired to describe the seamy side of Soviet life, its inadequacies, contradictions and failures, and the dilemmas and conflicts faced by its citizens. Although members of *Hart* and *VAPLITE*, like most writers of the time, considered themselves proletarian, their work often depicted disillusioned Communists and portrayed a peasant psychology that, on the whole, remained antagonistic to the regime. In short, they hoped to describe the real Soviet reality and, beyond that, the human condition in personal terms.[12]

Dovzhenko's membership in *Hart* and *VAPLITE* suggests that mass organisations aimed at attracting workers and peasants did not appeal to him. Despite his peasant origins, he never belonged to or supported peasant-oriented organisations after his membership in the UPSR, nor did he endorse the Red enlightenment movement promoted by the party. Instead, Dovzhenko 'always affiliated himself with those who believed in a distinct socialist Ukrainian culture, poised toward the high culture of Europe and liberated from Russian dominance'.[13]

Both Dovzhenko and Krylova-Dovzhenko made a favourable impression on like-minded Ukrainian artists and intellectuals. Their first apartment, a modest, but bright and sunny, clean and fragrant room, attracted Kharkiv's intelligentsia. Its dining table served as a work table. Two ottomans covered with Ukrainian *kylyms* and a reproduction of a Cézanne landscape evinced the Dovzhenkos' appreciation of native Ukrainian arts and a sophisticated knowledge of the wider world. The apartment contained an easel, hundreds of tubes of paints and brushes and many books, a multi-volume set of Gogol's works occupying a central place on the bookshelf.[14]

In Kharkiv Dovzhenko found an environment to nurture his creative nature, but his embrace of the city's artists, writers, poets, playwrights and theatre directors alienated him from Krylova-Dovzhenko. He 'often forgot about his wife, who suffered, waiting for his affection'.[15] She later recalled that when he worked at *Visti*, he often dined with his colleagues at the 'Red Hotel', forgetting that she had prepared a lunch for him at home.[16] One of their mutual friends concluded that they were not compatible, that their life together generated tensions.[17]

Dovzhenko always remained busy, always in motion. Even when relaxing, he created. Krylova-Dovzhenko remembered: 'He rarely rested, but even when he put his hands under his head and looked out the window at the sky, he devoted his thoughts to fantasy; he saw rocket ships landing on the moon, then heading towards Mars.'[18]

Dovzhenko's commitment to the world of creativity collided with reality when Krylova-Dovzhenko fell seriously ill. At the end of 1924, she, who had never possessed the best of health, became incapacitated. One day on a canoe trip with her husband, she accidentally hit herself on the knee with a paddle. At first she did not feel much pain. Later her knee began to throb. The pain worsened, becoming unbearable. Doctors did not understand her illness, possibly reflex sympathetic dystrophy or causalgia (a disorder wherein swelling, sweating, changes in local blood flow, or changes in the tissues accompany neuropathic pain; marked behavioural changes, including emotional instability, anxiety and social withdrawal, usually follow).[19]

Krylova-Dovzhenko's doctors diagnosed her condition as tuberculosis.[20] She needed extensive, uninterrupted treatments, and a long convalescence in bed.[21] Her lower leg became paralysed.

The apartment the Dovzhenkos shared with several others provided a singularly unsuitable environment for rest and treatment. In addition to her lack of privacy, Krylova-Dovzhenko felt obligated to take care of her husband, to do the housecleaning and cooking for him.[22] In addition to her physical pain, Krylova-Dovzhenko also suffered psychologically. Her illness complicated her life with him. She did not want him to see her suffer; her suffering paralysed him, prevented him from working on his art and on his caricatures for *Visti*.[23] She became depressed.

A sanatorium seemed to offer the best solution. In order to soothe, if not heal, her leg, Krylova-Dovzhenko needed rest and comfort without the burden of domestic responsibilities. And so the Dovzhenkos parted – as it turned out, permanently.

The uncertainty of Krylova-Dovzhenko's disease and her increasing handicap undermined Dovzhenko's moral bearings. Her illness saddened Dovzhenko and created a philosophical crisis for him. He left Krylova-Dovzhenko, as he explained to Mykola Bazhan and to Anatol and Larysa Petrytsky, his closest friends in Kharkiv, because he 'could not calmly watch his beloved wife's deformity and suffering, because his aesthetic feelings protested against it'.[24] As an artist, he sought beauty and harmony; he imagined that his wife's illness now presented him with a brutal dilemma.

For many artists and the public at large, the concept of beauty and health become, consciously and unconsciously, essentially interchangeable. Although Dovzhenko's films depict sick, dead and unhealthy bodies (such as the malnourished, blind and amputated in *Arsenal* and the dying grandfather in *Earth*) and although his 'aesthetic' embraced the dead and the sick as part of the beauty of life, at that time Dovzhenko shared this social perception equating health with beauty. In a letter to Elena Chernova, one of his future loves, he confided, 'I love only the healthy.'[25] He, according to one critic, 'romanticized and idealized Barbara, and to watch his ideal corroded, disgraced, and trampled upon before his eyes was unbearable'.[26] In Dovzhenko's mind, he had only two options: health and beauty or Krylova.

To pre-empt disappointment and to maintain his healthy environment, he initiated the separation, which occurred in early 1925. Although Dovzhenko suggested the separation, he suffered in his wife's absence. Bazhan, his flatmate, wrote that after the separation Dovzhenko walked around 'with a sullen look, looking dejected'.[27]

Even though the Dovzhenkos corresponded, the physical and psychological distance between them increased, especially in June 1926, when Dovzhenko moved from Kharkiv to Odessa, where he began work as a film director. In Odessa, Dovzhenko met two young and attractive actresses, Elena Chernova and Julia Ippolitovna Solntseva, and fell into their orbits.

Krylova-Dovzhenko's prolonged absence from Dovzhenko's life opened the door for Chernova and Solntseva. His new experiences in a new environment without her made his wife superfluous. He had now entered a new world; she represented the old. Correspondence might maintain their friendship, but it could not sustain their marriage.

Indeed, Krylova-Dovzhenko must have noticed a change in tone and emphasis in his letters to her, for she travelled to Odessa to see Dovzhenko in the spring of 1928. In a letter to Chernova, Dovzhenko described Krylova's visit:

> She came completely unexpectedly after a year and a half of silence. Enormous crutches stood before me like terrifying ghosts for two weeks. At every step, I stumbled across them. I feared walking around the room. I feared to touch things lightly. I thought that they would break and deform themselves from my touch. My room became small and tight. And on the bed my wife Barbara lay. She was pitiful, and worn out. This was the biggest absurdity I had ever felt in my life. I wanted to run out on the street and to shout loudly: 'No, this is not her, she was completely different'. Misfortune spread like a fog, in my room. I felt extremely sorry for this good woman ...[28]

Dovzhenko's reaction to Krylova's crutches reflected his uneasiness with her illness and his irrational identification of good health with beauty. He once loved her very much, but her illness transformed her beauty into a physical deformity and his love for her into pity.

They remained married – but only on paper. Although they separated in 1925, they did not divorce until 1955.

Dovzhenko's irrational reaction to his wife's illness, especially his perception of betrayal, traumatised him and led him to re-evaluate his life. He assessed his first three decades and found them wanting. The ideals he had sought – truth, justice, beauty and love – could not exist harmoniously; many proved mere illusions. The Ukrainian Revolution disappointed him, as did his progress as a painter and his marriage. In order to cope with these psychological burdens, he felt that he had to reinvent his life.

These deep disappointments challenged Dovzhenko's most basic assumptions about himself, prompting a dramatic inward quest to redefine himself. Startled by the realisation that a lifetime of hard work and adherence to rules had not paid off, he became shaken to his core. His separation from Barbara freed him from all personal responsibilities and allowed him to explore new avenues.

Dovzhenko and Film

Long before he left for Odessa, film had fascinated Dovzhenko. In the early 1920s, he did not consider it art. By the end of 1924, he had revised this view, and he completed his first screenplay the following year. By 1926 he began to direct films based on his screenplays. His interest in art and theatre, his viewing of American, European and Soviet film, his work for the All-Ukrainian Photo and Film Administration (VUFKU) and his long conversations with friends and roommates about cinema and its possibilities prepared him both pragmatically and psychologically. A career in film, Dovzhenko concluded, could best present his stories to the largest possible audience.

Following in his father's and grandfather's footsteps, Dovzhenko excelled at weaving tales. According to his friend Yury Smolych, Dovzhenko became a far better storyteller than a painter, a writer, or even a film director. 'Dovzhenko', Smolych asserted, 'did not paint, did not write, and did not create on film one one-hundredth of the quality of the stories he told and knew how to relate.'[29]

Until 1926 Dovzhenko considered himself first and foremost a painter. In addition to his political cartoons for *Visti*, Dovzhenko also studied at one of the art institutes in Kharkiv.[30] He displayed some talent but realised that he needed another ten or fifteen years of intensive preparation to become a good artist.[31] He aspired to a career as a professional painter, he wrote to Maksym Vovchenko in 1924, 'to be free, not bow to anyone, and not be dependent on anyone'.[32] For Dovzhenko, a work of art should contain clues to inspire a story in the mind of the viewer. Because painting consists of static images, it cannot furnish a narrative; its images cannot evolve or develop across time.

Initially he thought the theatre, a longstanding interest, might offer the best venue for introducing his stories to a larger audience. When he lived in Sosnytsia, he had participated in an amateur youth theatre group (see photo on p. 17) and saw many plays at the Sosnytsia theatre. Inspired by the German expressionistic plays he had seen in Berlin and by the theatrical experiments conducted by Vladimir Mayakovsky, Vsevolod Meyerhold, Ilya Ehrenburg and Les Kurbas, Dovzhenko thought that the theatre would give him the freedom he needed to express himself best.[33]

To learn about the artistry and techniques of stage production, Dovzhenko began to attend performances at the Ivan Franko Theatre in Kharkiv on a regular basis. He often joined Smolych, a theatre critic, and quizzed him about the theatre, theatrical techniques and the new experimental theatres in the USSR, especially Meyerhold's theatre in Moscow and Kurbas's Berezil theatre in Kiev. Inspired by Berezil, Dovzhenko viewed the theatre as an art of contrasts, as a dazzling coat of many colours, and, according to Smolych, as the most persuasive and the most expressive performance possible before an audience.[34]

Berezil revolutionised Ukrainian theatre, raising its provincial style, aesthetics and repertoire to the highest standards set by Western European theatre. Kurbas founded this company in Kiev in 1922 and with its 300 actors and crew members it became the most dynamic and most ambitious theatre troupe in Ukraine. Trained in Vienna before the war, he created a unique Ukrainian expressionistic theatre after a long period of experimentation. By brilliantly synthesising rhythm, movement and avant-garde theatrical and visual devices, including montage, he forced his audiences to think, not watch passively as had the ethnographically oriented Ukrainian theatre of the past. Although Kurbas's greatest creative achievements took place on the stage, in the early 1920s he also directed a number of films, which did not survive.

Before establishing itself permanently in Kharkiv in 1926, Berezil toured the Soviet Ukrainian capital in the summers of 1923 and 1924; the Kharkiv newspapers often published reviews of its new productions.[35] Moving to Kharkiv in August 1923 after his return from Germany, Dovzhenko may have missed Berezil's 1923 summer performance, but he most likely saw the 1924 production, which (like all of Kurbas's productions) contained radically contrasting episodes.[36]

Despite Dovzhenko's enthusiasm for Kurbas's achievements, his passion for the theatre faded quickly. The theatre was 'too small for those ideas and fantasies, which swirled in Dovzhenko's exuberant imagination', Smolych claimed. 'The art of the stage did not correspond to the concepts, to the temperament, and to the scale of his thinking.' Dovzhenko thought in broad and all-encompassing terms, and these visions and fantasies required depiction on a very large scale, larger than a theatrical stage. Dovzhenko also wanted his stories to run at a faster pace than the theatre allowed. His stories demanded rapid changes in the action, in the location of the action and in time. In presenting the interaction between image and movement, he wanted to utilise as many options as possible. He hoped to use montage, a rapid succession of contrasting images, to deliver his stories.[37] Inasmuch as film offered him the opportunity of employing the montage method, it attracted him.

Dovzhenko entered the film world thirty years after the first motion picture flickered onto a screen. Building on the kinetograph invented by Thomas A. Edison, Louis and Auguste Lumière constructed their own camera and projector. By 1905, ten years after the Lumières created an integrated system to project film for the mass audience, film-making had developed rapidly in the United States and Western Europe. Over the next two decades, pioneering film-makers experimented with the new medium and created networks to reproduce and distribute their films. In addition to its technological innovations, film introduced new ways of telling a story.

The Lumières recorded actual events, the earliest form of *cinéma vérité*, and Edison and Georges Méliès explored the illusionist aspect of film. They defined film 'as a mass medium'.[38] By creating a 'totally imaginary world on film' and by extending the length of film and introducing special effects, Méliès raised the role of narrative in fictional film to new heights.[39]

Movies achieved great popularity in the Russian Empire before the First World War, but Dovzhenko's introduction to the cinema remains unknown.[40] Despite all the detail provided in his autobiographies and diaries, Dovzhenko did not reveal the name of the first film that caught his eye, where he saw it, or what impressions it created on him. Perhaps he enjoyed this movie in Hlukhiv, Zhytomyr, or Kiev, the large cities in which he lived prior to his diplomatic posting to Poland in 1921.

Certainly, Dovzhenko viewed many films in Warsaw and Berlin. His friend Dmytro Kapka noted that Dovzhenko displayed a taste for European and American adventure films while in the Polish capital.[41] In Berlin, Dovzhenko continued to attend film screenings and sought out the creators and actors of the German film world. He befriended Hryhory Khmara, a Ukrainian actor from Poltava, who lived with Asta Nielsen, a prominent Danish-born actress. Dovzhenko frequented her salon, where he often met with directors Fritz Lang, Georg Wilhelm Pabst, Friedrich Wilhem Murnau, and actors Emil Jannings, Paul Wegener and Pola Negri.[42]

In the summer of 1922, Kapka came from Warsaw to Berlin to visit Dovzhenko. The two received free tickets to Berlin's movie theatres. After one screening, Dovzhenko said affably: 'Well, Kapochko, you saw what European cinema is; now you can go home!'[43]

The sophistication of the movie-making techniques mastered in Western Europe and in the United States excited Dovzhenko more than the stories these films portrayed. Still, the future film-maker did not perceive cinema as a serious art form or consider it a personal vocation.[44]

Nevertheless, Dovzhenko developed a good working knowledge of popular film. After moving to Kharkiv in August 1923, he kept up with the most recent films. Many, if not most of the films shown on Ukrainian screens, came from America or Western Europe.[45] In one instance, he put his knowledge of popular film to good, if comical, use. When a mysterious woman stalked Dovzhenko, he decided to drive her away by confronting her. Inspired by a recent Hollywood production, he shouted: 'I am a major international criminal, like the Thief of Baghdad!' The woman ran away, never to reappear.[46] In addition to films of this type, comedies with Buster Keaton and Harold Lloyd and romances starring Dorothy and Lillian Gish, Greta Garbo and others appeared on Kharkiv's screens, as did the first Soviet films.[47]

In addition to seeing the most recent American, European and Soviet releases in Kharkiv, Dovzhenko began to work for VUFKU, a part of the Soviet Union's highly decentralised film system, which the Soviet Ukrainian government created on 13 March 1922. Fiercely independent, the leaders of this organisation refused to submit to the plans of Sovkino, one of the main production companies operating in the Russian Republic, which wanted to rationalise the production and distribution of movies on an all-Union scale.[48] At this time, VUFKU maintained its headquarters in Kharkiv and its only studio, the largest 'film factory' in the USSR until the end of the 1920s, in Odessa.

At first, Dovzhenko made posters for VUFKU's films. Over the course of time, he became more involved with poster-making than drawing cartoons for *Visti*.[49] Oleksandr Hryshchenko, one of his closest friends in the 1920s, speculated on how VUFKU's assignments may have influenced the young artist:

> A person works on creating a film poster, and in his head a thought erupts about writing his own screenplay. At times he breaks away from his easel, and sits at his desk and writes something in a hurry. Deep in thought, he suddenly takes up the pen again. After working at the desk for a time, he throws down the pen and takes up the brushes, continuing his work on the poster.[50]

Dovzhenko most likely experienced this creative tension. Having seen many films, he began to imagine that he could create a better one – just for the fun of it, art or no art. Depicting scenes from film on canvas sharpened his critical faculties. He began to tinker mentally with other people's films, revising scenes on the posters before him. In time, the artist's playfulness matured. Instead of manipulating other people's completed films, he began to invent his own screenplays, with his own heroes, plots and action.

In addition to creating posters, Dovzhenko prepared titles for VUFKU's silent films, thereby supplementing his income. His friend, Maik Johansen, worked for VUFKU and hired him to help translate English- and European-language titles into Ukrainian. For Dovzhenko, title-making offered not only a means of making additional money, but another outlet for his creativity. In making these film titles, he established and developed his own style.[51]

Dovzhenko's posters and titles for VUFKU impressed its administrators, perhaps even Pavlo Nechesa, its deputy head and the main administrator for production.[52] Dovzhenko's good humour and extroverted nature gave him an influence at VUFKU far beyond his responsibilities, allowing him on at least one occasion to find employment for his friends in the newly emergent and expanding Ukrainian film industry. In 1925 Kapka asked the cartoonist to help him become an actor at the Odessa Film Studio. Dovzhenko went to VUFKU and the next day, according to Kapka, Dovzhenko 'got me a job in Odessa as a film actor with comic roles. I rejoiced and went to Odessa.'[53]

Between 1921 and 1925, Dovzhenko watched and criticised film from a distance, but his friendships with people in the film world, their interaction and their encouragement inspired him. Barbara Krylova-Dovzhenko inadvertently started this process. Her illness and its expenses led Dovzhenko to expand his moonlighting for VUFKU. Subsequently, her departure freed him from his marital obligations and provided him with more time to develop his interests and to socialise with friends. Most of his friends from this period eventually joined the film industry or became film critics.

Dovzhenko shared living quarters with the novelist Yury Yanovsky, the poet Mykola Bazhan, and the artist Stefan Melnyk. They met every morning for breakfast and often convened in the evenings.[54] Dovzhenko thought that the four 'bachelors' lived in a state of chaos. He set up a system for dividing the chores and cleaning the rooms. Each morning someone had to go to the store to buy four bottles of milk, eight rolls and 200 grams of butter. Dovzhenko then prepared breakfast. After the morning meal the roommates had to wash the bottles and glasses and clean the main room. Then, and only then, could they rush to work.[55] Organised and meticulous, Dovzhenko always emphasised order over chaos, not only in running a household, but also in his attempts to dissect the world of film and to establish with his friends a consensus on film-making.

These discussions persuaded Dovzhenko to enter the film world on a full-time basis. In his reaction to the leftist intellectuals grouped around the Moscow journal *LEF* (Left Front of Art), which stressed the primacy of 'documenting reality' in the first socialist state, Dovzhenko found rational reasons for his decision.[56] Although he did not completely agree with these leftist intellectuals, their advocacy of photography and journalism (which they claimed provided a more realistic portrayal of

the world) over painting and literature appealed to him. They provoked him to re-
assess his long-term commitment to portrait and landscape painting. Moreover, his
wife's illness and their *de facto* separation created a situation of flux in his personal
life. His compass could not provide the proper coordinates. Dissatisfied with his
position as a staff cartoonist for *Visti*, he wanted to find a more fulfilling profession.
His frustration compelled him to seek a change.

The Soviet film-making industry provided Dovzhenko with the opportunity he
needed. After Soviet Russia's Council of People's Commissars (Sovnarkom) eliminated private studios and film-distribution networks on 27 August 1919, Soviet
cinematography developed slowly. Its first products included newsreels and *agitki*,
'short films, from five to thirty minutes long, with extremely didactic content aimed
at an uneducated audience'.[57] After the Civil War, the number of Soviet feature films
expanded steadily from twelve in 1921 to 102 in 1926.[58]

Despite this progress, growth proceeded in spite of inadequate support from the
Soviet government, which did not provide the necessary funds to replace the
industry's inferior equipment or to buy raw film, which film-makers had to import
from abroad using precious convertible currency.[59] In order to make up for inadequate government subsidies, the Soviet film industry had to support itself and make
a profit. By importing and distributing foreign films, the industry financed its own
recovery by the late 1920s.[60] Showing European and American films, even those politically censored, acted as a double-edged sword. Although the Soviet studios
profited from these foreign pictures, audiences preferred Hollywood films to domestic productions. Crowds flocked to see *The Mask of Zorro*, *Robin Hood* and *The Thief
of Baghdad*. These and similar films enjoyed much wider appeal than the Soviet films
of the 1920s that later established themselves as classics of the world cinema.

Although the great majority of Soviet films from this period contained political
messages approved by the authorities, directors soon developed individual and characteristic styles. Each sought to expand the borders of the possible and the
permissible, asthetically if not politically.[61] Vsevolod Pudovkin's *Mother* (1926),
Sergei Eisenstein's *Strike* (1925) and *The Battleship Potemkin* (1925), Lev Kuleshov's
The Extraordinary Adventures of Mr West in the Land of the Bolsheviks (1924) and *By
the Law* (1926), and Dziga Vertov's *Cinema-Eye* (1924) not only explored new
themes, never before shown on the screen, but also employed radically new techniques to present their messages. Soviet audiences, hungry for entertainment, still
preferred escapist films over experimental art. On average, foreign films produced
ten times the profit of domestic ones.[62]

Although Dovzhenko most likely saw most of these films in Kharkiv, he never
recorded his reactions to them. At that time he still felt torn between the two creative avenues of painting and film. Both painting and the cinema dealt with images
and the construction of illusions, which appealed to Dovzhenko. The imagination

that had helped him deal with the death of his twelve brothers and sisters drove artistic impulses that cried out for expression in some form. Both media allowed Dovzhenko to translate his private dreams into public illusions, one on canvas and the other on celluloid. Although these images did not necessarily coincide with reality, they could represent reality.

Both painting and film belonged to the visual arts, but the two forms of expression differed in their scope. 'What can an artist show on canvas?' Dovzenko asked. 'Only a small part, an episode of what happens here. But film can capture everything completely, show it during its development, show its rhythm, breathing, and human fate ...'[63] These media also differed in their relationship towards movement. The canvas captured only a single static image, while film could portray thousands of images moving at various speeds. Film could set the images it captured in chronological order and provide a narrative. The possibility of creating a narrative in this new medium made it the most exciting and the most demanding of the arts.

In addition, film attracted Dovzhenko with its potential for reproduction and distribution to millions of viewers. A theatrical production, even the major stage spectacles popular in the 1920s, could attract at most several thousand spectators at one time in one place.[64] The new art form became the most 'democratic' art, a mass art.[65]

Because films could simultaneously reach millions, Dovzhenko believed the cinema could diminish the psychological boundaries between the city and the village, between important cultural centres and the provinces.[66] Audiences in rural areas saw the same images and followed the same on-screen plots as their counterparts in Kiev and Moscow. By providing diverse audiences with a common frame of reference, cinema could forge a new 'imagined community', a common culture for the diverse regions of the newly created Soviet Ukrainian Republic, which had become a founding member of the multinational Soviet Union in December 1922.[67]

In addition, film – according to Dovzhenko – had the responsibility to challenge the viewer.[68] To copy past trends manifested decadence, not creativity. 'We need', he wrote, 'to educate and to raise the people's artistic tastes.'[69] After making *Zvenyhora* in 1927, the director defined his creative principles:

> The task of art is not to slavishly reflect reality, but to search for new paths in art ...
> And if after leaving the movie theater, the viewer who did not understand what he saw
> in the film reflects on what he beheld, then in this manner his mind will be expanded.[70]

Dovzhenko's views on the social role of art reflected his adherence to the spoken and unspoken assumptions of the Ukrainian intelligentsia as well as those of the Bolsheviks. The *intelligent* worked for the common good, however he defined it. In order to overcome the legacies of tsarist national oppression and social and political injustice, the *intelligent* had to raise the people's standards by challenging the status quo and by introducing new possibilities. Aspiring to become a painter, then director, Dovzhenko still remained a teacher at heart.

Cinematography's revolutionary potential appealed to Dovzhenko and his friends, who discussed the role of cinema and movie-making techniques during their long evening conversations. These heated discussions often dealt with cinema's place in the arts. They disagreed over how a Ukrainian cinema could develop, but they all agreed that without this achievement, Ukrainian culture as a whole could not evolve.[71]

Film, according to Bazhan, 'entered our consciousness, occupying a place almost equal to literature'.[72] In fact, the cinema had the potential to surpass literary influences. The written word demanded a literate audience, but film did not. Because the overwhelming majority of the Soviet Ukrainian population could not read, film could help the Ukrainian intelligentsia communicate with both peasants in the countryside and Russified Ukrainian workers in the cities. Until 1932 only silent films appeared in Ukraine. Although these films employed Ukrainian- or Russian-language titles, they did not divide the audience by language, since the majority of the viewers could not read anyway. Movie theatres employed 'criers' who shouted out the titles to the audience. Only after the introduction of 'talkies' in 1932 did film administrators have to decide which language to record on film and which language to dub or subtitle.

Dovzhenko and his friends hoped to use the new medium to reach and influence the illiterate Ukrainian masses by challenging the conservative oral traditions and popular culture. Like their predecessors in the nineteenth century, the Ukrainian intelligentsia of the 1920s would 'go to the people', but not physically or via literature. Instead, they would reach their potential urban and rural audiences visually. This communication required a Ukrainian cinematography distinct from the American, the Western European and especially the Russian.

Until 1917 the documentary films produced in the Ukrainian provinces and distributed throughout the Empire developed in the shadow of film studios in Moscow and St Petersburg/Petrograd.[73] Beginning in March 1919, the studios in Kiev, Kharkiv, and Odessa generated agitational films. After the Civil War, the Yalta and Odessa studios began to produce feature films, though only a small number and of mediocre quality.

The few films that emerged from these studios failed to depict a distinct Ukrainian identity. Not surprisingly, the cities that hosted the film studios in Ukraine had very few Ukrainian activists in residence.[74] Most of the directors and film crews came from Moscow or Germany. The studios remained isolated not only from Ukrainian life, but also from the central film studios in Moscow and Petrograd, and from European cinematography. As a result, the Ukrainian studios maintained a very provincial outlook. At their evening conversations, Dovzhenko and his friends agreed that film-making standards had to improve and that the film industry in Ukraine needed to reflect Ukrainian culture.

Dovzhenko and his friends did, in fact, transform the film industry. Pavlo Nechesa, VUFKU's deputy director, came to head the Odessa Film Studio. Yury Yanovsky became an editor at VUFKU in Kharkiv in June 1925. A year later, Yanovsky took on the post of head editor at the Odessa studio.[75] Mykola Bazhan became the editor of the Ukrainian film journal *Kino*. Faust Lopatynsky began to direct films in Odessa. With Dovzhenko's first screenplay, *Vasia the Reformer* in 1926, the young cartoonist and poster-maker followed in their footsteps.[76]

In Odessa

When Yanovsky left for Odessa in the spring of 1926, VUFKU had approved Dovzhenko's first screenplay for filming, and Lopatynsky had agreed to direct it.[77] Unfortunately, Lopatynsky proved incompetent. He interfered with *Vasia the Reformer*'s production, damaged the film and held up its completion. In response, the Odessa Film Studio replaced Lopatynsky with the cameraman, Iosif Rona. This move only proved a stop-gap solution. To save the film, Dovzhenko had to review 75 per cent of the finished picture and reshoot several scenes.[78]

Dovzhenko initially planned to stay in Odessa for at least a month, beginning in late June 1926.[79] Arriving in 'the Hollywood on the Black Sea', he met Nechesa, Yanovsky, Kapka and Lopatynsky at the studio.

The Odessa Film Studio made its home in Ukraine's most multinational and least Ukrainian city. Created from a nationalised pre-revolutionary studio in 1919, it remained, as Lopatynsky asserted, 'a cultural Kamchatka', a backwater.[80] It lagged behind the Ukrainian cultural revolution, especially Ukrainianisation. In response Ukrainian party leaders, who understood cinema's importance in Ukrainianisation, demanded a remedy. In 1925, they passed a decree which encouraged many prominent Ukrainian writers, actors, theatre directors and designers to work in the film industry, which would train them.[81]

Despite his lack of experience in film-making, Dovzhenko fitted the bill. During his first few weeks at the studio, Kapka noted, his friend seemed 'very insecure' about his abilities to master the new medium. He knew what he liked on the screen but did not have a command of the techniques needed to produce what he envisioned. He had never even operated a camera. To complete *Vasia*, he had to learn fast. After perfecting his ability to record clearly focused, properly exposed images on film, Dovzhenko then had to learn to evaluate the different pictorial compositions, choose between the use of long shots and close-ups and assess the effects of different lenses and filters. After the completion of filming, he had to learn how to edit the film in order to create meaning and tone.[82] The mastery of each process required enormous amounts of time and energy.

At first, Dovzhenko walked around the film studio, inspected everything carefully, and visited the locations where his more experienced colleagues shot their scenes.[83] Over the weeks, Dovzhenko began to believe in himself. He wrote:

> One simple fact helped me in the beginning. I began to observe how one Odessa director conducted location shooting not far from the studio. What he did with his actors was so obviously bad that I immediately gained confidence. I thought to myself: if I can see that it's bad and know why it's bad, then I'm not so incompetent. What's more, I can just get up there and do better.[84]

Dovzhenko also had the opportunity to learn from the best and the brightest. Throughout the 1920s, VUFKU's only studio employed mostly pre-revolutionary directors and cameramen who had not emigrated after the revolution broke out. Highly competent directors, such as Pyotr Chardynin, Vladimir Gardin, Nikolai Okhlopkov, Georgy Tasin and Aksel Lundin worked at the Odessa Studio. Although they identified themselves as Russians or with Russian culture, they did not neglect Ukrainian themes in their films, as Gardin's *Ostap Bandura* (1924), and Chardynin's *Ukrazia* (1924) and *Taras Shevchenko* (1926) demonstrate.[85]

These directors did not supervise Dovzhenko's apprenticeship. Instead, Dovzhenko learned what he needed to know from VUFKU's cameramen: Iosif Rona, Danylo Demutsky and Boris Zavelev.[86] One of the Odessa Film Studio's senior cameramen, Nikolai Fedorovych Kozlovsky, took Dovzhenko under his wing. 'In your work never make compromises,' Kozlovsky advised his student. 'If you yield half a kopek, you soon will lose one hundred rubles.'[87] In another instance, Dovzhenko quoted Kozlovsky, 'There should not be any compromises in your work,' he said. 'To give up a thumb means to lose a hand.'[88]

Dovzhenko managed to complete *Vasia the Reformer* in Odessa. No copies of *Vasia* survive, but all accounts indicate that his first film satirised the social problems generated by the New Economic Policy (NEP), introduced by Lenin in March 1921.[89] By abandoning War Communism, the NEP allowed a mixed state-private economy, which brought social peace after seven years of war, revolution and civil war. The new policy also encouraged social irresponsibility, especially among the highly visible NEPmen, those traders and small entrepreneurs most people identified with greed and conspicuous consumption.[90]

Dovzhenko's protagonist, Vasia, a Young Pioneer, comes across as part Boy Scout, part Dennis the Menace. Through a series of slapstick adventures and misadventures, Vasia exposes and rectifies a number of social ills, including drunkenness, fraud, clerical dishonesty and marital strife. Although the film, which reveals the influence of Buster Keaton and Charlie Chaplin's comedies, takes a decidedly light-hearted, even farcical approach, it contains the roots of Dovzhenko's later cinematographic masterpieces.

Vasia incurs his Uncle Hryhory's wrath by catching a fishhook in the uncle's beard. Uncle Hryhory pursues Vasia across town but abandons the chase in order to go drinking in the pub. Vasia, in the meantime, goes fishing with his younger brother, Yury. Along the way, the two brothers find a pouch containing money, perfume, cosmetics and a factory manager's identity card written in Ukrainian. The pouch has blown out of the manager's car.

Uncle Hryhory then reappears, drunkenly stumbling into the river. Vasia rescues and revives him, but the uncle has not forgotten his earlier anger. He chases Vasia, who encounters the factory manager's car, abandoned while the manager conducts a non-business transaction with a young woman behind the bushes. Vasia accidentally starts the car, which then pursues the uncle. The amorous couple in the bushes, alerted by the sound of the car's engine, give chase but to no avail. The car crashes into Vasia's gate, sustaining serious damage.

The film progresses in a similar vein, as Vasia foils a robbery in his own house, convinces his uncle and other men to abandon their excessive drinking, denounces the corrupt factory manager and transforms the church into a cinema with the charlatan priest acting as a projectionist.[91]

Dovzhenko's first film belonged to a popular genre of Soviet films criticising the NEPmen, and NEP's negative social consequences.[92] It showed no traces of what would later emerge as his distinctive style. Nonetheless, even in this early, slapstick effort, a number of the film-maker's personal themes – family, community and the eventual triumph of right-minded simplicity – stand out. In a sense, Vasia represents the precursor to Dovzhenko's later eponymous *Ivan* (1932). Both characters represent a kind of accidental hero, achieving great deeds while remaining ordinary, simple men.

After completing *Vasia the Reformer*, Dovzhenko abandoned any idea of returning to Kharkiv and his former profession. As he gained confidence in his film-making abilities, he decided to become a full-time director. He immediately undertook another film, *Love's Berry* (1926), which approximated his first film in its style. Dovzhenko wrote:

> I locked myself in a room in a hotel for a week. I wrote the screenplay and rereading it laughed. I rejoiced that my comical screenplay turned out well. Later I began to film according to this scenario. At all times I could not stop laughing.[93]

Love's Berry, the first film Dovzhenko wrote and directed alone, dealt with sexual relations, public morality, courting rituals, family responsibility and marriage during the NEP era. Modelled on Hollywood comedies, it also attacked authority and pomposity. Its young protagonist, Zhan Kovbasiuk, works as a barber and hairdresser. Working in his shop, he receives a letter from Lisa, a girlfriend whom he has not seen in a long time, asking him to meet her at their favourite park bench.

When they meet, she pulls out a baby from under her coat. Zhan moves to run away and denies fathering the child, but he furtively examines it. He takes out a mirror, combs his hair and compares the child's physical features with his own in the mirror.

Lisa hands him the child, telling Zhan that she needs to drink some water. On the way to the water booth, she runs away. After Zhan realises that she has disappeared, he takes the child to the police station and lies about finding 'this abandoned baby'. One of the policemen carefully looks at the child, then at Zhan, noticing the resemblance between them. Realising the policeman's unspoken conclusions, Zhan rushes off with the child and experiences a number of misadventures in attempting to rid himself of it. Lisa, in the meantime, goes to the people's court and sets up a meeting with the court's investigator.

Zhan leaves the baby with a man in the park and returns to his normal routine in the barbershop, but then he receives a subpoena from the investigator at the people's court. It orders him to appear at the court with the child at 4 p.m.

Now Zhan desperately tries to find the baby. He accidentally reacquires the child when its latest recipient covertly slips it into Zhan's stolen baby carriage. Overjoyed, he rushes off to court, where he enthusiastically embraces Lisa before the

Marian Krushelnytsky and Margarita Chardynina-Barska play the barber Zhan Kovbasiuk and his girlfriend in Dovzhenko's second film, *Love's Berry* (1926)

investigator. After the meeting, he leaves the court with Lisa to register their marriage. Zhan carries the child, and an expression of pride and happiness appears on his face.[94]

Despite Dovzhenko's best efforts, his first two experiments in a new medium did not achieve critical or popular success. This failure should not have surprised Nechesa or VUFKU. Dovzhenko lacked film-making experience. Becoming a film director entailed more complicated effort and preparation than becoming a cartoonist. Dovzhenko could not easily transfer his humour to the big screen. Although he could not stop laughing while writing his script, minutes after he previewed *Love's Berry* before his colleagues and studio administrators, 'a funereal silence' prevailed in the hall.[95]

According to workers at the Odessa Film Studio interviewed by Rostislav Iurenev, Dovzhenko 'poorly conceptualized' and 'took an excessive fancy to the technical side' in his first two films.[96] VUFKU distributed these films in Ukraine (not in the Russian Republic), but critics and audiences ignored them. Even the Ukrainian film journal, *Kino* (edited by Bazhan, Dovzhenko's friend), which listed *Vasia* and *Love's Berry* in its film chronicle and reproduced several stills from them, did not review them.[97]

As a result of these two failures, Nechesa, a hard-nosed sailor who had stormed the Winter Palace in October 1917 and fought anti-Bolshevik armies in Ukraine during the Civil War, called Dovzhenko in and gave him an ultimatum.[98]

> Sashko! You do not know how to write screenplays and you are engaging in something you know nothing about. We need to throw you out of the movie-making business, but you are a talented person. Here's the screenplay by Zats and Sharansky, *The Diplomatic Pouch*. If you'll make a good film from this screenplay, then you'll be a happy man; if not, then excuse me, even though I am your friend, I'll throw you out![99]

After this meeting, Dovzhenko worked long and hard in creating this film, which he hoped would please Nechesa. When *The Diplomatic Pouch* became his first cinematic success, he listed it as his first film in his autobiographies and personnel forms.[100]

First Success

The February 1926 assassination of Theodore Nette, a Soviet diplomatic courier in Western Europe, by Russian émigrés with anti-Soviet sympathies inspired the screenplay for *The Diplomatic Pouch*. As a 'red detective' story, an ideologically motivated film genre with the qualities of a thriller, the film claims that the European working class wholeheartedly identified itself with the USSR and its well-being.[101]

The film takes place in Great Britain, where the Soviet Embassy orders two couri-

Dovzhenko (on the left) plays a coal stoker in *The Diplomatic Pouch* (1927)

ers to take a sealed diplomatic pouch to Leningrad by ship from Portsmouth. On the London-to-Portsmouth train, the British Secret Service's Inspector White and his partner intercept the couriers, kill one of them, and seriously wound the other, who miraculously escapes with the pouch. A short time later, a British rail worker finds the wounded courier near the railway tracks, takes him home and reveals his own Communist sympathies. Just before he dies, the courier explains his mission, and the worker's family promises to deliver the important documents to the USSR. The rail worker then passes on the pouch to his son, Harry, a seaman on the Portsmouth-to-Leningrad run. After tracing the pouch to Harry's ship, Inspector White boards it and tries to recover the pouch from the sailors with the help of a provocatively dressed dancer named Ellen. All of the seamen on Harry's ship resist White. At the end of the film, as Ellen performs her suggestive dances for the passengers, the sailors throw him and his partner to their deaths in the North Sea. The ship sails on to Leningrad; the sailors deliver the pouch to the Soviet authorities.[102]

Conforming to the Soviet vision of the world, *The Diplomatic Pouch* provides an unrealistic portrayal of the political situation in Western Europe. It presents stereotype after stereotype. According to Peter Kenez, 'British workers and sailors are class-conscious proletarians, who happily risk their lives in the service of the Soviet cause. The enemy is decadent and corrupt. We can tell that the representatives of the enemy are decadent because they dance with scantily dressed women. Class-conscious proletarians, on the other hand, are able to resist the allure of such females.'[103]

Although Dovzhenko employed an out-of-focus sequence of the wounded courier's hallucinations, distorted close-ups and a rhythmic portrayal of the ship engine's pistons (influenced by Eisenstein's *Potemkin*), very little in this film fore-shadowed the cinematic innovations of his later films, *Zvenyhora*, *Arsenal* and *Earth*. This ordinary action-thriller possessed an accessible narrative and followed the Soviet line. However unbelievable the pro-Soviet class consciousness of the British sailors, the film – with its cartoon-like characters and simple plot – achieved success and guaranteed Dovzhenko a future in the budding Ukrainian motion picture industry.

Conclusion

The impression that Dovzhenko and his friends created, that he managed to trans-form himself overnight from a political cartoonist into a successful director, forms an important part of the film-maker's myth. The seeds of Dovzhenko's career in film originated in his youth when he acted in amateur theatrical productions and pur-sued artistic interests. He frequented the cinema, especially in Warsaw, Berlin and Kharkiv. He may not have yet understood the theoretical intricacies of film as a syn-thetic art, but he engaged in long conversations with his friends and colleagues in Kharkiv about film.

His wife's illness tested Dovzhenko's resilience and undermined his commitment to her and to his past and present. After an eighteen-month psychological struggle, he enthusiastically reinvented himself as a master of illusions.

He did not just appear at the gates of the Odessa Film Studio and win a job as a director; VUFKU sent him there to revive his first screenplay, *Vasia the Reformer*. Although Dovzhenko did not know how to operate a camera, he did know several important people at the Odessa Film Studio and used his connections to enter the film world. In Odessa, he not only edited Lopatynsky's footage, but he also added scenes to it. Inspired by the many creative possibilities of film-making, he began to film *Love's Berry* after *Vasia*'s completion.

Although Dovzhenko's first two films sank into both cultural and popular obliv-ion, he redeemed himself with *The Diplomatic Pouch*. Dovzhenko learned from his mistakes. He discovered that funny screenplays do not necessarily make funny films. He mastered the camera, and he began to understand that making a film required cooperative effort. Most importantly, during the filming of *Vasia*, Dovzhenko met Danylo Demutsky, who became his long-term cameraman and creative partner. Together they created *Vasia*, *Love's Berry*, *Arsenal*, *Earth* and *Ivan*.[104]

The films Dovzhenko viewed in Warsaw, Berlin and Kharkiv and his occupation as a political cartoonist influenced his first three films, designed to attract viewers

away from the American and Western European films shown in Ukraine. In light of
his extensive discussions with his friends over the need to establish a Ukrainian cinema, it seems somewhat surprising that his first three films did not deal with
Ukrainian themes. Perhaps he recognised his inexperience at film-making and
anticipated working on Ukrainian themes after he mastered the new medium.

Dovzhenko's emergence as a film director coincided with the rapid expansion of
the Soviet film industry and the creation of many opportunities. In the mid-1920s,
individuals with little experience could become film directors with a little luck, talent and help from friends in the industry. Dovzhenko joined Sergei Eisenstein,
Vsevolod Pudovkin, Lev Kuleshov, Dziga Vertov, Grigory Kozintsev and Leonid
Trauberg, the masters of the first generation of Soviet film-makers. The film studios,
the Soviet government and the Communist Party tolerated the inevitable mistakes
involved in the introduction of a new, unmastered medium. Dovzhenko admitted
that 'the films that emerged were poor', but the administrators 'scolded us gently,
gave us other work, and after wasting several thousand rubles of state funds, we
became directors'.[105]

Notes

1. '1939 Autobiography', p. 17. Pavlo Nechesa, the director of the Odessa Film
   Studio, provides a slightly different account of Dovzhenko's metamorphosis.
   See P. Nechesa, 'Shchastia buty poruch', *PZh*, p. 216.
2. The relationship between Dovzhenko and Krylova after the summer of 1917,
   when Dovzhenko moved to Kiev, remains murky. Krylova apparently left
   Ukraine between 1917 and 1921, ending up in Prague, where Dovzhenko
   met up with her in 1922. See Mykola Kutsenko, 'Spovid' pro trahichne
   kokhannia', *Vitchyzna*, no. 4 (1991), pp. 181–94; and M. Vovchenko, 'Iakym
   ia znav O. Dovzhenka', *DMM*, File 8. Also see George O. Liber, ' "Till
   Death Do You Part": Varvara Krylova, Yuliya Solntseva and Oleksandr
   Dovzhenko's Muse', *Australian Slavonic and East European Studies*, 14, nos
   1–2 (2000), pp. 75–97.
3. The chronology in the last two paragraphs comes from Kutsenko, 'Spovid'',
   p. 187.
4. V. S. Dovzhenko, 'Moi vospominaniia ob Aleksandre Petroviche
   Dovzhenko', RGALI, 2081/1/1123, p. 6.
5. 'Pro zakhody zabezpechennia rivnopravnosti mov i pro dopomohu
   rozvytkovi ukrains'koi movy', in *Kul'turne budivnytstvo, tom I: Zbirka
   postanov pro ukrainizatsiiu (Tsentral'nykh i okruhovykh orhaniv kompartii i
   radvlady)* (Kherson, 1929), p. 243.
6. Ibid., I, pp. 242–7.
7. Gennadii Konovalov, 'Dovzhenko nachinalsia tak . . .', in B. N. Tarasenko

and G. M. Kapel'gorodskaia, eds, *Uroki Aleksandra Dovzhenko* (Kiev, 1982), pp. 126–9. For a sample of Dovzhenko's caricatures, see I. Zolotoverkhova and H. Konovalov, *Dovzhenko – khudozhnyk* (Kiev, 1968).

8. Bohdan Nebesio, 'The Silent Films of Alexander Dovzhenko' (unpublished PhD dissertation, University of Alberta, 1996), p. 60. A Ukrainian NKVD report from 1940 provides a slightly different interpretation of Dovzhenko's participation in these literary organisations. *D*, pp. 28–9; *ZA*, pp. 272–3.

9. A. Leites and M. Iashek, *Desiat' rokiv ukrains'koi literatury: 1917–1927* (Kharkiv, 1928), vol. 2, p. 374; cited in George S. N. Luckyj, *Literary Politics in the Soviet Ukraine, 1917–1934* (New York, 1956), p. 47.

10. Myroslav Shkandrij, *Modernists, Marxists, and the Nation: The Ukrainian Literary Discussion of the 1920s* (Edmonton, Alberta, 1992), p. 34.

11. Shkandrij, p. 103.

12. Shkandrij, p. 103.

13. Nebesio, pp. 75–6; pp. 61–2.

14. Mykola Bazhan, 'Mytets' shukaie puti', *PZh*, p. 174.

15. Kutsenko, 'Spovid'', p. 187.

16. Varvara Dovzhenko, 'Naidorozhche, vichne', *PZh*, p. 146.

17. P. M. Nyrkovskii, 'Vospominaniia ob A. P. Dovzhenko', RGALI, 2081/2/213, p. 14a.

18. V. S. Dovzhenko, 'Moi vospominaniia ob Aleksandre Petroviche Dovzhenko', p. 8.

19. Robert Berkow, Mark H. Beers, and Andrew J. Fletcher, eds, *The Merck Manual of Medical Information, Home Edition* (Whitehouse Station, NJ, 1997), pp. 289–90; and Robert J. Joynt and Robert C. Griggs, eds, *Clinical Neurology*, vol. 4 (rev. ed., Philadelphia, 1998), p. 15. Dr. Walter Brandner, MD, of Homewood, Alabama, suggested that Krylova-Dovzhhenko suffered from reflex sympathetic dystrophy.

20. Kutsenko, 'Spovid'', p. 187. Kutsenko claims that this boating accident happened in 1925. Most likely, however, this mishap occurred in 1924. Krylova-Dovzhenko and Dovzhenko separated in early 1925.

21. Serhii Plachynda, *Oleksandr Dovzhenko: Zhyttia i tvorchist'* (Kiev, 1964), p. 27.

22. Bazhan, p. 179.

23. Kutsenko, 'Spovid'', p. 187.

24. Leonid Cherevatenko, 'Z Dovzhenkovoho lystyvannia', *Dnipro*, no. 1–2 (1997), p. 162.

25. Letter 11, in Roman Korohods'kyi, ed., 'Visimnadtsat' lystiv pro kokhannia: Oleksandr Dovzhenko – Oleni Chernovii', *Kul'tura i zhyttia*, no. 49 (4 December 1996), p. 3.

26. Cherevatenko, p. 162.

27. Bazhan, p. 179.

28. Letter 16, in Korohods'kyi, 'Visimnadtsat' lystiv pro kokhannia', p. 3.

29. Iurii Smolych, 'Dovzhenko', *PZh*, p. 46. A more detailed memoir of Dovzhenko appeared in Smolych's *Rozpovid' pro nespokii* (Kiev, 1968), pp. 154–81. The Russian film-maker Sergei Yutkevich agreed with Smolych's assessment. See 'Vystuplenie S. Iutkevicha', *ZBK*, p. 100.

30. A. P. Iakovets, RGALI, 2081/1/1212, p. 51b.

31. '1939 Autobiography', p. 16.

32. Cited in M. Vovchenko, 'Iakym ia znav O. Dovzhenka', p. 7.

33. R. Iurenev, *Aleksandr Dovzhenko* (Moscow, 1959), pp. 13–14.

34. Smolych, 'Dovzhenko', *PZh*, p. 47.

35. Natalia Kuziakina, 'Oleksandr Dovzhenko i Les' Kurbas', *Ukrains'kyi teatr*, no. 6 (1989), p. 9.

36. Kuziakina, p. 10.

37. Smolych, 'Dovzhenko', *PZh*, pp. 47–8.

38. Douglas Gomery, *Movie History: A Survey* (Belmont, CA, 1991), pp. 8–10; quote comes from p. 10.

39. Gomery, p. 23.

40. On the popularity of movies in the Russian Empire before 1914, see Yuri Tsivian, *Testimoni silenziosi: film rusi, 1908–1919* (Pordenone, Italy, 1989); his *Early Cinema in Russia and Its Cultural Reception* (London and New York, 1994; Chicago, 1998); and Denise J. Youngblood, *The Magic Mirror: Moviemaking in Russia, 1908–1918* (Madison, WI, 1999).

41. Dmytro Kapka, 'Zvela mene dolia z Dovzhenkom', *PZh*, p. 158.

42. Hans-Joachim Schlegel, 'Berlin i Germaniia Aleksandra Dovzhenko', *KZ*, no. 31 (1996), pp. 143–4.

43. Kapka, p. 159.

44. Kapka, p. 158.

45. Nebesio, p. 73, n. 95, citing the works of Vance Kepley, Jr., Betty Kepley and Denise Youngblood, asserts that 'most films' shown in Ukraine in the 1920s did not come from the Soviet Union. See Vance Kepley, Jr., and Betty Kepley, 'Foreign Films on Soviet Screens, 1922–1931', *Quarterly Review of Film Studies*, 4, no. 4 (1979), pp. 429–42; and Denise Youngblood, 'The *Amerykanshchina* in Soviet Cinema', *Journal of Popular Film and Television*, 19, no. 4 (1992), pp. 148–56. But of the total of 283 movie posters produced in Ukraine between 1923 and 1932 and held by the Central Library of the Academy of Sciences of Ukraine, seventy-one (or one-quarter) depict foreign films. See I. I. Zolotoverkhova, *Ukrains'kyi radians'kyi kinoplakat 20–30-kh rokiv* (Kiev, 1983), pp. 55–100.

46. O. Hryshchenko, *Z berehiv zacharovanoi Desny* (Kiev, 1964), p. 130.

47. A. Mar'iamov, 'Razbeg', *Iskusstvo kino*, no. 9 (1964), pp. 25, 32.
48. Denise Youngblood, *Soviet Cinema in the Silent Era, 1918–1935* (Ann Arbor, MI, 1985), pp. 44, 180. 'Because of VUFKU's constant wrangling over distribution first with Goskino [Sovkino's predecessor] and now Sovkino, major films of Russian production were a long time coming to the Ukraine (if ever) and vice-versa. VUFKU insisted on outright purchase of Russian films instead of combining a rental price with a percentage at the box office, as was traditional' (p. 44).
49. Bazhan, pp. 181–2.
50. Hryshchenko, p. 63.
51. Bazhan, p. 180.
52. O. F. Svachko, *Rozpovidi pro suchasnykiv* (Kiev, 1983), p. 24.
53. Kapka, p. 159.
54. Bazhan, pp. 180–1.
55. Bazhan, pp. 181–2.
56. See Dziga Vertov's 'Kinoki. Perevorot', *LEF*, no. 3 (1923), pp. 135–43. Also see Sergei Eisenstein's 'Montazh attraktsionov', *LEF*, no. 3 (1923), pp. 70–5.
57. Peter Kenez, *The Birth of the Propaganda State: Soviet Methods of Mass Mobilization, 1917–1929* (Cambridge and New York, 1985), p. 109.
58. For statistics concerning Soviet film production, see Sergei Zemlianukhin and Miroslava Segida (compilers), *Domashniaia sinemateka: otechestvennoe kino, 1918–1996* (Moscow, 1996), p. 6.
59. Kenez, *Propaganda State*, pp. 206–7; Kristin Thompson, 'Government Policies and Practical Necessities in the Soviet Cinema of the 1920s', in Anna Lawton, ed., *The Red Screen: Politics, Society, and Art in Soviet Cinema* (London and New York, 1992), p. 28.
60. Thompson, pp. 19, 23, 28.
61. Kenez, *Propaganda State*, pp. 208, 209.
62. Peter Kenez, *Cinema and Soviet Society, 1917–1953* (Cambridge and New York, 1992), p. 72.
63. Iosif Shpipen, 'Tvorcheskoe edinstvo', in *DVVS*, p. 79.
64. See Katerina Clark, *Petersburg: Crucible of Cultural Revolution* (Cambridge, MA, 1995), especially chapter 4.
65. Vadym Skurativs'kyi, 'Kino i natsional'na kul'tura', in V. H. Horpenko and O. S. Musiienko, eds, *Zmina paradyhmy: Zbirnyk naukovykh prats', Chastyna 1* (Kiev, 1995), p. 12.
66. I. M. Tokarev, 'T. Dovzhenko!', *DMM*, File 8, p. 1.
67. The term 'imagined community' comes from Benedict Anderson, *Imagined Communities: Reflections on the Origin and Spread of Nationalism* (London, 1983).

68. O. Dovzhenko, 'Do problemy obrazotvorchoho mystetstva', in Iurii Lavrinenko, ed., *Rozstriliane vidrodzhennia* (Paris, 1959), p. 871.

69. Dovzhenko, 'Do problemy', p. 872.

70. *Vechirnii Kyiv*, no. 243 (1927); cited in *Storinky*, p. 49.

71. Bazhan, p. 180.

72. Bazhan, p. 182.

73. Iurenev, pp. 22–3.

74. K. Fel'dman, 'Zvenigora', RGALI, 2081/1/1200, p. 7.

75. 'Z lysta Iu. Ianovs'koho do Prezydenta *VAPLITE* M. Kulisha (28 August 1927)', TsDAVOVUU, 166/6/1494, pp. 116–17.

76. Heorhii Ostrovs'kyi, 'Pratsia O. P. Dovzhenka na Odes'kii kinofabrytsi (1926–1929)', *Literaturna Odesa*, no. 17–18 (1957), p. 248. Maria Romanivs'ka, a friend from Dovzhenko's Kharkiv period, claimed that Dovzhenko was near completion of a draft of his first screenplay on 1 January 1925. M. Romanivs'ka, 'Daleka nasha kinoiunist'', *Vitchyzna*, no. 11 (1969), p. 153.

77. Bazhan, p. 184.

78. 'Lyst O. Dovzhenka do biuro Korelisu z povidomlenniam do rishennia vyikhaty na kinofabryku dlia roboty nad kartynoiu "Vasia-reformator" (20 June 1926)', TsDAVOVUU, 166/6/8600, p. 94; Oleksandr Rybalka, ed., '"Moia trahediia iak khudozhnyka poliahaie v tomu . . ."', *Starozhytnosti* (Kiev), no. 13–14 (1993), p. 24.

79. 'Lyst O. Dovzhenka', p. 94.

80. The phrase 'cultural Kamchatka' came from Faust Lopatyns'kyi, 'Kopiia lysta do redaktora haz. "Komunist". Shanovnyi tovaryshu redaktore! (April 1927)', TsDAVOVUU, 166/7/252, p. 10.

81. 'Pro robotu VUFKU: Postanova TsK KP(b)U vid 25 kvitnia 1925 r.', in *Kul'turne budivnytstvo v Ukrains'kii RSR: Vazhlyvishi rishennia Komunistychnoi partii i radians'koho uriadu 1917–1959 rr.*, vol. 1 (Kiev, 1959), pp. 281–2, cited in Nebesio, p. 58.

82. Gerald Mast, *A Short History of the Movies* (Indianapolis, 1975), p. 10.

83. Kapka, pp. 159–60.

84. '1939 Autobiography', p. 18.

85. Ivan Koshelivets', *Oleksandr Dovzhenko: Sproba tvorchoi biohrafii* (Munich 1980), pp. 72, 73.

86. Nebesio, pp. 68–9.

87. A. P. Dovzhenko, 'Kratkaia avtobiografiia (1935)', RGALI, 2081/1/350, pp. 4, 10.

88. Quoted in RGALI, 2081/1/382, p. 27; *Les lettres Françaises*, no. 875 (11–17 May 1961), p. 7.

89. For surveys of NEP society, see Sheila Fitzpatrick, Alexander Rabinowitch and Richard Stites, eds, *Russia in the Era of NEP* (Bloomington, IN, 1991); Roger Pethybridge, *One Step Backward, Two Steps Forward: Soviet Society and Politics in the NEP* (New York, 1990); and Lewis H. Siegelbaum, *Soviet State and Society Between Revolutions, 1918–1929* (New York, 1992).

90. For an analysis of the NEPmen, see Alan M. Ball, *Russia's Last Capitalists: The Nepmen, 1921–1929* (Berkeley, CA, and London, 1987).

91. *Vasia the Reformer*'s screenplay appeared in O. Dovzhenko, *Tvory v p'iaty tomakh* (Kiev, 1964), vol. 2, pp. 341–83.

92. For an analysis of these films, see Denise J. Youngblood, *Movies for the Masses: Popular Cinema and Soviet Society in the 1920s* (Cambridge and New York, 1992).

93. G. A. Mariagin, 'Legendy k biografii Dovzhenko', RGALI, 2081/1/1158, p. 11.

94. Dovzhenko's screenplay appeared in O. Dovzhenko, *Tvory v p'iaty tomakh*, vol. 2 (1964), pp. 327–39.

95. Mariagin, p. 11.

96. Iurenev, p. 18.

97. Ostrovs'kyi, 'Pratsia O. P. Dovzhenka', p. 249.

98. O. F. Svachko, pp. 24–5, provides a short biography of Nechesa.

99. Aleksei Svachko, 'V kino prikhodit Dovzhenko', *DVVS*, p. 68; Oleksii Svachko, 'V kino prykhodyt O. Dovzhenko', *PZh*, p. 198. O. Svachko's 'Dozvol'te zniaty fil'm', *Druh chytacha* (Kiev), 9 September 1969, pp. 5–6, confirms Nechesa's account of Dovzhenko's cinematic failures before *The Diplomatic Pouch*. See Pavlo Nechesa, 'Shchastia buty poruch', *PZh*, p. 216.

100. 'Vystuplenie A. Dovzhenko', *ZBK*, p. 59.

101. *Service*, p. 110.

102. *Service*, pp. 37–8. I owe my synopsis of *The Diplomatic Pouch*'s plot to Professor Kepley, who provides a fuller analysis of the political climate surrounding the film.

103. Kenez, *Cinema and Soviet Society, 1917–1953*, pp. 66–8.

104. *Service*, pp. 169–70.

105. A. Dovzhenko, 'Vystuplenie na sobranie sotrudnikov kievskoi kinofabriki (Sept. 1936)', RGALI, 2081/1/371, p. 16.

5

Abundant Harvest

Dovzhenko's first three films represented his efforts at learning the craft of film-making. His next three – *Zvenyhora*, *Arsenal* and *Earth* – became his 'serious' films, rich in complexity and symbolism. Whereas his early pictures possessed coherent unilinear narratives, *Zvenyhora*, *Arsenal* and *Earth* introduced complex multilinear themes and narratives, which often confused his audiences. He situated his first three in the Soviet environment; he planted his next three in Ukrainian soil. Dovzhenko finally found his voice as a film-maker.

By the mid-1920s, most intellectuals who remained in the USSR, even those who had at one time or another actively opposed the Bolsheviks, accepted the necessity of coming to terms with the new Soviet political order. Some had joined the Bol-sheviks in the course of the Revolution and Civil War; others crossed the ideological Rubicon afterwards. Depending on their individual talents, temperaments, circum-stances and opportunities, each had to decide what he truly believed, how much he could reveal of himself and how actively he could participate in the cultural, politi-cal and literary transformations of the day.[1]

As a former member of the Ukrainian Party of Socialist Revolutionaries, of the Borotbists (even if for a very short time) and of the Communist Party of Ukraine, Dovzhenko did not have much room to manoeuvre. Since 1923, as a cartoonist and as a film director, he had become a public intellectual, always at the centre of atten-tion. His public statements did not necessarily reflect his true, private beliefs. His personal world appears more in his diaries, in the memoirs of his friends, in NKVD reports and in the oblique mirror of his films, which contain more contradictions and dualisms than the autobiographical statements he wrote for official reasons. Even these 'autobiographies' provide clues about his ambivalent reactions to the emergence and consolidation of the Stalinist order.

Zvenyhora

After the success of *The Diplomatic Pouch*, Dovzhenko planned to film *The Insur-rection of the Dead*. Boris Sharansky, one of the screenwriters for *The Diplomatic Pouch*, wrote a screenplay about a group of Russian counter-revolutionary soldiers. In the story, members of General Vrangel's anti-Bolshevik White Army stranded in

Bulgaria want to return to the Soviet Union. White officers take advantage of their naiveté and send them to Algiers before selling them to the French Foreign Legion and sharing the commission for doing so. The soldiers realise that their officers have betrayed them and rebel. In response, the officers set the ship on fire and all of the rebels die.[2]

Dovzhenko began to rewrite Sharansky's screenplay, but the Central Committee of the Communist Party of Ukraine abruptly stopped the project. It sent VUFKU a strong message: 'You cannot offer pity to the White Guard.'[3]

Although Dovzhenko never completed his version of the screenplay, his treatment appears to side with the rank and file soldiers who opposed the Soviet regime. In light of his own experiences during the Civil War, his assignment to persuade internees in Poland to return to Ukraine and the executions at Bazar, he wanted to present an idea: that ordinary soldiers could not act as true counter-revolutionaries. He wished to depict 'rebel' soldiers as the victims of the officers who misled and betrayed them. Dovzhenko suggested that the Soviet government could politically re-educate and rehabilitate such soldiers, but the party would not approve any sympathetic treatment of those it considered its enemies.

During Dovzhenko's negotiations with VUFKU over *The Insurrection of the Dead*, he also began to edit the screenplay for *Zvenyhora*, written by Maik (Mykhailo) Johansen and Yury Tiutiunnyk (Yurtyk in the film's credits), originally entitled *The Enchanted Place*.[4] Johansen, a Ukrainian poet and writer (1895–1937), played a prominent role in the literary organisations *Hart* and *VAPLITE* in the 1920s.[5] His colleague, Tiutiunnyk, had served as a general in the Army of the Ukrainian National Republic and led the disastrous campaign that ended at Bazar. After this defeat, he fled to Poland. In the mid-1920s he returned to Soviet Ukraine and requested amnesty. The authorities granted his request, allowing him to live in Kharkiv and to lecture at the School for Red Officers. With Johansen's help, Tiutiunnyk began to publish in the newly created Ukrainian-language journals and to work part-time at VUFKU. The screenplay penned by Johansen and Tiutiunnyk, according to the critic Ivan Koshelivets', became 'to a great extent an autobiography of Tiutiunnyk himself'.[6]

Inasmuch as the script contained 'a lot of devilry and blatant nationalism', Dovzhenko claimed in his 1939 autobiography to have completely rewritten the Johansen-Tiutiunnyk screenplay. After reading the revisions, Johansen and Tiutiunnyk – according to Dovzhenko's account – demanded that he remove their names from the credits.[7] This assertion is questionable but even if true, Johansen's name and Tiutiunnyk's pseudonym, Yurtyk, appear in the film's credits and in most publications.

In his 1939 autobiography, Dovzhenko characterised his conflicts with the two screenwriters as ideological. In all probability, he made this assertion for his own political purposes. By the 1930s both had become 'enemies of the people'; the security organs executed Tiutiunnyk in 1929 and Johansen in 1937. To protect himself, Dovzhenko most likely created a fictitious ideological conflict between himself and the two writers. Despite his portrayal of this conflict as political, the disagreements dealt with methodology, how best to transfer the screenplay to celluloid.[8] Their arguments produced creative results.

One eyewitness to Johansen and Dovzhenko's friendship characterised their creative collaboration as follows:

> Maik and Sashko argued and an episode appeared; Maik and Sashko came to an agreement and a new development occurred in the action; Maik and Sashko always argued and a new scene, a new treatment, a new view of the project emerged. Dovzhenko, as everyone knew, was not open to any suggestions or advice, intolerant as he was with any disagreement with his views. Johansen was also stubborn. I do not recall if he ever agreed to a treatment different from his own: he convinced himself that someone else's treatment contradicted his own ideas . . .[9]

Despite his stubbornness, Dovzhenko learned from Johansen and Tiutiunnyk's comments. After *Zvenyhora*, whenever he wrote something, he sought out a group of friends and colleagues and read his drafts to them, using their ideas to strengthen his work.[10] When Dovzhenko emphasised his ideological differences with the two screenwriters, he attempted to camouflage his agreement with much of their interpretation of the past.

Even with Dovzhenko's changes, however drastic, the screenplay remained controversial. The majority of the Odessa Film Studio's Artistic Council opposed filming it. Despite their opposition, Dovzhenko began.[11] His methods of filming *Zvenyhora* also aroused heated disagreements; his own film crew opposed him. His studio-appointed cameraman, Boris Zavelev, complained to his colleagues:

> Dovzhenko is undoubtedly an interesting person, but he has worked in cinema for only a short period of time. He doesn't understand the composition of the frame and montage. I want to teach him, but he is stubborn. And I am forced to do everything he wants. What will come of this, I do not know.[12]

Dovzhenko persevered. Nechesa, the studio director, recalled the battle:

> The filming started and every day conflicts broke out among the director, the cameraman, and the set designer (Professor V. H. Krychevsky). Neither the cameraman nor the set designer could agree in any case with the director's instructions. When the director demanded that the cameraman film an entire section out of focus, the

cameraman said: 'I have filmed for twenty years, but I have never encountered such idiocy. I do not want to film out of focus and to discredit myself across the entire Soviet Union'. And every day the cameraman wanted to film only beautifully composed frames, but the director asserted that the cameraman's understanding of what constituted beautiful shots would destroy the film. Often the administration of the studio had to intervene. It was the same with the set designer . . .[13]

Although *Zvenyhora* emerged as Dovzhenko's fourth film, most critics consider it his first real film, as well as his most intellectually challenging. It attempts to unite the legends of the Ukrainian past into one narrative, with complex, interwoven themes and elements of fantasy.

Sometime in the sixteenth or seventeenth centuries, an old grandfather leads a band of Cossacks to a heavily forested mountain, Zvenyhora, which he says contains 'our Ukrainian treasures'. After defeating a group of Poles in the area, the Cossack chief and the grandfather find a valuable chalice, but it immediately transforms itself into a broken bottle. An ancient monk with magical powers haunts the mountain and impedes their search for the treasure.

As the Cossacks leave Zvenyhora, the chieftain tells the grandfather, 'Let no enemies tread here. Let the treasure lie in peace!' For centuries the grandfather stands guard over the area where the treasures are located, reappearing in the twentieth century with his two grandsons, Pavlo and Tymish.

In surveying life in the village, Dovzhenko set the cinematic pattern for his future films, with shots of endless fields of grain, of people harvesting their crops, of people eating. The outbreak of World War I, in which 'nation rose against nation, country against country, brother against brother', disrupts this peaceful life. Dovzhenko skilfully contrasted the tranquil prewar period with the war, cinematographically transforming haystacks into stacks of rifles.

While Tymish fights in the ranks of the tsarist army, Pavlo and the grandfather search for the treasure still buried in Zvenyhora. In order to sustain the war effort, the tsar's army mines Zvenyhora, penetrating deep into the mountain. The grandfather protests, but to no avail. With the collapse of the tsarist order in 1917, Tymish joins the Bolsheviks, but the grandfather and Pavlo keep looking for the treasure. As they search, the grandfather tells Pavlo the ancient legend of Princess Roksana.

The action shifts to depict this legend. Tribute-demanding invaders capture Roksana and her people. She then 'betrays her nation' by falling in love with the foreign leader, but 'not for long'. She chokes her new husband and raises the cry for her people to rebel. The invaders, however, crush the rebellion and the invader chief, who did not die at Roksana's hands, places a supernatural curse upon her. The gold of tribute remains buried in Zvenyhora.

An anti-Soviet conspiracy in *Zvenyhora* (1928): Pavlo (Les Podorozhny) instructs his grandfather (Mykola Nademsky) on how to blow up a Soviet train

Inspired by the legend, Pavlo joins the Ukrainian nationalists fighting against Tymish and the Red Army troops. After the war, Pavlo, the 'Duke of Ukraine', emigrates to Western Europe and raises money from the 'respectable' bourgeoisie. He lectures on the Bolshevik destruction of Ukraine, then promises to shoot himself with his own revolver before the audience. He has developed this 'performance art' as an elaborate scam to finance another treasure hunt at Zvenyhora. He admits that members of his audience, especially the women, have no interest in Ukraine or the Bolsheviks, but have come to see him kill himself on stage. The police come and arrest him, to the frustrated fury of the cheated audience. The police, as it turns out, operate as Pavlo's accomplices.

In the final scene, Pavlo tries to persuade the grandfather to sabotage the railway tracks in order to derail a Soviet train carrying Tymish past Zvenyhora, but at the last moment the old man refuses. Pavlo then commits suicide. The train stops, a crowd emerges from the train. After they disarm the grandfather, Tymish and his friends invite the old man aboard the train and serve him hot tea and food. The young people accept the grandfather, even though they have caught him with a bomb in his hands, as a man misled by counter-revolutionaries. They believe they can politically re-educate him. As the train speeds off, they accept the grandfather into the new Soviet order.[14]

On the surface, Dovzhenko's *Zvenyhora* opposed Ukrainian nationalism and promoted the cause of a multinational working class in Ukraine in its struggle against national and class oppression.[15] His film asserted the common interests of the working classes of Ukraine and Russia, while at the same time claiming the cultural uniqueness of Ukraine.

As one of the first films to present Ukrainian myth, folklore and history on screen, *Zvenyhora* distinguished itself not only as the most identifiably Ukrainian picture, but also as the first 'historiosophical' movie in Ukrainian cinematography.[16] *Zvenyhora* did not portray a history based on documents, but a mythologised interpretation, in which Dovzhenko deployed a broad survey of Ukrainian history to an illiterate audience who shared a common concept of the past. The film's sensibility made it more 'Ukrainian' than prior film adaptations of Ukrainian literary classics. Shortly after its release, Ukrainian critics called *Zvenyhora* the cornerstone of a Ukrainian national cinema.[17]

Skilfully interweaving Ukrainian myths and folklore with historical events over the course of a millennium, Dovzhenko emphasised the uniqueness of Ukrainian history, a history separate from Russia's.[18] By connecting the Roksana legend (situated in the ninth and tenth centuries during the Varangian penetration) with the Cossacks of the sixteenth and seventeenth centuries and with Pavlo and Tymish in the twentieth century, Dovzhenko asserted the continuity of Ukraine's thousand-year history. His film closely followed Mykhailo Hrushevsky's interpretation of the history of Eastern Europe and the separate development of the Ukrainian, Russian and Belorussian cultures.[19]

Dovzhenko's use of Ukrainian historical themes within the film's narrative reflects the Borotbist approach to the Ukrainian past. Unlike his Russian colleagues, who presented history from a Marxist perspective (witness Eisenstein's *October* [1927] or Pudovkin's *The End of St Petersburg* [1927]), Dovzhenko showed pre-revolutionary Ukrainian history as an 'integral' component of the new Soviet Ukrainian identity. In *Zvenyhora*'s final sequence, the young Bolsheviks, instead of executing the grandfather, invite him to join them on the train of progress as it speeds towards the future. The Soviet Ukrainian revolution's embrace of the grandfather 'suggests that the grandfather and his stories can be reconciled with and useful to the new socialist state'.[20]

Zvenyhora, according to Bohdan Nebesio, pays far greater attention to the romanticised notion of history embraced by the Ukrainian nationalists than to the revolutionary Marxist agenda.[21] In the nationalist interpretation, the historical tales staged in the film represent two of the most glorious periods in Ukrainian history: the period of Kievan Rus between the tenth and the twelfth centuries and that of Cossack autonomy in the sixteenth and seventeenth centuries. During these two eras Ukrainian leaders oriented themselves culturally towards Europe rather than Russia. At the time of the Kievan princes, Muscovy and Russia had not yet emerged, and Rus enjoyed numerous links with European culture. During the Cossack period

Western influences mediated through Poland generated a renaissance of Ukrainian culture in the early modern period. Thus, Dovzhenko anchored his interpretation of the Ukrainian past in experiences separate from Russia. This focus followed Khvylovy's call for the Soviet Ukrainian creative intelligentsia to consider Western Europe, not Russia, as its cultural role model.[22]

Although Dovzhenko acknowledged the past, he did not want to return to a romanticised view of it. By presenting the historical tales in an ironic mode, the film-maker suggests that all Ukrainians should board the train of progress.[23]

In his first films, made in the mid-1920s, Dovzhenko ignored the past. He wrote: 'Do we need to narrow ourselves to the kingdom of our national past, or to ethnography ...? As an artist as well as a movie director, I categorically refuse to film historical pictures.'[24] With *Zvenyhora*, Dovzhenko abandoned his aversion to historical subjects and began to formulate and integrate his interpretations of the past, present and future. 'Disrespect for the past,' he wrote, 'for one's past, for the history of the people is a characteristic of the villainy of the rulers, which is harmful and antagonistic to the people's interests.'[25] He alluded to the Russian tsars who had limited the autonomy of the Ukrainian Cossacks in the seventeenth and eighteenth centuries and later restrained the growth of a Ukrainian culture separate from the Russian in the nineteenth. The expression of these ideas constituted a politically fraught minefield, even in the moderate 1920s, as Soviet authorities identified them with nationalist sentiments.

In *Zvenyhora* the grandfather connected past, present and future and set the tone for the series of grandfathers who appear in Dovzhenko's later films. The director lovingly patterned them after his own family's patriarch. He admitted, 'I cannot create films without grandfathers. I am lost without a grandfather. A grandfather is a prism of time.'[26] About the grandfather in *Zvenyhora*, Dovzhenko wrote: 'The grandfather is not merely a romantic portrait of the past of our people. Through him I wanted to show the ties between generations, and especially the old, which willingly retreats before the young.'[27] In *Zvenyhora*, the grandfather taught the younger generations, but in the end he learned about the new Soviet way of life from his grandson Tymish.

Playing a critical role as both teacher and student, the grandfather symbolised the history of Ukraine over the course of a thousand years. The grandfather – a peasant – represented all Ukrainians, inasmuch as peasants made up the overwhelming majority of the Ukrainian population.[28] Dovzhenko's illiterate grandfather possessed a natural intelligence and common sense formed by experience, decades of hard work and disappointment. Moreover, the white-haired grandfather acts as the guardian of ancient treasures, the thousand-year-old Ukrainian traditions.[29] The strong grandfather figure, who symbolises Ukraine's history and traditions, subverts *Zvenyhora*'s ostensibly anti-nationalist stance. The grandfather, after all, endures a thousand years of oppression by outsiders. In a sense, *he* is a mountain of treasures. Dovzhenko's technique, a precursor of Gabriel Garcia Marquez's 'magical realism', as expressed in *A Hundred Years of Solitude*, implies that the grandfather will survive the Soviets as well.

His grandsons, Pavlo and Tymish, represent different interpretations of their grandfather's traditions. The two brothers sharply differ, physically as well as mentally. Tymish (portrayed by Symon Svashenko) presents a slimmer and physically more attractive bearing than the stocky Pavlo (portrayed by Les Podorozhny). Dovzhenko portrayed Pavlo as an idle dreamer, Tymish as an industrious worker. Tymish possessed a sharper mind and quicker wits than Pavlo. Pavlo's consciousness occupied itself with folklore and mythology, while Tymish displayed a practical and utilitarian outlook. Pavlo represented the old world: the earth, the village, the countryside and agriculture; Tymish the new: steel, the cities and industry. While Pavlo looked to the past, Tymish looked to the future. Pavlo blindly adhered to old traditions. Tymish destroyed the present and built it anew.[30] Not surprisingly, the brothers' politics reflected their differing temperaments and worldviews. Pavlo became a Ukrainian nationalist and Tymish a Bolshevik. Dovzhenko presented Tymish as a committed Bolshevik who could and would successfully overcome any challenges.

The treasures buried at Zvenyhora constituted the heart of the struggle between the two brothers. Pavlo literally believed that Zvenyhora held gold; Tymish came to believe that his grandfather's stories symbolised a different treasure, the iron ore and coal that would power the Soviet industrial revolution.

According to Ivan Koshelivets', the grandfather's search for the hidden treasures also represented Ukraine's search for freedom: both metaphor and theme constituted popular elements in Ukrainian pre-literate popular culture.[31] This search for freedom became intimately connected with the search for their own identity. Divided between two empires, Ukrainians could not play an active role in this search. Foreign rulers and administrators constrained the Ukrainian search for self-definition. But the collapse of the repressive tsarist order, the Revolution and Civil War and the establishment of a Soviet power that tolerated and supported multiple cultures allowed Ukrainians a greater opportunity to define themselves. The policy of indigenisation, initiated in 1923, allowed the Ukrainians as well as the other non-Russians within the Soviet Union to develop their national identities.

In *Zvenyhora*, the way Pavlo and Tymish defined the treasure (either gold or iron ore/coal) reflected the way they defined themselves politically, by national identity or class identity. Committing themselves to their mutually exclusive choices, the brothers engaged in a conflict patterned on the struggles between Cain and Abel, and between Andry and Ostap from Gogol's *Taras Bulba*.[32]

At first, Dovzhenko's sympathies may have centred on his fellow dreamer, Pavlo. By the late 1920s, as his experience with *The Insurrection of the Dead* demonstrated, he could not provide a sympathetic portrayal of the Ukrainian nationalists who had opposed the Bolsheviks. Working under these political constraints, Dovzhenko thus satirised Pavlo, as well as all of the supporters of the Ukrainian National Republic.[33] If Pavlo represented Tiutiunnyk (and Dovzhenko's political views in 1917–20), then Tymish, who received his grandfather's approval in the final scene, symbolised a politically reborn Dovzhenko.[34]

Zvenyhora clearly establishes the division that characterised Dovzhenko's creative output until the very end of his life. He celebrated Ukrainian identity at the expense of Ukrainian nationalism. Although his public statements no longer reflected his private thoughts completely, some of his private interpretations may have conformed to the current political line. In his 1939 autobiography, Dovzhenko wrote:

> *Zvenyhora* has remained one of my most interesting pictures for me. I made it in one breath – a hundred days. Unusually complicated in structure, perhaps even eclectic in form, the film gave me, a self-taught production worker, the fortuitous opportunity of trying myself out in every genre. *Zvenyhora* was a catalogue of all my creative abilities.
>
> The [critics] were quite enthusiastic about *Zvenyhora* when it came out, but the people completely rejected it because it was difficult to understand. Yet I was proud of the film and even remember boasting that I was more a professor of higher mathematics than an entertainer. I seemed to have forgotten why I came to film.
>
> Was this a deception or a betrayal of film as a mass art? It was not. I did not know the rules yet and so didn't think I was making any mistakes. I did not so much make the picture as sing it out like a songbird. I wanted to broaden the horizons of the screen, to break away from stereotyped narrative, and to speak the language of great ideas. I definitely overdid it.[35]

Although Dovzhenko claimed in 1939 that he 'overdid' it, he did not take this critical view eleven years earlier, when he admitted to a friend that *Zvenyhora* represented his own personal characteristics: 'paradoxical, dreamy, at times wild, quivering from a sharp sensation of the contradictions and rhythms of all time.'[36]

Dovzhenko's paradoxes, dreaminess and contradictions on celluloid sparked controversy. Although many critics enthusiastically praised the film after its first public screening in Kiev in November 1927, audiences in Ukraine (much less in Russia) did not easily understand it.[37] According to Eisenstein's assistant Grigorii Aleksandrov (later a director in his own right), *Zvenyhora* confused Sovkino's head K.M. Shvedchikov so much that he invited several well-known directors, including Eisenstein and Pudovkin, to evaluate it for him.[38] Sergei Eisenstein attended the film's Moscow premiere in December and recalled his first impressions: 'Goodness gracious, what a sight! We saw sharp-keeled boats sailing out of double-exposures. The rump of a black stallion being painted white. A horrible monk with a lantern being either disinterred or buried – I am not sure which.'[39] In spite of these strange and confusing images, or perhaps because of them, Eisenstein and Pudovkin enthusiastically hailed Dovzhenko's film as a masterpiece and Shvedchikov agreed to distribute it in the Russian Republic.[40]

Leon Moussinac, the French Communist film critic, saw *Zvenyhora* in Kiev and reviewed it positively, praising the film's visual impact, not its complex narrative. 'The film was well-planned,' he wrote. 'In Comrade Dovzhenko, you have a young talented director who does not possess the superstitions which are tied with theatrical productions and who knows how to think cinematographically ...'[41]

The film's narrative, which demanded substantial knowledge of Ukrainian history and folklore, and its idiosyncratic form confused many viewers. *Pravda*'s and *Komsomolskaia pravda*'s film critics recognised Dovzhenko's talent but claimed his film's political message might have been better developed.[42] *Vecherniaia Moskva*, however, hailed it as the most significant film produced in Ukraine.[43]

'It is clear that the film is extraordinary and different from other films,' one viewer wrote. 'But its method is very new, difficult and incomprehensible, similar to a futurist poem, which contains unpronounceable parts of a sentence.'[44] Nevertheless, the film did demonstrate that a new film master, with an individual although not completely mature view of his own, had arrived on the scene.

Arsenal

In 1926 and early 1927, the party invited prominent film-makers to commemorate the forthcoming tenth anniversary of the Bolshevik Revolution and the Civil War. Sergei Eisenstein's *October* and Vsevolod Pudovkin's *The End of St Petersburg* and *Storm Over Asia* (1928) fulfilled this political assignment.

Dovzhenko constructed *Arsenal*, which celebrated the tenth anniversary of the failed January 1918 Bolshevik uprising in Kiev against the Central *Rada*.[45] After surveying the horrors of war and their effect on the military as well as on the civilian population, the film concentrates on the *Rada*'s effort to capture the 'Arsenal' munitions plant and the struggle of the pro-Bolshevik workers to defend it.

Dovzhenko started to work on *Arsenal* in the second half of June 1928.[46] He first planned to deal with the uprising of the Arsenal workers in Kiev and then the social and political conflicts in 1917 and 1918 throughout Ukraine. The victorious entry of the Red Army into Kiev in February 1918 would highlight the end of the film.[47] The director's initial plans followed the pattern set by Sergei Eisenstein's *The Battleship Potemkin*, in which the revolution rippled outward – in Eisenstein's case, from the ship, in Dovzhenko's from the arsenal.[48]

During filming, however, Dovzhenko reversed his plans. He dealt with the macroscopic issues first (the World War, revolution, class antagonism), and then zeroed in on the struggle between the pro-Bolshevik forces at the Arsenal and the troops loyal to the Central *Rada*.

Arsenal (1928): one of the opening scenes

Still from the opening sequence of *Arsenal* (1928). Amvrosy Buchma plays a gassed German soldier

Arsenal emerged as *Zvenyhora*'s sequel, according to one Ukrainian critic. In contrast to *Zvenyhora*, however, 'the time frame in *Arsenal* is shorter, altogether several days, possibly several hours – if one excludes the prologue concerning the horrors of the First World War'.[49] *Arsenal*'s shorter time frame made the narrative more comprehensible to the viewer and more focused. Just as *Zvenyhora* established Dovzhenko's reputation as a significant film director in Ukraine, *Arsenal* did the same within a Soviet context.[50]

The film depicts the horrors of World War I, the fraternisation of Tsar Nicholas II's and Kaiser William II's troops, and the desertion of the Russian army from the front. When the pro-Bolshevik deserters return to Kiev, they encounter Ukrainian nationalists who formed the Central *Rada* in the spring of 1917. The city's Bolsheviks react with great hostility to this political body. The nationalists then launch a strike at the city's arsenal, the Bolsheviks' headquarters. In a hail of bullets, the *Rada*'s troops storm the arsenal and execute all the Bolsheviks there. The victory proves short-lived. Although Dovzhenko did not include the victorious entry of Muraviev's Red Army into Kiev in February 1918 in his frames, *Arsenal*'s viewers knew who won the Civil War.

Overall *Arsenal* generally followed a realistic course, but in several scenes Dovzhenko shifted to the realm of folklore or fantasy. In the film's famous last scene,

Symon Svashenko plays the
Bolshevik Tymish in *Arsenal* (1928)

the main hero, Tymish (a Ukrainian Bolshevik, played by Svashenko, who may or may not represent *Zvenyhora*'s Tymish), defends the arsenal against the approaching Ukrainian nationalists. When his machine gun jams, the *Rada*'s troops overrun his position. Tymish then rips his shirt open and challenges his enemies to shoot him. They fire volley after volley into him, but their bullets fail to kill him. Then, in an extraordinary conclusion, the *Rada*'s soldiers literally disappear as a result of Tymish's defiance. His invulnerability stems from his uncompromising revolutionary idealism, triumphant even in death. Although Tymish's final stand provoked disbelief, Dovzhenko's intended message – that the Revolution will inevitably triumph – proved very compelling.

On the surface the film presented a politically correct interpretation of the Bolshevik Revolution in Ukraine. The Odessa regional Communist Party committee, for example, praised the film and claimed that audiences at closed screenings enthusiastically responded to it. 'Dovzhenko's previous film, *Zvenyhora*, which introduced Dovzhenko's name to the history of Soviet cinema, was criticized as a result of its obscurity and lack of clarity. *Arsenal* is free of these mistakes. *Arsenal* is simple. *Arsenal* is cinema and only cinema.'[51]

Stalin also enjoyed the film. Ihor Belza, the composer of the music for *Arsenal*, met Stalin at a screening of the film at a plenum of the Central Committee of the All-Union Communist Party in November 1928. According to Belza, Stalin called *Arsenal* a 'real revolutionary romantic film'.[52]

If the film enthusiastically endorsed the Bolshevik point of view, its subtext questioned the morality of Bolshevik revolutionary brutality. Examining the Revolution and Civil War in moral terms, Dovzhenko's film fluctuates, as Vance Kepley, Jr. pointed out, 'between a celebration of the revolutionary spirit and reservations about the turmoil and human misery caused by revolutionary violence'.[53]

Dovzhenko's moral ambiguity and his poking fun at Ukrainian nationalists alienated many Ukrainian intellectuals. According to Grigory Roshal, a prominent Moscow director, film-makers in the Soviet capital thought very highly of Dovzhenko's film and expressed surprise that Ukrainian film-makers and critics condemned the work. 'To our great amazement,' Roshal wrote, 'many who came out against this film found inaccuracies and a great retreat from the Ukrainian national theme on Dovzhenko's part.'[54]

According to Dovzhenko, many Ukrainian intellectuals misunderstood his intentions and denounced the film, which they felt satirised the Ukrainian bourgeoisie and Ukrainian nationalism as a whole. Some of his critics allegedly asserted that he had 'hyperbolised' the revolution and had 'vulgarly and brutally touched upon a painful wound' – that is, the political positions of the nationally conscious Ukrainian intellectuals during the revolutionary and Civil War period.[55] According to the film-maker:

For betraying 'Mother Ukraine', for profaning the Ukrainian nation and intelligentsia, for depicting the Ukrainian nationalists as provincial nonentities and adventurers, and so forth, the film was reviled in the press; I was boycotted for many years, and the [party] leadership treated me for a long time with cool reserve that I could not comprehend.[56]

Dovzhenko's account, written in 1939 after the extensive purges in Ukraine, sought to elicit sympathy from those who would approve his Communist Party membership. Here, he deliberately exaggerated his differences with the Ukrainian intelligentsia and the party leadership. In fact, according to one Canadian film historian, the majority of Ukrainian critics construed *Arsenal* as another great achievement of Ukrainian cinema and praised its 'realistic' portrayal of the Ukrainian Revolution.[57]

Undoubtedly, Dovzhenko's film contained scenes which may have offended nationalist sensibilities. His depiction of Taras Shevchenko (1814–1861), Ukraine's most important poet and hero to all nationally conscious Ukrainians, infuriated his critics. In the offending scene, Shevchenko's portrait comes to life in order to blow out a candle a Ukrainian nationalist has brought to honour him. Although Dovzhenko sought to make this scene comical, the significance of Shevchenko's action became immediately clear to all viewers: Ukrainian nationalists should not call upon Shevchenko to buttress their legitimacy.

The issue of legitimacy recurs several times in *Arsenal*. In one of the film's early scenes, a young Ukrainian nationalist officer confronts Tymish and his friends and yells out: 'In the name of the Ukrainian National Republic, I order you to surrender your arms!' Tymish defiantly stands his ground and replies, 'In the name of the Ukrainian people? Who said so?'

This question represented a more complex problem: who had the right to speak for the Ukrainian people? The Bolsheviks or the nationalists? As a Ukrainian, Tymish understood the oppression Ukrainians suffered, but he did not think national independence would necessarily free the poor from the curse of social inequality. 'We are workers – we also stand for the freedom of Ukraine,' Tymish asserted before a group of nationalists. 'But we demand the land for the peasants and factories for the workers. You who care only for national independence will let Ukraine go on as it has been for centuries under old Russia.'

Tymish's position made *Arsenal* a 'national film done in a Bolshevik manner'.[58] In the film, Bazhan noted, 'Dovzhenko speaks about the national within the social revolution; … the national does not hide its true social face from him.'[59] Despite Bazhan's assessment, *Arsenal* conformed more to the Borotbist interpretation of the Ukrainian Revolution than to the Bolshevik view.

In *Arsenal* Dovzhenko also criticises the notion of 'guilt by national affiliation'. In one scene, as the deserters from the front encounter Ukrainian nationalist troops, they hear an oft-repeated nationalist phrase: 'Russia oppressed us for 300 years.' One of the deserters, presumably a Russian, retorts, 'And I oppressed you for 300 years?'

The nationalist slogan and its rebuttal signified one of the greatest dilemmas for all politically aware people in Ukraine during the revolutionary period: how do you define your enemy? By national criteria? Class criteria? If *Zvenyhora* introduced the dilemma of national identity on the screen, *Arsenal* inserted the overlapping issue of the enemy. Once groups of people identify and group themselves, they create boundaries, dividing people into categories of 'us' or 'them', friend or foe.

For Ukrainians this question of 'us' and 'them' represented an important issue. Part of this quest for national identity focused on the allocation of blame for their social, economic and cultural backwardness. Did the Russian people as a whole share the guilt? The tsarist system? How could an ordinary Russian peasant or worker take responsibility for Ukraine's 300-year history of oppression? And if one could not assign group guilt and group responsibility, how could one define the enemy?

Dovzhenko provides several clues but no concrete solutions. In one scene Tymish is interviewd for a job by the arsenal's manager, who asks him: 'Are you a Ukrainian?' Tymish raises his eyebrow, but says nothing. At another point, he encounters a Ukrainian National Army recruitment officer, who tries to persuade him to join. The officer asks the film's hero, 'But you are a Ukrainian, aren't you?' Tymish replies, 'Yes, a worker.' He then glares at the officer and turns away. In the last scene, Tymish has run out of ammunition and offers himself for execution by nationalist troops. He defiantly yells out, 'A Ukrainian worker!'

This scene exemplifies Dovzhenko's most blatant attempt on screen to reconcile the two seemingly contradictory components of the Ukrainian Revolution, the national and the social. According to Nebesio, 'the mythologization of the Ukrainian worker as an indestructible force represents faith in the possibility of a Ukrainian workers' state', a state with a high degree of autonomy within the Soviet Union. By the end of the 1920s, this Borotbist-influenced interpretation raised the ire of the ascendant Stalinists. For this reason 'Tymish's national-revolutionary development never comes to the film's foreground.'[60]

Although Dovzhenko endorsed class as an important component of identity, he questioned the Bolshevik Revolution's consequences, which may have undercut *Arsenal*'s original commemorative assignment. The allusions that run through the film consistently equate the World War with the Revolution, casting moral doubt on the revolutionary effort. In many respects, the second part of the film, which includes material on the Revolution and Civil War, repeats the first part, which shows the last phases of World War I and its effects on Ukraine. By sacrificing innocent people, the revolutionary dream gave way to the brutal reality of a life or death struggle. Dovzhenko suggested that all groups, including the Bolsheviks, in some way shared responsibility for the general degradation that accompanied the Civil War.[61]

As Dovzhenko questioned the nationalist cause, he also questioned the morality of class warfare. In the middle of *Arsenal*, a worker at a political rally asks if it will 'be all right to kill officers and bourgeois in the street if we find them?' Protagonists in the film repeat this question two more times. As Kepley has observed, 'the question concerns more than tactics. It confronts the fundamental moral issue of the revolution: Given that there are class enemies, does the proletariat possess the moral authority to eliminate them systematically?'[62]

Dovzhenko appears to answer the question in one scene near the end of the film. A bespectacled Ukrainian nationalist captures one of Tymish's friends, stands him against the wall and prepares to execute him. 'Face the wall!' the nationalist yells. The Bolshevik walks towards the wall, then abruptly turns around and asks, 'Can't you do it looking in my eyes?' The nationalist reacts with paralysis, impotent politically as well as physically. The Bolshevik comes up to him, takes the gun from his hand, and says, 'I can.' He then shoots the nationalist at point-blank range.

With this scene, Dovzhenko provides a striking contrast between the Ukrainian nationalists' and the Bolsheviks' political wills. Although *Arsenal* celebrates Bolshevik triumph, the Bolsheviks' cold-bloodedness may have diluted the film's message.

Despite *Arsenal*'s unclear revolutionary message and its pacifist undertones, the film surprisingly received positive reviews. *Arsenal*'s release date in early 1929 may partially explain this good fortune. Still claiming to adhere to the party's 1923 Ukrainianisation programme, Stalinists had not yet declared open warfare on their perceived manifestations of Ukrainian nationalism.[63] One of the first signs of Stalin's skepticism regarding this programme appeared at his Kremlin meeting with Ukrainian writers on 12 February 1929, two days before *Izvestiia*'s reviewers praised Dovzhenko's film. In a rambling and informal discussion, Stalin asserted that national cultures with a socialist content had a future in the transition period from capitalism to socialism, but he sided with Russian chauvinists who criticised Ukrainianisation's cultural achievements.[64] The new Stalinist interpretation of the party's nationality policy did not emerge immediately after this meeting, which was not publicised. As a result, the reviewers in Moscow's papers did not discover the film's 'deviations'.[65]

In *Arsenal*, Dovzhenko focused on ordinary people – on their efforts and the extraordinary cost of the Revolution in their personal lives – rather than on the Bolshevik heroes of the Revolution. This focus drew sharp censure from the party, to which Dovzhenko replied: 'I wanted to make a film about the revolution, not the palace revolution, but the revolution of peasants, workers, and intellectuals who made the revolution and then did not get anything.'[66]

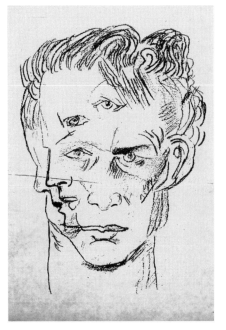

Dovzhenko's first drawing: a self-portrait   Dovzhenko's second drawing

Although he claimed *Arsenal* as a completely orthodox film, its lyrical interpretation of the war and Revolution muffled the official view. This film, moreover, reflects Dovzhenko's own feelings and inner conflicts about his nationalist past and his Communist present. By trying to acknowledge and to please both Ukrainian nationalists and Bolshevik sensibilities, he inevitably contradicted himself and risked offending both. He felt alienated.

His letters to Elena Chernova, an actress who played a minor role in *The Diplomatic Pouch* and to whom he dedicated *Arsenal*, reflect this struggle. In his eighteenth letter to her, written while he worked on *Arsenal*, Dovzhenko enclosed two drawings. The first superimposed multiple images of his face. Each stern face stared in a different direction. The second drawing showed him dressed in a peasant shirt and rolled-up trousers with hands in his pockets: he stares at the feet of a dead man lying on the ground, whose right leg is encased in a boot, his left in a sock. Two factories with billowing smoke stacks line the bottom of the drawing. Superimposed over Dovzhenko's head appears the raised head of a horse. Superimposed over the horse's head appears yet another head, Dovzhenko's, looking up.

Dovzhenko admitted to Chernova the strangeness of his drawings, which suggest the film-maker's isolation and the pressure to satisfy disparate expectations during *Arsenal*'s preparation and filming. These drawings, he claimed, reflected his 'soul'. In writing the screenplay and then shooting the winter scenes, he experienced

Dovzhenko and Julia Solntseva
(1928)

constant headaches and insomnia. He claimed that he hated his bosses, presumably because they interfered with his work.[67]

No records reveal how or why Dovzhenko's relationship with Chernova ended, but the vacuum she left did not remain long. Within months, Dovzhenko met another actress in Odessa, Julia Ippolitovna Solntseva, with whom he began a life-long relationship in 1928 and married in 1955.[68]

Political Changes

Dovzhenko's most famous film, *Earth*, appeared in early 1930, during the opening stages of Stalin's 'revolution from above'. The Soviet leader's introduction of the first Five Year Plan in late 1928 represented the beginning of the end of both the moderate nationality policies and the New Economic Policy introduced in 1921 and after.

Between 1927 and 1930, when the film-maker made *Zvenyhora*, *Arsenal* and *Earth*, the Communist Party of Ukraine experienced a bitter struggle over its sponsorship of the development of Ukrainian culture. Three factions within the CP(b)U vied for power. Dovzhenko's former patron, Shumsky, the Commissar of Education from 1924 to 1927, led the first faction, which consisted of former Borotbists who backed Khvylovy's demands to expand the role of Ukrainian culture into the Russified cities and working class. The second group, supported by party members from the highly-

Russified industrial regions of Ukraine, represented a pro-Russian and an anti-Ukrainian inclination. They opposed Ukrainianisation. Mykola Skrypnyk, who replaced Shumsky as the Commissar of Education in April 1927, commanded the third faction, which hovered between the first two. Until the Stalinists denounced Skrypnyk in early 1933, Skrypnyk's group remained the most powerful.[69]

Shumsky's removal from the Commissariat of Education and the party's corresponding attacks on Shumsky, Khvylovy and their followers in 1926 tainted Dovzhenko, who identified himself with both men and who had supported their ideas on the expansion of Ukrainian culture. After 1927 he distanced himself from writers' groups, such as *VAPLITE*, and did not actively take part in the discussions on Ukrainian culture.[70] Instead, he concentrated all his efforts on film-making.

As the industrialisation drive accelerated at the end of the 1920s, critics harshly attacked the Soviet film industry, which produced films with little ideological content. They called for a reduction in the share of foreign films in the market, deplored the Soviet production of romance and adventure stories, and demanded that the film industry create more agitational films. These critics also sharply criticised film directors, such as Eisenstein, Dovzhenko, Pudovkin and Vertov, for not making ideologically correct films that ordinary workers and peasants could understand. Although these film-makers did produce films with 'politically correct' messages, their experimental styles confused their audiences and obscured their films' political conclusions. The critics accused the leading members of the first generation of Soviet film-makers of 'formalism', a pejorative term used to describe 'any concern with the specifically aesthetic aspect of filmmaking, any deviation from a simple narrative line, and any artistic innovation'.[71]

The formal process of redefining the contours of Soviet film-making and of non-Russian national cinemas within the Soviet film industry began at a Moscow conference organised by the Central Committee's agitational and propaganda section in March 1928. At this meeting, the Communist Party decided to impose a 'correct' line on the Soviet film industry. Of the 200 people who attended, most represented the party, the government, trade unions and various film organisations – not film-makers. Of the dozens of film-makers who addressed the group, only a single director – Friedrich Ermler – spoke. The overwhelming majority of those who participated in this conference expressed an interest in film only as a political tool.[72]

Speaker after speaker asserted that no conflict should exist between ideological considerations and the production of genuinely popular films. Inasmuch as most Soviet citizens, like people everywhere, sought entertainment, not ideological lectures, they preferred romances, musicals and action-adventure stories; the party's orders remained contradictory and impossible to fulfil.[73] Although the party demanded films 'accessible to the millions', it did not desire the production of the types of films that millions would actually want to see'.[74]

Most importantly, this party conference condemned creative experimentation and ideological nonconformity. By demanding that film-makers produce films viewers could easily understand, the political leaders undermined the most imaginative among them. Inasmuch as the conference's vague pronouncements did not define clearly how politically-didactic films could attract a mass audience, they left some hope for future reconsiderations of this complex issue. Party officials, according to Kenez, 'knew much better what they did not like than what they did'.[75]

Just as Dovzhenko began to work on *Zvenyhora*, *Arsenal* and *Earth*, the Ukrainian film industry began to lose its highly prized autonomy. Despite Skrypnyk's vehement defence of the Ukrainian film industry at the March 1928 conference, I. Vorobiov, a man who favoured the centralisation of the Soviet film industry, replaced VUFKU's director, O. Shub. As the new film chief, Vorobiov postponed, then abandoned plans to create a Ukrainian film school. In its place, Moscow's All-Soviet State Institute of Cinematography (VGIK) would train film-makers for all of the Soviet republics. In 1930 Ukrainfilm replaced VUFKU; now a central planning body, Soiuzkino (located in Moscow) coordinated film production throughout the Soviet Union.[76] Although these measures reflected the centralising trends within the Soviet Union at the end of the 1920s and threatened the development of a Ukrainian national cinema over the long term, they did not affect the day-to-day operations of the Ukrainian film industry, especially not those of Dovzhenko, whose films received prior approval.

On the heels of Stalin's reinterpretation of nationality policy in February 1929, Soviet security organs arrested thousands of former leaders and prominent supporters of the Central *Rada* that following summer and accused them of forming an underground organisation, the Union for the Liberation of Ukraine (SVU). The Soviet Ukrainian government then placed forty-five men and women on trial in Kharkiv from 9 March to 19 April 1930. They accused Serhy Efremov, a prominent literary scholar, a former minister of the Central *Rada* and a member of the All-Ukrainian Academy of Sciences, of leading the organisation.

Most of the accused conformed to Efremov's profile. They were older Ukrainian intellectuals, mostly in their fifties. Many came from priestly families from the countryside and worked as scholars. During the Revolution they had joined Ukrainian, anti-Bolshevik political parties, such as the Socialist-Federalists, the Socialist Revolutionaries and the Social Democrats. They also had been prominent members of the Central *Rada*, Petliura's Directory and the Ukrainian National Republic.[77]

Efremov and his colleagues allegedly founded the SVU in 1926. According to the charges against them, these men and women infiltrated the All-Ukrainian Academy of Sciences and other scientific institutions in order to influence the young and to recruit members for their youth affiliate, the Union of Ukrainian Youth (SUM), and to prepare an armed struggle against Soviet power.

After an insurrection, assassination of prominent Communist leaders and mass terror against the Soviet Ukrainian intelligentsia, the SVU would set up a bourgeois order, modelled after the Ukrainian National Republic. After a complete capitalist restoration in Ukraine, the SVU allegedly would hand Right Bank Ukraine to the Poles and the Left Bank to the Germans.[78] At another point in the trial, the prosecutor accused SVU members of preparing a 'federation' of Ukraine with 'fascist Poland'.[79] Prosecutors claimed that SVU members propagated the idea of a Ukrainian 'agricultural mission' and could not come to terms with the Soviet first Five Year Plan.[80]

Highlighting the development of heavy industry and promising to transform the Ukrainian Republic into the Soviet Union's coal and steel centre, the plan (inaugurated on 1 October 1928) generated rapid urban growth throughout the USSR. To feed the expanding urban population and to pay for machinery bought abroad, the government sought to acquire low-priced grain from its peasants. Soviet central planners decided to collectivise agricultural lands as quickly as possible and by whatever means necessary.

The overwhelming majority of peasants in Ukraine did not want to give up their land holdings, however meagre. In response, the party worked to isolate the wealthier peasants (the so-called *kulaks*) from poorer peasants. Since the Bolsheviks had destroyed many of the old kulak families during the Civil War, the wealthier peasants of the late 1920s often represented former poor or middle peasants, who as result of their hard work, had prospered under the New Economic Policy.[81]

Branded 'enemies of the people' and presented as rich, 'blood-sucking usurers' and exploiters of their fellow villagers, these peasants possessed far fewer numbers and less power than the party claimed. A decree in May 1929 defined a kulak as someone with at least 300 rubles (or 1,500 rubles per household), who owned any kind of motorised farm machinery or employed hired labour. According to these criteria, at the time of the decree Soviet Ukraine contained only 71,500 kulak households, representing a mere 1.4 per cent of all households in Soviet Ukraine.[82] A wealthier peasant usually owned ten to fifteen acres, several horses and cows, and some sheep.[83] War invalids and widows, not well-to-do peasant entrepreneurs, headed most of the households that used hired labour. In short, the term 'kulak' and even the vaguer category of 'kulak ally' had less to do with a peasant's actual wealth than with the Soviet authorities' need for an all-purpose term with which to brand whomever they suspected of resisting their authority.[84] The Soviet authorities needed a scapegoat, and the kulaks fitted the bill.

Having defined their enemy, the authorities then reintroduced class warfare. In 1924, but especially after 1926, the Soviet government imposed heavy taxes on the kulaks. With the encouragement of the state and the party, members of the local Communist youth organisation (Komsomol) and the Committees of Poor Peasants mercilessly harassed them.[85]

De-kulakisation reached its peak during the winter of 1929–30. In January 1930 the Central Committee of the All-Union Communist Party in Moscow ordered 'the liquidation of the kulaks as a class'. With poor peasants unwilling to ruin their more prosperous neighbours and with a shortage of party members in the countryside, the government sent nearly 50,000 urban workers and Komsomol members, frequently Russian or Jewish Communists, to complete the party's mission.[86] Supported by local OGPU and army units, these Communists physically rounded up everyone (men, women and even children) identified as kulaks and shipped them off to Central Asia, Siberia and the Soviet Far East. During the forced transport, uncounted thousands died. By March 1930 the party had removed nearly 62,000 kulak households, an estimated quarter of a million people, from Soviet Ukraine.[87]

As the party de-kulakised the countryside, it introduced mass collectivisation. Generally, the creation of collective farms followed a pattern. Party workers entered a village and called a meeting, during which they intimidated several peasants into forming a collective. A party activist then opened the meeting by declaring: 'Anyone opposed to the collective farm is opposed to the Soviet government. Let's vote. Who is against the collective farm?' Few peasants would publicly express their dissent in front of their militant guests. After the establishment of a collective farm, the party activists then demanded that all villagers pool their land and surrender their livestock.[88] Peasants often responded by slaughtering their animals rather than turning them over to the collective.

Despite extensive peasant opposition, the party collectivised 65 per cent of the farms and 70 per cent of the livestock in Soviet Ukraine by March 1930.[89] After a brief respite that month, when the party allowed the peasants to leave the collective farms if they wished (and a majority did so), the party accelerated the pace of collectivisation. By 31 December 1932, at the end of the first Five Year Plan, the Soviet government had collectivised 70 per cent of all agricultural land in Ukraine.[90]

But Communist control of the countryside remained fragile. Peasant resistance to collectivisation transformed the party's war against the kulaks into a war against the peasants, which reached its peak with the famine of 1932–3, when millions of peasants died in Ukraine.[91]

Earth

In the summer of 1929, before the outbreak of large-scale violence in the countryside, Dovzhenko hoped to make a film 'that would herald the beginning of a new life in the villages' by praising the first stages of collectivisation.[92] He deliberately wanted to represent collectivisation as a voluntary process.

He began work on *Earth* in August 1929 and completed it in March 1930.[93] It featured a more straightforward narrative than his two previous films. In a normal chronological fashion, the film tells the story of a Ukrainian family, the Trubenkos,

The grandfather's (Mykola Nademsky) death scene in *Earth* (1930)

and their reaction to the collectivisation campaign in their village in 1929. The film opens with the death of the family patriarch, Grandfather Symon, in an orchard. His family and friends, including his son Opanas, his grandson Vasyl and his old friend Petro, surround Symon, who perceives these moments as his last ones. As he dies, the village's kulaks, led by the Bilokin family, vow to resist collectivisation. Although the film depicts the Trubenkos as middle peasants, Opanas opposes the creation of communal farms. His son, Vasyl, and the local Communist Youth League actively support the collective farm movement.

The conflict between the kulaks and their opponents divides the village. Vasyl exacerbates these tensions when he brings the collective's first tractor back from the city and ploughs through the fences of the kulak households. With the help of the tractor, the peasants bring in a successful harvest. One night while Vasyl celebrates his hard work and his love for his fiancée, Natalia, the kulak Khoma Bilokin murders him. Inspired by his son's martyrdom, Opanas then decides to support the collective and leads the funeral procession, which helps unite the village in support of the new system.

The film's plot and its three main characters – Vasyl Trubenko, Opanas Trubenko and Khoma Bilokin – who represent, respectively, the Komsomol activists in the villages, the confused middle peasants and the evil kulaks – conform to the party's interpretation of the social conflicts in the countryside.

But the film's visual impact, especially its poetic depiction of nature, overshadows this ideological framework. *Earth* celebrates the emergence of a new relationship, 'the harmonious unity of people with nature, something on the order of pantheism'.[94] From the opening scene, in which a girl stands next to an enormous sunflower, to one of the last scenes, in which the falling rain gently caresses the apples in the trees, Dovzhenko successfully presented this association on screen. Peasants working the land shared their lives with the soil and with its harvests. Now, with the common ownership of the land and the end of class conflict in the countryside, collectivisation would create an even more intimate relationship between the peasants and the land.

Dovzhenko fused the party's collectivisation drive with his own recollections of his childhood. As a child of peasants and now an urban resident longing for a sense of balance, the film-maker imposed his own reconstructed memories of his 'idyllic' childhood onto his scenes depicting life in the contemporary countryside. Conceived during the period of 'voluntary' collectivisation in 1929, *Earth* appeared during the most brutal period of de-kulakisation in the spring of 1930. The director brought out what Kepley calls 'his most understated work' at a time when the Soviet press was hysterically condemning the kulaks.[95] In contrast to the party's harsh political rhetoric and its violent implementation of de-kulakisation,

Earth (1930): the opening sequence

Dovzhenko's portrayal of man's relationship to the soil overshadowed his condemnation of the kulaks.

His celebration of nature made many of his scenes ambiguous, even controversial. Although *Earth* presents an enthusiastic endorsement of collectivisation, nature remains the root of life, death and rebirth. Nature's cycle, moreover, heals man's wounds and transforms him into an integrated person. In the last scenes, after a heavy rainfall, Dovzhenko depicts Natalia in the arms of another man. As she opens her eyes, she smiles. The rain has washed away her grief and pain over the death of Vasyl, whose sacrifice 'restores paradise to man'.[96]

According to the film-maker's view of the world, the introduction of the tractor represents the mechanisation and collectivisation of the countryside, but on peasant terms. With Vasyl driving the tractor, Dovzhenko shows the peasants collectively ploughing, tilling and harvesting grain and baking bread, all 'compressed into a symbolic day's work'.[97] *Earth* shows how man and machine coordinate their rhythms to produce a bountiful harvest. According to Gilberto Perez, this synthesis

> dances to a rhythm less of a machine than of the body, a brisk rhythm the machine makes possible but does not dictate, a rhythm that feels organic, even erotic, benefitting a true marriage in which the men and women at work are not pieces in the machinery but individuals robustly in concert with it. The old is not swept aside but assimilated into this organic rhythm of the new.[98]

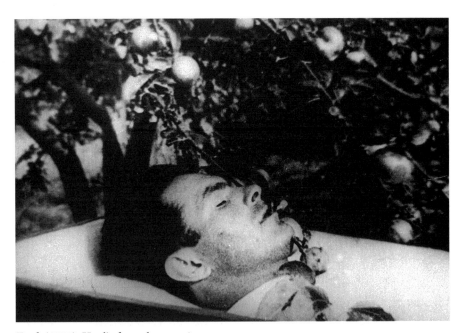

Earth (1930): Vasyl's funeral procession

Most of the villagers possess an internal rhythm, which they effortlessly coordinate with the rhythms of nature and of the new machines. Animate and inanimate power produce a rich harvest. Not surprisingly, the kulaks are not endowed with internal metronomes. They can not synchronise themselves to the new social order in the countryside.

Khoma's lack of internal harmony and rhythm manifests itself in a very concrete way, in an inability to dance. Walking along a road and totally drunk, Khoma begins to dance. Flailing his arms and legs, Khoma's movements lack cohesion and grace; alcohol makes them even more grotesque and inhuman. At Vasyl's funeral, Khoma voluntarily admits to the assembled villagers that he killed Vasyl, but no one listens to him; everyone already knew. He, after all, belonged to a kulak family and had a vested interest in killing this Komsomol activist. Khoma then engages in another dance, if one could call it that. Placing his head and feet on the ground, his body wildly swirls in an imperfect circle. His movements do not possess a rhythm, are only manifestations of anger and self-loathing.

For contrast Dovzhenko included a scene in which Vasyl, returning alone from an evening's romantic rendezvous with his fiancée, breaks into a spontaneous dance on a lonely, moonlit road. His simple steps start slowly, then move at a faster pace. His movements flow naturally and reflect not only his joy over his long day's labour, but also about his love for Natalia. Bursting with happiness, not only his legs, but his whole body and soul move in a rhythm at peace with the world.[99] In admitting to his murder of Vasyl, Khoma does not discuss the obvious social and political motivations that drove him. Instead, he simply asserts, 'I killed him in the night ... when everyone was asleep ... But he was walking down the lane and dancing.'

Although his depictions of peasants and kulaks conformed to the party's overall interpretation of the social divisions in the countryside, Dovzhenko's cinematic interpretation emphasised life, love and death over the class struggle. Other scenes quickly aroused controversy. Dovzhenko's presentation of Vasyl's entry into the village on the collective's new tractor reminds the viewer of Jesus's Palm Sunday entry into Jerusalem on a donkey. In *Earth*, however, the tractor, the 'Communist steel horse', not a mystical religious figure, becomes the village's saviour. At the edge of the village, the tractor abruptly stops. After examining the engine, Vasyl realises that the water in the radiator has evaporated. He then orders his friends to urinate into the radiator. 'Let her fly!' he yells. After filling the radiator in this unorthodox manner, Vasyl starts up the tractor and drives it to its new home.

The second controversial scene depicts Natalia's emotional breakdown after learning of her fiancé's murder. Seeing Vasyl's body at the Trubenko home, she returns to her room, cries, tears off her clothes, clutches her breasts, mercilessly beats her pillow and then pounds on the walls. Dovzhenko became one of the first Soviet directors to film a nude female body. Although his portrayal of Natalia did not reveal much by today's standards, it shocked audiences as well as critics in his day.

Eisenstein, for example, claimed that Dovzhenko's effort to use the naked Natalia to re-emphasise by metaphorical montage the film's life-affirming opening scenes failed.[100] According to Perez, Eisenstein enthusiastically approved of Dovzhenko's ode to life but not his requiem for the dead; his preference for the first over the second fuelled his criticism of *Earth*.[101]

The third controversial scene shows Vasyl's mother in labour. Dovzhenko's cameras concentrate on the vivid pains and joys reflected in her face during delivery. At the very hour of Vasyl's funeral, she delivers a healthy child, Vasyl's replacement. Although he did not film the newborn or the baby's bloody journey from the mother's womb to this world, Dovzhenko's realistic presentation of a woman's facial expressions while giving birth upset his orthodox critics, as had Dziga Vertov's *Man with a Movie Camera* in 1929.

When Dovzhenko began to shoot *Earth* in 1929, his political message conformed to the Communist Party's interpretation. By the spring of 1930, however, this same message had become suspect. In reaction to his search for harmony in an increasingly violent and brutal environment, Dovzhenko's critics began to question his political motivations.

Even before VUFKU released Dovzhenko's film, the Soviet and Soviet Ukrainian film censorship boards demanded that the film-maker cut the scenes depicting urination and nudity. The director, however, 'categorically refused to edit the film'.[102] His artistic integrity would come to haunt him.

Dovzhenko later recalled how shortly after the film's first public screening in Kharkiv in early March, the Ukrainian Central Committee called him in and told him that 'I had brought shame on Ukrainian culture with my work and behavior and was called to order. A statement of repentance was demanded from me ...'[103] In spite of this demand, Dovzhenko did not repent publicly.

At a 20 March 1930 screening of *Earth* in Moscow organised by the Association of Workers of Revolutionary Cinematography (ARRK), the audience greeted Dovzhenko warmly but did not offer unanimous praise.[104] Many enjoyed the lyrical film, but others criticised it for celebrating the primacy of nature over politics. In his closing statement, Dovzhenko did not address the critical points raised against him. Instead, he diplomatically spoke about his next project, a comedy.[105]

Dovzhenko's charm, however, did not appease his critics. The furore over *Earth* did not abate. On 29 March 1930, *Pravda* published the first major critical review of *Earth*. Its author, Petr Bliakhin, criticised Dovzhenko's film for showing the kulaks as isolated and unimportant, and for creating the impression that collectivisation had no powerful enemies. Bliakhin also misrepresented the film, claiming that it did not show the class characteristics of the protagonists.[106]

Less than one week later, Demian Bedny, one of Stalin's favourite poets, brutally criticised *Earth* in the pages of *Izvestiia*, the news organ of the Soviet government. He branded Dovzhenko's film as 'unnatural', 'cynical' and a 'kulak' picture. In contrast to Bliakhin's criticism, Bedny claimed that Dovzhenko presented the kulak as all-powerful and showed him as the film's victor. Natalia's nude scene outraged Bedny's puritanical sensibilities. The film, he said, savoured 'sexual perversity'.[107] And because *Earth* did not highlight the brutal social conflicts in the countryside, Bedny considered the film deeply misguided.[108]

Bedny's criticism caught Dovzhenko off guard. In his 1939 autobiography, the film-maker recorded his reaction:

> I was so stunned by his attack, so ashamed to be seen in public, that I literally aged and turned gray within several days. It was a real emotional trauma for me. At first I wanted to die. But a few days later I found myself at the crematorium in the honor guard at the funeral of Vladimir Mayakovsky, with whom I had always been on good terms. Bedny stood in front of me. I stared at his greasy head and passionately thought to myself: 'Die!' But he was immune. So we left the crematorium alive and unharmed.[109]

The denunciations and criticisms of *Earth*, especially from Bedny, drained and depressed Dovzhenko. He needed a break. On 19 June 1930 he left for a tour of Western Europe. During the next four and a half months, he met colleagues in the film world, showed his films and learned about the 'talkies', which Hollywood introduced in 1927.[110]

This visit to the major European film-making capitals did not restore Dovzhenko's emotional equilibrium. Months after Bedny's attack, Dovzhenko remained psychologically wounded. In a letter to Sergei Eisenstein from Berlin in July 1930, he wrote: 'My heart became tired ... I already can not walk as quickly as in the past. And I have completely stopped laughing.'[111] In an undated letter, written to Barbara Krylova-Dovzhenko some time between 1930 and 1932, the film-maker admitted that he had 'experienced a substantial psychological trauma'. Although he did not describe the nature of this emotional wound, the political denunciations he received in this period may have generated it. This strain, he claimed, transformed him into 'the most exhausted and the most down-trodden person in the country'.[112]

Dovzhenko survived the denunciations and trauma, but *Earth* did not. After it premiered on 8 April 1930, the Soviet film industry's censorship board recalled the film on 17 April.[113] Censors then cut the three controversial scenes from the film.[114]

The elimination of these critical scenes weakened the film's emotional power. The new Stalinist puritanism had triumphed over the Soviet tolerance for the experimentation of the 1920s. Dovzhenko's film employed his distinctive style, which emphasised nature and the separation of images from their social context. This artistic style struck authorities as an ideological heresy of the highest order.

Conclusion

Zvenyhora, *Arsenal* and *Earth* developed Ukrainian themes, presented the tensions between the national and the social, and explored the boundaries of class and national hatred. Unlike Dovzhenko's previous works, each of these films contained complex turns, ambiguities and self-doubts. The film-maker raised important questions about the relationship between the old and the new, between tradition and revolution, between the countryside and the cities, between life and death, and between people and the soil. These questions, Dovzhenko asserted, did not yield easy answers.

Complex in structure, charged with associative imagery and full of abrupt transitions in time and place, the films comprising Dovzhenko's Ukrainian trilogy did not conform to the traditions of the realistic narrative. Inasmuch as viewers could not passively filter his films, they found them difficult to follow. Audiences resisted experimentation, demanding a familiar repertoire of ethnographic realism, stereotypical roles, and the Russian classics.[115] They demanded entertainment, not engagement.

Dovzhenko's trilogy, moreover, promoted a poeticised, ideological vision increasingly at odds with the Stalinist vision now consolidated in Moscow. If *Zvenyhora* and *Arsenal* interpreted Ukrainian history through a Borotbist prism, *Earth*'s visual impact suggested that man's harmonious relationship with nature – the root of life, death and rebirth – remained more important than his class orientation.

As a film-maker in the Soviet Union at the end of the 1920s, he experienced great tensions. He wanted to do his part, to use his film-making vocation on behalf of the Soviet people, but he could not succeed. He sought to concentrate on exploring his art and to use film as a vehicle to show reality as he interpreted it, but with every step he took, he offended someone – the emergent Stalinist political order and sometimes even the very tradition and history he identified with.

By embracing complexity and ambiguity, Dovzhenko began to alienate groups with a monochromic orthodox view of the world. Many Ukrainian intellectuals denounced Dovzhenko's harsh criticism of Ukrainian nationalism, as exemplified by the protagonists in *Zvenyhora* and *Arsenal*. Orthodox Communists criticised Dovzhenko's ambivalence regarding the Revolution and social change, as in *Arsenal* and *Earth*. By the end of the 1920s, Stalin's Soviet Union could not tolerate moral ambiguity.

Notes

1. Ivan Koshelivets', *Oleksandr Dovzhenko: Sproba tvorchoi biohrafii* (Munich, 1980), pp. 90–1.
2. Koshelivets', p. 81.

3. Quoted in A. Mar'iamov, *Dovzhenko* (Moscow, 1968), p. 109; cited in *Service,* p. 50.

4. Heorhii Ostrovs'kyi, 'Pratsia O. P. Dovzhenka na Odes'kii kinofabrytsi (1926–1929)', *Literaturna Odesa*, no. 17–18 (1957), p. 253.

5. For excellent analyses of these organisations, see George S. N. Luckyj, *Literary Politics in the Soviet Ukraine, 1917–1934* (New York, 1956) and Myroslav Shkandrij, *Modernists, Marxists and the Nation: The Ukrainian Literary Discussion of the 1920s* (Edmonton, Alberta, 1992).

6. Koshelivets', pp. 81–3.

7. '1939 Autobiography', p. 19.

8. Iurii Ianovs'kyi, *Tvory v p'iaty tomakh* (Kiev, 1959), vol. 5, p. 131.

9. Iurii Smolych, *Rozpovid' pro nespokii* (Kiev, 1968), p. 160; also cited in Koshelivets', pp. 84–5. Although Smolych did not include Tiutiunnyk (who was still a 'non-person' in 1968) in his memoir, the former nationalist general also must have helped create this film.

10. Koshelivets', p. 85.

11. Pavlo Nechesa, 'Shchastia buty poruch', *PZh*, pp. 217–18; *Storinky*, p. 47.

12. Quoted in Lazar Bodyk, 'Kinokadry zhyttia i strichky', *Kriz' kinoobiektyv chasu: Spohady pro veteraniv ukrains'koho kino* (Kiev, 1970), p. 259; cited in Koshelivets', p. 87. Zavelev, a superb cameraman, had made over thirty films before *Zvenyhora*. Bodyk's quote, a part of the post-1956 Dovzhenko myth-creating process, depicts *Zvenyhora* as a battle between the 'innovative' new director and the old professional. In light of Zavelev's bold visual style, which also appears in *Zvenyhora*, this is not necessarily the case. I am grateful to Yuri Tsivian for pointing this out to me.

13. Pavlo Nechesa, 'Iak stavyly "Zvenigoru"', *Teatr i kino*, no. 22 (30 November) 1927; *DMM*, File 7; *SDM*, A-196.

14. *Service*, p. 47.

15. K. Fel'dman, 'Zvenigora', RGALI, 2081/1/1200, p. 13.

16. Raymond John Uzwyshyn, 'Between Ukrainian Cinema and Modernism: Alexander Dovzhenko's Silent Trilogy' (unpublished PhD dissertation, New York University, 2000), p. 78; Oleh Buriachkivs'kyi, '"Zvenyhora" O. Dovzhenka: istoriosofiia Ukrainy,' in V. H. Horpenko and O. S. Musiienko, eds, *Zmina paradyhmy: Zbirnyk naukovykh prats'*, *Chastyna 1* (Kiev, 1995), p. 22.

17. Nebesio, 'The Silent Films of Alexander Dovzhenko: A Historical Poetics' (Ph.D. dissertation, University of Alberta, Edmonton, 1996), p. 89.

18. Koshelivets', pp. 87–8.

19. See Mykhaylo Hrushevsky, 'The Traditional Scheme of "Russian" History and the Problem of a Rational Organization of the History of the Eastern

Slavs', *The Annals of the Ukrainian Academy of Arts and Sciences in the U.S.*, II, no. 2 (1952), pp. 355–64. First published in *Zbornik statei po slavianovedeniiu*, vol. 1 (St Petersburg, 1904).

20. Nebesio, p. 86.
21. Nebesio, p. 86.
22. Nebesio, pp. 86–7.
23. Nebesio, p. 87.
24. Cited in O. Buriachkivs'kyi, '"Zvenyhora" O. Dovzhenka: istoriosofiia Ubrainy', p. 49.
25. B. Stepanyshyn, 'Triumf i kaskad trahedii', *Kul'tura i zhyttia*, 13 August 1994; cited in Buriachkivs'kyi, p. 49.
26. Cited in *DIS*, p. 88. The phrase, 'A grandfather is a prism of time', also appears in '1939 Autobiography', p. 8.
27. Cited in *DIS*, p. 88.
28. Buriachkivs'kyi, p. 27.
29. Buriachkivs'kyi, p. 29.
30. *Service*, p. 56.
31. Koshelivets', p. 88; Buriachkivs'kyi, p. 23.
32. Buriachkivs'kyi, p. 32.
33. Koshelivets', p. 90.
34. Buriachkivs'kyi, pp. 29–30.
35. '1939 Autobiography', pp. 19–20.
36. Letter 2, in Korohods'kyi, 'Visimnadtsat' lystiv pro kokhannia: Oleksandr Dovzhenko – Oleni Chernovii', *Kul'tura i zhyttia*, no. 48 (27 November, 1996), p. 3.
37. See M. Bazhan, 'Pro "Zvenyhoru"', *Teatr i kino*, no. 31 (14 February 1928), especially pp. 2–3 and RGALI, 2081/1/1099; and K. Fel'dman, 'Zvenigora', RGALI, 2081/1/1200. Also see Bazhan's 'Lehendy ta istoriia', *Kino*, no. 21–2 (1928); and *Zhyttia i revoliutsiia*, no. 1 (1928).
38. Denise Youngblood, *Soviet Cinema in the Silent Era, 1918–1935* (Ann Arbor, MI, 1985), p. 181.
39. Sergei Eisenstein, 'The Birth of an Artist', in his *Notes of a Film Director* (New York, 1970), p. 142. For a slightly different account, see the memoirs of G. V. Aleksandrov, *Epokha i kino* (Moscow, 1976), p. 240.
40. Youngblood, p. 181.
41. *Kino*, no. 19–20 (1927), p. 4; cited in *Storinky*, p. 48.
42. Kh. Khersonskii, 'VUFKU na perelome', *Pravda*, 10 February 1928, p. 3; and B. Allers, 'Neosushchestvlennyi zamysel', *Komsomol'skaia pravda*, 22 May 1928, p. 3.
43. *Vecherniaia Moskva*, no. 118, 23 May 1928; cited in *Storinky*, p. 56.

44. Cited in Ostrovs'kyi, 'Pratsia', p. 255.

45. '1939 Autobiography', p. 20.

46. *Storinky*, p. 57.

47. *Teatr i kino*, no. 37 (1928); SDM, A-196.

48. *Service*, p. 63.

49. Ian Kuchera, 'Spivets' revoliutsii', *DIS*, pp. 70–1.

50. Nebesio, p. 102.

51. *Shkval*, no. 49 (1928); SDM, A-196.

52. Ihor Belza, 'Avtor "Arsenalu"', *PZh*, p. 212; *Storinky*, p. 59.

53. *Service*, p. 62.

54. Grigorii Roshal, 'Tvorchyi podvyh', *PZh*, p. 430.

55. Smolych, *Rozpovid' pro nespokii*, pp. 162–3.

56. '1939 Autobiography', pp. 20–1.

57. Nebesio, pp. 99–100.

58. Bazhan, 'O. Dovzhenko', in O. Babyshkin, ed., *Oleksandr Dovzhenko: Zbirnyk spohadiv i statei pro mytsia* (Kiev, 1959), p. 46.

59. Bazhan, 'Monolitnyi film', RGALI, 2081/1/1099, p. 7.

60. Nebesio, p. 97.

61. *Service*, pp. 63–5.

62. *Service*, pp. 66–7.

63. Nebesio, p. 103.

64. Leonid Maximenkov, ed., 'Stalin's Meeting with a Delegation of Ukrainian Writers on 12 February 1929', *Harvard Ukrainian Studies*, 17, no. 3–4 (1992), pp. 361–431.

65. Nebesio, p. 103.

66. A. P. Dovzhenko, *Sobranie sochinenii v chetyrekh tomakh* (Moscow, 1966), vol. 1, p. 256; cited in *Service*, p. 74.

67. Letters 16 and 18, in Korohods'kyi, 'Visimnadtsat' lystiv', *Kul'tura i zhyttia*, no. 49 (4 December 1996), p. 3.

68. Julia Solntseva (1901–89), the lead actress for *Aelita* (1924) and *The Cigarette Girl from Mosselprom* (1924), met Dovzhenko at the Odessa Film Studios, where she was shooting a film. She became his primary assistant director and closest collaborator on *Earth* and played a minor role in it. Only one skimpy biography of her exists: N. Tolchenova, *Iuliia Solntseva* (Moscow, 1979). Also see George O. Liber, '"Till Death Do You Part: Varvara Krylova, Yuliya Solntseva and Oleksandr Dovzhenko's Muse', *Australian Slavonic and East European Studies*, 14, no. 1–2 (2000), pp. 75–97.

69. The best study of these factions still remains James E. Mace's *Communism and the Dilemmas of National Liberation: National Communism in Soviet Ukraine, 1918–1933* (Cambridge, MA, 1983).

70. Nebesio, p. 78.

71. Peter Kenez, *Cinema and Soviet Society, 1917–1953*, (Cambridge and New York, 1992), p. 103.

72. Kenez, pp. 103–4.

73. Kenez, p. 104.

74. Kenez, p. 104.

75. Kenez, p. 105.

76. Nebesio, p. 82.

77. George O. Liber, *Soviet Nationality Policy, Urban Growth, and Identity Change in the Ukrainian SSR, 1923–1934* (Cambridge and New York, 1992), p. 161.

78. *'Spilka Vyzvolennia Ukrainy'. Stenohrafichnyi zvit sudovoho protsesu* (Kharkiv, 1931), vol. 1, pp. iii, v.

79. *'Spilka Vyzvolennia Ukrainy'*, vol. 1, p. 153.

80. *'Spilka Vyzvolennia Ukrainy'*, vol. 1, p. 25.

81. Orest Subtelny, *Ukraine: A History* (Toronto and Buffalo, 1991), p. 410.

82. Paul Robert Magocsi, *A History of Ukraine* (Seattle, WA, 1996), p. 557.

83. Subtelny, p. 410.

84. Magocsi, p. 557. Also see Moshe Lewin's 'Who Was the Soviet Kulak?' in his *The Making of the Soviet System: Essays in the Social History of Interwar Russia* (New York, 1985), pp. 121–41.

85. Magocsi, p. 557.

86. Subtelny, p. 410.

87. Magocsi, p. 557. Also see Robert Conquest, *Harvest of Sorrow: Soviet Collectivization and the Terror-Famine* (London and New York, 1986), chapter 6.

88. Subtelny, p. 411. For a Communist activist's vivid description of collectivisation in Ukraine, see Lev Kopelev, *The Education of a True Believer* (New York, 1978).

89. Magocsi, p. 555.

90. Magocsi, p. 555.

91. The exact number of deaths due to the famine in Ukraine is unknown. Estimates range from 3 million (S. G. Wheatcroft, 'Ukrainian Famine', *Problems of Communism*, 34, no. 2 [1985], p. 134) to 7.5 million (James E. Mace, 'Famine and Nationalism in Soviet Ukraine', *Problems of Communism*, 33, no. 3 [May–June, 1984], p. 39). Robert Conquest claims that 5 to 7 million died (Conquest, *Harvest of Sorrow*, p. 239). The controversy over the number of deaths due to the famine correlate to the reasons for the outbreak of the famine. Those who provide the higher figures claim that Soviet authorities planned the famine; those who provide the lower figures

generally claim that the famine developed accidentally. Also see Dana Dalrymple, 'The Soviet Famine of 1932–1934', *Soviet Studies*, 15, no. 3 (1964), pp. 250–84; Roman Serbyn and Bohdan Krawchenko, eds, *Famine in Ukraine, 1932–1933* (Edmonton, Alberta, 1986); James E. Mace, 'The Famine of 1932–1933: A Watershed in the History of Soviet Nationality Policy', in Henry R. Huttenbach, ed., *Soviet Nationality Policies: Ruling Ethnic Groups in the USSR* (London, 1990), pp. 177–205; Steven Rosefielde, 'Excess Collectivization Deaths, 1929–1933: New Demographic Evidence', *Slavic Review*, 43, no. 1 (1984), pp. 83–8, with subsequent commentary and rejoinders by Stephen G. Wheatcroft, Steven Rosefielde, Barbara A. Anderson and Brian D. Silver, *Slavic Review*, 44, no. 3 (1985), pp. 505–36; Mark B. Tauger, 'The 1932 Harvest and the Famine of 1933', *Slavic Review*, 50, no. 1 (1991), pp. 70–89; and R. W. Davies, M. B. Tauger and S. G. Wheatcroft, 'Stalin, Grain Stocks, and the Famine of 1932–1933', *Slavic Review*, 54, no. 3 (1995), pp. 642–57.

92. '1939 Autobiography', p. 21.

93. *Storinky*, pp. 67, 73.

94. Ann Filip, '"Zemlia" – tse velyka i hlyboka pisnia', *DIS*, p. 53. On *Earth*'s visual impact, see Robert Warshow, *The Immediate Experience: Movies, Comics, Theatre and Other Aspects of Popular Culture* (New York, 1964), pp. 210–12; Gilberto Perez, 'All in the Foreground: A Study of Dovzhenko's *Earth*', *Hudson Review*, 28, no. 1 (1975), pp. 68–86; and *Service*, pp. 75–84.

95. *Service*, p. 84.

96. Uzwyshyn, pp. 477–8.

97. Gilberto Perez, *The Material Ghost: Films and Their Medium* (Baltimore and London, 1998), p. 178.

98. Perez, p. 178.

99. On the evolution of Vasyl's dance, see Semen Svashenko, 'Charivnyk', in *PZh*, pp. 245–50.

100. Sergei Eisenstein, 'Dickens, Griffith, and the Film Today', in his *Film Forum: Essays in Film Theory*, edited and translated by Jay Leyda (New York, 1977), pp. 241–2.

101. Perez, p. 189.

102. L. Bodyk, *Dzherelo velykoho kino. Spohady pro O. P. Dovzhenka* (Kiev, 1965), p. 87.

103. '1939 Autobiography', p. 21. Dovzhenko did not provide the date when the Central Committee summoned him or reveal who led the charge against him. Kutsenko's chronology of the film-maker's life asserted that he visited Kharkiv during the first week of March 1930. See *Storinky*, p. 73.

104. For some of the comments made at this meeting, see Mikh. D., 'Prekrasnyi khudozhnik, prekrasnaia kartina', *Komsomol'skaia pravda*, 2 April 1930.

105. *Storinky*, p. 74.

106. P. Bliakhin, 'Zemlia', *Pravda*, 29 March 1930.

107. Demian Bedny, 'Filosofy', *Izvestiia*, 4 April 1930. Republished, with analysis, in *KZ*, no. 23 (1994), pp. 151–62.

108. Demian Bedny, '"Kononizatsiia" ili "chto i trebovalos' dokazat"', *Izvestiia*, 6 April 1930.

109. '1939 Autobiography', p. 21. Fifteen years later, in 1945, Dovzhenko encountered Bedny at the Kremlin polyclinic. Bedny greeted Dovzhenko and allegedly said: 'I do not know, I already forgot why I ripped your *Earth* to shreds. But I will tell you that I never saw such a film before or after. It was great art.' O. P. Dovzhenko, *Tvory v p'iaty tomakh* (Kiev, 1966), vol. 5, p. 209; cited in Koshelivets', p. 153.

110. RGALI, 1923/1/1784; and Bodyk, p. 88. Dovzhenko's departure date appears in *Storinky*, p. 77.

111. Quoted in *Storinky*, p. 79.

112. Cited in M. V. Kutsenko, 'Spovid' pro trahichne kokhannia', *Vitchyzna*, no. 4 (1991), p. 190.

113. *Izvestiia*, 17 April 1930.

114. Roman Savyts'kyi, Jr., 'Pomiry "Zemli" O. Dovzhenka', *Suchasnist'*, no. 7–8 (1975), p. 107.

115. Shkandrij, *Modernists, Marxists and the Nation*, pp. 169–70.

6

Stalin's Client

In spite of Dovzhenko's questionable political reliability, Soviet authorities allowed him to leave the USSR in June 1930. Accompanied by Julia Solntseva and Danylo Demutsky, he travelled to Poland, Czechoslovakia, Germany, France, and Great Britain. During his trip, he met the French director Abel Gance, H. G. Wells, Albert Einstein and other celebrated artists and intellectuals. These meetings comprised a fringe benefit to his travels. He undertook the trip with the primary purpose of investigating new trends in film-making, especially the rise of sound film, which became very popular with audiences after its introduction in American newsreels in 1927. By January 1929, the major American film studios began to release all of their feature presentations as 'talking pictures' and the Soviet film industry needed to follow suit.[1]

Sound on film revolutionised film-making. Wedded to the technology of silent film, Soviet studios fell behind the American and West European industries. Hoping to raise Soviet standards, Dovzhenko concentrated his attention on the new technology, its impact on cinematography and how he could integrate these innovations into his own work. In a letter from London to his friend Ivan Sokoliansky, the director of Kharkiv's Research Institute for the Deaf and Dumb, Dovzhenko gave these new trends high marks: 'I saw the power of sound films. A few of them are not bad. All with stupid content. But technically they are very strong.'[2] He then expressed the hope that Soviet directors would master sound film and remain among the best film-makers in the world.

The trip stimulated Dovzhenko's creativity. In another letter to Sokoliansky, he described his thoughts about the future:

> I have a head full of new production plans ... Cinema is only now beginning to emerge from its childhood. In three years we will be participants in and eyewitnesses to such miracles that all that was done and is being done up to now will be remembered as naive games ... I want to live a hundred years with a hundred lives, in order to do all this and to see all this ...[3]

Dovzhenko's optimism proved unrealistic. His enthusiasm for the unlimited possibilities unleashed by the introduction of sound film soon clashed with the new Stalinist political regimentation.

Political Pressures

By the end of the 1920s, Stalin and his allies had neutralised two of his major opponents, Nikolai Bukharin and Leon Trotsky, and gained unprecedented power within the Communist Party and the Soviet state. As Stalin and his men consolidated their rule, the Soviet Union's political, social, cultural and economic priorities changed. Collectivisation, industrialisation and socialist realism now became the order of the day. As resistance to these changes intensified, Soviet leaders discovered enemies everywhere, and political life became harsher, especially for the peasants, former oppositionists, and the non-Russians.

As the Stalinists undermined policies established a decade earlier, they dismantled Ukrainianisation, which had promoted Ukrainians into the trade unions, the party and the Soviet Ukrainian state bureaucracy. By 1933 Ukrainians constituted 60 per cent of the membership of the Communist Party of Ukraine and the majority within the working class and trade unions.[4] The Soviet Ukrainian government spent scarce resources to teach its illiterate population how to read and write, and most adult literacy courses focused on the Ukrainian language. By the 1932–3 school year, 88 per cent of all elementary and secondary school students in Soviet Ukraine received instruction in Ukrainian. By 1930, nearly 80 per cent of all books published appeared in Ukrainian, as did nearly 90 per cent of all newspapers by 1931.[5] As millions of Ukrainian peasants migrated into the urban centres, the cities developed a more Ukrainian character. These transformations encouraged a number of prominent Ukrainian communists to demand greater 'home rule' from Moscow.

This claim, Stalinists asserted in the late 1920s, threatened the political integrity of the Soviet Union. After the trial of the Union for the Liberation of Ukraine (SVU) in 1930, the Stalinists began to limit the Communist Party of Ukraine's authority. By 1932 and 1933, at the height of the struggle to collectivise the countryside, the central party began to purge the CP(b)U, accusing its leaders of 'bourgeois nationalism' and of 'wrecking', even if they had joined the Bolsheviks decades before the revolutions of 1917 and had loyally served the party. Once painted with this brush, nothing could save them.

Between 1934 and 1938, the security organs arrested nearly 150,000 party members, one-third of the total membership of the Communist Party of Ukraine.[6] Shumsky's successor as Commissar of Education, Mykola Skrypnyk, an old friend of Lenin and the driving force behind Ukrainianisation, became one of the most prominent victims of this policy's reversal. He cheated Stalin by committing suicide on 6 July 1933.

The arrests, trials and denunciations of 1929–33 prepared the way for the Great Terror of the 1930s. Despite occasional pronouncements by high party officials that they would not hold a person's 'political past' against him, former political allegiances generally served as a predictor of an individual's fate.[7] Present conformity and usefulness to the Soviet state, however, could mitigate an unsavoury political history.

How would Dovzhenko fit into this new political climate? He himself did not know. Shortly after the appearance of *Earth*, Felix Kon, the head of the Main Arts Administration (*Glaviskusstvo*), divided his 'fellow travelling' artists into two categories: those who professed allegiance to the Communist Party in order 'to use us' and those who honoruably 'follow us, but do not know how to do this'. He advised that the Communist Party should fight against the first group and attempt to bring the second 'closer to us, not repulse them'. Dovzhenko, Kon claimed, belonged to the second group.[8]

The Ukrainian film-maker understood that a thin line separated Kon's first group from the second. He must also have realised that party officials, especially during periods of political crisis and ideological exuberance, moved this line arbitrarily.

By producing a new film, he hoped to resurrect his own tarnished reputation in the eyes of Soviet officials. Although his trip to Western Europe stimulated his creativity and encouraged him to try new technologies and techniques, he experienced a creative lapse, a 'writer-director's block', for nearly seven months after his return. He searched for an appealing subject, but he found that the new political environment limited his choices. He described his dilemma thus:

> When I came back from the foreign assignment I suggested to the administration of Ukrainfilm a screenplay that had been taking shape in my mind about our heroes in the Arctic based on the tragedy of Nobile and the death of R. Amundsen. The administration turned down the idea and demanded that I write 'something similar' about present-day life in Ukraine. I hastily put Amundsen out of my mind and in twelve days wrote the unsuccessful script *Ivan* and set about shooting it. I found it difficult to work on *Ivan* because Bedny's feuilleton continued to weigh heavily on my mind.[9]

Bedny's criticism and the rejection of his first screenplay proposal since *Earth* served as a warning to Dovzhenko. He realised that he could no longer make films dealing solely with the Ukrainian countryside and Ukrainian peasants. He quickly understood that he had to focus his attention on the Ukrainian working class.

He began to film *Ivan* in June 1931 and completed it on 30 October 1932.[10] Dovzhenko spent more time on this film than on any of his previous projects. In addition to adhering to his own demanding standards, he needed to master new techniques while employing old equipment. Most importantly, he had to overcome his reputation as 'an unreliable fellow traveller who could be tolerated' and to satisfy his political critics, who expected much from the new film.[11] As Dovzhenko planned and filmed *Ivan*, the pressures on him only intensified.

In response to these pressures, the film-maker grew nervous and irritable, possibly experiencing a nervous breakdown. He sublimated his frustration over his career through criticism of architecture and civil engineering. According to his 1939 autobiographical statement, the Brest-Litovsk Highway, which led to the film studio in Kiev, played 'an important, but malevolent role' in his everyday life.

> I don't like this highway and have complained about it daily for ten years. All that time, during every trip over that highway, I felt disgust. It became the focal point of my disorder. Every day for ten years I tore down in my mind from that broad, beautiful road all five unsightly rows of telegraph, telephone, and tramway poles and buried the cables underground. I filled in the ditches and levelled the bumps, making the road even. I replaced the tramcars, which were always breaking down, with buses and trolleybuses all the way to Sviatoshyne and poured asphalt over a concrete base. The street became wide and straight as an arrow. I tore down the wretched huts all along the highway and in their place built handsome low buildings. I reconstructed the Galician Market, the most disappointing spot in Kiev, and made a lake on the site with a graceful embankment. I convinced myself that only when this was done would directors make good films.[12]

Dovzhenko's complaints about the Brest-Litovsk Highway and his plans to redevelop it and other streets and squares symbolised his efforts to deal with the political guidelines hampering his creativity. He transfered his frustrations over his powerlessness into politically acceptable suggestions. In his mind's eye, he bulldozed crumbling and ugly structures and constructed 'handsome low buildings' in their place, symbols of the artistically pure films he longed to create.

In public, he suggested improvements. Never satisfied with mediocrity or the status quo, he believed that he could negotiate anything, including the spoken and unspoken restrictions the authorities placed on his creative projects. One thing he could not negotiate, however was the deadline to complete the film for the fifteenth anniversary of the November 1917 revolution. He had to work at break-neck speed:

> The demand that I submit the film by October [1932] was almost impossible to meet. It was my first sound film, made with very bad equipment that the sound technicians had not mastered yet. Nevertheless I did manage to turn the film in on time, although at the end I had to work at the cutting table for eighty-five hours without getting up from it. The film came out raw and shapeless.[13]

In spite of Dovzhenko's claims, the problems with *Ivan* did not stem solely from the tightness of the deadline.[14] When he started filming in June 1931, he already knew the time frame. *Ivan* took nearly seventeen months to complete. By contrast, he only spent about a year making each segment of his earlier Ukrainian trilogy. Because Dovzhenko knew that this film would determine his future, he devoted long hours to it, but his hard work did not pay off. Although *Ivan* muted the themes and the scope of his Ukrainian trilogy, it raised serious questions about his political and artistic reliability.

Ivan

Unlike *Zvenyhora*, *Arsenal* or *Earth*, *Ivan* did not reflect Dovzhenko's personal memories or the myths and folklore of the Ukrainian peasantry.[15] Although he left the theme of the soil, which had defined his creative vision, he did not abandon his love of nature. Instead, he integrated this concern into his celebration of a brave new industrial world under construction at the rapids of the Dnieper River, which had protected the Ukrainian Cossacks for four centuries.

As part of the first Five Year Plan inaugurated in 1928, Soviet central planners sought to construct a massive dam and hydroelectric complex on the Dnieper River in central Ukraine. They wanted to subdue the dangerous river, irrigate parts of the neighbouring countryside and supply electric power for future industrial growth in this area. This government-sponsored undertaking initiated the communist regime's series of large-scale projects to industrialise the country. Investing more labour and capital in building the dam than in any other construction project to date, the Soviet government considered the Dneprostroi project one of the most important foundations of its new centrally planned economy.[16]

Dovzhenko sought to glorify this project by examining its social, political and psychological impact on the workers who had only recently migrated from the countryside. He wove his narrative around a single Dneprostroi worker, the eponymous Ivan, and traced the evolution of his working-class consciousness and his transformation into a new Soviet man.

The film opens with a long shot of the Dnieper River in the early spring, prior to the dam's construction. In his lectures on the art of combining visual images and sound, Eisenstein highly praised this visually poetic opening. He considered Dovzhenko's melding of the visual expanse of the river with the sound of the waters and the melting ice crashing against the protruding rocks one of the best examples of combining sight and sound in cinematography.[17]

After this poetic introduction, the film shows the hydroelectric dam under construction. In another scene, a Soviet official visits a Ukrainian farm village to recruit volunteers to work on the construction site. Ivan, a strong, lanky, young man, and a lazy fellow named Stepan Huba set out for the project. Subsequent scenes portray the daily routine at the project, where Ivan works hard driving rail spikes while

Petro Masokha plays Ivan (*Ivan*, 1932)

Huba becomes a 'slacker'. One day a worker dies in a construction accident, and his mother mourns his death. Later, Ivan strives to earn the honour of 'shock worker', but he becomes frustrated and angry when he loses an organised 'socialist competition', a contest to determine who could drive the most rail spikes. He begins to feel insignificant when other workers receive honours and recognition, and he does not. The film's climax occurs at a mass meeting of the workers, when the leaders of the construction project inform them that a critical section of the dam threatens to collapse. After the workers rush out to meet the challenge and save the day, Ivan realises that he needs a proper technical education. He enrolls in courses to raise his qualifications. He optimistically envisions promotion and perhaps even membership in the party.

In contrast to Dovzhenko's Ukrainian trilogy, *Ivan* strikes the viewer as an ordinary film which may have taxed Dovzhenko's use of political symbols, but not his creative powers. Dovzhenko created a case study of a single worker in order to highlight the problems of adjusting to modern working conditions. The film-maker named his protagonist Ivan, the most common East Slavic name, with the intent of portraying an 'everyman', a representative of the millions of new workers who had migrated from the countryside to the mines, construction sites and factories.

Despite Dovzhenko's best efforts, *Ivan* failed to refurbish his political reputation. The overwhelming majority of critics compared Dovzhenko's *Ivan* with Friedrich Ermler and Sergei Yutkevich's *Counterplan*, which also premiered in November 1932. The latter film deals with the problems of production in a modern factory, where the workers express their enthusiasm for the party's vision of industrialisation by presenting their own counterplan, a more ambitious programme than that of the factory's managers. After many trials and tribulations, the workers successfully implement their project.[18]

In contrast to *Counterplan*'s single-minded focus, commentators interpreted *Ivan* as a retrospective that emphasised the poetic nature of silent films and included complex metaphors and philosophical pathos. Several of Dovzhenko's colleagues, such as Pudovkin, Yutkevich and Nikolai Shengelaia, praised *Ivan*, claiming that the socialist realist method included a number of different styles and provided freedom of creativity.[19] Most reviewers, however, considered *Counterplan* more understandable to viewers and hence more 'progressive' than *Ivan*.[20]

Despite Dovzhenko's goal to make a film worthy of the fifteenth anniversary of the Bolshevik Revolution, *Ivan* did not present a clear message. Visual and thematic ambiguities and contradictions marked the film's frames. Although *Ivan* highlighted Dneprostroi's economic and political importance, it possessed an ambivalent subtext, which reflected the film-maker's own tensions. In following the party's guidelines, he experienced problems in reconciling his perspective of reality with the party's interpretations.

Conforming to the positivist nature of the emerging socialist realist model of film-making, Dovzhenko's depiction of Dneprostroi presented a false picture of reality. The Ukrainian peasants who came to constitute the majority of the site's work force did not arrive voluntarily. As the collectivisation drive accelerated in 1932, famine broke out. By joining the Dneprostroi work force, these 'volunteers' escaped starvation, collectivisation, possible exile in Siberia, or even death. They entered a new world radically different from their old peasant existence. Torn from the land of their forefathers and the natural rhythm of the seasons, the new workers had to acclimatise themselves to a new and brutal industrial discipline, learn to use primitive technology and work at a dangerous pace. As a result, thousands died or suffered serious injuries while constructing the dam.[21] The transformation of the peasants into productive members of the working class did not occur as quickly or as painlessly as Dovzhenko depicted in *Ivan*, much less in Ermler and Yutkevich's *Counterplan*.

While Dovzhenko's cinematic sanitising of industrial brutality appeared straightforward, the depictions of the power of nature and the film's use of Ukrainian presented ambivalent messages. The powerful opening scenes of the wild Dnieper crashing through the rapids demonstrate the mighty force of the river and the challenges that confront anyone who attempts to harness that force. Shot lovingly by Danylo Demutsky, Dovzhenko's long-time cameraman, this opening scene mutes the message of the rest of the film. The river surges with such raw power that the viewer finds it difficult to imagine the men and women of the film, with their flaws and weaknesses, taming it.

Dovzhenko directing Danylo Demutsky (his cameraman) to shoot the rapids scene (*Ivan*, 1931–2)

In another scene, the highly agitated mother of the dead worker runs through seven sets of doors to get to the construction foreman. When she finally reaches his office, she overhears a telephone conversation he is conducting with one of his subordinates. As if reading her mind, the manager admonishes his junior colleague to fix the problem that caused the young man's death. His demand satisfies the mother.

Although many sets of doors and walls separate the dam's manager from his workers, Dovzhenko suggests that the foreman had the best interests of his workers at heart. The first part of the scene, which appears to criticise the increasing bureaucraticisation of Soviet society, contradicts the second part. This ambiguity violated socialist realism's principle of simple and easily understandable messages. Dovzhenko, moreover, never portrayed the completed dam, only the efforts and sacrifices expended by the workers to build it.[22] Without a final product, their work and suffering appear wasted.

As the first sound film to use the Ukrainian language, Dovzhenko's *Ivan* garbled the party's message. On the surface, the film presents the reality of industrialisation's impact on Soviet society. As the new factories, mines, and construction projects demanded more workers and as the collectivisation drive accelerated in the countryside, more Ukrainian peasants abandoned the land to join the industrial work force, which hitherto had contained primarily Russians. Dovzhenko's selection of only Ukrainian-speaking actors for his first sound film emphasised the Ukrainianisation of the working class.

Dovzhenko defended his use of Ukrainian by claiming that Kiev had a dearth of good actors, and the best actors at his disposal spoke no Russian. Under these conditions, it became impossible to find someone who could dub the film into Russian.[23] This claim did not fit with reality: during the 1926 census, the majority of residents of Kiev declared Russian as their native language.[24]

After Dovzhenko released the film, he admitted that the use of Ukrainian posed problems. The closeness of the Ukrainian and Russian languages, their cognates, and their near mutual understandability actually undermined the film's accessibility to Russian-speaking audiences. The Russian viewer frequently assumed incorrectly that he could understand the Ukrainian language in the film. According to Dovzhenko,

> When you watch an English film, you immediately abstract yourself from the language and turn your attention to other aspects. But it's different with regard to the Ukrainian language. The viewer's semi-knowledge of the language is the problem. This half-knowledge introduces to the viewer's consciousness inhibitory elements which irritate the viewer. This lowers the quality of the film'.[25]

The Russian critic V. Grossman-Roshchin agreed: 'our semi-knowledge of the Ukrainian language is far worse than our not understanding it at all.'[26]

Dovzhenko's use of Ukrainian in *Ivan* raised a serious issue with regard to the use of non-Russian languages in the Soviet film industry, one far more critical than the use of non-Russian titles in silent films. As sound film became commonplace, dialogue expanded and took on a more critical role in the success of the narrative. Soviet film heroes of the 1930s, such as Chapaev, Shchors and Alexander Nevsky, gave long speeches that reflected the current party line.[27] If a viewer could not understand the dialogue, then he could not comprehend the film's message. If the party wanted to communicate its view of the world to the masses, it had to insure that audiences could understand its films. The language question grew into a hotly contested issue. Not only did the medium of film constitute a message in and of itself; the language of the film also became a message, which party leaders realised they needed to assess carefully.

The portrayal of Ivan as an 'unheroic' hero, the ideological ambiguity of certain scenes, and the use of Ukrainian galvanised critics to write harsh reviews. Most damningly, Dovzhenko's film failed to conform to the emerging model of 'socialist realism' and its primary component, the positive hero.

In order to put an end to factional strife 'on the artistic and cultural front' and to subordinate all cultural activity to the party leadership in Moscow, the Central Committee on 23 April 1932 issued a decree, which disbanded all independent artistic groups. In their place, the party established highly centralised 'creative

unions' of writers, artists, composers, architects and film-makers, who would present their works through the prism of 'socialist realism'.[28] First coined on 17 May
1932 by Ivan Gronsky, the head of the organisational committee of the newly
founded Soviet Writers' Union, socialist realism remained a vague concept even
until the union's first congress in late August 1934.

At this meeting, the writers and the Communist Party hierarchy enshrined the
model for all artists, who thereafter would create the 'truthful, historically concrete
representation of reality in its revolutionary development'.[29] How artists would
incorporate this 'modal schizophrenia' into their works without a specific set of rules
remained unclear.[30] Although the leadership of the Writers' Union and the party
issued pronouncements that socialist realist literature should be optimistic, accessible to the masses and party-minded, most novels from the mid-1930s conformed
to a single master plot, which represented a synthesis of the plots of several 'exemplary' novels (primarily Maxim Gorky's *Mother* and Fedor Gladkov's *Cement*).[31]
According to Katerina Clark, the master plot defines socialist realism.[32]

In the evolution of the master plot which integrated Soviet politics and Communist ideology, on the one hand, and Russian literary traditions, on the other, the hero
of the novel acquires or strengthens his Communist consciousness by overcoming a
serious socio-political-economic challenge. The main protagonist usually arrives at
a new place and realises that the state-given plan is not being fulfilled properly.
Instead of accepting this status quo, the migrant becomes a socialist crusader and
makes plans for correcting the problem. Inevitably, the local authorities rebuke him,
asserting that the hero's solution is Utopian. The protagonist then mobilises 'the
people', addressing them at a mass meeting, and inspiring them to follow his plan.
Despite the personal problems he encounters on his journey to fulfil the plan, he
succeeds in overcoming all obstacles and gains a full-blown Communist consciousness.[33] This positive hero resembles a fairytale protagonist as well as the model
presented in Joseph Campbell's *The Hero with a Thousand Faces*.

By observing and interpreting reality only within the framework of the long march
toward Communism, the creative intelligentsia became 'engineers of human souls'
and servants of the Soviet state. Artists, composers, architects, writers and film-
makers sought to raise the political consciousness of their audiences. Conforming to
the spirit of socialist realism, they portrayed current and historical events in a revisionist spirit calculated to lend support to the present Soviet regime. They provided
their audiences with an ideal depiction of present reality and a vision of the future,
as 'it is bound to become, when it bows to the logic of Marxism'.[34] In addition, these
'engineers' strove to portray the seeds of this bright future in the present, which ordinary men and women, enmeshed in their daily routines, could not see. Socialist
realism's juxtaposition of 'what is' and 'what ought to be' represented 'an impossible
aesthetic'.[35]

These Soviet artists endeavoured to introduce the Communist ideal into the consciousness of Soviet citizens and convince them of the value of that ideal, whatever the reality, by moulding and tranforming their audiences' consciousness.[36] Long before socialist realism emerged as the primary literary model in the 1930s, many Soviet literary groups in the 1920s accepted the idea that 'the subconscious dominates human consciousness and can be logically and technically manipulated to construct a new world and a new individual'.[37] Socialist realism built on their ideas and predispositions.

These socialist realist artists relied to a great extent on the celebration of the positive hero, a paragon of Bolshevik virtue, as a role model for readers and viewers. The hero's life should 'show the forward movement of history in an allegorical representation of one stage in history's dialectical progress'.[38] The positive hero, as the Russian critic Andrei Siniavsky defined him:

> [He] is not simply a good man. He is a hero illuminated by the light of the most ideal of all ideals … He firmly knows what is right and what is wrong; he says plainly 'yes' or 'no' and does not confuse black with white. For him there are no inner doubts and hesitations, no unanswerable questions, and no impenetrable secrets. Faced with the most complex of tasks, he easily finds the solution – by taking the shortest and most direct route to the Purpose.[39]

Although Ivan, a 'good man' at the beginning of the film, becomes a productive Soviet citizen, he never evolves into a positive hero. According to Dovzhenko, Ivan became an integral part of a much larger biography. 'Placing him in a larger framework, I do not want to make him a hero who leads the picture, but I made him a hero who is led.'[40] Dovzhenko described his title character as an 'unheroic hero', one who 'did not repel bullets nor sacrifice himself for the commune: he simply drove spikes on a rail spur, nothing more'.[41]

Although Ivan became a conscious member of the working class at the film's conclusion, his political self-actualisation did not develop clearly. In a period when politicians and intellectuals hotly debated socialist realism and its characteristics, Ivan's hesitance and self-doubt disqualified him as worthy of emulation.

Although the statutes of the Writers' Union reassured its members that socialist realism, with its emphasis on the positive hero, guaranteed 'excellent opportunities for the display of creative initiative and choice among its various forms, styles, and genres', they did not provide a clear set of rules instructing artists how to produce such works.[42] In the late 1920s the party had launched a campaign against 'formalism' and the avant-garde, which narrowed the choices for the creative masters. Although the party demanded clarity, an emphasis on the socialist present and the Communist future, and adherence to the party line, these criteria provided no specific artistic guidelines. Employing them would not necessarily attract the masses, especially in the field of cinema, which demanded a skilful coordination of sight, sound and message.

To present the Communist Party's ideological messages to a mass audience weaned on imported comedies and action-adventure films, Soviet directors had to create films with simple plots and unambiguous characterisations. Hollywood-style films with a Communist point of view attracted the average peasant and worker, who sought entertainment, not art on a grand scale. The leading Soviet directors, however Communist in their points of view, sought to explore the boundaries of art frame by frame. By the early 1930s, Stalin's party would no longer tolerate avant-garde or experimental films. Although such films had won Soviet cinematography international acclaim, very few peasants or workers could understand them. The Stalinist party leadership, moreover, hated avant-garde art as well escapist entertainment. They wanted to educate the masses politically, to communicate the 'message that there was only one way to look at the world, their way, and that every deviation from their point of view was necessarily hostile'.[43] Films had to be comprehensible, even to the half-educated. They had to portray the party's version of reality.

Soviet socialist realist film-making slowly evolved over the course of the 1930s as the party and film-makers revised, reinterpreted, and renegotiated the implementation of this ideology on film. Directors felt reticent at first, but they soon learned from their mistakes and successes. Easily understandable films with party-approved political messages then emerged on the screens. These films dealt with contemporary themes: the socialist construction in the city and in the countryside, the struggle with class enemies and the legacy of the past in the people's consciousness.[44] *Chapaev* (1934), directed by Sergei Vasiliev and Georgi Vasiliev (unrelated), became the most popular and most influential socialist realist film ever made in the Soviet Union, selling over 50 million tickets.

Chapaev proved that directors could create a popular film conforming to the principles of socialist realism. Competently made and easy to understand, this exciting action film, depicted the relationship between V. I. Chapaev, an uneducated peasant Soviet partisan commander, and D. A. Furmanov, his political commissar, during the Civil War. Chapaev, a courageous fighter, possesses good political instincts and understands that the Bolshevik party represents the future. These qualities alone do not suffice; Chapaev requires the ideological guidance of Furmanov to achieve victory. Under the commissar's supervision, Chapaev's class consciousness grows and he wins on the battlefield. Although he dies in battle at the end of the film, his Red division triumphs and his death marks him as a hero who makes the ultimate sacrifice.

Audiences could readily identify with *Chapaev*'s characters. Although a drama, the film included many humorous touches. Most importantly, this film, 'popular in form', featured a plot 'socialist in content'. In a subtle manner, it promoted three

Bolshevik myths concerning the Revolution and Civil War. The guiding role of the Bolsheviks in the struggle against all counter-revolutionaries constituted the most important post-revolutionary invention. Although successful on his own, Chapaev would not have achieved his greatest victories without the commissar, the party's representative. In dealing with the relationship between workers and peasants in Chapaev's ranks, the film celebrates another fiction, the 'worker-peasant alliance', or more accurately, the hegemony of the workers over the peasants, who by all Marxist accounts displayed a less-developed class consciousness than the workers. The film, moreover, concludes with an allusion to the fantasy of the 'radiant Communist future'. After Chapaev dies a heroic death in a struggle with the Whites, his troops avenge his death by vanquishing their enemies. The hero might die, but the Bolshevik cause (as in *Arsenal* and *Earth*) marches on.[45]

Chapaev took its place as an exemplary socialist realist film not only because it presents two positive heroes, Furmanov (the Bolshevik) and Chapaev (the proto-Bolshevik), but because it successfully harnessed the past, even revolutionary turmoil, to the Stalinist present and to the Communist future.[46] Communism, it asserted, constituted the grand design of history. The leading role of the Bolsheviks in the Revolution and Civil War, in effect, legitimised the Stalinist political system.

Ivan, which appeared two years before *Chapaev*, did not present such a clear message. Not surprisingly, Dovzhenko found it difficult to adopt the emerging, but poorly defined, socialist realist model. Conforming to the new principles of film-making presented enormous problems for him, as well as for other Soviet directors, such as Grigory Kozintsev, Leonid Trauberg, and Sergei Eisenstein. Each had begun their careers in the 1920s. Critics recognised them as 'innovators' with 'authentic and original voices'. When forced to conform to the contours of the new model, which despite its promises did not tolerate originality or experimentation, they experienced great psychological and political strains. Although they displayed a willingness to satisfy the new needs of the Stalinist state, they had a hard time changing their artistic approaches and compromising their standards.[47] Although critics brutalised Dovzhenko's film for failing to show a heroic and positive hero, *Ivan* represented a stage not only in Dovzhenko's evolution towards socialist realism, but in the evolution of the style in general.

Moving to Moscow

Dovzhenko completed *Ivan* on 30 October 1932. Even before its official premiere on 6 November, it drew controversy. Its first public screening took place in Kiev on 2 November; its second screening in Kharkiv on 3 November.[48] In Kharkiv, according to one of Dovzhenko's friends, the critics condemned *Ivan*. Although Ivan Sokoliansky did not provide any details, in a letter written to Solntseva twenty-four years later he recalled how 'idiots attempted to ruin Sashko's beautiful work'.[49]

The specific charges remain unclear, but in light of the film's ambiguities, critics raised the issue of Dovzhenko's Ukrainian nationalism. No one could point out specifically how Ukrainian nationalism appeared in Dovzhenko's films, but his equivocal scenes led critics and party officials to suspect a hidden Ukrainian nationalist subtext.[50]

As the film contained many scenes open to multiple interpretations, viewers as well as critics experienced difficulties understanding *Ivan*'s plot. Although the authorities may have had misgivings about *Ivan*, they allowed its release. On 5 November 1932, a special commission created by the 'leading institutions' met, viewed the film, and cut its most politically inconsistent frames.[51] Shivarov, the Ukrainian GPU censor, saw *Ivan* at a closed screening the next day and interpreted several scenes in a negative light. In his view, the film portrayed the Soviet industrial revolution as chaotic in nature, presented the peasant-workers as unhappy and depicted Stepan Huba, the slacker, in a favourable manner. Although Shivarov could not comprehend some of the film's critical scenes because he did not know Ukrainian, he approved the film. In his interpretation, Dovzhenko's depiction of the transformation of the peasant psychology under the leadership of the proletariat overshadowed the film's flaws.[52] Although Shivarov did think the film could have been more persuasive, he recommended its release.

The censor's approval, however, did not guarantee a positive reception. Articles critical of Dovzhenko soon appeared. Fedir Taran, a former Borotbist now in the Communist Party's good graces, sharply attacked *Ivan* in the pages of *Kino* and *Komunist* for 'distorting Ukrainian reality' and for 'not being Bolshevik enough'.[53] He did not provide details. Maxim Gorky, the future head of the Soviet Writers' Union, later called *Ivan* 'chaotic'.[54] In his 1939 autobiographical statement, Dovzhenko claimed that Skrypnyk accused him of fascism.[55] He never revealed on what grounds.

Ivan represented Dovzhenko's opportunity to redeem himself politically after *Earth*, an opportunity he failed to grasp. The film-maker, according to his radical Ukrainian critics, had not achieved political reliablity. That said, no matter how damning their charges, they could not torpedo the film.

Ukrainfilm's administrators became nervous. Aware that any decision they would make might haunt them in the future, they ordered Dovzhenko, Solntseva and Hryhory Zeldovych, the film's editor, to travel to Moscow and wait there until members of the 'highest circles' decided *Ivan*'s fate.[56] Beginning in mid-November, the trio spent nearly six weeks in the Soviet capital.[57] They lived at the Metropol Hotel on Sverdlov Square and waited for the decision. While Solntseva entertained her friends at the hotel, Dovzhenko and Zeldovych visited the Tretiakov Gallery on a daily basis. According to Zeldovych, Stalin and the Politburo reviewed *Ivan* and approved its release.[58]

Despite the Stalinist elite's approval, the Ukrainian authorities continued to harrass Ukraine's most famous film director. After *Ivan*, the Kiev Film Institute refused to allow Dovzhenko to direct a seminar on its premises. Slowly and quietly, the Kiev Film Studio removed him from his administrative positions and dispersed his regular film crew. Dovzhenko became isolated. According to one of his biographers, he experienced 'daily nerve-racking encounters with the authorities, petty insults, false accusations, and reproaches'.[59]

By the end of 1932, Dovzhenko began to fear for his life. According to two of Dovzhenko's biographers, the security organs in Ukraine prepared a warrant for his arrest. The film-maker found out about this warrant as well as a list of Ukrainian cultural figures 'to be liquidated', in which his name appeared among the first few entries.[60] For some unexplained reason the leaders of the security organs hesitated and their indecision saved the film-maker, who left for Moscow.

On 30 December 1932 Dovzhenko spent an evening at Eisenstein's, where he met the Russian playwright Vsevolod Vishnevsky. In his diary, Vishnevsky mentioned that the Ukrainian film-maker spoke about his problems with *Ivan* and said that the attacks on the film upset him.

> He thinks: what should I do? He has ideas about new films, *Nicholas II* (a tragic satire), *Siberia*, and about the 1914–1918 war (in order to commemorate its twentieth anniversary). He is searching for new ways to present words (by soundtrack plus by special titles). He speaks bitterly of the film community.[61]

Although Dovzhenko's colleagues in Ukraine denounced the film-maker, those in Moscow and Georgia may have saved his life. After spending November and December of 1932 in Moscow waiting for the appropriate committees to review and release *Ivan*, he received an invitation from Georgian film-makers to visit them. In early January 1933, Dovzhenko travelled to the Caucasian republic to lecture, screen his new film, and edit a Georgian film-maker's latest project.[62]

After concluding his consultations in Tbilisi, he travelled to Abkhazia, where he planned to stay at a sanatorium in Sukhumi until 20 January 1933.[63] In Sukhumi, the capital of Abkhazia and a resort on the Black Sea, Dovzhenko's health deteriorated. Here he learned that the collective farm in Sosnytsia had expelled his aged parents.[64]

In a letter to Sokoliansky, the film-maker admitted that his own actions most likely led to his parents' expulsion. Feeling badly about placing his parents in harm's way and fearing for his own life, Dovzhenko fell into a deep depression.[65] He could not work creatively and claimed that he possessed 'feelings of hatred and unending grief. I have lost my balance and peace ... I often feel that I am not capable of anything ... I expected to work for another fifty years.' In addition to this emotional distress, Dovzhenko experienced a dangerous enlargement of his heart.[66]

Questions concerning his health and survival tortured Dovzhenko. By December 1932 the security organs expanded their work in Ukraine.[67] They arrested many of Dovzhenko's friends and colleagues, most prominently Danylo Demutsky, his favourite cameraman.[68] In Sukhumi, the film-maker had to make a difficult choice. He loved Ukraine as his home, his birthplace, his psychological sanctuary and the source of his creativity. He could not imagine living anywhere else but he realised that to return to Ukraine meant certain arrest, imprisonment and possibly execution. In his letter to Sokoliansky, he predicted that the Ukrainian party leadership 'will accuse me of sabotage and wrecking. I do not expect much good for myself. I'll tell you more. Whenever I think that I need to return to Kharkiv, I become ill.'[69]

Bowing to circumstances, Dovzhenko moved to Moscow. The Soviet capital offered not only a refuge from persecution in Ukraine, but also an opportunity to work creatively. He had close friends and respected colleagues there. The Moscow Film Studios might offer him a position, and Solntseva, moreover, possessed a Moscow residence permit.

Although these factors played an important role, they took on a secondary status in light of the high-level intervention that took place on his behalf. One of Dovzhenko's biographers claimed that Boris Shumiatsky, the head of Souizkino from 1930 to 1937, invited him to Moscow and introduced him to Stalin.[70] No other source verifies this assertion. In the above-mentioned letter to Sokoliansky, Dovzhenko wrote, 'Stetsky told me that I should work in Moscow.'[71]

A. I. Stetsky headed the Central Committee's Agitation and Propaganda Committee.[72] As the party's man in charge of cultural matters (including the cinema), a field in which officials outside Stalin's inner circle played an important role in formulating policies, he, according to Dovzhenko, helped the film-maker.[73] We do not know the date or the substance of this alleged conversation in which Stetsky advised Dovzhenko to relocate to Moscow. Stetsky's suggestion may have originated from Stalin's proposal.[74] It remains unclear whether Shumiatsky, Stetsky, or both in tandem approached Dovzhenko, or if Stalin knew about this invitation.

Dovzhenko remained confused in January 1933. Physically and psychologically exhausted, he expressed his frustration to Sokoliansky: 'I do not know. I repeat that at this point I am not capable of working.'[75] He may have felt unable to work creatively, but his sense of self-preservation demanded that he take action.

Ultimately, Dovzhenko's decision to move to the Soviet capital centred not on the creative possibilities in Moscow, but on the question of survival. In order to create, he needed to survive. In order to survive, he needed to compromise his vision. He knew that the authorities in Moscow would closely monitor and limit his artistic expression, but he may have justified his move by imagining that he would improve upon these limitations, in the same way that he planned to redevelop the Brest-Litovsk Highway and other streets and squares in Kiev. The film-maker would accept the price of constant negotiation in order to place his narratives on the screen. In his mind, the act of creation, however hampered, remained superior to no creation at all.

By the end of January 1933, Dovzhenko had left Abkhazia for Moscow. Because the political authorities in Ukraine 'hated and continually harassed' him, he 'fled to Moscow'.[76] He wrote:

> Immediately after arriving in Moscow, I wrote a letter to Comrade J. Stalin with great emotion and asked him to protect me and help me develop creatively. Comrade Stalin heard my plea. If I had not appealed to him promptly, I would have certainly perished both as an artist and as a citizen. I would no longer be alive. I did not immediately grasp this, but now I shall never forget it, and every time I think of this great and noble man I am filled with a feeling of profound filial gratitude and respect for him.[77]

Writing a letter to a potential patron, especially one as powerful as Stalin, became the Soviet intelligentsia's standard way of communicating requests by the early 1930s. Letter writers needed to compose carefully each letter's salutation, contents, and ending. They needed to pay serious attention to its overall tone.[78]

The film-maker never disclosed when he wrote this letter to Stalin. He never summarised its contents. Moreover, he did not reveal whether he wrote it on his own initiative or whether someone, perhaps Stetsky or Shumiatsky, suggested that he do so.[79] Dovzhenko understood that Stalin knew of him and had seen his films, *Arsenal* and *Ivan* at least, and possibly *Earth*.[80] He had nothing to lose by turning to the general secretary, by becoming a supplicant. Whatever its origins and exact contents, the letter succeeded in its mission. Dovzhenko joined the Moscow Film Studio (Mosfilm) shortly after he wrote his letter and experienced no immediate political problems in Moscow.[81]

After years of harassment in Ukraine, Dovzhenko desired to fit in and desperately sought physical and psychological security. He turned to Stalin, and the general secretary probably saved Dovzhenko's life.

Eisenstein and Dovzhenko

Stetsky's and Shumiatsky's investment in Dovzhenko paid off. By 1935 Dovzhenko, desperate to avoid arrest, yielded to the new faith and rehabilitated himself politically. Already, in 1934, the Ukrainian film-maker had started to work on *Aerograd*, which promised to become his most socialist realist film. In January 1935 he addressed the conference of Soviet cinematographers.

The All-Union Conference of the Creative Workers of Soviet Cinematography met in Moscow from 8 to 13 January 1935. Intended as a belated celebration of the fifteenth anniversary of the August 1919 decree nationalising the film studios, and as a means of establishing for film-makers the guidelines on socialist realism adopted at the First Congress of Soviet Writers in August 1934, this conference began two months after *Chapaev*'s successful release. Here, Communist Party leaders and film administrators sought to motivate the members of the first Soviet generation of film-makers, especially Eisenstein, to make socialist realist films.

Eisenstein's political career in the 1930s paralleled Dovzhenko's. Eisenstein had been abroad from August 1929 until May 1932 and despite his best efforts in Hollywood and in other movie capitals had not produced a film since *The Old and the New* in 1929. After his return to the USSR, he taught the course on film direction at Moscow's All-Union State Institute of Cinematography (VGIK), and proposed several projects to Shumiatsky, who vetoed them. He continued to prepare his theoretical publications and did not make any progress in making a new film. By January 1935 Eisenstein had been back two-and-a-half years and still did not have a film in production.

After the party's spokesman opened the meeting, Eisenstein gave a rambling talk on theoretical matters, not practical ones, as everyone had expected. Most damagingly, he did not provide enough self-criticism.[82] In response, Eisenstein's colleagues sharply attacked the man most closely identified with the beginnings of Soviet film art.

Different directors, at different stages of rehabilitation, responded differently to the conference's mission. Some merely confessed previous errors and promised to

Dovzhenko with Sergei Eisenstein at the First All-Union Conference of the Creative Workers of Soviet Cinematography (January, 1935)

create socialist realist films in the future. Others, such as Leonid Trauberg, who with Grigory Kozintsev directed the politically acceptable *Alone* (1931) and *Maxim's Youth* (1935), took the lead in criticising those who had yet to pass the threshold. Trauberg accused the pioneers of Soviet film-making – Eisenstein, Dovzhenko, Pudovkin, Kuleshov, and Vertov – of becoming 'wax figures', who coasted on the accomplishments of their past but who had yet to produce socialist realist films.[83]

Although the conference speakers criticised each other, they concentrated their fire on Eisenstein, 'the genius master and often-mistaken theoretician'.[84] Most of the speakers knew of Shumiatsky's critical attitude towards this 'difficult' artist and expressed their remarks with a mixture of love, pity, fear and political correctness.[85] Although everyone praised *Potemkin*, they expressed regret, irritation and anger with the director's inability to produce a socialist realist film. Inasmuch as the party defined socialist realism in broad, almost incomprehensible terms, the conference's participants hoped to persuade Eisenstein to join them in their search to master the new orientation. They, after all, had much to learn from each other's mistakes and achievements.

Dovzhenko's talk at the conference reflected this delicate balance. Although he acknowledged that Soviet cinematography should have accomplished more in its fifteen-year existence, he criticised Trauberg's perspective of evaluating the achievements of the past from the vantage point of the present. Identifying the problems in Soviet cinema with his own problems, he asserted: 'I do not want to assess our creative history as a series of errors and mistakes, which I should spit on. I want to view it as approaching the truth. From this perspective, even mistakes are dear to me, just as are my achievements.'[86]

Dovzhenko's position, albeit unwilling, as a propagator of the official Stalinist position brought considerable stress, both external and internal. Not only did he have to adjust to a sea of political vicissitudes, but also had to endure the emotional and physical distress resulting from his various efforts of compromise and adaptation. At times he became moody, introspective and harshly critical of his own work:

> ... every one of my films brought me serious problems. I am to blame for this in many ways. I still dream about creating an authentic, great Bolshevik-minded, healthy in content, deep and vigorous film ... If I improve and extend my future work, I will be happy. But if my work and my sincerity does not produce the necessary results, I will regard this as my tragedy ...[87]

For Dovzhenko, the road to socialist realism built on the achievements of the past and on those of the present, such as *Maxim's Youth* and *Chapaev*. He then applied this perspective to Eisenstein, who had always supported his work:

We know Eisenstein's place in cinematography, we know his past and present. We await his further contributions to cinematography. But yesterday, his report disturbed me. On the one hand, Eisenstein presented himself as a deeply principled master and thinker ... but on the other hand, Eisenstein failed [to tell us what he plans to do]. At this point he does not occupy the position in cinematography that he could. Standing here by his side and loving him devotedly, I will tell you and him my views of his creative work. I do not want Eisenstein to tell us about Polynesian women. All of this is too far from our concerns ... life is too short. I think that Eisenstein should examine the living women who surround us. They are closer to us and they are much more important. Comrades, I hope that you will understand the metaphor as intended. When I listened to Eisenstein's talk, I feared that he knows so much, that he has a very logical mind and that it looks as if he will not produce another film. If I knew so much as he does, I would die [laughter, applause]. You laugh in vain. I hope that Eisenstein will not chew up his own tail. I am also afraid that his laboratory may blow up from an overwhelming confusion of complicated, mysterious, and enigmatic material.

I'm convinced that in more ways than one his erudition is killing him. No! Please excuse me, that's the wrong word. I do want to say: disorganizing him. I think that Eisenstein's work, a new film, is absolutely necessary for us and for him. Sergei Mikhailovich, if you do not produce a film within a year, then do not work on one at all. After a year's time, it won't be needed by you or by us. But now it is necessary for us, like air. With your film you should untie all the disputed knots around your person. You should unravel the entire 'Freudian complex'. It is necessary to put an end to it all. I think the film you will make will have an enormous impact ...

Trauberg's dispute with Eisenstein is unpleasant for me. I am uncomfortable with what I will say. I have done everything to soften what I wanted to say so that S. M. does not feel too badly. But it is necessary for him to understand that there is a tremendous job ahead of him. For me, Sergei Mikhailovich, your picture is worth ten times more than all of your theories. I will exchange all talk about Polynesian women and all of your unfinished scripts for one of your films, which you will show us without an introduction.[88]

Taken in their complete context, Dovzhenko's comments at the conference appear kinder and contain more respect for Eisenstein than those expressed by the other speakers.[89] Riding on the success of *Chapaev*, Sergei Vasiliev, Eisenstein's former student, claimed that his former teacher should abandon his interest in 'exotic' films and should establish contact with the masses in order to make films understandable to them.[90]

Other film-makers, such as Lev Kuleshov, sent Eisenstein mixed messages. Referring to Dovzhenko's and Yutkevich's criticisms of Eisenstein's intellectual interests, Kuleshov asserted: 'Dear Sergei Mikhailovich, no one ever burst from too much knowledge, but from too much envy.'[91] Despite his recognition of the personal

factor in criticism directed against Eisenstein, Kuleshov claimed that directors need
to follow party directives concerning the arts and that they should construct a 'Bolshevik cinematography'. He then asserted:

> And all those who do not understand this will be swept (*sketenye*) away by the
> revolutionary socialist leadership, just as the cans in Pudovkin's *Genghis-Khan* were
> swept away. Life is ruthless toward those who are not able to go into the night with the
> party. These people, perhaps even the most individually talented people — will be
> struck out of Soviet cinematography.[92]

These rhetorical remarks, delivered in early January 1935, six weeks after the
assassination of Sergei Kirov, the head of the Leningrad party organisation, and after
the first wave of mass arrests, dovetailed with Dovzhenko's criticisms.

Dovzhenko's comments regarding his colleague at the cinema conference appear
unheroic from our current vantage point, when it is easy to make moral judgments.
Having been brutally humiliated after *Earth* and *Ivan*, the Ukrainian film-maker
sought rehabilitation and speaking out in defence of Eisenstein could have placed his
career and life in considerable jeopardy. He could no longer use his surroundings to
negotiate a more favourable outcome for himself. Now he could only react and hope.

Dovzhenko's attempt to rehabilitate himself by rehabilitating Eisenstein demonstrates the tenuousness of his situation, which constantly changed in the Stalinist
environment. Because of his nationalist background and his experiences with *Earth*
and *Ivan*, he could not support Eisenstein during the 1935 cinema conference, during the heated attacks on Eisenstein's *Bezhin Meadow* in March 1937, and certainly
not during the attacks on Eisenstein's *Ivan the Terrible, Part Two* in 1946.

At the 1935 cinema workers' conference, Eisenstein's colleagues demanded that
he join the socialist realist bandwagon. The Soviet government agreed. On 11 January 1935 Soviet newspapers announced that the Soviet government issued awards
marking the fifteenth anniversary of Soviet film-making. Eisenstein did not receive
the highest honour, the Order of Lenin, which Shumiatsky, G. Vasiliev, S. Vasiliev,
Pudovkin, Dovzhenko, Kozintsev, Trauberg, and others collected. Eisenstein did not
acquire the Order of the Red Star, which Vertov won. Instead, Eisenstein earned
the lowest honour, the title of Honoured Art Worker.[93]

This public slight reflected Shumiatsky's dislike of Eisenstein as well as the director's failure to prove himself as a socialist realist director. Eisenstein had not yet got
into the programme. Dovzhenko had.

Aerograd

After the Ukrainian film-maker moved to Moscow, he hoped to make films dealing
with historical topics. Having received tremendous criticism for *Earth* and then *Ivan*,

films set in the present, Dovzhenko must have realised that he could better inter-
pret the politics of the past than decipher the subtle twists and turns of the Stalinist
leadership.

Mosfilm, however, demanded a film dealing with a contemporary subject. After
several months spent assessing his options, in June 1933, Dovzhenko decided to
film a narrative set in the Soviet Far East and revealed his decision to his friends.
On 25 July 1933 Dovzhenko spoke at the All-Union Conference for Planning
Themes in Feature Films in Moscow about his film, titled *Aerograd*.[94]

At the same conference, Alexander Fadeev, the former head of the Russian Association of Proletarian Writers (RAPP), a former critic of Dovzhenko's *Arsenal*, and the
future general secretary of the Soviet Writers' Union (1939–54), delivered a presentation on the need to include depictions of the Far East in literature and
film-making.[95] Previousy, he had written *The Rout* (1927), a novel in which Red partisans fought the Whites and the Japanese in this desolate region. In 1933 he began
to write *The Last One from Udege*, a novel also dealing with the Far East. Dovzhenko
and Fadeev decided to collaborate.

The two planned to work on a screenplay about events in the Far East, a politically
safe topic. In light of the Japanese invasion of Manchuria in 1931, the Soviet Far
East's 5,000 kilometre border with China, Manchuria and the Pacific Ocean needed
reinforcement.[96] This immense area, rich with natural resources, had never before
served as the setting for a film. Dovzhenko understood that the majority of Soviet citizens did not 'know what a colossal territory it is, equaling . . . six or seven Ukraines'.[97]

This collaborative effort with Fadeev and the choice of setting reflected a brilliant
move on Dovzhenko's part. Working with Fadeev, Dovzhenko bolstered his own
political reliability in the eyes of his critics. The Ukrainian director and the Russian
author, representing two of the most important arts, 'united their creative aspirations in fulfilling the tasks of the party', especially in popularising the Soviet need
to secure the Far East.[98] More importantly for Dovzhenko, *Aerograd* would not deal
with Ukraine, a politically suspect subject. By concentrating on the Soviet Far East,
Dovzhenko would demonstrate his loyalty as a Soviet citizen, avoiding the taint of
Ukrainian nationalism. As things turned out, however, Dovzhenko kept Ukraine at
centre stage.

On 6 September 1933 Dovzhenko began a four-month expedition with Fadeev and
Solntseva to explore the Far East. They arrived in Khabarovsk and then visited Biro-
bidzhan, Nikolaevsk-on-the-Amur, Sakhalin, Vladivostok, Suchan and Kashkarovka,
returning to Moscow on 10 January 1934.[99] In his 1939 autobiography, Dovzhenko
wrote:

> This trip was a radiant event in my life. I was enraptured by the country's vast spaces,
> incredible riches, and beauty. I traveled five hundred kilometers along the Pacific Coast

and never ceased to be amazed at what I saw. Standing on the shore of the Pacific Ocean and looking west, I thought of Ukraine. In my mind's eye it rose to its true grandeur somewhere far away in the southwest. The vision strengthened my pride in being a citizen of the vast Soviet country.[100]

Reacting like most strangers in a strange land, he sought to find something familiar. Not surprisingly, Dovzhenko sought out Ukrainians who had migrated east at the end of the nineteenth century and the beginning of the twentieth. Solntseva wrote in her memoirs, 'We decided to go see the Far East, to the Green Wedge, where many Ukrainians who once left Ukraine lived … We passed many villages and saw much. Here the majority of the population consisted of Ukrainians and Old Believers and the villages had names such as Kiev, Poltava, and Uman.'[101] Even in the isolated Far East, Dovzhenko tried to find a connection with Ukraine and with Ukrainians. But because the Soviet authorities considered Ukrainian culture politically suspect by the early 1930s, Dovzhenko judged these Ukrainian connections – even in the Soviet Far East – too dangerous to include in his film.

While Dovzhenko considered the Far East foreign and exotic, Fadeev called it home; he had been born there. When the writer returned to his native village, the poverty depressed him. As Fadeev saw it, the Far East had not yet experienced the socialist construction that had occurred in the European part of the Soviet Union. Wanting to help his compatriots, the writer sought a realistic portrayal of the Soviet Far East's poverty in the planned screenplay.[102]

Dovzhenko's creative criteria would not allow this depiction. In his film, he wanted to portray this exotic and geopolitically important region as an integral part of the radiant Communist future, not to deal with the poverty of the present.[103] Having learned from the political criticisms of *Earth* and *Ivan*, the film-maker understood the principles of socialist realism far better than Fadeev.

In the course of this trip, Dovzhenko and Fadeev could not agree on the script. Dovzhenko had always been a difficult collaborator and often refused to compromise. He would not make an exception for this film, which he saw as a vehicle for his political rehabilitation. Believing that he could best define the film and write its script alone, he parted ways with Fadeev. The film-maker had gathered the material he needed, he had used Fadeev as a political cover, and now he understood what he needed to do to shoot a politically successful film.

Dovzhenko and Solntseva returned to Moscow in early January 1934. The film-maker then wrote the screenplay in two and a half months. After Mosfilm approved his script in the spring, he left Moscow for the Far East at the end of June with a new film crew to shoot several scenes.[104] Edward Tisse, Eisenstein's cameraman, replaced Dovzhenko's long-term friend and associate, the politically suspect Danylo Demutsky.[105]

Dovzhenko (behind the camera) and his film crew shooting *Aerograd* (1934 or 1935)

The hero, Stepan Glushak (Symon Shahaida), guards
the Soviet frontier (*Aerograd*, 1935)

The director and his crew completed their second expedition to the Far East on 4 November 1934.[106] After a year's editing, *Aerograd* premiered in Moscow on 6 November 1935 and in Kiev on 9 November.[107] Why it took Dovzhenko nearly a year to edit his film remains unclear, but it seems reasonable to assume that he, who felt rushed in editing his last films, needed breathing space. He wanted to make sure that this film would work politically as well as creatively.

Dovzhenko created *Aerograd* as a contemporary frontier adventure set in the Soviet Far East, an isolated region often penetrated by the Japanese after their invasion of Manchuria in the 1930s. The film deals with the efforts of the hunter Stepan Glushak, a Civil War veteran, and his neighbours to secure their heavily forested region. As the film opens, Glushak ambushes a group of Japanese infiltrators. He then trails one of the surviving Japanese officers through the taiga to the home of Vasily Khudiakov, Glushak's oldest friend, who hides the enemy. When Glushak asks Khudiakov if he has seen any strangers recently, Khudiakov, like the apostle Peter, denies any encounter whatsoever three times. Having known Khudiakov for fifty years, Glushak does not challenge his friend's claim, but he feels uneasy as he heads home. He realises that either his once-sharp eyes or Khudiakov have deceived him.

Meanwhile, in a neighbouring village dominated by Old Believers, an anti-establishment sect, a Russian counter-revolutionary persuades the villagers to form a paramilitary unit and join forces with Khudiakov and the Japanese officer in his protection. Once Glushak and his neighbours uncover the conspiracy, they attack

Another anti-Soviet conspiracy: a Japanese infiltrator allies himself with counter-revolutionaries by kissing the Old Believer priest's crucifix (*Aerograd*, 1935)

the Old Believer village and crush the uprising. After the fierce battle, Glushak cold-bloodedly executes Khudiakov, paving the way for the Soviet government to build the modern city of Aerograd, which in turn would secure control of the Soviet Far East.[108]

Building on the ideological underpinnings, assumptions, and presuppositions of the Vasilievs' film, *Aerograd* reflected the political hysteria fanned by the Stalinists after Kirov's murder on 1 December 1934, when the secret police went on the political offensive, arresting, trying and executing all suspected enemies.[109] Mass xenophobia and paranoia became commonplace. With the emergence of Fascist Italy, Nazi Germany and Imperial Japan by the mid-1930s, the Soviet leadership reassessed its political isolation in the world. By promoting films with 'wreckers, saboteurs, spies, traitors, Trotskyites, and foreign opponents', Soviet cinema raised the level of political anxiety in the USSR, preparing to repeat the orchestrated 'war scare' of 1927.[110]

Aerograd fitted this model. By narrating the settlement of the Far East and the threat of foreign (especially Japanese) intervention, Dovzhenko helped Soviet audiences visualise the danger of 'capitalist encirclement'. In addition to raising tensions about foreign interventionists, *Aerograd* presented the issue of domestic enemies and their collaboration with potential invaders. At the heart of this film lies the question of political loyalty, not only of the fictionalised characters on the screen, but of Dovzhenko as well.

'Whose side are you on?' Dovzhenko asked. In an era when the Soviet mass media relentlessly praised Pavlik Morozov, the boy who denounced his parents to the secret police, and when one could face imprisonment for failing to denounce a family member's disloyalty to the Soviet state, Dovzhenko probed the long-term friendship between Glushak and Khudiakov. Would their friendship induce Glushak to ignore Khudiakov's treason?

'No,' Dovzhenko replied resoundingly. In a scene reminiscent of that in *Arsenal* in which the Bolshevik executes the Ukrainian nationalist at point-blank range, Glushak shoots his friend in the same manner. Inasmuch as killing one's friend entails a certain personal sacrifice, Glushak's action represents a greater service to the state than the Bolshevik's in *Arsenal*. *Aerograd*'s main protagonist emerges as a 'positive hero', who possesses a higher class-consciousness than Ivan. Glushak, after all, possesses nerves of steel and does not question the necessity of executing his oldest friend, who has betrayed the USSR. Adherence to the Soviet state supercedes loyalty to one's friends or family, the film self-righteously declares. Traitors deserve execution at point-blank range.

Dovzhenko propagated this message to demonstrate his own devotion to the new Stalinist order. Exhausted from the attacks on *Earth* and *Ivan*, he learned from the successes and failures of his colleagues at implementing the socialist realist model on screen.

Although *Aerograd* presented a politically correct message, the film failed artistically. Dovzhenko could not decide on the basic theme of the film. He concentrated on the exotic aspects of the Far East, such as the expansive forests, the saboteurs and the fanatical Old Believers, and not on the construction of the new city of Aerograd, which never appeared in his film. Although critics praised the poetic nature of the film, *Aerograd* did not attract a large audience. Some viewers, according to the Russian film critic Rostislav Iurenev, found its complex metaphorical language difficult to understand.[111] Other viewers, such as Hryhory Kostiuk, found Dovzhenko's message depressing. Kostiuk, a Ukrainian literary critic, saw *Aerograd* while imprisoned in the Vorkyta concentration camp, where he served his sentence from 1935 to 1940. In his memoirs, he described his reaction:

> I left the screening hall in a disturbed state. The film contained everything: a talented depiction of the beauty and immensity of the open spaces of the Soviet Far East, the iron columns of the frontier troops, their commanders' menacing features, the superhuman docility of the soldiers, the diligence of the NKVD informers, the power of aerodromes, and the fearlessness of the Soviet squadrons which patrol the Pacific Ocean under the clouds and which secure the USSR's borders. In one word, the film contained everything which government propaganda needed, but it did not show the creator of *Earth* and *Ivan*. There was no great artist, there were no living, psychologically complex, but always moving Dovzhenko heroes. I left the theater in a sad state. I had the feeling that I had attended the funeral of our great 'poet of the cinema'.[112]

The same factors that disappointed Kostiuk helped *Aerograd* become Dovzhenko's first film in nearly a decade to open without controversy.[113] Inasmuch as it celebrated Soviet patriotism and presented Glushak's execution of his best friend as a 'positive' act, some critics called it 'one of the most significant films of our cinematography'.[114] Even before its release, this film had politically rehabilitated Dovzhenko and revived his career.

Moving to Moscow paid off. Not only did he save himself, he continued to create. In order to do so, he had to tame his creative voice and embrace the constraints of a hazily defined model of film-making. His transformation came slowly and painfully. While *Aerograd* marked Dovzhenko's political comeback, his next film, *Shchors* (1939), manifested his political triumph.

Notes

1. *Storinky*, pp. 77–82. In light of the critical evaluation of Dovzhenko by the security organs in 1930, it is unclear who allowed him to travel abroad. For this negative assessment, see *D*, pp. 34–5; *ZA*, p. 257. For trends in the film industry, see Douglas Gomery, *Movie History: A Survey* (Belmont, CA, 1991), pp. 166–7.

2. O. Dovzhenko, *Tvory v p'iaty tomakh* (Kiev, 1966), vol. 5, p. 329; *Storinky*, p. 81.
3. Dovzhenko, *Tvory*, vol. 5 (1966), pp. 333–4; *Storinky*, p. 83.
4. George O. Liber, *Soviet Nationality Policy, Urban Growth, and Identity Change in the Ukrainian SSR, 1923–1934* (Cambridge and New York, 1992), chapters 4–5.
5. Paul R. Magocsi, *A History of Ukraine* (Seattle, WA, 1996), p. 564.
6. Repression 'had reduced the membership of the Ukrainian party from 433,500 in 1934 to 285,800 in 1938'. *Ocherki po istorii Kommunisticheskoi partii Ukrainy* (Kiev, 1964); cited in Roy Medvedev, *Let History Judge: The Origins and Consequences of Stalinism* (rev. and expanded edition, New York, 1989), p. 412.
7. For an example of such a pronouncement, see 'Stenogramma vystupleniia tov. Postysheva P. P. na zasedanii orgburo ot 8. III. 1936 g. po voprosy o rabote Soiuza pisatelei (Ukrainy)', RGASPI, 88/1/603, pp. 5–8.
8. 'Kartina ogromnoi khudozhestvennoi tsennosti. Tov. Feliks Kon o rabote tov. Dovzhenko', *Komsomol'skaia pravda*, 8 April 1930.
9. '1939 Autobiography', p. 22.
10. *Storinky*, pp. 86, 87.
11. G. A. Mariagin, 'Legendy k biografii Dovzhenko', RGALI, 2081/1/1158, pp. 15–16.
12. '1939 Autobiography', p. 23.
13. '1939 Autobiography', p. 23.
14. Dovzhenko repeated this interpretation in another place: 'I needed to work on this film for another two months. I made mistakes in the selection of actors'. RGALI, 2081/1/363, pp. 18–19.
15. Ian Kuchera, 'Spivets' revoliutsii', *DIS*, p. 84.
16. *Service*, p. 89; Anne D. Rassweiler, *The Generation of Power: The History of Dneprostroi* (New York and Oxford, 1988).
17. Sergei Eisenstein, *Iskusstvo kino*, no. 4 (1955), p. 86; for memoirs of the filming of the scenery for *Ivan*, see Leonid Kokhno, 'Ivan', *DMM*, File 5.
18. Peter Kenez, *Cinema and Soviet Society, 1917–1953* (Cambridge and New York, 1992), p. 168.
19. V. Pudovkin, 'Liniia ogromnogo soprotivlenniia', *Kino*, 26 November, 1932, p. 2; S. Iutkevich, 'Puti razvitiia', *Kino*, 26 November, 1932, p. 2; and N. Shengelaia, 'Filma obrazov i idei', *Kino*, 26 November, 1932, p. 2.
20. R. N. Iurenev, *Aleksandr Dovzhenko* (Moscow, 1959), p. 59; Serhii Plachynda, *Oleksandr Dovzhenko: Zhyttia i tvorchist'* (Kiev, 1964), p. 116.
21. Ivan Koshelivets', *Oleksandr Dovzhenko: Sproba tvorchoi biohrafii* (Munich, 1980), pp. 167–8.

22. Workers had actually finished the first stage of Dneprostroi's construction, the installation of five generators, on 10 October 1932, three weeks before Dovzhenko completed editing *Ivan*. See Rassweiler, pp. 10, 188; and *Storinky*, p. 87.
23. RGALI, 2081/1/354, pp. 28–9.
24. TsSU SSSR, otdel perepisi, *Vsesoiuznaia perepis' naseleniia 1926 goda* (Moscow, 1929), vol. 11.
25. A. Dovzhenko, 'Pochemu "Ivan"?', *Kino* (M), 24 November 1932, p. 2.
26. V. Grossman-Roshchin, 'Malenkoe ili bol'shoe?', *Kino*, 26 November 1932, p. 2.
27. Barbara D. Leaming, 'Engineers of Human Souls – The Transition to Socialist Realism in the Soviet Cinema of the 1930s' (unpublished PhD dissertation, New York University, 1976), p. 207.
28. Boris Groys, *The Total Art of Stalinism: Avant-Garde, Aesthetic Dictatorship, and Beyond* (Princeton, NJ, 1992), p. 33.
29. *Pervyi Vsesoiuznyi s'ezd sovetskikh pisatelei 1934: Stenograficheskii otchet* (Moscow, 1934; reprint: Moscow, 1990), p. 712.
30. Katerina Clark coined this phrase in analysing the paradox of socialist realism. See her *The Soviet Novel: History as Ritual*, 3rd ed. (Bloomington, IN, and London (as no other publishers mentioned) 2000), p. 37.
31. Clark, pp. 4–5.
32. Clark, p. 6.
33. Clark, pp. 255–60.
34. Abram Tertz [Andrei Siniavsky], *The Trial Begins and On Socialist Realism* (New York, 1960), p. 200.
35. See Regine Robin, *Socialist Realism: An Impossible Aesthetic* (Stanford, CA, 1992).
36. Matthew Cullerne Bown, *Art Under Stalin* (New York, 1991), p. 90.
37. Groys, p. 19.
38. Clark, *The Soviet Novel: History as Ritual*, 1st ed. (Chicago, 1981), p. 46.
39. Tertz, pp. 172–3.
40. A. Dovzhenko, 'Pochemu "Ivan"?', p. 2.
41. *Service*, p. 90.
42. 'Ustav Soiuza sovetskikh pisatelei SSSR', in *Pervyi Vsesoiuznyi s'ezd sovetskikh pisatelei 1934*, p. 712.
43. Kenez, *Cinema and Soviet Society*, p. 158.
44. After Iutkevich's and Ermler's *Counterplan* emerged as the first model Soviet socialist realist film in 1932, Ivan Kavaleridze's *The Kolii Rebellion* (1933) Arnold Kordium's *The Last Port* (1934) and Leonid Lukov's *Youth* (1934) became the first socialist realist films produced in Ukraine. A. E. Zhukova,

'Ukrainskoe sovetskoe kinoiskusstvo (1930–1934)', RGALI, 2081/1/1130, p. 18.

45. Kenez, *Cinema and Soviet Society*, pp. 172–6.

46. Leaming, pp. 128–9.

47. Leaming, p. 137.

48. *Storinky*, p. 88.

49. Ivan Sokoliansky to Julia Solntseva (December 1956), RGALI, 2081/1/1547, p. 7.

50. One of Dovzhenko's friends recounted an apocryphal account (which he undoubtedly received from the film-maker himself) of a conversation the director allegedly had in 1933 with Vsevolod Balytsky, the head of the Ukrainian GPU, a member of the Communist Party of Ukraine's Politburo, and the man who cleaned up the Soviet Ukrainian Embassy in Warsaw in late 1921. 'You know, Alexander Petrovych,' said Balytsky, 'a number of people are not pleased with your success in film-making … Many well-known people tie your name with nationalism. Of course, it's absurd, no one can concretely say how it manifests itself.' Mariagin, 'Legendy k biografii Dovzhenko', p. 17. Inasmuch as Dovzhenko left Ukraine in November 1932 (returning only for a short visit in May 1933, not coming back until 28 April 1935), and Balytsky arrived in Ukraine on or after 24 January 1933 (and served until late May 1937), this talk did not occur in 1933, if at all. Nevertheless, this alleged comment revealed much about the tensions between the film-maker's creative vision and Stalinist realities. On Dovzhenko's whereabouts between 6 November 1932 and 28 April 1935, see the best (but incomplete) account, *Storinky*, pp. 88–107 and *ZA*, p. 273. On Balytsky's – see R. Conquest, *Harvest of Sorrow* (London and New York, 1986), pp. 241–2, and Iurii Shapoval, Volodymyr Prystaiko and Vadim Zolotar'ov, *ChK-HPU-NKVD v Ukraini: osoby, fakty, dokumenty* (Kiev, 1997), pp. 21–78. Also see Dovzhenko's diary entry for 18 August 1949, where he cryptically refers to this incident, but places it in 1938 (an impossibility, inasmuch as the security organs arrested Balytsky in July 1937 and executed him on 27 November 1937). *UVOKShch*, p. 350; *Hospody*, p. 345; and *ZDUVOShch*, p. 471.

51. TsDA-MLMU, 1196/2/6, p. 1. For a set of documents describing how the central party organs evaluated films in 1933, see V. S. Listov, 'Nazvanie kazhdoi kartiny utverzhdaetsia komissiei orgbiuro', *KZ*, no. 31 (1996), pp. 108–30.

52. TsDA-MLMU, 1196/2/5, pp. 1–2.

53. F. T. 'Z pytan' pro fil'm "Ivan" O. Dovzhenka', TsDA-MLMU, 535/1/1000; *Kino* (Kiev), no. 19–20 (1932), pp. 10–13; and *Komunist*, 12, 15, 16 September 1932.

54. A. M. Gorky, 'Literatura i kino', *Literaturnaia gazeta*, 15 April 1935, p. 1.

55. '1939 Autobiography', pp. 22–4. I have not been able to find Skrypnyk's article. Dovzhenko's 1939 assertion sought to distance himself from his former chief six years after his suicide. As the People's Commissar of Education, Skrypnyk oversaw the Ukrainian film industry.

56. Hryhorii Zel'dovych, *'Zemlia' i liudy*, MDFS, p. 2.

57. *Storinky*, pp. 88–90.

58. Zel'dovych, p. 2.

59. Plachynda, *Oleksandr Dovzhenko*, p. 117.

60. Leonid Cherevatenko and Anatolii Lemysh, 'Dovzhenko v pritsele VChK-OGPU-NKVD-KGB: K stoletiia so dnia rozhdeniia A. P. Dovzhenko', *Kievskie vedomosti*, 3 September 1994. The authors, unfortunately, do not provide a source for this assertion.

61. Vsevolod Vishnevskii, *Stat'i, dnevniki, pis'ma o literature i iskusstve* (Moscow, 1961), p. 283.

62. See Dovzhenko's letter to Sokoliansky in Dovzhenko, *Tvory*, vol. 5 (1966), pp. 335–6; also cited in *Storinky*, p. 90. Both of these publications claim that the Ukrainian film-maker wrote this letter in December 1932 when he was in Georgia. But a Georgian film-maker places Dovzhenko's visit to his republic in January 1933: Siko Dolidze, 'To, chto dorogo sertsu', *Literaturnaia Gruziia*, no. 10 (1964), pp. 88–90; cited incorrectly in *Storinky*, p. 90, as appearing in *Literaturnaia Rossiia*, no. 10 (1964). I am grateful to Orest Pelech, the Slavic Bibliographer at Duke University, who provided me with the proper citation. Due to Dovzhenko's appearance at the All-Union State Institute of Cinematography (VGIK) in mid-December and at Eisenstein's on 30 December 1932, Dolidze's chronology is most likely more accurate.

63. Dovzhenko, *Tvory*, vol. 5 (1966), p. 335.

64. Dovzhenko, *Tvory*, vol. 5 (1966), p. 335. One author asserted that officials, claiming that Petro Dovzhenko was a 'kulak', expelled him from the collective farm. His neighbours opposed this measure, but could not overturn the decision. Petro Dovzhenko still worked hard and did not curse his neighbours. After Alexander Dovzhenko's intervention (Zasenko did not record the date), the authorities readmitted his father to the collective farm in Sosnytsia. Oleksa Zasenko, *Dorohi moi suchasnyky* (Kiev, 1983), pp. 143–4. I have been unable to verify this account. According to published NKVD documents, the Ukrainian Central Executive Committee in Kharkiv overturned the local decision to de-kulakise P. S. Dovzhenko. *D*, p. 33; *ZA*, p. 244.

65. Dovzhenko to I. O. Sokoliansky, TsDA-MLMU, 690/3/7, pp. 22–3; Dovzhenko, *Tvory*, vol. 5 (1966), pp. 335–6.

66. TsDA-MLMU, 690/3/7, p. 23; Dovzhenko, *Tvory*, vol. 5 (1966), p. 336.

67. There are many monographs on the repressions and purges in Ukraine. See, for example, Hryhory Kostiuk, *Stalinist Terror in the Ukraine: A Study of the Decade of Mass Terror (1929–1939)* (New York, 1960); '... *Z poroha smerti ...': Pys'mennyky Ukrainy – zhertvy stalins'kykh represii* (Kiev, 1991); O. I. Sydorenko and D. V. Tabachnyk, *Represovane 'vidrodzhennia'* (Kiev, 1993); and Ivan H. Bilas, *Represyvno-karal'na systema v Ukraini, 1917–1953: Suspil'no-politychnyi ta istoryko-pravovyi analiz* (Kiev, 1994), vol. 1, pp. 5–107 and vol. 2, pp. 9–128; and Ivan Il'ienko, *U zhornakh represii: opovidi pro ukrains'kykh pys'mennykiv (za arkhivamy DPU-NKVS)* (Kiev, 1995).

68. Demutsky's 1932 arrest is noted in his 1935 NKVD interrogation, TsDAHOU, 263/1/57017, k 1388, p. 14. See note 105.

69. TsDA-MLMU, 690/3/7, p. 23; Dovzhenko, *Tvory*, vol. 5 (1966), p. 336.

70. V. Pryhorovs'kyi, 'Dovzhenko i Stalin', *Komsomols'kyi hart* (Chernihiv), 4 June 1988, p. 7.

71. O. Dovzhenko, *Tvory*, vol. 5 (1966), p. 336.

72. Between 1930 and 1938, Aleksei Ivanovich Stetsky headed the Agitation and Propaganda Committee of the Central Committee of the All-Union Communist Party (VKP[b]). At the same time he served as the editor-in-chief of the theoretical journal, *Bolshevik*. Between 1934 and 1937 he served as a member of the Organisational Bureau (Orgburo) of the Central Committee of the CPSU. Biographical sketches of him appeared in RGASPI, 124/1/1859; *Geroi oktiabria: Biografii aktivnykh uchastnikov podgotovki i provedeniia Oktiabr'skogo vooruzhennogo vosstaniia v Petrograde* (Leningrad, 1967), pp. 444–5; V. K. Piatnitskii (compiler), *Golofa: Po materialam arkhivno-sledstvennogo dela no. 603 na Sokolovu–Piatnitskuiu Iu. I.* (St Petersburg, 1993), p. 154; and A. D. Chernev, *229 kremlevskikh vozhdei* (Moscow, 1996), p. 274. Stetsky, a renowned follower of Nikolai Bukharin, defected to Stalin, in March 1929. See Stephen F. Cohen, *Bukharin and the Bolshevik Revolution: A Political Biography, 1888–1938* (New York, 1973), pp. 220, 308.

73. I have been unable to verify if Stetsky had actually met with Dovzhenko. For the role of lower-ranking Communist officials in the creation of Soviet cultural policy, see A. Kemp-Welch, *Stalin and the Literary Intelligentsia, 1928–39* (New York, 1991), especially pp. 262–3, 268.

74. Koshelivets', p. 190.

75. TsDA-MLMU, 690/3/7, p. 23.

76. '1939 Autobiography', p. 24.

77. '1939 Autobiography', pp. 23–4.

78. Sheila Fitzpatrick, 'Intelligentsia and Power. Client–Patron Relations in Stalin's Russia', in Manfred Hildermeier and Elisabeth Muller-Luckner, eds,

Stalinismus vor dem Zweiten Weltkrieg. Neue Wege der Forschung/Stalinism Before the Second World War. New Avenues for Research (Munich, 1998), p. 45.

79. I have been unable to locate this letter. Perhaps it remains in the Stalin Archive at the Archive of the President of the Russian Federation.

80. At the November 1928 plenum of the Central Committee of the All-Union Communist Party in Moscow, Stalin – according to *Arsenal*'s composer, Ihor Belza – complimented Dovzhenko's film: 'A real revolutionary romance.' Ihor Belza, 'Avtor "Arsenalu"', *PZh*, p. 212. Zel'dovych implied that Stalin, a member of the 'highest circles', may have seen *Ivan* and decided its fate. On the possibility that Stalin saw *Ivan*, see Zel'dovych, '*Zemlia' i liudy*, p. 2.

81. '1939 Autobiography', p. 24, and A. P. Dovzhenko, 'Uchitel' i drug khudozhnika', *Iskusstvo kino*, no. 10 (1937), p. 15.

82. 'Vystuplenie K. Iukova', *ZBK*, p. 126.

83. 'Vystuplenie L. Trauberga', *ZBK*, pp. 55–6.

84. 'Vystuplenie S. Yutkevicha', *ZBK*, p. 100.

85. Jay Leyda, *Kino: A History of the Russian and Soviet Film,* 3rd ed. (Princeton, NJ, 1983), p. 318.

86. 'Vystuplenie A. Dovzhenko', *ZBK*, p. 71.

87. 'Vystuplevie A. Dovzhenko', *ZBK*, p. 72.

88. 'Vystuplenie A. Dovzhenko', *ZBK*, pp. 72–3.

89. A number of prominent Eisenstein biographers have butchered Dovzhenko's remarks at this conference and misinterpreted them completely. See Marie Seton, *Sergei M. Eisenstein: A Biography* (New York, 1960), pp. 336–7; Leyda, *Kino*, pp. 318–19; Yon Barna, *Eisenstein* (Bloomington, IN, 1973), p. 190; Norman Swallow, *Eisenstein: A Documentary Portrait* (New York, 1977), pp. 114–15; and David Bordwell, *The Cinema of Eisenstein* (Cambridge, MA, 1993), p. 24. Compare their citations of Dovzhenko's remarks with 'Vystuplenie A. Dovzhenko', *ZBK*, pp. 72–3.

90. 'Vystuplenie S. Vasilieva', *ZBK*, pp. 112–13.

91. 'Vystuplenie L. Kulesheva', *ZBK*, p. 121.

92. 'Vystuplenie L. Kulesheva', *ZBK*, p. 120.

93. Leyda, p. 319.

94. *Storinky*, p. 91.

95. Aleksandr Rutkovskii, 'Grad nebesnyi Aleksandra Dovzhenko', *Zerkalo nedeli* (Kiev), 9 December 1995, p. 14.

96. A. P. Dovzhenko, 'Iazykom mysli', *Kino*, 22 April 1934.

97. See Jonathan Haslam, *The Soviet Union and the Threat from the East, 1933–1941: Moscow, Tokyo, and the Prelude of War* (Pittsburgh, 1992) and John J. Stephan, *The Russian Far East: A History* (Stanford, CA, 1994).

98. Rutkovskii, p. 15.

99. *Storinky*, pp. 92–94.
100. '1939 Autobiography', pp. 24–5.
101. Quoted in Rutkovskii, p. 14. Ukrainians did constitute a significant percentage or a majority of the population in the areas Dovzhenko visited. Nearly half listed Ukrainian as their native language in 1926. For a summary of the Ukrainian population in the Soviet Far East in 1926, see *Ukraintsi: Skhidna diaspora: Atlas* (Kiev, 1993), pp. 11, 12.
102. Rutkovskii, p. 15.
103. Quoted in Rutkovskii, p. 14.
104. *Storinky*, pp. 95–7.
105. In 1930, the Ukrainian GPU began to investigate Demutsky. In 1932, the GPU arrested him and held him for four months. The security organs accused him of attempting to send abroad Lopatynsky's 'counter-revolutionary' screenplay, *Ukraine*. But because of lack of evidence he was released. On 19 December 1934, the NKVD arrested him again, charging him with being a 'socially dangerous individual'. The NKVD then exiled him to Kazakhstan for three years. He left Ukraine on 29 April 1935 for Tashkent, where he worked in its film studios. On 11 January 1938, the Uzbek NKVD arrested him. After seventeen months' imprisonment, this security organ freed him. In 1944, Demutsky received the title of Honoured Activist of Arts from the Uzbek SSR, the Stalin Prize in 1952 and in 1954, shortly before his death, he received the award, Honoured Activist of the Arts of the Ukrainian SSR. By July 1946, he returned to Kiev and lived less than two blocks from Polina Dovzhenko's apartment, which Alexander Dovzhenko often visited after 1948. TsDAHOU, 263/1/57017, k 1388, pp. 14–29; DMTMKU, Fond 'R' (D. Demutsky Archive), Inventory nos 7738, 7732.
106. *Storinky*, pp. 96, 98.
107. *Storinky*, p. 112.
108. O. Dovzhenko, 'Aerograd', in his *Tvory* (1964), vol. 2, pp. 71–99; and *Service*, p. 107.
109. Leaming, p. 93.
110. *Service*, p. 107.
111. Iurenev, p. 69.
112. Hryhorii Kostiuk, *Okaianni roky: Vid Luk'ianivs'koi tiurmy do Vorkuts'koi trahedii (1935–1940 rr.)* (Toronto, 1978), p. 114.
113. See '"Aerograd". Novyi fil'm rezhissera A. Dovzhenko', *Pravda*, 5 November 1935; '"Aerograd". Novyi fil'm rezhissera A. Dovzhenko', *Pravda*, 12 November 1935; and I. Bachelis, 'Poema o kryl'iakh', *Komsomol'skaia pravda*, 5 November 1935.
114. B. Reznikov, 'Zamechatel'nyi fil'm', *Pravda*, 12 November 1935.

7

(Re)creating *Shchors*

In his 1939 autobiography, Dovzhenko appraised his recently released film *Shchors* as his best:

> Working on the script for *Shchors* and shooting the film was the most satisfying experience of my life. It took eleven months to write the script and twenty months to film it. It was a whole lifetime. I put to full use in *Shchors* all the knowledge and experience acquired in twelve years of hard labor. I made it with all my love and strength as a memorial to the people, a token of my love and deep respect for the hero of the great Ukrainian October. I felt that my creative urges were being expressed not in flimsy celluloid, but in durable stone or metal fated to survive the centuries. I wanted to be worthy of the people and of the trust placed in me by the great man. When I fell ill during the work I could not bear the thought that I might not be able to finish it.[1]

In reality, Dovzhenko's filming of *Shchors* involved more convolution and more frustration than this description implies. In a letter to a close friend written on 8 December 1939, several days after writing his autobiography, he admitted: 'I completed *Shchors*. It was a very difficult film to make and took a good five years of health from me. And I still have not gotten over it.'[2]

Dovzhenko did not leave a complete summary of the filming of *Shchors*.[3] Only fragmentary, sometimes hagiographic, descriptions exist in accounts written by others. Reading between the lines of these narratives, it becomes obvious that creating *Shchors* presented Dovzhenko with his greatest challenge yet. Among other things, Stalin's personal involvement restricted the full expression of Dovzhenko's creativity. In response, the film-maker became very frustrated, angry, depressed and ill, and he even considered suicide. Despite official delays and emotional outbursts that paralysed his work, Dovzhenko completed his project and created his most successful socialist realist film.

The film portrays Ukrainian resistance to the German intervention in 1918, the Polish invasion in 1919 and to Petliura's Ukrainian nationalist army during the Civil War. Led by the young Mykola Shchors and by the old peasant Vasyl Bozhenko, Ukrainians join the pro-Bolshevik cause under Shchors's command.

After Kaiser William II's abdication in November 1918, German soldiers stationed in Ukraine hope to return home, but their officers oppose them. Shchors then initiates a policy of fraternisation between the Ukrainian and German enlisted men, which undermines the authority of the German officers and clears the way for the Germans to leave Ukraine.

After Petliura takes command of the Ukrainian nationalist army on behalf of the Directory (the same army in which Dovzhenko served in 1918–19), Shchors defeats him at Chernihiv and soon conquers Kiev. A nationalist counter-offensive forces Shchors to retreat, and he becomes wounded in battle at Berdychiv. Recuperating with other partisans, Shchors shares his dreams of the future with them. When Bozhenko learns that counter-revolutionary agents have murdered his wife, Shchors consoles him. The two leaders then regroup and rout the Polish invaders. This victory, however, quickly succumbs to a new threat. In the summer of 1919, General Denikin's White Army troops sweep across Ukraine. Mortally wounded during Denikin's attack, Bozhenko dies. As his men carry him to his grave, Shchors delivers the eulogy. The film ends with Shchors reviewing the troops at his school for Red Army officers twenty years later.[4]

Although it suffered from an unevenly developed plot, *Shchors* conformed to the guidelines of socialist realism. Dovzhenko's film depicts a dedicated, selfless and zealous revolutionary hero who overcomes great odds through his faith in Lenin and the force of his will. As a politically and militarily infallible protagonist, Shchors dominates the film. When the film appeared in 1939, it joined a group of films, such as the Vasilievs' *Chapaev* and Eisenstein's *Alexander Nevsky* (1938), that celebrated heroes from the Russian and Soviet past, who presaged and legitimised Stalin's authority.[5]

In creating *Shchors*, Dovzhenko skilfully negotiated the conflicting demands of his own creative muse and Stalin's interpretation of the Revolution and Civil War. In doing so, he took great risks and managed to square the circle, but at tremendous emotional cost.

Stalin's Initiative

As Dovzhenko edited *Aerograd* at the end of 1934, he planned to start shooting two new films in 1935, *Tsar* ('a social satire based on the Imperialist War of 1914–1918') and *Paradise Lost and Found* ('about a new ice age').[6] Stalin had other plans for the film-maker.

When M. I. Kalinin, the head of the Central Executive Committee (TsIK) and the nominal president of the USSR, awarded Dovzhenko the Order of Lenin on 27 February 1935, Stalin, who stood close to the podium, allegedly said of the film-maker: 'He has an obligation – to create a Ukrainian Chapaev.'[7] In suggesting that Dovzhenko make a film about a 'Ukrainian Chapaev', Stalin proposed a highly sensitive topic, the Revolution and Civil War, which the party had steadily reinterpreted along increasingly Stalinist lines since the mid-1920s.

After the presentation of the awards, Stalin asked Dovzhenko if he knew about Mykola Oleksandrovych Shchors. When Dovzhenko affirmed that he did, the Soviet leader then said, 'Think about him.'[8] Stalin's suggestion made it impossible for the film-maker to dissociate himself from his past.

Dovzhenko had little choice but to agree to Stalin's proposal. On 12 March 1935, he publicly revealed that his next film would deal with Shchors, a heretofore little-known Bolshevik leader in Ukraine.[9]

Before 27 February 1935, most Soviet journalists and scholars could not have identified Shchors. After *Pravda* published Stalin's remarks from the anniversary's conclave on 5 March, they began to publicise Shchors and re-evaluate his contributions to the Bolshevik cause. Suddenly, he emerged as 'one of the organizers and commanders of the first units of the Red Army in Ukraine'. Together with the help of the 'fraternal Russian people and the heroic units of the Red Army', this Ukrainian Bolshevik liberated Ukraine from 'counter-revolution'.[10]

These hyperbolic declarations contradicted historical reality. Born in the village of Snovsk in the Chernihiv Province in 1895, Shchors came from a working-class family headed by a railway mechanic. He completed his education at a school run by the Imperial railway administration and then received training as a military medic. At the beginning of World War I, he served in the medical corps. After completing officer training school in 1915, he became a junior officer in the tsarist army.[11]

Although the beginnings of Shchors's Bolshevik sympathies have never come to light, he clearly identified with the Communist cause by September 1918, when he formed the pro-Soviet Bohun Brigade. In February 1919 his unit helped capture Kiev, and in March 1919 he became the commander of the First Soviet Ukrainian Division.[12]

Although Shchors did participate in the Revolution and Civil War, he did not play the central role the party assigned to him after February 1935. Shchors, in fact, presented real problems as a hero. In August 1919, shortly before his death a month later, Red Army military inspectors claimed that Shchors, who had objected to former tsarist officers giving him orders, had an inflated sense of self and did not possess the necessary qualifications of a division commander.[13] These inspectors claimed that Shchors should take the blame for his unit's recent defeat and stand trial before a revolutionary court.[14]

Despite these historical facts, the Stalinist political machine insisted on representing Shchors as a selfless Bolshevik revolutionary hero. Reviving a secondary figure from the memory of the Civil War, Stalinist ideologists exaggerated Shchors's accomplishments, much as they inflated the General Secretary's own feats. Now Dovzhenko had to capture this new Stalinist vision on film.

To portray this myth, Dovzhenko had to gather details about the new Bolshevik hero and create a coherent interpretation. His research required extensive interviewing and travel. By mid-March Dovzhenko met with veterans from Shchors's division living in Moscow and listened 'attentively' to their stories, as well as to those of Hryhory Shchors, Mykola's brother. Dovzhenko also allegedly received over 13,000 letters and brief memoirs from all across the USSR from those who had served under Shchors.[15]

On 28 April 1935 Dovzhenko travelled to Kiev to examine materials that Ukrainfilm's Historico-Literary Bureau had recently gathered on Shchors.[16] As his first extensive trip to Ukraine since his departure in late 1932, it went well. With Stalin's blessing to create a film about Shchors publicised extensively, he arrived triumphantly.[17] For nearly a year, until March 1936, Dovzhenko travelled back and forth between Moscow and Kiev. As he researched Shchors, he continued to edit *Aerograd* until November 1935.[18] Working on two projects simultaneously undoubtedly exhausted the film-maker.

These meetings, letters and research trips generated an enormous amount of 'facts' concerning Shchors. According to one newspaper correspondent who observed him, Dovzhenko often selected only a phrase or an allusion from these mountains of paper in order to create the Bolshevik commander's largely fictionalised personal and professional characteristics.[19] After receiving thirty-eight thick files on Shchors, the film-maker claimed that they described 'the same things six, eight, and ten times, but in different ways ... I am beginning slowly to become aware that those who remember, "remember" for a certain reason ... I must admit that there is not one exact episode. I created everything'.[20]

Dovzhenko quickly perceived inconsistencies in the reminiscences and narratives written shortly after Stalin embraced Shchors. In light of the public campaign, the respondents delivered positive versions of the past, providing 'facts' and vignettes they expected to please those collecting the memoirs. These 'facts' could not provide a workable basis for the character. Dovzhenko needed to establish a coherent vision of his own.

Building on the memoirs' hyberbole, Dovzhenko established a framework for Shchors's revolutionary activities. In doing so, he created a fiction greater than Stalin's. For personal and professional reasons, he hoped that Stalin would be pleased.

Dovzhenko had good reason for concern. Between 27 February 1935, when Stalin first presented his idea to Dovzhenko, and March 1939, when the film finally appeared, the party leader met with Dovzhenko several times. The first meeting took place in Stalin's Kremlin office on 22 May 1935. At first, the Soviet leader asked the film-maker questions about *Aerograd*. He then focused on *Shchors*.[21] Stalin, according to Dovzhenko's account, repeated that he had only suggested that the film-maker consider making a film about Shchors. Dovzhenko should feel no obligation to do so, Stalin claimed. If he had other plans, then he should work on them.

Dovzhenko thanked him for his concern but claimed that the idea to make a film about Shchors excited him. At this meeting Stalin spoke much about Shchors, about the differences between Shchors and Chapaev, and about the challenges in creating a film about this Civil War hero.[22]

Stalin believed that the film should portray the struggle of the Ukrainian people with the 'Ukrainian counter-revolution and with the German and Polish occupiers for their social and national liberation'. At the same time, the film should strive 'to show the Ukrainian people, especially their national character, their humor, their beautiful songs and dances'.[23] Stalin's paternalistic representation of Ukrainians consigned them to the category of peasant nation, an exotic but backward people. Most importantly, the Soviet leader wanted to remind the film-maker that *Shchors*, Dovzhenko's first attempt at a Ukrainian topic in three years, should reflect the new Soviet interpretations of the Ukrainian past.

According to Stalin's guidelines, the film would present a revisionist message – that the Ukrainians played an integral part in the Bolshevik Revolution and that they, assisted by the 'fraternal Russian people' and the 'heroic units of the Red Army', led a victorious struggle against Ukrainian, Polish and German counter-revolutionaries. *Shchors* would celebrate a Ukrainian Bolshevik leader and suggest that the primary source of the Communist triumph in Ukraine came from the Ukrainians themselves and not from Bolshevik intervention from Russia. At the end of the meeting, Stalin mentioned a recently released record of Ukrainian folk songs. 'Have you heard this record?' he asked the film-maker.

'No, I haven't', Dovzhenko replied. 'I don't have a record player.'

An hour after Dovzhenko returned home from the Kremlin, the film-maker received a record player, a present from the Soviet leader. In an interview published shortly after this meeting, Dovzhenko claimed that he would keep the record player to the end of his life. 'In what other country would workers and artists, scholars and authors feel such a direct intimacy with their beloved leader and feel our glorious party's and Comrade Stalin's daily concerns?' he asked rhetorically.[24]

In the company of his closest friends, however, Dovzhenko claimed that Stalin gave him the record player and the Ukrainian record to remind the film-maker of his nationalist past.[25] Stalin certainly knew of Dovzhenko's service in Petliura's army and of his arrest and conviction in 1919.[26] Stalin's gift represented a warning shot. If Dovzhenko did not produce a film that conformed to Stalin's standards, trouble would follow.

Searching for an Interpretation

Not surprisingly, *Shchors* experienced problems. In the course of its production, Dovzhenko's emotional stability deteriorated. Fears, anxieties and feelings of insecurity weakened him. He often fell ill for long periods. In late August 1938, he

Yevgeny Samoilov plays Shchors
(*Shchors*, 1939)

experienced a serious automobile accident, which almost killed him. According to
an NKVD report, Dovzhenko's driver noticed after the accident that someone had
cut the steering column, leaving a thin piece of metal, which broke at the turn
of the wheel. Suspecting foul play on the part of the security organs, Dovzhenko
became depressed for a long period.[27] His panic, his wish to conform and his desire
to preserve his own creative integrity may have caused his illnesses.[28]

In seeking to implement Stalin's suggestions, Dovzhenko feared that the actors he
had selected, especially those in the primary roles, might not please the Soviet leader.
After completing half the film with one actor in the title role, Dovzhenko started anew
with another.[29] Finally, in the autumn of 1937, Dovzhenko chose a third actor,
Yevgeny Samoilov, to play Shchors.[30] One NKVD intelligence officer provided a very
perceptive analysis of the director's inability to find a good actor to play Shchors: 'I
think that Dovzhenko's dissatisfaction with the actors who played Shchors has a more
complex reason than the incompatibility of this or that actor. Dovzhenko's creative
dissatisfaction with the image of Shchors caused this hypercriticism.'[31]

The historical context behind Shchors's image constantly changed after 1935. During the mid-1930s, Soviet historians repeatedly revised the official history of the

Dovzhenko (right) giving instructions to Ivan Skuratov (who plays Bozhenko) and Yevgeny
Samoilov (*Shchors*, 1938)

Revolution and Civil War in response to the frequent purges. As the security organs
arrested prominent party officials and former heroes, their actions simply disappeared
from official accounts of the Revolution. Dovzhenko's project became an integral part
of this revisionist process. Censors arbitrarily altered sequences to conform to the
latest changes in the official record.[32] Most importantly, the film-maker had to sec-
ond-guess the contours of the continuously shifting politically acceptable.

This same set of circumstances caused Dovzhenko's problems with *Earth* and
Ivan. He started his films with one set of political assumptions. Over the course of
their production, the party changed course and left Dovzhenko, who could not
transform his films as quickly as the Politburo could issue decrees, open to attack.

The Stalinist hyper-regimentation of the late 1930s forced the film-maker to submit every decision and every episode to groups of people 'who knew what Stalin
wanted'. Some critics, for example, noted that Stalin wished Dovzhenko to show
the superiority of Shchors's staff over Chapaev's. Others claimed that the Soviet
leader wanted the director to depict a peasant insurrection in the film. Still others
hoped that he would use Stalin's remarks concerning the national question. And
another group strongly suggested that Dovzhenko make Shchors the leading political representative of the Leninist–Stalinist nationality policy in Ukraine.[33]

D. V. Petrovsky, a writer, a veteran of the First Soviet Ukrainian Division and a
man who knew Shchors personally, reviewed the screenplay and excerpts from
scenes Dovzhenko had shot during the summer of 1937. He pointed out that the

director fleshed Bozhenko out more than he did Shchors and that Arkady Kisliakov, the second of the three actors who portrayed Shchors, did not fit the role and needed replacement. Most importantly, Petrovsky claimed that the portrayal of Shchors dying in the arms of his second-in-command (Ivan Dubovy), the climactic moment in the 1937 version of the film, proved highly unsatisfactory. 'It does not lift up the viewer,' a key ingredient in the socialist realist recipe. In order to arouse the viewer's enthusiasm, Dovzhenko should add a revolutionary call to arms, such as 'Let's recapture Kiev!', to this scene. Then in the film's final frames, the First Soviet Ukrainian Division, inspired by Shchors's death, should take Kiev. This, according to Petrovsky, would represent the proper cinematic response.[34]

In addition to these critics, Dovzhenko endured more late-night meetings with Stalin, some of which were not as pleasant as the first few. According to Jay Leyda, Dovzhenko told him about one frightening incident in Stalin's office, when the Soviet leader refused to speak to the film-maker and Beria accused him of joining a nationalist conspiracy.[35]

Dovzhenko's situation certainly became more precarious after the arrest of Dubovy, Shchors's former deputy, in early 1938 and his execution on 29 July 1938. An important Red Army officer, Dubovy commanded the First Soviet Ukrainian Division, which he handed over to Shchors in the spring of 1919. After Shchors's death, Dubovy again commanded the division. From 1924 he commanded the Kiev Rifle Corps. In 1929 he became deputy commander of the Ukrainian Military District (under Yona Yakir). Following a reorganisation in 1935, he took command of the Kharkiv Military District.[36] He befriended Dovzhenko in 1935 and became a military consultant for *Shchors* as well as a character in the film.

Dubovy's relationship with Yakir marked him. After the arrest, trial and hasty execution of Yakir, along with Marshal Mikhail Tukhachevsky, the deputy commissar of defence, and other important military commanders on 11 June 1937, Stalin called for the extermination of 'enemies of the people' in the Red Army.[37] Stalin's subordinates suspected that Dubovy had engaged in unauthorised contact with Germans and Ukrainian nationalists abroad.[38] Arrested in early 1938, Dubovy confessed, perhaps under torture, to killing Shchors in battle 'in order to take his place as commander of the division'.[39] His arrest, confession and execution placed the Ukrainian film-maker in an extremely vulnerable position, especially since the arrest took place in Dovzhenko's presence at the Kiev Film Studio.[40]

This Kafka-esque turn of events not only complicated the completion of the film, but also placed Dovzhenko in great danger. Before Dubovy's arrest, the director had envisioned Shchors dying on the battlefield and passing his command to Dubovy. Now in order to save his own skin, he had to rewrite and refilm *Shchors*.[41]

Dubovy became Dovzhenko's central problem. Shchors's deputy could not appear in the film unless the director presented him as 'an enemy of the people', but Dovzhenko saw Dubovy as the victim of unjust repression and resisted demonising him in celluloid.[42] The film-maker clearly did not want to portray Dubovy killing Shchors. If he did not want to incorporate the official reinterpretation, he had to edit Dubovy out of the film. Once he excluded Dubovy, Shchors's alleged killer, the cinematic Shchors could live beyond 30 August 1919.

Although Dovzhenko did not have much room to manoeuvre, he sought to deal honestly with other issues beyond Stalin's representation on the screen and Dubovy's relationship with Shchors. Despite the fiction of the film's overall message (that nationally conscious Ukrainians constituted the core supporters of the Bolshevik victory in Ukraine), Dovzhenko's use of Ukrainian folklore Ukrainianised the film. Although the film met the guidelines, 'national in form, socialist in content', the Ukrainian songs and dances undercut its intended political message. *Shchors*'s national form appears more vibrant than its socialist content.

At the end of the screenplay and the film, Shchors observes a parade of future Red Army officers at the military academy he heads. In the screenplay, before a group of visiting inspector generals who want to send his students into hopeless battle, Shchors asserts: 'I will not send my school of Red commanders into battle. I will lose a division, but will save my commanders, and I'll have a division! A corps! An army!'[43]

In one of the versions of the film, a narrator's voice concludes: 'If Red Army commanders exist, then there is a Red Army.' In and of itself, the statement reflected reality, but by the late 1930s, when the security organs arrested and executed tens of thousands of Soviet military leaders, this statement may have represented a subtle dig against the Stalinist repressions of the Soviet military.[44]

Although Dovzhenko did not have much creative flexibility under Stalin's shadow, his artistic ability, personal charisma and stubborn persistence allowed him to present his own subtle differences with the official Soviet interpretation of history on the screen. Although he adhered to the overall Stalinist interpretation given to him, he muted the film's overall message. He succeeded in completing the film and achieving a compromise between his own artistic vision and the official party line, but he did so at the cost of his own physical health and his own emotional equilibrium.

Emotional Breakdown

By the summer of 1938, Dovzhenko could not disguise his rage against the restrictions that the Stalinist system placed on him, especially when he became drunk. In a conversation recorded by the Kharkiv Oblast NKVD and forwarded to Beria, Dovzhenko expressed his fury against the Soviet authorities, Ukrainians and the party. In light of the purges, he claimed that he could not distinguish between the legitimate Soviet authorities and the enemies of the people, who lived everywhere. He cursed Dubovy, whose arrest forced him to reshoot his nearly completed film. He cursed the Ukrainians, whom he branded 'traitors'. They did not possess a culture because the authorities feared the emergence of a Ukrainian culture independent of the Russian and considered the creators of Ukrainian culture as 'potential enemies'. As a result of these suspicions, Ukrainian cultural workers became 'martyrs at Golgotha'. Dovzhenko then cursed the party. 'What kind of party is this? Why does it contain so many traitors? All of its leaders are traitors.' Dovzhenko claimed that Shchors had an easier task to get rid of the Germans in 1918 than Dovzhenko did to make a film about the Bolshevik hero. 'Let them let me work!' he cried out.[45]

During a meeting of party members at the Kiev Film Studio on 19 October 1938, Dovzhenko's colleagues criticised the film-maker for his lack of self-criticism, his slow pace, his waste of film and his cost overruns. Dovzhenko snapped and retorted that he would prefer 'to die than to listen to such criticism'.[46] Responding hysterically to his critics, he shouted, 'I hate you!'[47] Inasmuch as a director no longer had the right to change the screenplay during the actual shooting of the film, Dovzhenko claimed that this rule 'restricts his creative possibilities'. Upset by these constraints, Dovzhenko threatened to change careers. After regaining his composure, he admitted that directors needed to follow this rule, but he claimed that he did not have the strength to do it at the present time. He promised that he would finish the picture as soon as he could, but no one had the right to rush him. He then abruptly walked out of the meeting.[48]

Not surprisingly, he claimed that he found life 'very difficult' during this period. He often declared that he did not want to live.[49] Dovzhenko often threatened suicide, before and after Dubovy's arrest.[50] Suicide, he imagined, would free him from the conflict between his private desires and Stalinist expectations. Solntseva claimed that the film-maker often did not sleep at night and kept telling her that he felt persecuted and that death threatened him. When he slept, he often spoke in Ukrainian and became 'involved in politics'. Dovzhenko, in her opinion, understood that 'his star has set politically'.[51] In the Soviet environment of the 1930s, physical death often followed political decline.

In the course of creating *Shchors*, Dovzhenko held many discussions with leading party and government officials, in addition to Stalin. They included Panas Liubchenko (who committed suicide in 1937 after authorities accused him of heading a counter-revolutionary nationalist organisation in Ukraine), Vsevolod Balytsky (executed in 1937), S. V. Kossior (killed in 1938), P. P. Postyshev (executed in 1938), B. Z. Shumiatsky (shot in 1938), Nikolai Yezhov (arrested in 1939 and killed in 1940) and Nikita Khrushchev, who served as the First Secretary of the Communist Party of Ukraine from 1938 until 1949.

These meetings at the height of the purges must have heightened Dovzhenko's sense of insecurity and fears for his future. As he read his morning newspapers with their denunciations of those purged, he may have felt happy about the demise of some of his tormentors. He did not understand the logic of Stalinism's capriciousness.

Eventually, though, he must have come to the realisation that if the security organs arrested, tried and executed his supervisors, then he became vulnerable as well – once on a list, always on a list.

Success

Dovzhenko completed the filming of *Shchors* in the autumn of 1938 and immediately started editing the raw footage. On 4 March 1939 he brought his final version to the Cinematography Committee in Moscow for approval.[52] When the first official viewing of his film took place, he lay on the sofa in an adjoining room and cried.[53] Semen Dukelsky, the man who replaced Shumiatsky, saw the film with his assistant but abruptly left the screening room at the end without discussing the film with Dovzhenko. He immediately took the film to his superiors. Only after they praised Dovzhenko's final version did Dukelsky admit that he had enjoyed the picture.[54]

Two weeks later, on 19 March 1939, delegates to the Eighteenth Congress of the All-Union Communist Party in Moscow saw *Shchors* for the first time.[55] The film officially premiered on 2–3 April 1939 at the House of Cinema in Moscow. The audience, which included Sergei Eisenstein and other famous Soviet directors, responded enthusiastically.[56] One critic called *Shchors* the work of a 'great master'.[57] In his view, Dovzhenko captured on film 'giants, born during the people's struggle, and great people in the best meaning of the word, who . . . the Leninist party inspired to rise to the heights of valor, courage, liberty, and honor'.[58] Another critic claimed

Dovzhenko speaking before a crowd of Ukrainian villagers in Eastern Galicia, after the Soviet occupation of Poland (Autumn, 1939)

that Dovzhenko's movie represented not only a wonderful 'poem about the civil war', but the art of 'great optimism, the belief in the victory of good over evil'.[59]

On 1 May 1939 *Shchors* premiered in Kiev and gained popularity throughout the USSR, selling 31 million tickets.[60] Dovzhenko took pride in his accomplishment and considered it his best film.[61] Stalin agreed.

Dovzhenko's completion of *Shchors* resuscitated Soviet officialdom's faith in the film-maker and brought him many rewards. In the spring of 1939, he became a member of the Soviet Writers' Union. In November he received the title of Honoured Activist of the Arts of the Ukrainian SSR. In December he won election to the Kiev City Council. In the autumn of 1940, the All-Union Committee on Cinematography appointed Dovzhenko artistic director of the Kiev Film Studio. In March 1941 he received the Stalin Prize, First Class, for *Shchors*.[62] Most importantly, after his completion of *Aerograd* in November 1935, the authorities allowed Dovzhenko to live and work in Ukraine. Only one prize eluded Dovzhenko – reinstatement in the Communist Party. *Shchors* became Dovzhenko's political triumph, but at great psychological cost.

Stalin and Dovzhenko

In his 1939 autobiography, Dovzhenko claimed that his meetings with Stalin 'strengthened my spirit and multiplied my creative ability. I made *Shchors* on the advice of the great teacher.'[63]

In actuality, the film-maker navigated a far more convoluted and dangerous course. Dovzhenko wanted to cooperate, but Stalin and his agents directed and thwarted his creativity. They frequently questioned his loyalty and reliability to the Soviet state and to the ideals of the Communist Party. In addition to Stalin's own interference, bureaucrats constantly supervised and micromanaged the director. In light of the purges and annihilation of the Ukrainian intelligentsia during the 1930s, Dovzhenko – not surprisingly – feared for his life.

He tempered his fears with creativity. Despite his adherence to the assigned interpretation of Shchors's career, Dovzhenko's film presented several scenes and points of view mitigating the official interpretation. He made the film within a Stalinist framework, but he made it on his own terms.

In light of Dovzhenko's unpredictable behaviour and stubbornness, it appears surprising that the Stalinist machine saved him in 1933 and then tolerated him for the next twenty years, but the leaders imagined that Dovzhenko could serve their purposes. Stalin and his colleagues understood the potential of film as a powerful and widely disseminated medium. In 1924, at the Thirteenth Party Congress of the All-Union Communist Party, Stalin announced that the cinema 'is the greatest means of mass agitation. Our problem is to take this matter into our own hands.'[64] Films, according to Stalin, should not only advocate specific actions, but should also propagate the superiority of the Soviet system. The government recognised the wisdom of tapping into the unsurpassed political impact of this mass medium. One of the leaders of the Soviet film industry claimed that in the 1930s Stalin asserted: 'Every film has a great social and political significance' and 'A good picture equals several divisions'.[65]

Beyond the political importance of film-making, Stalin savoured watching movies very much. By the 1930s he saw Soviet and foreign films one or two nights per week, often accompanied by other members of the Politburo. In foreign films Stalin enjoyed action-adventure stories, especially detective and cowboy movies.[66]

By the 1930s Stalin began to intervene actively in the creation of films, not just historical films portraying the Bolshevik Revolution and its heroes, but almost every film shown to Soviet audiences.[67] He first met with cinematographers as a group in 1929, then engaged some of them individually in the 1930s. In this decade, he became the most important critic of the medium. Stalin's presence in the film-making process radically transformed it. Dovzhenko's vocation would no longer constitute the Ukrainian film-maker's refuge, much less his escape, from the external pressures of the world.

Starting with Mikhail Romm's *Lenin in October* (1937), which presented Lenin and Stalin together in dramatic roles, Stalin began to occupy centre stage in many films. Directors and writers rewrote the past and always presented Stalin in leading roles and advanced Stalin's cult of personality. By the 1930s Dovzhenko too had to conform to the Stalin cult.

Stalin and his colleagues realised that they needed directors who could present persuasive revolutionary films to the tens of millions of potential viewers in the USSR and abroad. Stalin recognised Dovzhenko's talents and sought to harness them for the Soviet cause. He and his inner circle may have also taken an interest in Dovzhenko because they hoped that the director would make a film praising Stalin and his role in the Revolution and Civil War.[68]

Dovzhenko's autobiographies and diaries did not mention that by moving to Moscow in 1933, he had struck a deal with the most powerful man in the Soviet Union. Primarily because of Dovzhenko's potential usefulness to the Soviet state and to its leader, Stalin never withdrew his support from the film-maker, even though the latter often disappointed him. Dovzhenko, moreover, was prepared to conform and compromise.

In the period between November 1928 (when Stalin first saw *Arsenal*) and 5 March 1953 (when Stalin died), Dovzhenko may have met the Soviet leader as many as seven times. In his 1939 autobiographical statement, he claimed that Stalin made arrangements to see him five times before November 1939.[69] Between 1939 and the general secretary's death, the film-maker may have encountered Stalin a few more times. The Soviet leader met Dovzhenko in his Kremlin office more often than he did any other Soviet film director.[70] Each of these meetings exercised a profound effect on Dovzhenko's psychological well-being.

Dovzhenko met his most important critic for the first time a year after moving to Moscow. After he completed the screenplay for *Aerograd* in April 1934, he wrote a letter to Stalin asking permission to read it to him personally.[71] Shortly afterwards, Stalin invited Dovzhenko to his Kremlin office.[72] On 14 April 1934 the film-maker spent seventy minutes there.[73] Several years later, Dovzhenko enthusiastically recorded his first meeting with Stalin. Whatever the film-maker's private doubts or fears, he presented a public image of Stalin as a charismatic benefactor:

> The great Stalin received me that day, at the Kremlin like a kind master, introduced me, excited and happy, to Comrades Molotov, Voroshilov, and Kirov, listened to my reading, gave his approval, and wished me success in my work. When I came away from him I saw that the world had changed for me. With his paternal solicitude Comrade Stalin had lifted from my shoulders the burden of many years' standing, when I had felt creatively, and therefore politically, inferior, a feeling instilled in me over many years by my environment. My subsequent four meetings with Stalin strengthened my spirit and multiplied my creative ability.[74]

At this first meeting, Dovzhenko claimed that Stalin impressed the film-maker by taking him seriously:

> Inquiring about the Far East, Comrade Stalin asked me if I could show him on a map where I would build a city if I were a builder, not a film director. I replied that I could. Then he led me to his small office, which contained maps on the wall. I showed him the place and explained why I thought that way ... To now, I recall with great pleasure that Joseph Vissarionovich asked me about it.[75]

If these passages truly reflect Dovzhenko's emotional universe, his first meeting with Stalin overwhelmed him emotionally. Dovzhenko wanted the burden of persecution and criticism he had experienced in Ukraine lifted, and the singular or combined influences of Stalin, Stetsky, or Zhdanov did so. Dovzhenko wanted recognition, and he found it. He wanted respect, and he received it. He wanted approval, and he won Stalin's blessing. He heard everything that he wanted to hear, perhaps even more. Stalin may have asked the film-maker where he would construct the future city of Aerograd. Coming from the most powerful man in the Soviet Union, this question won Dovzhenko over. As the above-mentioned passage implies, Dovzhenko may have imagined that he had won a degree of respect from the party hierarchs not accorded to any other Ukrainian intellectual or Soviet film-maker. This attention must have turned his head.

Stalin's flattery and support eroded the Ukrainian film-maker's ability to resist the secretary general's charisma. Beyond obligation, Dovzhenko sought internal peace by complying with Stalin's expectations.

In his memoirs, Yury Smolych, who met Dovzhenko in the 1920s and befriended him over the next thirty years, recounted Dovzhenko's reactions to his meetings with Stalin. Until Dovzhenko met Stalin, the film-maker perceived the general secretary not as a living person, but rather as a certain symbol. 'For all of us as well as for Sashko,' Smolych recalled thirty years later, 'Stalin was the original embodiment of the party, of party politics, party activities, and party concepts. Stalin represented stability, perseverance, firmness ... But ... Stalin was a certain abstraction as a human being.'[76]

After this visit and his conversation with Stalin, Dovzhenko ceased to see the general secretary as an abstraction. The film-maker began to view him as a human being, as someone with whom he could communicate. According to Smolych, 'Dovzhenko perceived and evaluated people on how they treated him.'[77] This human characteristic, the emotional equivalent of Newton's third law of thermodynamics, provides a key to understanding why Dovzhenko enjoyed the company of Stalin, Voroshilov, Khrushchev and Zhdanov. Initially, they – especially Stalin – treated him very cordially.

Dovzhenko, like many writers, artists and film-makers, gained access to privileged party circles, which encouraged him to participate directly in the Stalinist apparatus. At their meetings, the party leaders provided the creative intelligentsia with insights on how to mould reality. Party leaders expected the artists to assimilate Stalinist mores in their works and learn to perceive the ever-evolving will of Stalin and his inner circle, Stalinism's real creators. The creative intelligentsia, after all, participated as junior partners in the Stalinist construction of a new socialist reality.

In order to acquire the Stalinist mindset, Dovzhenko had to master his fear of Stalin and the political hierarchy. 'I am afraid of him,' Dovzhenko, referring to Stalin, admitted to Smolych, '... but he also charms me.'[78] The film-maker's coexisting fear of Stalin the symbol and his attraction to Stalin the man persisted throughout the course of their relationship. If first impressions are the most important, then Stalin's courtesy 'excited Sashko, enraptured him especially as a person, as someone with a human disposition, as an individual ...'[79]

Conforming to the nineteenth-century peasant interpretation of the tsar as the distant but good father, Dovzhenko believed, according to Smolych, that Stalin did not know of the problems prevalent in the Soviet state and of the crimes committed in his name. If someone brought these critical matters to Stalin's attention, then Stalin would act decisively to solve them. Smolych recalled:

> From that time, whenever our conversations began to deal with some problems in the country (especially the various successive disasters during the collectivization and the political practices in the countryside), or about some immediately incomprehensible

efforts of the party or the government, Sashko began to believe that these events happened because Stalin did not know about it. Stalin could not be concerned with completely everything, with every detail. 'I need to point this out to Stalin, I need to write to Stalin', Sashko said in these instances.[80]

In the first half of the 1930s, Smolych asserted, 'many people sought to explain events which they did not understand in this manner'.[81] Dovzhenko's meetings with Stalin and his belief that he could communicate with and establish a rapport with the Soviet leader led the film-maker to construct an Orwellian 'double-think' mentality, the ability to hold two diametrically contradictory points of view simultaneously and not notice the contradiction. The film-maker may have imagined that Stalin saw him as more than just a client, that the leader actually respected him and his opinions.

Protected by the general secretary, Dovzhenko often spoke his mind outside Stalin's inner circle. He apparently felt safe to do so. Although he criticised many aspects of the new Stalinist order, he never challenged Stalin in public. He may have justified to himself his public affection for Stalin by believing that he could bring matters of serious importance to Stalin's attention, matters no one else could. In an emergency, he could inform Stalin of grave problems and the leader would listen and accept Dovzhenko's words. Whether or not he actually tested this belief, he certainly exaggerated his importance to Stalin to himself, if not to others.

Dovzhenko's personal circumstances help to explain his uncritical attitude towards Stalin, although they cannot totally justify it. The film-maker knew of the famine of 1932–3, the purges of the Ukrainian intelligentsia and party and the political convulsions throughout the USSR. Logic dictated that Stalin, as the country's unchallenged leader, must have had some hand in these events. On an emotional level, however, Dovzhenko felt overwhelmingly grateful to the general secretary, grateful enough not to challenge him. Stalin-the-symbol had saved the young film-maker from arrest and possible execution in Ukraine and provided him with refuge in Moscow. Stalin-the-symbol then revealed himself in human form to Dovzhenko. In his first meetings with the film-maker, the party leader played the affable host. He was polite, pleasant and attentive. In response, the film-maker expressed great enthusiasm for Stalin, at least initially.

After his conversations with Stalin and after receiving the Order of Lenin in February 1935, Dovzhenko spoke warmly about the party leader. In defending the arrests and purges in Ukraine, he accepted the Stalinist construction of reality. When Bazhan and Yanovsky, the film-maker's closest friends, claimed that the mass of arrests of the Ukrainian intelligentsia represented a manifestation of Russification and the strangulation of Ukrainian culture, Dovzhenko argued the Stalinist case. According to NKVD informers, the film-maker asserted that smoke did not appear without fire, that the political situation had become very complex, and that the industrialisation of the USSR remained its most important political priority. According to one NKVD report, he gradually convinced Bazhan and Yanovsky of his position.[82]

Dovzhenko's relationship with Stalin developed through several phases. His initial meetings with the Soviet leader may have seduced him. Building on the tsar-father archetype, typical of his peasant upbringing, and on the fact that he owed his life to Stalin, the film-maker's imagination reinforced the charismatic appeal the party leader projected. Dovzhenko's creative process often allowed him to erase, or at least blur the borders between the real and the imagined. As he admitted in his 1939 autobiography, 'my dreams and imagination were so strong that at times I lived on two levels – the real and the imaginary – which struggled with each other and yet seemed reconcilable'.[83]

In conformity with Dovzhenko's conscious role as an artist, he possessed a flexible interpretation of the truth. For him, the truth, like the process of film-making, did not lie in the details, but in the overall interpretation. 'We do not need ordinary words, daily motions, probable details,' he asserted, 'just the clean golden truth.'[84] In his cinematic biography of Shchors, just as in his later film about the botanist Ivan Michurin, the film-maker emphasised this higher truth. In one of his diary entries for 1944, Dovzhenko wrote about Michurin: 'Maybe he was not like this; most likely he was not. I threw out the entire sum of small, private, ordinary truths, and oriented the screenplay toward the single main truth of this person.'[85] This emphasis on the most basic reality predisposed him to conform to the principles of socialist realism, which demanded the same.

As an artist, Dovzhenko believed that he possessed a poetic licence. The truth held importance, but it remained secondary to beauty. Paraphrasing Anatole France, the film-maker wrote in a 30 April 1944 diary entry:

> If one has to choose between truth and beauty, I choose beauty. It has a more profound verity than the naked truth has. Only the beautiful is true. And if we don't comprehend beauty, we shall never perceive truth in the past, present, or future. Beauty teaches us everything. It is the supreme teacher. Painters, sculptors, architects and poets prove this. What would we have left from Rome or the Renaissance if it were not for them? Yet this simple observation has been ignored, especially by the enemies of lofty thoughts and feelings. In everything human I want to search for beauty, that is, for the truth.[86]

These noble words remained his public credo. They also justified the revisionist stance he took with his own history.

During the filming of *Aerograd*, Dovzhenko began to imagine that he had created a new reality. As he admitted,

In this manner *Aerograd* was not an invention of an artist, but a reality of our days. Even if this city did not exist, it did not mean anything ... When I first came upon this word, which I invented, it began to live in my consciousness as an inevitable reality.[87]

Directing a film promoting the importance of the defence of the USSR from internal and external enemies, Dovzhenko pretended that he and his film crew protected Soviet borders. He came to believe that

I myself am not at all a director, but a partisan, a hunter, a Chekist, that I should not make films, but reconstruct the country, uncover its riches and defend our distant borders from the enemies of the working people.'[88]

Conforming to these illusions, the director ordered naval uniforms for members of his film crew (see p. 143). During the shoots they all marched in columns, singing military songs.[89] In Dovzhenko's world, imagination overpowered reality.

He believed that artists not only presented reality, but also interpreted it and constructed it. Most importantly, artists should restructure reality. In his address to the First All-Union Conference of Soviet Cinema Workers in 1935, he declared that artists needed to do more than 'illustrate' party and governmental decrees:

I dream about an artist who would write a novel. The Politburo would read this novel and issue the following order: 'We decree that beginning tomorrow we will implement this novel in life, exactly, as if it were a screenplay'. And that's how some new White Sea Canal project will be built![90]

Before Dovzhenko's success with *Aerograd*, his imaginary world and the real world occupied separate realms. But after this film rehabilitated him, he may have imagined that he could use his charm and influence to persuade those in the highest circles to transform his dreams into reality. Not only did Dovzhenko's films create illusions that reached millions, but he also became an active member of many commissions, such as the committee editing the 1937 Soviet Ukrainian constitution and the Kiev City Council, which sought to construct and to refine the nature of Stalinism's realities.[91]

Dovzhenko's Anti-Semitic Outbursts

Just as Dovzhenko made expediently complimentary comments about Stalin after his disillusionment during *Shchors*'s filming, he also expediently expressed a number of anti-Semitic remarks. In January 1937, for example, in a speech before the Fourteenth Extraordinary Meeting of the Soviets of Ukraine, he described his reaction to the trial of Yury Piatakov, Karl Radek, Grigory Sokolnikov and others, former followers of Trotsky. The Soviet government accused these Old Bolsheviks of belonging to a 'Parallel Centre', which allegedly conspired to commit acts of terrorism, worked as spies for foreign powers and attempted to provoke a war with Germany and Japan in order to produce a Soviet defeat.[92] In his talk, Dovzhenko described these men with Jewish backgrounds as 'damned degenerates', 'villains', 'Judas Iscariots' and as 'Christ-sellers', who sickened him.[93]

Although he had criticised the notion of guilt by national affiliation in *Arsenal*, he employed this reprehensible and illogical idea ten years later. In the Stalinist political language, the party considered all of its enemies 'Judases', traitors who had to be eradicated. Dovzhenko's harsh remarks mirrored the Stalinist hegemony of the public discourse in the late 1930s. Men and women with a Jewish background comprised a high percentage of the leadership of the Old Bolsheviks, those who had joined the party prior to the outbreak of the 1917 revolutions, and the purges hit them very hard. As the Stalinist leadership reconstructed the Communist Party membership in the 1930s, it began to associate itself more closely with Russian national interests.[94]Whereas the party condemned anti-Semitism as a major enemy during the Civil War, by the late 1930s the party identified prominent Jewish members of the Old Guard as the main enemy and tied them to Trotsky. Although this anti-Jewish animosity remained muted rather than openly expressed, it became closely connected with the war hysteria after the spring of 1935, when the Soviet Union adopted its Popular Front line.[95]By the late 1930s Stalinist authorities arrested prominent Jewish leaders and dismantled Jewish cultural organisations. An officially sanctioned, silent anti-Semitism emerged during the war; the government publicly introduced anti-Jewish measures only in the late 1940s.

In light of Dovzhenko's troubles filming *Shchors*, he must have felt it necessary to attack publicly the enemies of the Soviet state. Never a supporter of Trotsky, who rarely raised the banner of the non-Russians as Stalin had during his rise to power, Dovzhenko joined in the condemnation enthusiastically. In September 1936, in a talk before the Kiev Studio's workers, Dovzhenko attacked Trotsky and defended himself against charges that he had hired Trotskyists in his film crew.[96] Although he may have had a dread of coming under suspicion as a Trotskyist sympathiser and reacted to this fear, his 1937 comments regarding the 'Parallel Centre' contained unnecessary anti-Semitic barbs.

In the spring of 1940, he completed an addendum to his 1939 autobiographical statement, which he prepared for his reapplication to the Communist Party. After the secretaries at the Kiev Film Studio retyped his autobiographical statement, Dovzhenko wrote in his own hand:

> ... various repulsive rumors spread among the Yids at the studio. Apparently, they were
> terribly anxious to keep me from becoming a party member. I didn't see at the studio

any hands to which I could entrust my application. And so I decided to create the cause of Lenin and Stalin for the people according to the voice of my heart and my mind, without having anything to do with the despicable tradesmen whom I despise as much as they hate me. The time will come when people will curse the lies told by the betrayers of Christ, Lenin, and Stalin.[97]

This passage alludes to the unrecorded problems that Dovzhenko experienced after his homecoming at the Kiev Film Studio in 1935. Having turned against him after the party's criticism of *Earth* and *Ivan*, many of the studio's 1,000 film workers, including its Jewish personnel, may have felt uneasy about Dovzhenko's return under Stalin's protection.[98] The security organs arrested many of the studio's employees after Dovzhenko came back following *Aerograd*'s release.[99] Dovzhenko's role in these purges, if any, has never come to light. Whatever his responsibility, the film workers felt trepidation as to what direction Dovzhenko's actions might take. Even if he did not avenge the actions of his persecutors, he still posed a danger. Although he had revived his career with *Aerograd* and *Shchors*, he had a reputation as a 'loose cannon' and could endanger them in the future. Few, if any, members of the studio's party cell wanted to recommend Dovzhenko for party membership. Their recommendations, they foresaw, would haunt them in the future.

The attitudes of those who considered Dovzhenko a problem must have become more critical after the Communist Party of Ukraine's Central Committee appointed him the studio's artistic director, third in command after the two main administrators, in October 1940.[100] As the new artistic director, he expressed great ambitions. At the party-production conference at the Kiev Film Studio in April 1941, he announced that he hoped, with the construction of another film studio in Kiev, to produce thirty films per year by 1945, more than five times what the Kiev Film Studio planned to produce in 1941.[101] He denied charges that in his new role he refused three Jewish directors permission to film their own projects. He claimed that he respected good workers, but despised lazy and drunken ones who undermined one film after another. Referring to such a person, he declared, '... Even if he were my brother ... I would ask him to go somewhere else.'[102]

As the new artistic director, Dovzhenko had a low opinion of the films his studio had produced over the last decade. He asserted that the Kiev Film Studio did not possess a 'distinct creative visage because it lacked a national face in the best Bolshevik understanding of the term'. Without this national aspect, Ukrainian cinematography remained 'provincial and uninteresting'.[103]

This lack of a 'national face' at the Kiev Studio bothered Dovzhenko. In July 1938, for example, the NKVD noted that he, in a conversation with his friends outside Kiev, rhetorically asked, 'Why do Georgians produce films in Georgia and Russians in Russia, but in Ukraine, Georgians, Russians and Jews make films, but not Ukrainians?' Dovzhenko then answered his own question by asserting that 'if we dismiss the Georgians, Russians and Jews from our film-making industry, then there'd be no one working there; there are no Ukrainians'. The NKVD official added that Dovzhenko concluded that the authorities maintained these discriminatory hiring practices on purpose, in order to limit the development of Ukrainian culture.[104]

In his 1941 talk, Dovzhenko provided several reasons for this poor state of affairs at the Kiev Film Studio. Inasmuch as few Ukrainian actors or directors worked at the studio, the majority of the films produced there used the Russian language. He felt caught in a paradox. He could not make Ukrainian films without Ukrainian actors, he asserted, but he could not attract Ukrainian actors without a commitment to making Ukrainian films. In order to overcome this impasse, he recommended that the Kiev Film Studio hire more Ukrainian theatre actors and train new cadres of Ukrainian directors. He labelled many of the old directors 'sent to us from Moscow' second- and third-rate film-makers who came to Kiev to make money, not to produce quality films.

Dovzhenko then repeated what Khrushchev, the current head of the Communist Party of Ukraine, had allegedly told him, that the nationality of directors – whether Ukrainian, Russian, or Jewish – held no importance, as long as they made films using the Ukrainian language. According to Dovzhenko's account, Khrushchev supported his idea that all films produced at the Kiev Film Studio contain Ukrainian materials and themes and that new Ukrainian cadres be admitted and promoted there.[105] The Ukrainian film-maker, according to the NKVD account, claimed that this achievement emerged as a result of the conversations he had had with Stalin and Khrushchev.[106]

Putting this prescription into action, of course, proved extraordinarily difficult, inasmuch as few of the non-Ukrainian directors associated with the Kiev Film Studio understood Ukrainian culture or wished to learn more about it. Reacting to Dovzhenko's goal of radically increasing the production schedule and to his emphasis on the use of Ukrainian, many directors resented him and his vision. But because of Dovzhenko's proximity to Khrushchev and Stalin, they could not remove him, only obstruct his plans in subtle ways.

The war, moreover, overturned these plans and Dovzhenko reacted bitterly against all those who hampered or inefficiently administered Ukrainian cultural work in Soviet Central Asia. In a report sent on 22 March 1943 to Khrushchev, Serhienko, the Ukrainian People's Commissar of Internal Affairs, discussed how dissatisfied the Ukrainian writers had grown with Natan Rybak, the deputy head of the Ukrainian Writers' Union. Ukrainian writers, according to Serhienko, expressed many anti-Semitic comments when criticising Rybak, a Jew. One of the most characteristic criticisms, according to the Internal Affairs Commissar, came from Dovzhenko, who allegedly asserted:

Many little Jews harm Ukrainian culture. They hated us, hate us, and will continue to hate us. They attempt to worm themselves into everything and grab everything for themselves. It is scandalous that Rybak, a mangy little Jew, heads the Ukrainian Writers' Union ...[107]

Dovzhenko, a member of the Ukrainian Writers' Union since 1939, undoubtedly disliked Rybak. The deputy head of the Union, according to Serhienko, had alienated the Ukrainian intelligentsia. Many of its members complained that he did not satisfy the needs of the writers, had become involved in providing only for himself, and surrounded himself with a group of Jewish writers whom few Ukrainians respected. Many felt that he lacked the qualifications to serve as the second most powerful official within the Writers' Union. Although he wrote in Ukrainian, they did not respect him as a writer. He acted in an arrogant manner and did not consult with any of the organisation's most prominent writers or poets.[108]

Yury Yanovsky, a novelist, claimed that Rybak generally did 'what he wants. He's a dictator. A Napoleon.' Because members of the Writers' Union depended on him for their basic needs in Ufa, 'everyone fears him'.[109] According to many writers, Alexander Korniichuk – a prominent Ukrainian playwright and writer, former head of the Ukranian Writers Union (1938–41) and a man with political connections to Stalin's inner circle – protected Rybak. According to Maksym Rylsky, 'Ukrainian literature is Korniichuk and Rybak.'[110] The Union's bureaucracy, its publishing house and even its party organisation came under the control of Rybak, who – asserted Rylsky – possessed a two-faced character and always lied. All the Ukrainian writers living in Ufa lived poorly, but Rybak, taking advantage of his position, lived very well, as Serhienko summarised the views of Ukrainian writers in Ufa.[111]

The Ukrainian Commissar of Internal Affairs concluded his report by recommending that Khrushchev remove Rybak, who had few friends among the writers, from his position within the Ukrainian Writers' Union.

Although Dovzhenko's remarks about Jewish Old Bolsheviks reflected those of the Stalinist hierarchy, his comments about Rybak and Brodsky and Tsap, who worked at the Kiev Film Studio's party organisation, came from a more personal and professional antagonism. They were consistent with Dovzhenko's own view of his mission and of his self-anointed role as the 'Napoleon' of the Kiev Film Studio.

In his mind, Dovzhenko, as a Ukrainian *intelligent*, served the Ukrainian people as a film-maker. As a Ukrainian, he could understand Ukrainian interests far better than his non-Ukrainian colleagues, and he knew how best to present them on the screen. He would have found it impossible to conceive of a scenario such as the one whereby Sergei Paradzhanov, an Armenian raised in the Georgian city of Tbilisi's large Armenian community, trained as a film-maker in Moscow, worked at the Kiev

Film Studio, and came to direct the most famous postwar Ukrainian classic, *Shadows of Forgotten Ancestors* (1964).

Having survived *Earth*, *Ivan* and *Shchors*, Dovzhenko thought that he knew how to manoeuvre within a Stalinist environment. As the studio's artistic director, Dovzhenko believed that he could use the studio as his tool in presenting his vision of a Ukrainian past, present and future. In order to do so, he had to marshall the studio's limited resources, coordinate the work of his colleagues and pacify external overseers. He wanted to raise the quantity and the quality of the films produced and to transform them into Ukrainian films, not just films produced in Ukraine. In his efforts to accomplish these goals, he actively crossed swords with those who opposed him, among them a number of Russians and Jews, suspicious of Dovzhenko's efforts to Ukrainianise the film industry and apprehensive of their future.[112]

He interpreted the opposition to his plans as anti-Ukrainian and blamed his opponents' ethnic backgrounds. But Dovzhenko did not discriminate against Jews or members of other national groups; he employed many in his film crews.[113] He even enjoyed good relations with his Jewish students from the Kiev Film Institute.[114] In a position of authority as the studio's artistic director, he appeared to emulate the contradictory persona of Stalin and the Soviet state.

Despite his competition with Jewish film-makers in Ukraine, Dovzhenko did not participate in the officially sponsored anti-Semitic campaign of the late 1940s and early 1950s. He did not speak at the February 1949 conference at Moscow's Cinema House, which assessed Soviet cinematography's achievements in 1948 and its future plans. In their appraisals, many speakers at this symposium criticised Jewish film-makers and film critics.[115] Although in good favour with the recent release of *Michurin* (1948) in January, Dovzhenko spent 27 February to 25 March 1949 at a sanatorium at Barkhivka, a few kilometres outside of Moscow's city limits.[116] His efforts to create *Michurin* exhausted him; his heart troubled him.

At this meeting, Bolshakov, the Minister of Cinematography, accused Leonid Trauberg, the prominent Leningrad film director and the man who led the charge against Eisenstein in January 1935, of leading an 'anti-patriotic group of bourgeois cosmopolitans' in the Soviet film industry. At a time when the Soviet Union embraced a strident Russian nationalism at the start of the Cold War period, Bolshakov accused Trauberg and his fellow critics of claiming that American, French and German directors, cameramen and actors played an important role in the development of Soviet cinematography.[117]

Following Bolshakov, thirty-one of the most prominent Soviet film directors (including Yutkevich, Sergei Vasiliev, Pudovkin, Romm and Kuleshov), critics and administrators spoke at this meeting. They attacked the pernicious influence of American films on Soviet film-makers and advocated the need to create Soviet films which would celebrate the Russian national character, Russian folklore and Russian nature. According to the assessment Bolshakov and the others provided, prominent Jewish directors and critics did not show the proper respect for Russian culture.

Had Dovzhenko attended this conference, what would he have said? It is an open question. Having lived in Poland and Germany in the early 1920s, he most likely would have agreed that the large numbers of American, French and German films he saw there influenced him and the other members of the the first Soviet generation of film-makers, however indirectly. But in February 1949 would he have publicly defied Bolshakov and the major tenets of the 'anti-cosmopolitan' and 'Russia first' campaigns? Most likely not.

He fought his battles in a different arena. As the champion of Ukrainian culture, Dovzhenko fought to expand its contours. Within the increasingly russocentric environment of the late 1930s, he could not publicly condemn those Russians who opposed him as Russians, but he could identify his Jewish opponents as Jews or 'Zionists'.

He could make harsh comments about Jews as a way of expediently airing his grievances over the creative restrictions he experienced. By the late 1930s this type of comments about Jews became more socially acceptable in Soviet society than in the 1920s. Now he could express his political and artistic disagreements with Stalinist constraints in veiled terms.

Inasmuch as Ukrainian culture differed more from Jewish culture than from Russian culture, Dovzhenko's remarks represented a greater anti-Russian than anti-Jewish stance. As the self-appointed Napoleon of Ukrainian culture and cinema, he sought to protect his perimeters. With the end of Ukrainianisation, and in a period of political uncertainty after the Stalinist annihilation of the Ukrainian creative intelligentsia in the 1930s, the competition for control of the film-making industry in Ukraine fuelled Dovzhenko's perception of the animosity between Ukrainians and Jews. Although racial and religious differences remained secondary issues in the struggle with his Jewish critics in Ukraine, the film-maker's comments betray a prejudiced and intolerant mindset.[118] But his bigotry did not extend to Jews outside Ukraine.

Just as the purges provided a scapegoat for the Soviet state's contradictions and problems, his anti-Semitism offered him a scapegoat for the problems and conflicts he had expressing his own creativity within the Soviet state. Although Dovzhenko's anti-Semitic remarks sought to strengthen his political position at the film studio, they did not bring him party membership.

Whereas prominent Soviet film directors such as Pudovkin (1939), Romm (1939), Mikhail Chiaureli (1940) and Kuleshov (1945) became members of the Communist Party, Eisenstein, Kozintsev, Trauberg, Vertov and Dovzhenko did not.[119] In spite of becoming Stalin's client and a recognised servant of the Soviet state, the Ukrainian film-maker never regained his party card.

Conclusion

Stalin the patron and Dovzhenko the client established a Byzantine relationship, a 'lopsided friendship'.[120]At times, it appeared as if they played the roles of father and son, at other times those of teacher and student. Although the general secretary and the film-maker did not meet on a regular basis, Stalin's subordinates often played the role of intermediaries between the two. As usual in such cases, unequal power defined the Stalin–Dovzhenko relationship.

As the subordinate half of this pair, Dovzhenko feared letting Stalin down. He read about the arrests of high party leaders. He surely knew about the arrests and executions of his former collaborators, Yury Tutiunnyk, Faust Lopatynsky, Maik Johansen and Ivan Dubovy, and of his actors, Mykola Nademsky (who played the grandfather in many of his early films) and Symon Shahaida (who played the hero Glushak in *Aerograd*). The film-maker also knew about the arrests of Ostap Vyshnia, his friend from Kamianets-Podilsk, who became a prominent humourist in the 1920s and early 30s, and of his closest collaborator, Danylo Demutsky.[121]He also knew about the arrests of members of the Georgian intelligentsia.[122]

In response to these arrests, Dovzhenko began to express his dissatisfactions with the Stalinist order, according to NKVD informants. In private, he claimed that the Soviet Union could not possess so many internal enemies. When he learned that the authorities freed and rehabilitated some of those arrested, he concluded that the secret police, in reaction to the Stalinist hysteria of the 1930s, had overwhelmingly arrested the innocent. When he heard rumours that security organs tortured prisoners during their interrrogations, he began to curse the NKVD, asserting that sadists and enemies of the Soviet state worked there. The film-maker now contended that local authorities made foolish decisions, could not distinguish between the innocent and the guilty and sacrificed the innocent without any qualms.[123]

The change in Dovzhenko's attitudes towards the arrests fuelled his critical evaluation of the whole Soviet order: the schools, the Komsomol, social organisations, the relationship between Communists and non-party members, the draconian anti-abortion law of 1936, censorship in the arts and press, the purges of the military command, collectivisation, the persecution of religion and the whole tone of Soviet life built on 'hurrah-patriotism' and dogmatism.[124] As he nursed doubts about the Stalinist system during the last stages of his work on *Shchors*, he continued to mask them by highlighting his speeches and articles with praises of Stalin.[125]

On the eve of the outbreak of the German–Soviet war, Dovzhenko mourned, according to one NKVD informant, the prevalence of lies, 'the tragedy of our times'. He claimed that art 'lies, people lie to one another in their conversations, they fear each other, newspapers are full of boastful phrases, everyone with great effort presents the image that they are happy, that life is truly wonderful, but in their souls they are sick'.

When the informant asked Dovzhenko when all of this might change, the film-maker replied: 'In order for lies to disappear, fear should disappear first. And I don't see the end of fear. Perhaps when these wars will come to an end and an era of worldwide socialism will begin, not sooner.'[126]

By the end of the 1930s the Ukrainian film-maker abandoned many (but not all) of the illusions he acquired after moving to Moscow in 1933. On the eve of the war, Dovzhenko claimed that the Soviet Union needed a multiparty system. 'Communism and fascism are philosophical brothers, and both are totalitarian regimes,' he asserted to an NKVD informer.[127]

Despite Dovzhenko's doubts, Stalin protected Dovzhenko. In return, the most prominent Ukrainian film-maker became Stalin's client. He could live, he could create, but he could not translate all of his own visions onto the screen. In order to survive, Dovzhenko had to rein in the expressions of his imagination and falsify his political preferences in public. Forced to reside in Moscow, he lived in a golden cage, but a cage it remained. His creative interpretations of the truth made life under the party hierarchy's protection bearable. But even though Dovzhenko owed his life and career to Stalin, he remained a difficult client.

Notes

1. '1939 Autobiography', pp. 25–6.
2. TsDA-MLMU, 690/3/7, pp. 16–17; O. P. Dovzhenko, *Tvory v p'iaty tomakh* (Kiev, 1966), vol. 5, p. 343.
3. According to Dovzhenko's diary entry of 10 April 1944, he experienced serious difficulties in making this film: 'Write down the story of how *Shchors* was filmed from beginning to end: the parts played by Shumiatsky, Panas and Koshara; the talk with Budyonny at Panas' summer cottage; reading the script at the Ukrainian Politburo; shooting the film; Dubovy's arrest; X's phone call about the new version of Shchors's death; the trip to Moscow to see Stalin; how I conceived the ending of the film, etc., while filming *Shchors* I came down with a chest ailment; the film in Moscow; the 'reception' at Dukelsky's; the reception at Stalin's.' *PF*, p. 106; *UVOKShch*, p. 262; *Hospody*, p. 241; *ZDUVOShch*, p. 365. Dovzhenko, unfortunately, did not describe all of his experiences filming *Shchors*.
4. Dovzhenko's screenplays of *Shchors* appeared in: A. Dovzhenko, *Izbrannoe* (Moscow, 1957), pp. 94–160; Oleksandr Dovzhenko, *Tvory v tr'okh tomakh*, vol. 1 (Kiev, 1958), pp. 129–214; O. Dovzhenko, *Tvory v p'iaty tomakh*, vol. 2 (Kiev, 1964), pp. 101–79; A. Dovzhenko, *Sobranie sochinenii v chetyrekh tomakh*, vol. 1 (Moscow, 1966), pp. 180–252; O. Dovzhenko, *Tvory v p'iaty tomakh*, vol. 1 (Kiev, 1983), pp. 161–233; and O. Dovzhenko, *Kinopovisti, opovidannia* (Kiev, 1986), pp. 83–159. *Service*, p. 122, provides an excellent summary.

5. *Service*, pp. 122–3.

6. *Kino* (M), no. 59 (1934); cited in *Storinky*, p. 100.

7. 'Ukrainskii "Chapaev"', *Pravda*, 5 March 1935, p. 6.

8. 'Ukrainskii "Chapaev"', p. 6.

9. *Storinky*, p. 104.

10. I. L. Hoshuliak, *Ukrains'kyi istorychnyi zhurnal*, no. 6 (1985); cited in Oleksandr Fesenko, 'Iak tvoryvsia mif pro "ukrains'koho Chapaeva"', *Literaturna Ukraina*, 17 August 1989, p. 8. The most popular interpretation of Shchors appeared in *Bol'shaia sovetsakaia entsiklopediia* (cited hereafter as *BSE*), 2nd ed., vol. 48 (Moscow, 1957), p. 277.

11. *BSE*, 2nd ed., vol. 48, p. 277.

12. *BSE*, 2nd ed., vol. 48, p. 277.

13. See the quote in Fesenko, 'Iak tvoryvsia mif', p. 8.

14. 'Nikolai Shchors – legenda i real'nost', *Iskusstvo kino*, no. 9 (1990), p. 116.

15. *Storinky*, p. 104; and 'Narodzhennia fil'mu pro Shchorsa', *Proletars'ka pravda*, 17 April 1936; cited in *Storinky*, p. 119. 'Thirteen thousand letters' are hyperbolic and should not be accepted at face value.

16. *Storinky*, p. 106; Fesenko, p. 8.

17. Aleksandr Rutkovskii, 'Grad nebesnyi Aleksandra Dovzhenko', *Zerkalo nedeli* (Kiev), 9 December 1995, p. 15.

18. *Storinky*, p. 118.

19. 'Narodzhennia fil'mu pro Shchorsa'; cited in *Storinky*, p. 119.

20. Fesenko, 'Iak tvoryvsia mif', p. 8. A group of four surviving veterans from the 44th Soviet Ukrainian Division (later renamed the First Soviet Ukrainian Division) in 1918–20 confirmed that the memoirs collected in the 1930s were 'full of lies' and 'historically unfounded' (p. 109), 'Nikolai Shchors', pp. 109–17. These veterans provided a point-by-point archival refutation of many of the myths surrounding Shchors, including the 'fact' that Shchors met Lenin (p. 110), that he received telegrams from the Soviet leader (p. 112) and that he became a member of the Bolshevik Party in the autumn of 1918 (p. 111).

21. The only accounts of this meeting are Dovzhenko's and should be accepted critically: 'Na prieme u tovarishcha Stalina. Beseda s rezhisserom A. Dovzhenko', *Vechernaia Moskva*, 26 May 1935; and A. P. Dovzhenko, 'Uchitel' i drug khudozhnika', *Iskusstvo kino*, no. 10 (1937), pp. 15–16. Stalin's Kremlin office appointment book confirms this meeting: 'Posetiteli kremlevskogo kabineta I. V. Stalina: Zhurnaly (tetradi) zapisi lits, priniatykh pervym gensekom, 1924–1953 gg.', *Istoricheskii arkhiv*, no. 3 (1995), p. 167.

22. Dovzhenko, 'Uchitel', p. 15.

23. Dovzhenko, 'Uchitel', p. 16.

24. Dovzhenko, 'Uchitel'', p. 16.

25. This passage appeared in the unpublished memoirs of F. Soluianova, cited in Rutkovskii, p. 15.

26. The documents compiled by the Cheka and the NKVD on Dovzhenko were published only recently (unfortunately, not completely) in Ukraine: 'Zakliuchenie po delu no. 112 na Dovzhenko Aleksandra Petrovicha, 25 let' and 'Sovershenno sekretno. Spravka', in *ZA*, pp. 237–9, 241 and 242; and *D*, pp. 21–60.

27. *ZA*, p. 264. Seven years later, Dovzhenko described a nightmare involving a similar car accident in his diary. See *UVOKShch*, pp. 289–90; *Hospody*, pp. 274–5; *ZDUVOShch*, p. 399.

28. In the spring of 1937, Dovzhenko experienced sclerosis of the blood vessels, especially in his head and aorta, after Shumiatsky ordered him to stop shooting his film's winter scenes before the authorities completely approved his screenplay. After another four-month illness (from September 1937 until January 1938), he started to film more scenes. Then, coronary disease confined Dovzhenko to bed for three months in 1938. After completing *Shchors* in March 1939, he became sick and did not recover until September 1939. Dovzhenko, *Tvory v p'iaty tomakh*, vol. 5 (1966), p. 337; *Za bil'shovyts'kyi fil'm*, no. 7 (1938); cited in *Storinky*, p. 130; Also see Aleksander Dovzhenko, 'Ia poterpel bol'shoi uron v zhizni', *Iskusstvo kino*, no. 9 (1990), p. 124n; '1939 Autobiography', p. 26n; and Ivan Koshelivets', *Oleksandr Dovzhenko* (Munich, 1980), p. 220.

29. '1939 Autobiography', p. 26n.

30. The Kiev theatre actor Mykola Makarenko (February–March 1937), the Moscow theatre actor Arkady Kisliakov (May–Summer 1937) and, finally, the Moscow actor Yevgeny Samoilov (Autumn 1937–1938) played Shchors. Lazar Bodyk, *Dzherela velykoho kino. Spohady pro O. P. Dovzhenka* (Kiev, 1965), pp. 95–124; Aleksei Mishurin, 'Na s'emkakh "Shchorsa"', in *DVVS*, pp. 103, 107 and 108; and O. Mishurin, 'Polum'iane sertse', in M. Kovalenko and O. Mishurin, *Syn zacharovanoi Desny* (Kiev, 1984), pp. 148, 170 and 196–8.

31. *ZA*, p. 260.

32. *Service*, p. 122.

33. RGALI, 2081/1/941, pp. 2, 4, 5, 11, 12, 13, 15, 16.

34. RGALI, 2081/1/941, pp. 2, 4, 5, 11, 12, 13, 15, 16.

35. Jay Leyda, *Kino: A History of the Russian and Soviet Film*, 3rd ed. (Princeton, NJ, 1983), p. 354. This account, unfortunately, is unverifiable.

36. For an outline of Dubovy's career, see Borys Lewytzkyj, compiler, *The Stalinist Terror in the Thirties: Documentation from the Soviet Press* (Stanford, CA, 1974), pp. 117–18; and Koshelivets', p. 209. For a standard Soviet

biography, see N. S. Kheryshev, *Komandarm Dubovoi* (Kiev, 1986). Kheryshev's biography does not mention Dubovy's arrest or execution.

37. Roy Medvedev, *Let History Judge: The Origins and Consequences of Stalinism* (rev. and exp. ed., New York, 1989), pp. 420, 421.

38. Pavel Sudaplatov and Anatoli Sudaplatov, *Special Tasks: The Memoirs of an Unwanted Witness – A Soviet Spymaster* (Boston and New York, 1994), pp. 21–2.

39. N. S. Khrushchev, *Khrushchev Remembers*, with an introduction, commentary and notes by Edward Crankshaw (Boston, 1970), p. 88.

40. Tatiana Derevianko, the head of the Museum at the Dovzhenko Film Studios in Kiev, told me this during the summer of 1996.

41. Koshelivets', pp. 209–10.

42. Bodyk, *Dzherela*, p. 107. Shortly before his own death in November 1956, Dovzhenko expressed his pleasure that the party had rehabilitated Dubovy.

43. O. Dovzhenko, *Tvory v p'iaty tomakh*, vol. 2 (1964), p. 178; and O. Dovzhenko, *Kinopovisti, opovidannia*, p. 149.

44. Leonid Cherevatenko and Anatolii Lemysh, 'Dovzhenko v pritsele VChK-OGPU-NKVD-KGB: K stoletiia so dnia rozhdeniia A. P. Dovzhenko', *Kievskie vedomostei*, 3 September 1994, p. 3.

45. TsDA-MLMU, 1196/2/7, pp. 1–6; also cited in *ZA*, pp. 261–3.

46. TsDA-MLMU, 1196/2/8, p. 1 and 1196/2/4, pp. 1–6; also cited in *ZA*, pp. 261–3.

47. TsDA-MLMU, 1196/2/4, p. 4; *ZA*, pp. 261–3.

48. TsDA-MLMU, 1196/2/4, pp. 4–5; *ZA*, pp. 261–3.

49. TsDA-MLMU, 1196/2/4, p. 3.

50. Koshelivets', pp. 207–8. See Dovzhenko's April 1937 letter to Vsevolod Vishnevskii, in Dovzhenko's *Tvory*, vol. 5 (1966), pp. 336–9.

51. *ZA*, p. 263.

52. *Moskovskii bol'shevik*, 5 March 1939; cited in *Storinky*, p. 134.

53. I. Rachuk, 'Esteticheskie vzgliady Aleksandra Dovzhenko', *Baikal*, no. 1 (1962), p. 116.

54. Bodyk, p. 151.

55. *Kino*, no. 14 (1939); cited in *Storinky*, p. 135.

56. *Storinky*, p. 135. Also see L. Arnshtam, 'Shchors', *Pravda*, 25 January 1939; Vsevolod Vishnevskii, 'Fil'm "Shchors"', *Pravda*, 5 March 1939.

57. I. Bachelis, 'Rozhdenie "Shchorsa"', *Izvestiia*, 4 March 1939.

58. I. Bachelis, 'Poema o Shchorse', *Izvestiia*, 5 March 1939.

59. I. Agranovskii, 'Boguntsi idut v ataku', *Komsomol'skaia pravda*, 9 May 1939.

60. RGALI, 2409/1/56; cited in *Storinky*, p. 137.

61. '1939 Autobiography', p. 25.

62. *Storinky*, pp. 133–53.
63. '1939 Autobiography', p. 25.
64. I. V. Stalin, *Collected Works* (Moscow, 1948), vol. 6, p. 217.
65. G. Mar'iamov, *Kremlevskii tsensor: Stalin smotrit kino* (Moscow, 1992), pp. 48–9.
66. Evgenii Gromov, *Stalin: vlast' i iskusstvo* (Moscow, 1998), pp. 182, 213. Andrei Konchalovsky's English-language film, *The Inner Circle* (1992), depicts Stalin's love of movies.
67. For a brief survey of Stalin's relations with Soviet film-makers and his reactions to their films, see Gromov, pp. 181–223; G. Mar'iamov, *Kremlevskii tsensor*; and B. Z. Shumiatskii, '"Ochen' sil'no i kul'turno skomponovannaia veshch ...": O chem dumal i govoril tov. Stalin pri prosmotre otechestvennykh kinofil'mov', *Rodina*, no. 9 (1995), pp. 89–92.
68. See S. Plachynda's review of Hryshchenko's 'Polumiana dusha', *DMM*, File 5.
69. '1939 Autobiography', p. 25.
70. 'Alfavitnyi ukazatel' posetitelei kremlevskogo kabineta I. V. Stalina', *Istoricheskii arkhiv*, no. 4 (1998), pp. 16–203. Stalin, of course, also met film-makers away from his Kremlin office.
71. '1939 Autobiography', p. 25; *Storinky*, p. 94.
72. A. P. Dovzhenko, 'Uchitel'', p. 15. Here, Dovzhenko claimed that Stalin issued his invitation 'twenty-two hours' after the film-maker dropped his letter into the letterbox. Dovzhenko's account probably exaggerated how quickly he received an appointment to see Stalin.
73. 'Posetiteli kremlevskogo kabineta I. V. Stalina', *Istoricheskii arkhiv*, no.3 (1995), p. 129.
74. '1939 Autobiography', p. 25; Dovzhenko, 'Uchitel'', p. 15.
75. Dovzhenko, 'Uchitel'', p. 15.
76. Iurii Smolych, *Rozpovid' pro nespokii* (Kiev, 1968), p. 166.
77. Smolych, p. 164.
78. Smolych, p. 166.
79. Smolych, pp. 166–7.
80. Smolych, p. 167.
81. Smolych, p. 167.
82. *ZA*, pp. 259, 274.
83. '1939 Autobiography', p. 9.
84. Quoted in Rutkovskii, p. 15; and in Maksym Ryl's'kyi, 'Narodnyi mytets'', *PZh*, p. 22.
85. *PF*, p. 103; *UVOKShch*, p. 258; *Hospody*, pp. 236–7; *ZDUVOShch*, p. 361.
86. *PF*, p. 106; *UVOKShch*, p. 261; *Hospody*, p. 240; *ZDUVOShch*, p. 364.
87. Rutkovskii, p. 15.

88. Rutkovskii, p. 15.

89. Rutkovskii, p. 15.

90. 'Vystuplenie A. Dovzhenko', *ZBK*, p. 66.

91. *Storinky*, pp. 122, 142.

92. Medvedev, *Let History Judge*, p. 361.

93. RGALI, 2081/1/392, p. 1.

94. See Frederick Barghoorn, *Soviet Russian Nationalism* (New York, 1956) and David Brandenberger, 'The "Short Course" to Modernity: Stalinist History Textbooks, Mass Culture, and the Formation of Popular Russian Identity, 1934–1956' (unpublished PhD dissertation, Harvard University, 1999).

95. Alfred D. Low, *Soviet Jewry and Soviet Policy* (Boulder, CO, 1990), p. 54.

96. A. P. Dovzhenko, 'Vystuplenie po sobranii sotrudnikov kievskoi kinofabriki', RGALI, 2081/1/371, pp. 14–15.

97. '1939 Autobiography', p. 27.

98. According to M. Kovalenko, 'Idu za Dovzhenkom', DMM, File 8, p. 33, nearly 1,000 men and women worked at the Kiev Film Studio on the eve of the German invasion.

99. Jerzy Plazewski, 'Poslednii iz troitsy', RGALI, 2081/1/1169, p. 5.

100. *Storinky*, p. 32. According to Kovalenko, the Central Committee appointed Ia. Lynniichuk as the studio's main administrator, Kovalenko as the deputy administrator in charge of film production and Dovzhenko as artistic director two to three weeks before the German invasion. Kovalenko, p. 32.

101. TsDA-MLMU, 690/2/11, p. 3, and RGALI, 2081/1/389, pp. 4, 5.

102. TsDA-MLMU, 690/2/11, p. 9, and RGALI, 2081/1/389, p. 14.

103. RGALI, 2081/1/389, p. 8.

104. *D*, p. 23.

105. RGALI, 2081/1/389, pp. 9–11.

106. *D*, p. 25.

107. TsDAHOU, 1/23/685, p. 82.

108. TsDAHOU, 1/23/685, p. 83.

109. TsDAHOU, 1/23/685, p. 84.

110. TsDAHOU, 1/23/685, p. 85.

111. TsDAHOU, 1/23/685, p. 85.

112. See, for example, the anonymous letter the Soviet Ukrainian Commissariat of Internal Affairs and NKVD received in 1940 accusing Dovzhenko of being not just 'an enemy of the people', but possibly a German spy, a Polish spy, or a German-Polish spy in the Soviet film industry. *ZA*, pp. 264–5. Because the author of this letter referred to Dovzhenko's earlier interest in German expressionist film, he or she may have been an employee of the Kiev Film Studio.

113. His film crews included Lazar Bodyk (assistant director), Yury Yekelchyk
     (cameraman) and Ivan Shmaruk (assistant to the director), among others.
     See Bohdan Y. Nebesio's casting and crew credits in his *Alexander
     Dovzhenko: A Guide to Published Sources* (Edmonton, Alberta, 1995).

114. On Dovzhenko's relations with his Jewish students, see Sulamif Tsybul'nyk,
     'Pershi uroky', *Dnipro*, no. 9–10 (1994), p. 67.

115. E. Levin, 'Piat dnei v 49-m', *Iskusstvo kino*, no. 1 (1990), pp. 93–9; no. 2
     (1990), pp. 93–101; no. 3 (1990), pp. 77–89.

116. *Storinky*, pp. 242–3.

117. Ivan Bolshakov, "Razgromit' burzhuaznyi kosmopolitanizm v kinoiskusstve',
     Pravda, 3 March 1949, p. 3.

118. These ideas build on Henry Abramson, 'The Scattering of Amalek: A Model
     for Understanding the Ukrainian–Jewish Conflict', *East European Jewish
     Affairs*, 24, no. 1 (1994), pp. 39–47. The words 'bigoted' and 'intolerant'
     come from Carynnyk's comments to his '1939 Autobiography', p. 7. See, for
     example, Dovzhenko's complaint in 1945 that fourth-class Jews at the Kiev
     Film Studio poisoned his life and persuaded his countrymen (ostensibly
     because of the *Ukraine in Flames* fiasco) to expel him from the studio.
     UVOKShch, p. 279 ; *Hospody*, p. 262; *ZDUVOShch*, p. 386.

119. S. I. Iutkevich, ed., *Kinoslovar' v dvukh tomakh* (Moscow, 1966–1970) and
     S. I. Iutkevich, ed., *Kino: Entsiklopedicheskii slovar'* (Moscow, 1986). I am
     grateful to Richard Taylor for citing the second encyclopedia.

120. Robert D. Putnam, *Making Democracy Work: Civic Traditions in Modern Italy*
     (Princeton, NJ, 1993), p. 174. The term, 'lopsided friendship', comes from
     Julian Pitt-Rivers, *The People of the Sierra* (London, 1954), p. 40.

121. Anatolii Latyshev, 'Poimenno nazvat'', in L. Kh. Mamatova, ed., *Kino:
     politika i liudy. 30-e gody* (Moscow, 1995), p. 158. On Vyshnia's return from
     the camps and his visit with Dovzhenko in Moscow in December 1943, see
     UVOKShch, p. 241; *Hospody*, p. 215; *ZDUVOShch*, p. 339.

122. *ZA*, p. 261.

123. *ZA*, p. 274.

124. *ZA*, pp. 240, 243, 274–5, 280.

125. See A. P. Dovzhenko, 'Stat'i ob I. V. Stalina. Varianty i chernovye nabroski
     (October 1937–March 1953)', RGALI, 2081/1/374.

126. *ZA*, pp. 267–8.

127. *ZA*, p. 243.

8

Dovzhenko's War

After the German invasion of the Soviet Union on 22 June 1941, Soviet leaders encouraged a limited revival of the non-Russian identities, including the Ukrainian, within the russocentric Soviet framework that emerged in the late 1930s.[1] For the majority of Soviet citizens who had escaped German occupation, many – encouraged by the authorities – came to believe that with the victory over Nazi Germany, the USSR would modify the harsh social, political, economic, cultural and national policies it imposed in the late 1920s and 30s.[2]

Buoyed by the first major Soviet military victories – at Stalingrad in February 1943 and Kursk in July of the same year – Stalin and his men changed course and returned to his policy of placing 'Russia first'. Between 1943 and 1945, the policy promoting non-Russian identities introduced at the beginning of the war and the policy of promoting Russia first came into conflict. Dovzhenko became one of the most prominent victims of this ideological contention, inasmuch as he – a patriot of the Soviet Union – identified himself primarily as a Ukrainian.

At the Front

Whatever misgivings Dovzhenko may have had about previous Soviet policies, at the outbreak of the war, he mobilised for both the front lines and the home front quickly, wholeheartedly and enthusiastically.[3] He continued to work creatively during the course of the war but changed his choice of weapons from the camera to the pen, becoming a journalist, a publicist and a propagandist for the Soviet war effort. In 1942–3 he wrote and published several short stories describing the horrors of war. He began his autobiographical tale, *The Enchanted Desna* and – most importantly – started a series of notebooks and diaries covering the period from 1941 to 1956.[4] He also became a popular speaker who often appeared at anti-fascist rallies. Denouncing the German invasion and calling on all citizens to defend the Soviet Union, he also frequently spoke over the radio.[5]

As the Soviet defence of the western regions of the USSR quickly collapsed in the summer of 1941, the Soviet Ukrainian government in Kiev began to evacuate political officials and public figures to Central Asia in July. Dovzhenko, however, did not want to leave Ukraine. He wanted to work close to the action, even at the front.

Alexander Dovzhenko (right) with his father Petro Symonovych (late 1930s)

Instead of creating feature films, he wanted to film documentaries chronicling the war.[6] Despite his objections, the leadership of the All-Union Committee of Soviet Cinematographers ordered him to evacuate Kiev.

During the chaotic Soviet withdrawal, Dovzhenko could not take his mother and father, who had moved to the Ukrainian capital in the 1930s to live with him.[7] In June 1941 they had already left for their dacha outside Kiev. When the Soviet Ukrainian government decided to leave Ukraine several weeks later, the evacuation commission allegedly could not find Dovzhenko's parents.[8] They then fell under German occupation. For the next two years the film-maker experienced great emotional strain. In addition to this burden, Dovzhenko accumulated others in Central Asia.

The authorities sent Dovzhenko and Solntseva to Ufa, the capital of Bashkiria, which became the home for evacuated Ukrainian writers and scholars. After living in Ufa for nearly three months, on 26 October 1941, they moved to Ashkhabad, nearly 1,900 kilometres to the south.[9] The Cinematography Committee's leaders insisted that Dovzhenko, as the artistic director of the Kiev Film Studio, move to the capital of Turkmenia, where the Kiev Film Studio had set up shop.

Two months after arriving in Ashkhabad and taking up his responsibilities at the Kiev Film Studio, Dovzhenko completed the first draft of his screenplay *Ancestors of the Zaporozhian Cossacks*, which describes the life of a collective farm family in the

1930s.[10] Despite his hard work, Dovzhenko remained restless. He did not want to make films in the safety of Central Asia. Instead, he hoped to join his colleagues at the front.[11] In common with most Soviet intellectuals, he enthusiastically volunteered to work near the battle lines and place his life in danger. A sense of responsibility for his homeland and for his parents, the cornerstone of his identity, prompted him to do so. The German enemy clarified his loyalty to the USSR and distracted him from his prewar misgivings about the Soviet system.

At the end of January 1942, Dovzhenko left Ashkhabad to travel to Kuibyshev for a meeting of the literature and arts subcommittee of the Stalin Prize Selection Committee.[12] After completing his official duties there on 5 February 1942, he left for Moscow, where he wanted to meet with Ivan Bolshakov, the head of the Cinematography Committee, and with members of the party's Central Committee.[13]

He hoped that Bolshakov and the others would give him permission to spend a month at the Southwestern Front headquartered in Voronezh. After Voronezh, he planned to return to Moscow to write about what he had seen there.[14] They granted his wish.

Arriving in Voronezh at the end of February, he stayed at the Southwestern Front for the next six and a half months. In this city, Dovzhenko met with a group of Ukrainian writers and correspondents. After hearing their stories about the horrors of war at the front, he asserted: 'I will go with you to the front. I want to see everything with my own eyes.'[15]

He wanted to visit the battle lines immediately, but heart pains and severe headaches delayed him. Inasmuch as Dovzhenko always sought to influence the policies of the Soviet government and the Communist Party, his physical ailments at this point appear as a reaction to Soviet 'reality'. When his afflictions subsided in the spring of 1942, Dovzhenko visited the front and wrote about his experiences there. Initially he became a war correspondent and a member of the editorial board of the Southwestern Front newspaper, *Krasnaia Armiia*.[16] Not surprisingly, his writings dealt with life at the front.[17]

With the war, Dovzhenko could not divorce his creativity from the surrounding political context. He believed that he needed to subordinate his creative energies to the Soviet struggle against the Nazis. In a letter dated 2 May 1942, he informed Solntseva that he would soon become a member of the Political Administration of the Southwestern Front and would not return to Ashkhabad.[18] He claimed that he could do more for the Soviet war effort against Germany at the front than working at the studio in Ashkhabad.

While visiting this Front, Dovzhenko won the support of General S. F. Galadzhev, the head of the Front's Political Administration. He appointed the film director, who did not belong to the party, the head of *Krasnaia Armiia*'s political section.[19] Between the end of May and the beginning of June 1942, Dovzhenko officially became a manager (*intendant*), second class (a military rank for political and administrative officers) in the mobilised reserve of the Political Administration of the Southwestern Front.[20] In this capacity, he also served as an instructor and as a war correspondent.

Dovzhenko's urge to serve at the front comprised the most important, but certainly not the only reason that led him to leave Ashkhabad. In the evacuation from Kiev to Soviet Central Asia, Dovzhenko, the studio's artistic director, came into conflict with the studio's main administrator, Lynniichuk, and his allies. Although the details of this conflict present difficulties in reconstruction, a sketch of its broad outlines follows.

By the end of December 1941, Lynniichuk (with Bolshakov's approval) had removed Dovzhenko from his position as artistic director and fired Solntseva and Dovzhenko's two assistant directors, Lazar Bodyk and I. Ihnatovych.[21] A. Soroka, the head of the screenplay department of the Kiev Film Studio, had organised an effort to remove Dovzhenko on the grounds that he had 'deserted' Kiev and disrupted the work of the studio in Ashkhabad. Soroka persuaded Lynniichuk and Bolshakov, whose relations with Dovzhenko were tense, of these unfounded charges (the responsible authorities, after all, had evacuated Dovzhenko to Central Asia).[22]

With the approval of Moscow's Cinematography Committee, Lynniichuk temporarily replaced (on or before 14 March 1942) Dovzhenko as the studio's artistic director with M. I. Romm. Because the Ukrainian film-maker had to collect large amounts of material for his new screenplay, *Ukraine in Flames*, and write and film it, Lynniichuk explained, Dovzhenko did not have the time to devote to his duties as the studio's artistic director.[23] This explanation did not, however, tell the complete story.

In a report to D. S. Korotchenko, a secretary of the Central Committee of the CP(b)U, Vasyl Kostenko, the deputy head of cadres at the Ukrainian Central Committee, wrote on 22 October 1942 that the story of Dovzhenko's release from his position posed a big and complex question.[24] Unfortunately, he did not explain.

Perhaps the underlying reason for Dovzhenko's dismissal related to his insubordination. The film-maker, most likely, did not receive Bolshakov's or Lynniichuk's permission to leave the Kiev Film Studio in Ashkhabad to join the Southwestern Front. General Galadzhev's appointment of Dovzhenko to the Front's Political Administration must have come about over Bolshakov's and Lynniichuk's objections. By obtaining permission directly from Galadzhev, Dovzhenko bypassed Soviet cinematography's chain of command.

In light of Dovzhenko's poor relations with his colleagues, his audacity in taking such a step presents no great surprise. He hated Bolshakov and Lynniichuk. In April 1942, he asserted that he had two major enemies – Hitler and Bolshakov. In May 1942 he claimed that Lynniichuk was 'an internationalist in form, but a scoundrel in content'.[25] In addition to Bolshakov and Lynniichuk, he despised the directors

Romm and Ihor Savchenko with great passion. In a letter to Solntseva dated 4 June 1942, he predicted that dealing with these men would cause him to die prematurely in the course of a year or two.[26] One month later he asserted that he would not subordinate himself to Bolshakov, Romm and Lynniichuk. 'I cannot and do not want to tolerate these petty nothings and scoundrels. But most importantly, I cannot leave the army and do not want to. This is where I should be when the Ukrainian people are living in captivity.'[27] Most of all, Dovzhenko enjoyed contributing to the war effort by writing. He felt appreciated by his readers. 'The soldiers like my articles,' he wrote to his long-term companion. 'This is more important than Savchenko's films and all of Alma-Ata.'[28]

Perhaps the film-maker's problems with his superiors derived from more fundamental issues than a clash of personalities. In a March 1942 letter to F. A. Redko, the deputy chair of the Council of People's Commissars of the Ukrainian SSR, Dovzhenko asserted that Bolshakov had told him that the Soviet film industry did not need any new Ukrainian cinematographic cadres. 'Let them fight,' Bolshakov allegedly told Dovzhenko. 'Now there is no Ukraine, there is no Ukrainian Central Committee or Council of People's Commissars, and we do not need any cadres or films in Ukrainian. When we'll retake Kiev, then you'll train them.'[29] In his 4 June 1942 letter to Solntseva, Dovzhenko lamented that 'if by now the Ukrainian nation does not exist for them and if Ukrainian cadres are not necessary for their bureaucrats, then I am also unnecessary. I prefer to stay here – at the front.'[30]

Inasmuch as Dovzhenko insisted on maintaining the Kiev studio's Ukrainian identity, its use of the Ukrainian language and themes and its employment of Ukrainian film-makers, disagreements over the studio's mission and its role in Central Asia seriously divided Dovzhenko from Lynniichuk and Bolshakov. Whatever the exact nature or origins of their differences, the war exacerbated them and made Dovzhenko reconsider his film-making career. On 10 April 1942, he recorded the following observations in his diary:

> I often think how my life has been wasted. What a great mistake I made when I went to work in film. Sixteen years of penal servitude in this ... bourgeois dustbin where I am forced to cooperate with pitiful wretches who hate me and whom I profoundly despise as unqualified and amoral brutes without a shred of decency or holiness, wretches who hate my [people] and make it miserable. How much health and happiness have I lost because of people whom I can't stand! If I had applied all my strength and passion in these sixteen years to writing, I'd have at least a dozen volumes of real literature behind me ...[31]

In light of these frustrations, how could Dovzhenko craft a meaningful life for himself? The best way, he decided, did not involve returning to the Kiev Film Studio in

Ashkhabad. After completing his military service at the Southwestern Front in October 1942, he moved to Moscow. Four months later he completed his active tour of duty and became a member of the Red Army reserve, attaining the rank of colonel on 31 March 1943. In early April 1943 the Central Committee of the CP(b)U appointed him a member of the Ukrainian Commission Investigating German War Crimes.[32]

Living in Moscow, Dovzhenko became involved with his old colleagues from the Kiev Film Studio who worked in the Soviet capital. The Secretariat of the Central Committee of the Communist Party of Ukraine approved the idea that the men and women from the Kiev Film Studio stationed in Moscow could organise a branch at the Moscow Film Studio (Mosfilm). Until 1944, when the authorities re-established the Kiev Film Studio in Kiev, the studio remained divided between Moscow and Ashkhabad; Dovzhenko headed the Moscow branch.[33] Meanwhile, Alexander Valentynovych Horsky, a man more sympathetic to Dovzhenko, replaced Lynniichuk as the head of the Kiev Film Studio in 1943.[34] He may have reappointed the filmmaker to his position as the studio's artistic director.

Documentary Film-maker

In the course of the Second World War, Dovzhenko became a documentary filmmaker. After the Soviet invasion of Poland on 17 September 1939 and the occupation of its Belarussian- and Ukrainian-inhabited lands, he travelled to the soon-to-be annexed territories to give talks to the local Ukrainian populations there. He began to chronicle the reunification of these territories under a single government on film.

Entitling his film *Liberation* (1940), he captured the historical episodes: the departure of the unemployed in Lviv for work in the Donbass mines, the elections to the People's Assemblies in Lviv and Bialostok, the speeches of the delegates from Western Ukraine and Western Belarus at a session of the All-Union Supreme Soviet at the Kremlin and the enthusiastic applause these newly elected parliamentarians gave Stalin.[35] *Izvestiia*'s critic asserted that *Liberation*, 'a talented, lavish, and persuasive work, provided an excellent depiction of the national, political, and social oppression Belarussians and Ukrainians experienced under Polish rule'.[36]

Dovzhenko's next documentary, *The Battle for Our Soviet Ukraine* (1943), created with Solntseva and Avdiienko, dealt with events from June 1941 until the beginning of 1943. According to Peter Kenez, this film

> contrasted the 'peaceful and happy lives of the Soviet people before the war' with the difficult present. Dovzhenko's highly individual style, characterized by lyricism and attention to the beauties of the Ukrainian landscape, was very much in evidence. He

was among the first to utilize captured German newsreels in order to make his points. He undercut smiling German faces and the depiction of the suffering of the conquered people.[37]

Izvestiia's critic asserted that this film transcended the framework of documentary film-making to become 'a modern man's chronicle of events and a heroic song'.[38] *Pravda*'s critic claimed that *The Battle*'s visual impact went beyond the narrow confines of a documentary film. 'By visually depicting the horrors of the war, especially German war crimes, Dovzhenko's work not only recorded events, but encouraged hatred of the Germans,' which critics hailed as a positive accomplishment.[39] *Komsomol'skaia pravda*'s critic complimented the intimate relationship between the film's frames and Dovzhenko's text. He asserted that the frames 'not only illustrated the text, but also melded with it to produce a single artistic whole'.[40]

Produced after Stalin's denunciation of Dovzhenko on 30 January 1944, *Victory in Right-Bank Ukraine* (1945) emerged as the Ukrainian film-maker's last war documentary. Although Dovzhenko must have experienced difficulties in completing this film, Maksym Rylsky, the head of the Ukrainian Writers' Union, wrote a positive review for *Izvestiia*. He claimed that Dovzhenko produced a good text and that the film 'confirmed the greatness of the Soviet people, the greatness of the Great Fatherland War, and the greatness of our leader, Stalin'.[41]

Becoming a Writer

Over the course of the war, Dovzhenko also began to write short stories. In light of the long production and censorship delays associated with film-making, even with the creation of wartime documentaries, writing articles and short stories became the fastest way he could express his creativity and deliver it to a mass audience.

In a short period of time, he wrote the stories 'Victory', 'Life to Bloom', 'Night Before Battle', 'At the Barbed Wire', 'Mother', 'Stop, Death, Stop' and others. Seeking simply to raise the morale of the troops, his stories lacked subtle psychological nuances. Instead, they dealt with the war in black and white, with life and death.[42] Dovzhenko incorporated a number of these short stories into his screenplays *Ukraine in Flames* and *The Chronicle of the Flaming Years*.[43]

In his articles, films and speeches, Dovzhenko expressed his concern for the Soviet soldiers fighting at the front and for those living under German occupation. Dovzhenko's empathy for his parents transferred to all who had remained behind.[44] Most of all, the war allowed him to express publicly his Ukrainian patriotism, his love for his homeland.

At the Third Pan-Slavic Meeting in Moscow on 5 May 1943, Dovzhenko claimed that the war had brought disaster to all Slavs.[45] Of the Slavs, Dovzhenko asserted, Ukrainians suffered disproportionately: 'During this war the forty million Ukrainians experienced heavier losses and more destruction than any other people.'[46] Dovzhenko's interpretation did not take into account the German annihilation of 2–3 million Soviet Jews, who generally did not appear in the Soviet media. The Soviet agitation and propaganda machine almost never revealed that the Nazis had a special policy toward the Jews.[47] Throughout the brutal war on the Eastern Front, Soviet authorities did not differentiate the sufferings of the Soviet people by nationality. They defined German brutalities against Soviet citizens as crimes against the Soviet people as a whole.[48] By singling out the Ukrainians, the film-maker violated Soviet policy. As Dovzhenko emphasised Ukrainian uniqueness in his short stories, his views came to the attention of the party's ideological guardians. His short story 'Victory' and his screenplay *Ukraine in Flames* ultimately provided the Soviet authorities with the ammunition to accuse him of Ukrainian nationalism.

Dovzhenko completed 'Victory' on 28 October 1942, in Moscow.[49] His short story contained two controversial passages. Captain Vasyl Kravchyna, a Ukrainian and the commanding officer of a Soviet artillery unit fighting German tanks, rhetorically asks his soldiers on the eve of a major battle, 'What are we fighting for? What are we dying for?' Kravchyna then responds to his own question: 'We are fighting for something priceless, for Ukraine ... For the honorable Ukrainian people ... For forty million Ukrainians ... For our people torn to pieces, for our splintered people'.[50] At another point, Kravchyna repeats his question. His response becomes more focused: 'For the great peoples of the Soviet Union and for our Ukrainian state from the Subcarpathian Rus to this field of battle ... Remember,' he tells his soldiers, 'whatever fronts we fight on today, wherever Stalin would send us – to the north, to the south, to the west, to the four corners of the earth, we are fighting for Ukraine.'[51]

At the end of 1942, the editorial board of the journal *Znamia* accepted 'Victory' for publication. According to Georgy Aleksandrov, the head of the Central Committee's Directorate for Agitation and Propaganda (Agitprop), Dovzhenko's short story remained incomplete and carelessly constructed. It contained many 'exaggerated episodes' and 'ambiguous expressions'.[52]

Most importantly, Dovzhenko's 'Victory', according to Aleksandrov, reflected politically incorrect and harmful views, interpretations contradicting Bolshevism and its nationality policies. Inasmuch as no non-Ukrainian names appeared among Dovzhenko's protagonists, the author – according to Aleksandrov – gave the impression that only Ukrainians fought to free Ukraine from the Germans. Not once in his short story did Dovzhenko refer to Ukraine as Soviet Ukraine. Dovzhenko gave a completely false reason for the Red Army's retreat from Ukraine in 1941 – because the Soviet Union 'did not possess a cultured way of life, relations, or a cultured way of war'.

In Dovzhenko's story, Soviet soldiers win their battle against the Germans, but lose most of their unit's members. According to Aleksandrov's interpretation of his short story, the soldiers died because the Red Army did not train them properly, because of their commanders' incompetence and because of the bureaucratism of the military specialists. Not surprisingly, the Agitprop head recommended banning this short story.[53] Politburo member A. A. Andreev also read 'Victory' and agreed with Aleksandrov.[54]

Dovzhenko, however, did not grasp the essence of why he had angered the authorities. Perhaps he did not know of the ban. In any case, he committed an even more serious set of ideological mistakes in his next screenplay, *Ukraine in Flames*.

The film-maker-turned-writer, according to one of his colleagues, first used the phrase 'Ukraine in flames' in late 1941 in Ashkhabad. Three months later, he completed an article with the same title, which *Izvestiia* published on 31 March 1942.[55] *Ukraine in Flames* also served as the title of a Ukrainian literary almanac that first appeared in Ufa in 1942.

The party's censors claimed to find deviations from the party's political line in Dovzhenko's article. In reaction, in September 1942 Agitprop, on the orders of A. S. Shcherbakov, a candidate-member of the Politburo and the head of the Main Political Administration of the Red Army, secretly prohibited the republication of the article 'Ukraine in Flames' in Ukrainian and central Soviet publications.[56] Whether or not Dovzhenko knew of this prohibition, he continued to write in this vein.

Already in early 1942, he had begun work on the screenplay for *Ukraine in Flames*, a radically different version of his *Izvestiia* article.[57] After he completed his project at the end of the summer of 1943, Dovzhenko read excerpts to troops and front line correspondents on the outskirts of Kharkiv, which the Soviet army was preparing to storm.[58] On the night of 28 August, Dovzhenko personally read his screenplay to Khrushchev.[59] The party boss praised it highly and recommended that Dovzhenko publish it as a separate book in Russian and Ukrainian. 'Let them read it,' the film-maker–writer quoted Khrushchev as saying. 'Let them realise that it's not so simple.'[60] Two months later, on the eve of the Red Army's capture of Kiev, Dovzhenko recounted in his diary how Khrushchev assuaged the author's misgivings about certain critical passages in *Ukraine in Flames* and gave him permission to publish it 'completely and without delay'.[61]

If Dovzhenko's account of Khrushchev's reactions carries any veracity, then a serious difference of opinion may have emerged between the party leadership in Moscow (who, according to Khrushchev, thought in simple categories) and the party leadership evacuated from Ukraine (who saw the complexities of the internal situation in Ukraine) over the course of the war. Khrushchev, famous for his impulsive decisions, clearly miscalculated in this case.

Ukraine in Flames includes vignettes of Ukrainians who experience the war under German occupation and of those who fight the Germans. In its depiction of the brutalities of war, the Nazi occupation and the Soviet response, Dovzhenko's screenplay criticised the Soviet Union's treatment of those who had lived under the Nazi occupation. Each character in the screenplay has a different experience, but generally their encounters with Soviet authorities before and after the German occupation follow a negative pattern.

Dovzhenko also condemned the harshness and hypocrisy of Soviet officials who had retreated during the German advance only to punish those who could not escape on their return years later. In his diary entry of 29 November 1943, he wrote:

> One of the paradoxes of our age is that many people have the idea of liberating the Fatherland from the Nazi yoke without understanding the essence of the idea. There are commanders and political instructors who shed their blood for two years, suffering enormous difficulties as they fight to liberate the country, and then, when they have liberated some bloody, ravaged piece of it treat the people crudely and even cruelly, as if they were guilty in some respect. They forget that the Fatherland is not just land, it is also people, flesh of whose flesh they are.[62]

Khrystia, one of the screenplay's heroines, experiences this brutal treatment. During her interrogation after the return of Soviet troops, she recalls an earlier encounter with her interrogator from the summer of 1941, after the Germans had invaded. As Soviet officials prepared to retreat, she asked him if the Germans would soon occupy her village. If so, perhaps she should flee. He angrily called her question a provocation. Khrystia remained in the village. Shortly afterwards the Germans arrived.

This same Soviet officer now returns with the advancing Soviet Army and labels her a traitor and whore. She turns to him and sarcastically retorts: 'You are innocent, but I am not.' He then threatens to execute her.[63]

Two other passages in *Ukraine in Flames* attracted political controversy. Dovzhenko included Kravchyna's 'What are we fighting for?' speech, which had previously appeared in 'Victory'. In another passage, the German Colonel Kraus provides a lengthy and negative evaluation of Soviet citizens. Speaking to his son, he asserts:

> Well, Ludwig, you should know that among these people, their Achilles heel is never covered. These people are absolutely without the ability to forgive one another for their differences, even in the name of common and higher interests. They do not possess state instincts. You know, they do not study history. It is amazing. They have been living for twenty-five years with negative slogans, denying God, property, families, and friendship! For them the word nation (*natsiia*) remained only a negative. They do not have any eternal truths. This is because, among them, there are so many traitors ...

There is no reason for us to destroy them all. You know, if we are smart about it, they will exterminate each other.[64]

These remarks contributed to Dovzhenko's undoing. Censors and the party's ideological guardians could not distinguish where the author's imagination started and ended. Was he presenting his own interpretation of the Communist Party, the Soviet Union and the Soviet leadership, or merely portraying an enemy's perspective? They concluded that his artistic licence did not extend to such outrageous statements, even if attributed to the enemy.

By going to the front and by recording the events there, he thwarted his own desire to support the Soviet cause. He returned to his original dilemma: expressing the realities of the Ukrainian people, as he understood them, challenged the Soviet interpretation of that reality.

The Screenplay's Reception

As Dovzhenko steered his screenplay through the proper channels in Moscow in the autumn of 1943, he learned that the leading governmental and party leaders had reached conflicting interpretations of his work. Recognising that he might have problems receiving official approval for it, the film-maker met with Georgy Malenkov, a secretary of the party's Central Committee and a member of its Politburo. At this meeting, Malenkov promised Dovzhenko publication of his screenplay and permission to create a feature film based on it.[65]

As Dovzhenko presented his case for *Ukraine in Flames*, his first war documentary, *The Battle for Our Soviet Ukraine*, premiered in Moscow on 25 October 1943, to great acclaim.[66] Dovzhenko's conversation with Malenkov and the praise that he received at his documentary's premiere may have reinforced his idea that the authorities would approve *Ukraine in Flames*.

Two weeks later, on 6 November 1943, Dovzhenko, accompanying Marshal Georgy Zhukov, General M. F. Vatutin, N. S. Khrushchev, Solntseva and a number of Ukrainian writers and poets, entered Kiev, after Soviet troops had liberated it from the Germans.[67] He recorded the horrors he encountered:

Most of the population is gone. Only a small group of impoverished, exhausted people left. No children, no girls, no young men. Only old women and cripples. The world has not seen anything like this in centuries. Before the war Kiev had a population of one million; now there are only fifty thousand people among the ruins.[68]

In this devastation, Dovzhenko sought out his parents. He found his elderly mother. His father, he learned, had died of starvation during the German occupation.[69] He lay unburied for six days, until his wife sold the remains of her clothes, made him a

Nikita S. Khrushchev (left), the head of the Communist Party of Ukraine, with Dovzhenko during the war (1943)

coffin, and took him to the graveyard by herself.[70] Thus did Dovzhenko experience the terrible tragedy of the war at the most personal and intimate level.

After Dovzhenko returned to Moscow with his mother on 26 November 1943, he could not escape his grief by working harder. His political fortunes had changed for the worse. Upon arriving in the city, Oleksy Shvachko, Dovzhenko's young assistant, no doubt told Dovzhenko about the problems he had encountered in delivering the director's manuscript to the publisher.

Dovzhenko had asked Shvachko to stay behind in Moscow, complete the corrections and deliver the last draft of *Ukraine in Flames* to the *Znamia* editorial offices. After retyping and proof-reading the manuscript, Shvachko took the screenplay to the editor, Vsevolod Vishnevsky, who in the recent past had enthusiastically published Dovzhenko's works.[71] *Znamia*'s editorial staff had since changed their minds. They claimed that a temporary problem had held up publication. They promised Shvachko that *Znamia* would publish the screenplay shortly after Dovzhenko's return to Moscow, but the problem proved more than a temporary delay.[72]

After the film-maker returned from Kiev, he contacted Bolshakov, who told him that Stalin did not like *Ukraine in Flames* and had forbidden it to be published or screened.[73] Between 5 November, when Dovzhenko left Moscow for Kiev, and 26 November, when he returned, events transpired to doom his screenplay.

On 19 November 1943 the managing editor of *Znamia*, E. Mikhailova, sent a copy of the page proofs of *Ukraine in Flames* (scheduled to appear in the November 1943 issue of the journal) to Shcherbakov, one of the party's most rigid ideologues.[74] In addition to the proofs, she enclosed a brief note, which asserted that Dovzhenko had ignored the journal's editorial corrections and restored his original text.[75]

Although a number of Politburo members had read Dovzhenko's screenplay, Mikhailova's letter may have set off an alarm among those, such as Shcherbakov, who suspected Dovzhenko of ideological nonconformity, if not subversion. Indeed, as Soviet authorities grew increasingly sensitive late in the war, Shcherbakov viewed Dovzhenko's criticism of Soviet unpreparedness and military incompetence in 1941 as slanderous, even treasonable. Whereas a number of Politburo members may have approved Dovzhenko's screenplay during private conversations with him, they probably had not read it and would not necessarily defend it if one of their colleagues, such as Shcherbakov, created a political issue over it. After Shcherbakov received the letter from Mikhailova, he must have apprised Beria and then Stalin of the ideological undercurrents in Dovzhenko's screenplay.[76]

According to Khrushchev's memoirs, Stalin met with several members of the Politburo on 30 December 1943 to discuss Dovzhenko's screenplay.[77] At this meeting:

> Shcherbakov presented the case for the prosecution. He was obviously trying hard to
> fan Stalin's anger against Dovzhenko by harping on the charge that the film scenario
> was extremely nationalistic. Malenkov sat silently through this whole discussion, even
> though he had already given the scenario his blessing. Stalin didn't let the matter drop
> there. He told me to convene a meeting of the Ukrainian Party and governmental
> leaders, including the Central Committee secretaries in charge of propaganda. He told
> us to prepare a ... resolution about the unsatisfactory state of affairs on the Ukrainian
> ideological front.[78]

As Stalin prepared to give Dovzhenko a fierce dressing down, the film-maker wavered. Between 26 November 1943 and 30 January 1944, Dovzhenko experienced a surge of conflicting emotions, including anger, defiance, resignation and hope. He did not know what to do.[79] He sought reassurance from Khrushchev, his patron, but the head of the Ukrainian party, who had enthusiastically praised *Ukraine in Flames* only months earlier, now refused to meet with the film-maker.[80] Only on 3 January 1944 did Dovzhenko speak with Khrushchev, a dry run for his subsequent meeting with Stalin on 30 January 1944. According to Dovzhenko, the encounter with Khrushchev turned into an emotionally-draining meeting:

It seemed as if he wasn't N. S. [Khrushchev] and I wasn't myself ... There was a cold, merciless atheist and judge, and a guilty, amoral criminal, and enemy of the people, i.e. me.

And I understood that no arguments, even those pronounced with the anguish of a heavy heart and reflecting the most honest self-analysis, had changed his mind over anything, nor would they ... I left N. S. with the feeling that my life was ruined. 'We'll come back to a consideration of your work', he said. 'We won't just leave it as it is. No, we'll come back to it yet'. So I have to live and function under the oppressive and unbearable threat of eventual judgment. They will tear me apart before the people, and all of my many years of labor will be nullified and even turned into a dishonest trick. Lord, give me strength. Don't let me fall into grief and sorrow, lest my heart dry up and my soul turn bitter. Send me the wisdom to forgive the good N. S., who showed himself to be ... a weak person.[81]

Dovzhenko challenged the Soviet interpretation of the war. At the same time, he trusted high Soviet officials at many levels who he believed would defend him. Once Stalin objected to his screenplay, Dovzhenko's 'friends' disappeared.

By 21 December he decided to revise his screenplay.[82] The prospect of official prohibition from publishing or film-making inspired Dovzhenko to reconsider his truth and how he could save it.

Dovzhenko's Meeting with Stalin

Stalin sought to do more than simply ban Dovzhenko's screenplay. As a film critic who emphasised the primacy of socialist realism, and as the most important interpreter of Soviet nationality policies, the Soviet leader, along with important colleagues, clearly felt that the film-maker's recent work impugned the Soviet government's highest goals and beliefs. Stalin had protected and encouraged him, but Dovzhenko still nurtured an artistic and political vision at variance with that of the party hierarchy. The general secretary must have felt that the Ukrainian had not only ignored his advice, but also betrayed his trust. Stalin then invited him to the Kremlin.

Dovzhenko's meeting with Stalin occurred on 30 January 1944 and lasted from 9.05 p.m. until 10.20 p.m.[83] In addition to Stalin, half of the members and candidate-members of the Politburo attended this meeting.[84] Besides Khrushchev, the first secretary of the Communist Party of Ukraine and the new head (as of 1 February 1944) of the Ukrainian Council of People's Commissars, Stalin invited other leading Ukrainian party and governmental figures, including Alexander Korniichuk, who had a personal axe to grind with Dovzhenko.[85]

After greeting everyone, Stalin explained that he had called this meeting to discuss Dovzhenko's *Ukraine in Flames*. He turned to Dovzhenko and told him that his screenplay could not see publication.[86] At first, Stalin stated that he had considered publishing a critical review of the screenplay in the press, but he had declined to do so because he felt sorry for its author. He claimed that Dovzhenko had included in his screenplay a number of ideas that attempted to revise Leninism, and which came out against the party, against Soviet power, against collective farmers and against the government's nationality policies. The screenplay, in short, attacked the Soviet order.[87]

According to Stalin, Dovzhenko had committed serious mistakes of an anti-Leninist character. Stalin accused the film-maker of opposing the class struggle, the party's policy of liquidating the kulaks as a class and collectivisation itself. The screenplay's author, in Stalin's view, did not realise that the Soviet struggle against the Germans also represented a class war, a conflict between the oppressors and the oppressed. Dovzhenko, moreover, had dared to criticise the Communist Party's and the Soviet government's preparations for war. Stalin then pointed out that his client used the phrase 'thin armour' often, especially in his description of Soviet tanks. The general secretary accused the film-maker of asserting that the Soviet state failed in preparing its people for war.

Stalin then criticised Dovzhenko's view of the leadership of the party, government and Red Army. The film-maker had characterised them as careerists, selfish and stupid, isolated from the people. According to Stalin, the Soviet people had great faith in their officers and generals, party and governmental workers and loved them because they represented the best of Soviet society.

In his portrayal of the romance between Olesia Zaporozhets, the daughter of a hard-working collective farmer, and the Soviet Army officer Kravchyna, the author violated Soviet standards of propriety and tact. The inclusion of a scene in which Olesia asks Kravchyna to sleep with her, Stalin and the others alleged, slandered the virtue of Ukrainian women.

Worst of all, according to Stalin, Dovzhenko did not attempt to conceal his Ukrainian nationalism, as revealed by Kravchyna's response to his rhetorical question, 'What are we fighting for?' Dovzhenko presented the politically unacceptable view that his protagonists fought only for the defence and honour of their native Ukraine.

The screenplay portrayed only Ukrainians fighting against the Germans. All the peoples of the Soviet Union, according to Stalin, fought the Germans and defended Ukraine. Stalin then concluded: 'Dovzhenko's screenplay is a platform of narrow-minded and limited Ukrainian nationalism, which is opposed to the policies of our party and the interests of the Ukrainian and Soviet people.' In Stalin's view, Dovzhenko's nationalist ideology sought to weaken the unity of the Soviet people.[88]

At 10.20 p.m. Stalin dismissed Dovzhenko and the Ukrainian delegation.[89] Khrushchev and the other members and candidate-members of the Politburo stayed behind. They left Stalin's office at 11.10 p.m.[90] They left no record of what they discussed during the fifty-minute period between Dovzhenko's dismissal and the end of the meeting

Dovzhenko's Isolation

After 30 January 1944 Stalin and his lieutenants isolated Dovzhenko and marginalised his creativity. On 8 February 1944 Shcherbakov issued an order to Khrushchev, to the Ukrainian provincial party leaders, to the editors of prominent Moscow-based literary journals and to the directors of various publishing houses not to publish Dovzhenko's works without Agitprop's special permission.[91]

By the summer of 1944, Dovzhenko had lost his membership in the Artistic Council of the All-Union Cinema Committee.[92] By mid-February 1944, the Politburo of the Communist Party of Ukraine excluded Dovzhenko from the Pan-Slavic Committee and from the Stalin Prize Selection Committee. Members of the Ukrainian Politburo also removed the film-maker from the editorial board of the journal *Ukraina* and fired him from his position as the artistic director of the Kiev Film Studio.[93] To add insult to injury, the authorities demoted Dovzhenko from the rank of director first class to director third class.[94] He also lost access to the Kremlin polyclinic.[95] Given his history of heart trouble, this last punishment had the potential for the greatest harm. According to Peter Kenez, none of the prominent directors during the war experienced comparable abuse.[96] Dovzhenko became completely isolated. Official denunciations heightened this isolation.

After the Politburo's January 1944 meeting with Dovzhenko, the press and major party officials publicly criticised the film-maker. An article in *Bolshevik*, the theoretical organ of the Central Committee of the All-Union Communist Party, accused Dovzhenko of committing serious mistakes. The article asserted that the film-maker incorrectly portrayed the relationships among the peoples of the USSR, and gave a mistaken and essentially slanderous evaluation of the struggle of the Soviet people against the German-fascist invaders.[97]

Repeating Stalin's main accusations, Aleksandrov attacked Dovzhenko at the Ninth Plenum of the Executive Committee of the Soviet Writers' Union on 9 February 1944. Lacking the proper Leninist–Stalinist understanding of the world, Dovzhenko's worldview, Aleksandrov concluded, became seriously flawed.[98]

K. Z. Lytvyn, the CP(b)U's secretary for ideological matters, spoke at a Ukrainian meeting dealing with propaganda on 15 March 1944. He claimed that Dovzhenko had not completely reformed his nationalist convictions and repeated Stalin's accusation that his screenplay 'represented a volley against our party, against Soviet power, against collective farmers, and against our nationality policy'.[99]

At a 12 March 1944 meeting of the Kiev branch of the Soviet Writers' Union, Mykola Bazhan, Alexander Korniichuk and Lytvyn sharply criticised Dovzhenko's anti-Leninist, hostile views. Bazhan, Dovzhenko's former flatmate from the 1920s, had risen to the posts of Deputy Prime Minister of the Ukrainian SSR, its Commissar of Education and the CP(b)U Central Committee secretary in charge of cultural matters. Bazhan claimed that in *Ukraine in Flames*, Dovzhenko's representations of Soviet government, the Communist Party and Red Army officials did not conform to the positive hero model.[100] Korniichuk, Dovzhenko's sworn enemy, called the screenplay a filthy stain on Soviet reality, and he asserted that the author did not believe in 'our victory'.[101] Lytvyn branded the film-maker a political liability.[102]

In addition to these three officials, a number of prominent writers, including Pavlo Tychyna, Leonid Novychenko and Oleksandr Kopylenko, condemned Dovzhenko's work as hostile to the people and the Soviet government itself. Luka Palamarchuk, the managing editor of the official government newspaper, *Radians'ka Ukraina*, asserted that Dovzhenko had pretensions to be a prophet, to teach everyone everything, which led him to write a libellous screenplay against the Soviet people.[103]

Most damagingly, Khrushchev, who had acted as Dovzhenko's patron in Ukraine since 1938, condemned his former client. He stated that 'our politics won. This is our strength and the Dovzhenkos will be destroyed by the Ukrainian people.'[104] In light of Stalin's anger towards the film-maker, Khrushchev could not have done otherwise.

Although Dovzhenko's friends and colleagues in Ukraine may not have completely understood the party's charges against him, they did not dare publicly defend him.[105] Moreover, they tried to avoid him. Most of them lived in Kiev, and they could safely skirt meetings with the film-maker when they visited Moscow. Dovzhenko's friends in Moscow at first kept their distance, but as the film-maker slowly rehabilitated himself, they re-embraced him. Only Yury Yanovsky, who lived in Kiev, Ivan Kozlovsky, a Ukrainian opera singer at Moscow's Bolshoi Theatre, and his closest assistants from Mosfilm regularly visited Dovzhenko's apartment. These displays of loyalty, however, could not counterbalance the attacks against him. As one of his assistants admitted, 'we could not obviate his grief.'[106]

Conclusion

Dovzhenko's *Ukraine in Flames* angered the Stalinist leadership for three major reasons. First, the author did not adhere to the guidelines established for socialist realism. The flawed, all-too-human main characters did not fit the positive hero paradigm. The screenplay, moreover, did not present the Germans in the darkest of terms. Dovzhenko did not show the Communist Party or its leadership as infallible.

Second, Dovzhenko's portrayal of Ukraine diverged from the Soviet interpretation of reality, especially after Stalingrad. Ukraine constituted an integral part of the USSR, but Dovzhenko insisted on emphasising its uniqueness. Stalin and Aleksandrov considered Kravchyna's rhetorical question – 'What are we fighting for?' – provocative. This question demanded a different response from that offered by the screenplay's hero. According to Stalin, the commander should have responded in the following manner:

> Wherever the Soviet government will send you – whether to the north, to the south, to the west, or to the east – remember that you are fighting together with all brotherly Soviet peoples ... for ... our Soviet Union, our common Fatherland. To defend the Union of Soviet Socialist Republics means to defend Soviet Ukraine. When Ukraine, an independent state, is defended, it will become stronger, and will develop only in the presence of the Soviet Union as a whole.[107]

Dovzhenko's emphasis on the centrality of Ukraine, one of the major agricultural and industrial centres of the USSR and the largest non-Russian region lost to the Germans, ran counter to the party's ideological line. The screenplay's recognition of Ukraine's rapid loss in the first months of the war demonstrated the fragility of Soviet control over Ukraine. The author's protagonists criticised the Soviet socialisation of youth, the ignorance of history among Soviet soldiers and the unpreparedness of the Red Army. These factors, in Dovzhenko's opinion, led to the massive defeats of the first year of the war.[108]

Third, and most importantly, the screenplay's criticism of Soviet mistakes, especially the rapid withdrawal from Ukraine in 1941, implicitly blamed Stalin and the party. Intellectuals may have delicately criticised some aspects of Soviet policies before February 1943, but after Stalingrad and Kursk – with victory in sight – Soviet leaders did not want to discuss failures at all.

The war provided an officially sanctioned opportunity for Dovzhenko to concentrate on Ukraine again. The Germans became his and the Soviet state's common enemy, but they left the film-maker exposed in his adamant defence of Ukraine and its victims. His father's death only expanded the gulf between his perceptions and the Soviet interpretation of war and its core supporters.

Furthermore, Dovzhenko violated the unofficial strictures of Stalin's cult of personality. Although he peppered his stories and his screenplay with Stalinist pieties – 'Stalin gathered together and united our people for the first time'; 'Centuries passed and Stalin lifted our people's truth, almost dead from a long sleep, from the grave'; and 'For Stalin!' – not all of the screenplay's scenes complimented Stalin.[109]

Dovzhenko, moreover, did not include any scenes with Stalin in them. At a time when the German invasion threatened the very existence of the Soviet Union and international Communism, the Soviet leader did not make an appearance in his recently released *The Battle for Our Soviet Ukraine* or in the pages of his screenplay *Ukraine in Flames*.

Mikhail Chiaureli, a prominent Georgian film director and a friend of Beria, accosted Dovzhenko after January 1944 and angrily asserted:

> You couldn't spare ten meters of film for the Leader. Didn't make a single episode in any of your films for him. Couldn't spare them! Didn't want to show the Leader! You were eaten up with pride. Well, now you are going to die ... You! You don't know how to make films! What's your talent? Pah! I spit on your talent ... It doesn't mean anything if you don't know how to work. You do as I do: think what you will, but when you're making a film, you put in what is liked. Here a hammer, there a sickle, here a hammer, there a sickle, here a hammer, there a star.[110]

Chiaureli's accusation most likely reflected the views of Stalin's inner circle, perhaps even Stalin himself. The general secretary had befriended Dovzhenko in the early 1930s and saved him from possible arrest, but the director had failed to live up to his part of the deal. He continued to make films and to write short stories and screenplays emphasising Ukraine's uniqueness, and he did not always adhere to the guidelines of socialist realism. Dovzhenko's creative choices upset the Stalinist leaders, who felt betrayed and very angry.

In response Stalin derailed not only his career in film-making, but also his potential role as a symbol of a moderate non-Russian orientation during the war. Khrushchev, the head of Ukraine's Communist Party, may have initially promoted this potential role. Even after his evacuation in 1941, Khrushchev remained the party leader responsible for Ukraine and in this capacity addressed groups of Ukrainian intellectuals, seeking to establish good relations with them after the purges of the 1930s. By advocating the expansion of the public role of the Ukrainian language after the war, he gained their goodwill.[111]

Khrushchev did not elaborate how he planned to enhance Ukrainian, or whether he had Stalin's approval to make such promises, but having served in Ukraine, he understood that the national situation there involved far more nuances than his Moscow-based colleagues imagined. His recommendations may not have satisfied all of the Ukrainian intelligentsia, but in contrast to the brutal Soviet policies of the 1930s, Khrushchev's promises to increase the role of Ukrainian generated the intelligentsia's goodwill towards the Soviet regime and the Communist Party at minimal cost.

In addition to expanding the public role of the Ukrainian language, Khrushchev may have considered electing Dovzhenko to the Ukrainian Supreme Soviet and then appointing him as its head. According to one unverifiable account, he would have replaced Hrechukha, a Ukrainian who had served as the Ukrainian Supreme Soviet's chair since 1939, but who did not speak Ukrainian.[112] Some of the most prominent members of the Ukrainian intelligentsia did not think highly of

Hrechukha.[113] The appointment of Dovzhenko (who spoke Ukrainian in public and publicly identified himself as a Ukrainian) to this post would signal that the party had ameliorated its hard, russocentric line in Ukraine.

Rumours of this appointment may have provoked opposition from Hrechukha and his allies. This opposition may have intensified after Stalingrad and as the Soviet Army liberated Kiev. The end of the war approached. With victory in sight, the Stalinist leadership no longer felt it necessary to make concessions to Ukrainian national feelings.

Instead, the party sought to lean on the Russians, the most populous and powerful national constituency within the Soviet Union. The government expanded its prewar russocentric policies. The party's complete identification of the Russian people with Bolshevism 'whitewashed over' the contributions of the non-Russians to the party and state and 'blurred the difference between the Russian Empire and the Soviet socialist union'.[114] The German invasion had severed large, non-Russian areas from the Soviet Union and, according to the official line, revealed the 'disloyalty' of the non-Russians. Only the Russian core of the Soviet Union had remained loyal. According to Stalin's logic, it made sense to champion the Russians and punish the non-Russians. The general secretary and his inner circle aimed to rally the Russians to the Soviet flag by recognising the Orthodox Church and Russian primacy throughout tsarist and Soviet history.

For a few months in 1943, the policy to promote non-Russians uneasily coexisted with that of 'Russia first'. Many non-Russian intellectuals, including Dovzhenko, nurtured the hope that the party would soften its harsh prewar policies. These illusions inspired Dovzhenko's *Ukraine in Flames,* but by the time Dovzhenko submitted his screenplay for publication, the party's need to reach an accommodation with the non-Russians, especially the Ukrainians, had come to an end.

Stalin's criticism of Dovzhenko compromised Khrushchev, who had been on good terms with the film-maker and with the Ukrainian intelligentsia. Even though Stalin knew that Khrushchev had read Dovzhenko's screenplay, the Ukrainian party chief dreaded Stalin's wrath and did not want the general secretary to remember this fact.[115] At the January meeting in the Kremlin, Khrushchev feared that Dovzhenko might reveal that the Ukrainian party leader had read *Ukraine in Flames*, praised it and recommended it for publication. Although Stalin asked, 'Who read your work?', Dovzhenko did not give Khrushchev or anyone else away. After the meeting, Khrushchev allegedly met Dovzhenko in the corridor, shook his hand, and thanked him, stating 'I will never forget this, never.' He did forget, of course.[116] Malenkov also forgot.

After Dovzhenko's 'crucifixion' (as the director referred to his meeting with Stalin and his lieutenants), the film-maker feared for his life. Following the pattern set in 1919 and in 1932–3, he expected arrest, imprisonment, exile or execution, but

Stalin's agents only curtailed the film-maker's civic and creative responsibilities. Although they prohibited Dovzhenko from returning to Ukraine, they never arrested or imprisoned him. Exiled in Moscow again, Dovzhenko lived where Stalin's subordinates could monitor him closely. Although the most cosmopolitan city in the Soviet Union, Moscow represented a world far from the Ukrainian sources of Dovzhenko's creativity. The city and Mosfilm depressed him. Despite his best efforts to maintain an even keel, he experienced uneasiness, depression, defiance and writer's block.

The war had destroyed his homeland, and his father had died during the German occupation. The *Ukraine in Flames* debacle exacerbated Dovzhenko's emotional losses and undermined his creative powers.

Notes

1. TsDAVOVUU, 1/1/396. Also see David Brandenberger's 'The "Short Course" to Modernity: Stalinist History Textbooks, Mass Culture, and the Formation of Popular Russian National Identity, 1934–1956' (unpublished PhD dissertation, Harvard University, 1999), especially chapters 7–9.

2. See Alex Inkeles, *Public Opinion in Soviet Russia: A Study of Mass Persuasion*, 2nd ed. (Cambridge, MA, 1950) and Alex Inkeles, *Social Change in Soviet Russia* (Cambridge, MA, 1968).

3. Iurii Barabash, 'Stsenarii A. P. Dovzhenko "Ukraina v ogne"', RGALI, 2081/2/210, p. 1.

4. These notebooks became Dovzhenko's only outlet for recording his impressions and reactions to the turbulent world around him. It is unknown whether he shared them with his friends or with Solntseva. After his death in 1956, excerpts from his diaries and notebooks appeared in Soviet journals and collections of his writings, but in highly selective and heavily censored form. The original diaries and notebooks are in RGALI, but they are closed until January 2009. The first and only English-language publication of Dovzhenko's notebooks and diaries appeared in *Alexander Dovzhenko: The Poet as Filmmaker: Selected Writings*, edited and translated by Marco Carynnyk (Cambridge, MA, 1973), pp. 25–270. In critical places, Carynnyk's version (based on materials published in the 1960s) differs significantly from *UVOKShch*, *Hospody* and *ZDUVOShch*.

5. Barabash, pp. 1-2; Mykhailo Kovalenko and Oleksii Mishurin, *Syn zacharovanoi Desny* (Kiev, 1984), pp. 15, 32; *Storinky*, pp. 155, 164–5.

6. RGALI, 2081/1/695, cited in *Storinky*, p. 155.

7. RGALI, 2081/1/1212, cited in *Storinky*, p. 129.

8. RGALI, 2081/1/695, cited in *Storinky*, p. 155.

9. *Storinky*, p. 156.

10. *Storinky*, p. 156.

11. RGALI, 2081/1/717, cited in *Storinky*, pp. 155–6.

12. Kovalenko and Mishurin, p. 32.

13. *Storinky*, p. 158.

14. Dovzhenko to Solntseva, 13 February 1942, TsDA-MLMU, 690/3/9.

15. Cited in Kovalenko and Mishurin, p. 33.

16. *Storinky*, p. 158; Kovalenko and Mishurin, pp. 12–15; Oleg Lasunskii, *Volshebnoe zertsalo* (Voronezh, 1981), pp. 92, 96.

17. David Ortenberg, 'Gody voennye', *DVVS*, p. 147.

18. O. Dovzhenko, *Tvory v p'iaty tomakh* (Kiev, 1966), vol. 5, pp. 347–8; also cited in *Storinky*, pp. 165–6.

19. Ortenberg, pp. 146–7; *Storinky*, pp. 169, 171.

20. *Storinky*, pp. 169, 171.

21. Serhii Kot (compiler), 'Neopublikovani avtohrafy Oleksandra Dovzhenka', *Dnipro*, no. 9–10 (1994), p. 73.

22. Kot, p. 77; *Narysy istorii ukrains'koi intelihentsii (persha polovyna XX st.). U 3-kh knyhakh* (Kiev, 1994), knyha III, p. 76. Kot refers to the head of the screenplay department as 'Syrota'; *Narysy istorii* – A. Soroka. I have been unable to verify his proper name.

23. TsDAHOU, 1/70/66, p. 28.

24. TsDAHOU, 1/70/65, p. 13.

25. *UVOKShch*, pp. 160, 169.

26. TsDA-MLMU, 690/3/9, p. 13.

27. TsDA-MLMU, 690/3/9, p. 17.

28. TsDA-MLMU, 690/3/9, p. 18.

29. Quoted in Kot, p. 75.

30. TsDA-MLMU, 690/3/9, p. 9; Dovzhenko, *Tvory*, (1966), vol. 5, pp. 347–8.

31. *PF*, p. 54; *UVOKShch*, p. 132; *Hospody*, p. 86; *ZDUVOShch*, p. 204.

32. *Storinky*, pp. 187, 189.

33. RGALI, 2081/1/955, p. 5; cited in *Storinky*, p. 184.

34. 'Hors'kyi Oleksandr Valentynovych', in V. Kudryts'kyi, ed., *Mystetstvo Ukrainy: Biohrafichnyi dovidnyk* (Kiev, 1997), p. 170.

35. 'Osvobozhdenie', *Trud*, 7 July 1940.

36. T. Nikolaeva, 'Novyi fil'm A. Dovzhenko', *Izvestiia*, 7 July 1940.

37. Peter Kenez, 'Black and White: The War on Film', in Richard Stites, ed., *Culture and Entertainment in Wartime Russia* (Bloomington, IN, 1995), p. 162.

38. I. Bachelis, 'Bitva za nashu Sovetskuiu Ukrainu', *Izvestiia*, 22 October 1943.

39. Nikolai Tikhonov, 'Bitva za nashu Sovetskuiu Ukrainu', *Pravda*, 20 October 1943.

40. D. Zaslavskii, 'Za rodnuiu mat' – za Ukrainu!' *Komsomol'skaia pravda*, 23 October 1943.

41. Maksym Ryl's'kyi, 'Pobeda na Ukraine', *Izvestiia*, 1 June 1945.

42. R. N. Iurenev, *Aleksandr Dovzhenko* (Moscow, 1959), p. 98.

43. Barabash, p. 2.

44. V. S. Kostenko, 'Vernyi syn naroda', RGALI, 2081/1/1146, p. 6.

45. RGALI, 2081/1/414.

46. RGALI, 2081/1/413, p. 1.

47. Even 'when the Red Army liberated some of the death camps during the last year of the war, the newsreels never pointed out the nationality of its victims'. Kenez, 'Black and White', p. 162. For the best analysis of the evolution of the German Army's war crimes on the territories of the Soviet Union, see Omer Bartov, *The Eastern Front, 1941–1945, German Troops and the Barbarisation of Warfare* (New York, 1986), especially chapter 4.

48. See, for example, 'Rech' deputata L. R. Korniets. Preniia po dokladu o Gosudarstvennom biudzhete SSSR na 1944 goda', *Pravda*, 31 January 1944, p. 2, and *Izvestiia*, 4 February 1944, p. 2. Korniets, the head of the Soviet Ukrainian government (Khrushchev replaced him on 1 February 1944), revealed that the Germans executed over 70,000 (recent numbers put the figure at over 150,000) people at Babi Yar during their twenty-six-month occupation of Kiev, but did not disclose that the Nazis primarily targeted Jews. In addition to the Jews, the Germans also executed Soviet prisoners of war, Soviet partisans, Ukrainian nationalists and gypsies. On how and why Soviet authorities sought to universalise the Holocaust and to diminish the quality and quantity of Jewish suffering, see Zvi Gitelman, ed., *Bitter Legacy: Confronting the Holocaust in the USSR* (Bloomington, IN, 1997), pp. 14–42. For a catalogue of Nazi crimes against Soviet Jews, see the work compiled by Ilya Ehrenburg and Vasily Grossman during the war, but only now published in its entirety, *The Complete Black Book of Russian Jewry* (New Brunswick, NJ, 2002).

49. A. P. Dovzhenko, 'Pobeda', RGASPI, 17/125/212.

50. RGASPI, 17/125/212, pp. 40, 41.

51. RGASPI, 17/125/212, p. 43.

52. G. Aleksandrov, 'O povesti A. Dovzhenko "Pobeda"', RGASPI, 17/125/212, p. 1.

53. G. Aleksandrov, A. Puzin, A. Egolin, 'Sekretariu TsK VKP(b), tov. Malenkovu G. M.', RGASPI, 17/125/212, pp. 147–8, 159–60.

54. Iu. Kobylets'kyi, 'Moi zustrichi z O. P. Dovzhenkom', *DMM*, File 1, p. 10.

55. Kovalenko and Mishurin, pp. 34–5.

56. G. Aleksandrov, 'Sekretariu TsK VKP(b) tov. Scherbakovu A. S.', RGASPI, 17/125/212.

57. TsDAHOU, 1/70/60, p. 144.

58. Excerpts from the screenplay appeared in the newspaper *Literatura i iskusstvo* (under the title of 'Vozvrashchenie') on 18 September 1943 and in the journal *Smena*, no. 18, 1943. Iurenev, pp. 99–100.

59. See TsDA-MLMU, 690/3/9, p. 2, and TsDAHOU, 1/23/448, p. 21. Also see N. S. Khrushchev, *Khrushchev Remembers* (Boston, 1970), p. 172; and Bohdan Ryl's'kyi, 'Vbyla nenavist' i zlo', *Literaturna Ukraina*, 4 January 1990, p. 3.

60. *PF*, p. 90; *UVOKShch*, p. 221; *Hospody*, p. 191; *ZDUVOShch*, p. 314; Borys Polevoi, 'Nezabutnie', *DMM*, File 2, p. 2; Mykola Zhulyns'kyi, 'Pechal' dyshi i sviatist' bosonohoho dytynstva', *Holos Ukrainy*, 14 September 1994, p. 4.

61. *UVOKShch*, p. 223.

62. *PF*, pp. 95–6; *UVOKShch*, pp. 229–30; *Hospody*, pp. 201–2; *ZDUVOShch*, pp. 324–5.

63. RGALI, 2081/1/136, p. 115.

64. RGALI, 2081/1/140, p. 20.

65. M. Kovalenko, 'Idu za Dovzhenkom', *DMM*, File 8, p. 50; also see *Khrushchev Remembers*, p. 172.

66. *Storinky*, p. 199.

67. Kovalenko and Mishurin, p. 123.

68. *PF*, p. 93; *UVOKShch*, p. 224; *Hospody*, p. 195; *ZDUVOShch*, p. 318.

69. *PF*, p. 97; *UVOKShch*, p. 231; *Hospody*, p. 204; *ZDUVOShch*, p. 327.

70. *PF*, p. 94 (censored); *UVOKShch*, p. 227; *Hospody*, p. 199; *ZDUVOShch*, p. 322.

71. M. Kovalenko, 'Idu za Dovzhenkom', p. 49.

72. O. Shvachko, 'V kino prykhodyt' Oleksandr Dovzhenko', *DMM*, File 3, pp. 13–14.

73. *PF*, p. 94; *UVOKShch*, p. 226; *Hospody*, p. 197; *ZDUVOShch*, p. 320.

74. Khrushchev had a very low opinion of Shcherbakov, whom he called 'a poisonous snake'. *Khrushchev Remembers*, p. 171.

75. E. Mikhailova, 'Sekretariu TsK VKP(b) tov. A. S. Shcherbakovu', RGASPI, 71/125/293, p. 171; the page proofs may be found in RGASPI, 17/125/293, pp. 173–204 (over), 211–12 (over), 215–17 (over), and 219–21.

76. Ivan Bolshakov presents a different version of how Shcherbakov became aware of the screenplay's problems. In his version, Bolshakov plays a central role in bringing the contentious issues in Dovzhenko's screenplay to Shcherbakov's attention, but his depiction does not follow the established chronology of events. See I. Bol'shakov, 'Spohady', *Dnipro*, no. 9–10 (1994), pp. 69–70.

77. This meeting may have happened on 30 December 1943, when Stalin met

with Khrushchev, Malenkov and Shcherbakov, the men mentioned in
Khrushchev's memoirs. See 'Posetiteli kremlevskogo kabineta I. V. Stalina',
Istoricheskii arkhiv, no. 3 (1996), p. 86.

78. *Khrushchev Remembers*, p. 172.

79. *PF*, p. 94; *UVOKShch*, p. 226; *Hospody*, pp. 197–8; *ZDUVOShch*, p. 320.

80. *UVOKShch*, p. 248; *Hospody*, p. 224; *ZDUVOShch*, p. 348.

81. *UVOKShch*, p. 250; *Hospody*, pp. 226–7; *ZDUVOShch*, pp. 350–1. The
English translation of this diary passage appears in Iurii Shapoval, 'The
Ukrainian Years, 1894–1949', in William Taubman, Sergei Khrushchev and
Abbott Gleason, eds, *Nikita Khrushchev* (New Haven and London, 2000),
pp. 29–30.

82. *PF*, p. 101; *UVOKShch*, p. 246; *Hospody*, p. 222; *ZDUVOShch*, p. 345.

83. 'Posetiteli kremlevskogo kabineta I. V. Stalina', *Istoricheskii arkhiv*, no. 4
(1996), p. 67.

84. They included V. M. Molotov, G. M. Malenkov, L. P. Beria, A. I. Mikoian,
A. S. Shcherbakov and P. K. Ponomarenko. See 'Posetiteli kremlevskogo
kabineta I. V. Stalina', p. 67.

85. The Ukrainian delegation included D. S. Korotchenko, a secretary of the
CP(b)U; M. S. Hrechukha, the chair of the Presidium of the Supreme
Soviet; L. R. Korniets, the head of the Council of People's Commissars of
Ukraine; V. F. Starchenko, the deputy head of the Council of People's
Commissars; M. P. Bazhan; O. O. Bohomolets; A. Ie. Korniichuk; and M. T.
Rylsky, the head of the Ukrainian Writers' Union. TsDAHOU, 1/70/282,
p. 200 and 'Posetiteli kremlevskogo kabineta I. V. Stalina', p. 67.

86. *Iskusstvo kino* published the remarks that Stalin delivered on 30 January
1944 only in 1990. These remarks, however, may not have been Stalin's.
Shcherbakov, or Shcherbakov's office, may have prepared them. Compare
I. V. Stalin, 'Ob antileninskikh oshibkakh i natsionalisticheskikh
izvrashcheniiakh v kinopovesti Dovzhenko "Ukraina v ogne"', *Iskusstvo kino*,
no. 4 (1990), pp. 89–95; RGASPI, 17/125/293, pp. 20–35; and RGALI,
2081/1/140. As Political Commissar of the Armed Forces, Shcherbakov may
have suspected Dovzhenko and received his information on Dovzhenko's
activities from others, possibly Korniichuk, who worked as a senior
propagandist in his office.

87. TsDAHOU, 1/70/282, pp. 200–3.

88. I. V. Stalin, 'Ob antileninskikh oshibkakh', p. 95; and RGASPI, 17/125/293,
p. 35.

89. Besides TsDAHOU, 1/70/282, and I. V. Stalin, 'Ob antileninskikh
oshibkakh', see *Khrushchev Remembers*, p. 172; and the second-hand
accounts by Viktor Pertsov, 'Vospominaniia o Dovzhenko', RGALI,

2081/1/1167, especially pp. 13–14; Bohdan Ryl's'kyi, 'Vbyla nenavist' i zlo', *Literaturna Ukraina*, 4 January 1990, p. 3; and Oleksandr Pidsukha, 'Dlia bil'shoi iasnosti', *Literaturna Ukraina*, 21 June 1990, p. 4. These last three accounts confirm the meeting's general outline. Pertsov's account, however, contradicted the outcome of the meeting. Dovzhenko did not win Stalin over. With the exception of how Stalin parted with Dovzhenko, Rylsky's and Pidsukha's accounts generally confirm each other. Rylsky's account made it seem as if the two parted on good terms, whereas Pidsukha presented an angry Stalin. Dovzhenko's accounts in his diary reflect this confusion.

90. 'Posetiteli', p. 67.
91. RGASPI, 17/125/293, pp. 1–5. A number of Dovzhenko's works, already scheduled for publication, were not published. Compare, for example, the earlier and later versions of the Ukrainian State Publishing House's plans for 1944. TsDAHOU, 1/70/244, pp. 10–14 and TsDAHOU, 1/70/27, pp. 151–75.
92. G. Aleksandrov, 'Sekretarem TsK VKP(b) tov. Zhdanovu A. A., tov. Malenkovu G. M.', RGASPI, 17/125/291, p. 108; for a list of the Artistic Council's members, see RGASPI, 17/125/291, p. 111.
93. TsDAHOU, 1/6/715, p. 34; O. S. Hryshchenko, *Z berehiv zacharovanoi Desny* (Kiev, 1964), pp. 196–7.
94. M. Kovalenko, 'Idu za Dovzhenkom', p. 52.
95. Ivan Bolshakov, to his credit, opposed this measure. He claimed that an ill Dovzhenko needed uninterrupted medical help. See I. Bolshakov, 'Sekretariu TsK VKP(b) tov. Shcherbakovu A. S.', RGASPI, 17/125/291, p. 101.
96. Kenez, 'Black and White', p. 175.
97. I. Tikhonov, 'Otchestvennaia voina i sovetskaia literatura', *Bolshevik*, no. 3–4 (1944), p. 36.
98. See RGASPI, 1/30/84, especially pp. 89, 93, 95.
99. 'Stenogramma soveshchaniia po propagande pri TsK KP(b)U (kniga 4-ia)', TsDAHOU, 1/70/200, p. 86.
100. 'Z protokolu zahal'nykh zboriv pys'mennykiv Kyieva, zhurnalistiv ta pratsivnykiv mystetstv (12 March 1944 r.)', TsDAHOU, 1/23/858, p. 21.
101. TsDAHOU, 1/23/858, p. 22.
102. TsDAHOU, 1/23/858, p. 29.
103. TsDAHOU, 1/23/858, pp. 27–8; 'Radians'ka Ukraina: Informatsiia', p. 176.
104. Cited in 'Zapiski o Dovzhenko' (after 30 January 1944), TsDAHOU, 1/70/282, p. 192.
105. See 'Zapiski o Dovzhenko', p. 191.

106. O. Shvachko, 'V kino prykhodyt' Oleksandr Dovzhenko', p. 15. This statement does not appear in Shvachko's memoir in *PZh*, pp. 196–201.

107. Stalin, 'Ob antileninskikh oshibkakh', p. 94.

108. Pidsukha, 'Dlia bil'shoi iasnosti', p. 4.

109. RGALI, 2081/1/413; RGASPI, 17/125/212; RGALI, 2081/1/395, p. 12 and RGALI, 2081/1/136.

110. *PF*, p. 233; *UVOKShch*, p. 379; *Hospody*, p. 378; *ZDUVOShch*, p. 505.

111. See Khrushchev's speech at the plenum of the Union of Soviet Writers of Ukraine, 12 March 1944, TsDAHOU, 1/23/450, p. 46 and TsDAHOU, 1/70/43, p. 149.

112. Oles' Honchar, 'Koly dumaiesh pro Dovzhenka', *Kul'tura i zhyttia*, 10 September 1994, p. 2. Born to a Ukrainian peasant family, Hrechukha became a member of the Communist Party in 1926. From 22 July 1939 until January 1954, he remained the head of the Presidium of the Supreme Soviet of the Ukrainian SSR. See TsDAHOU, 39/4/45.

113. On 4 December 1944 Volodymyr Sosiura, a prominent poet and Dovzhenko's companion in the nationalist ranks at Kamianets-Podils'k in 1919, wrote Hrechukha a letter, admonishing him for not speaking Ukrainian. According to the poet, the head of the Ukrainian state considered the use of Ukrainian beneath his 'dignity as a senior governmental official'. Sosiura claimed that Hrechukha forgot what Stalin had asserted in 1929, that it was 'stupid to develop non-Russian cultures on the basis of Russian'. He then asked Hrechukha: 'Are you not ashamed?' Manuscript Division, T. H. Shevchenko Institute of Literature of the National Academy of Sciences of Ukraine (Kiev), f. 139, d. 75, pp. 2, 14. It is unclear if Sosiura sent this letter.

114. Brandenberger, 'The "Short Course" to Modernity', p. 183.

115. On Khrushchev's admission to Stalin that he read *Ukraine in Flames*, see *Khrushchev Remembers*, p. 172.

116. O. Honchar, 'Koly dumaiesh pro Dovzhenka', p. 1.

9

Internal Exile

In his account of Dovzhenko's reactions to his 1944 meeting with Stalin, Yury Smolych noted:

> The screenplay died. Even worse: not only the screenplay, but also Sashko's good reputation and Stalin's trust in him came to an end. Everyone understood what it meant to lose Stalin's trust in those times. All governmental and party institutions from top to bottom also lost their trust in him ... In the final analysis, he claimed that he was not a writer, but a film director above all! – Yes, this is how Sashko cheered himself up then: his job was to mount films. But would they now let him create films? He said this in anger, but at this moment he did not recognize and did not consider this a serious problem. He was wounded by something else: Stalin! Stalin, in whom he believed so much, wounded him most painfully. And not only because he rebuked him – he abused him sharply, unbearably, brutally. Not only because he ruined Sashko's work – his screenplay. And not only because Sashko considered Stalin's criticism untrue, unjust, and offensive. All of this was unpleasant and painful, but ... there was another matter, which wounded Sashko even more. 'The truth is unnecessary! You understand – unnecessary!' said Sashko and his eyes became moist with tears.[1]

Even after creating false versions of events and personalities of the past and present in his films, Dovzhenko still considered himself a servant of the truth. He fervently believed that *Ukraine in Flames* constituted the most honest account of the disaster that befell the Soviet Union and Ukraine, and he wanted to bring this truth to Stalin. In light of the Soviet Union's losses in the first two years after the German invasion, he became upset that Stalin and his colleagues displayed such unwillingness to think critically about the experience.

Dovzhenko considered himself, according to NKVD sources, 'unjustly suffering on behalf of the truth'.[2] If at first Dovzhenko blamed Stalin for his misfortune, the film-maker, conforming to the peasant view of the tsar as a 'good father', created a more politically convenient interpretation of why Stalin banned the screenplay.[3] 'Stalin could not have acted otherwise,' the NKVD informants surrounding him reported him saying. 'If he had approved it, he would have admitted that many who had followed his instructions over the last fifteen years acted improperly and brought great unhappiness to the people. So, it was not to be expected for Stalin to allow my screenplay to be published.'[4] NKVD analysts claimed that even this rationalisation of Stalin's role in this affair constituted a provocative statement.

Dovzhenko desperately sought to understand the reason for Stalin's denunciation. Having won the Soviet leader's favour with *Aerograd* and *Shchors*, he had developed a false sense of security. Stalin's rejection of *Ukraine in Flames* caught the Ukrainian film-maker by surprise. As his emotional world fluctuated between accommodation and resistance, and all points in between, he became psychologically unstable.

At times, he admitted that he had made a mistake with *Ukraine in Flames*, but he characterised this mistake as an honest one. Siko Dolidze, a Georgian director, met Dovzhenko in Moscow shortly after the fateful meeting with Stalin, but before the Ukrainian film-maker left for the front to find footage for his documentary *Victory in Right-Bank Ukraine*. In his brief memoir, Dolidze noted that Dovzhenko looked completely worn out and older than his fifty years. He complained about his heart and the injustice of Stalin's treatment. In making *Ukraine in Flames*, Dovzhenko claimed that he had possessed 'no malicious intentions and did not make any mistakes. But if it really was a mistake, then a person's entire life should not be cancelled out because of one mistake . . .'[5]

At other moments, Dovzhenko – in the sanctuary of his diary – challenged Stalin and his allies to prove him a 'Ukrainian nationalist'. He protested that his feelings of deep concern for his fellow Ukrainians did not make him a nationalist. Pride in one's national identity, the film-maker asserted, did not necessarily contradict Marxist–Leninist internationalism. In his diary entry from 27 July 1945, he wrote:

> My dear Comrade Stalin, even if you were God, I would not take your word that I am a nationalist who must be slandered and imprisoned. If there is no hatred in principle, and no scorn, and no ill feelings toward a single nation on earth, how can love for one's own nation be nationalism? Is it nationalism to refuse to connive with stupid functionaries and cold-blooded speculators? Is it nationalism when an artist cannot hold back his tears because his nation is suffering? Why have you turned my life into suffering? Why have you deprived me of joy? Why have you crushed me under your boot?[6]

Of course, Dovzhenko confined his protestations to his diary. Within the refuge of those pages, he could indulge in self-pity and defiance of his persecutors while maintaining a public image of conformity to their demands. He knew, after all, that he needed to regain their trust in order to create. No other alternative existed. Within a month after Stalin's denunciation, he wrote:

Enough suffering and repenting of my sins against Stalin. I must get down to business
and prove to him with my work that I am a Soviet artist … and not an odious talent
with a 'limited ideology'. I must take myself in hand, [encase] my heart, my will, and
my nerves in steel and … create a scenario and a film worthy of our great role in a great
historical age.[7]

Dovzhenko's need to win back lost political trust vied with his desire to express his
vision of the war.[8] He considered *Ukraine in Flames* his most forthright attempt to
deal with the Soviet collapse after the German invasion. After its ban, Dovzhenko
– who could not satisfy himself by 'writing for the drawer' – wanted to revise this
screenplay so that the authorities would publish it.[9] With great effort he transformed
Ukraine in Flames into *The Chronicle of Flaming Years*.

Dovzhenko's claim that 15 million Ukrainians (twice the most recent estimate)
died or became exiled lay at the centre of his efforts to expose Nazi brutalities and
Soviet blunders.[10] Wherever Dovzhenko obtained these statistics, he frequently
used them to drive home the obvious fact that Ukraine suffered disproportionate
deaths and physical destruction relative to the Soviet Union's total losses. In spite
of his inflated statistics, the film-maker had a point. Due to their location at the epi-
centre of the Eastern Front, the Soviet Ukrainian and Belarussian republics suffered
more severely than the other Soviet republics. Bearing in mind that the USSR suffered greater losses than its American and British allies, the Ukrainian fate in the
war appears especially harsh. From Dovzhenko's point of view, the enormity of this
suffering demanded a serious accounting, one that he hoped to provoke with
Ukraine in Flames and *The Chronicle of Flaming Years*.

Dovzhenko reworked his banned screenplay by September 1945.[11] Although *The
Chronicle* emerged as a weak variation of *Ukraine in Flames*, it did not meet the
'demands of our era', as the authorities euphemistically evaluated it.[12] The new
screenplay did not adhere to the Soviet leadership's political priorities. On 16 October 1945 the film-maker described the reaction:

The Chronicle of Flaming Years scares the leadership. Bolshakov avoided speaking to me
after he read it. Polikarpov accepted it but did not express his opinion, stating only that
it's difficult to understand. Kalatozov, who previously pretended to be full of
enthusiasm for it, is now afraid of it. The Lord have mercy on them. I had better send it
to Stalin. I'll send it and ask him to give me a sign because I cannot go on living this
way. In this inertia of suspicion and degradation one loses not just one's talent, but
one's sanity and desire to go living.[13]

Dovzhenko did ask Stalin to approve *The Chronicle of Flaming Years*, but the Soviet
leader declined to do so. In his place D. Yeromin, the director of the screenplay

section at the Cinematography Committee at the Council of Ministers, harshly crit-icised *The Chronicle* on 17 October 1945.[14]

This criticism further isolated Dovzhenko. Over a two-year period, Stalin and his men had personally rejected two of Dovzhenko's screenplays. Since early 1944 friends and colleagues had been avoiding him. On three different occasions Bol-shakov, the head of the Cinema Administration, rudely replied to Dovzhenko's enquiries regarding the screenplay. These responses, according to the Ukrainian film-maker, became contagious 'enough for all the lesser bigwigs, assistants, editors, and all the hirelings and lackeys to begin avoiding me and whispering behind my back. Even Kalatozov pretended he hadn't read it. That's how loathsome I am!'[15] This isolation heightened Dovzhenko's physical and emotional vulnerability. As an extrovert and a forceful personality, Dovzhenko chafed miserably under his imposed quarantine. He wanted to play a useful public role in Soviet society, but his duty to the truth (as he interpreted it), isolated him from his environment.

Once again Dovzhenko became *persona non grata*, a politically tainted individual who could not rehabilitate himself. Despite his best efforts, the creation of 'a sce-nario and a film worthy of our great role in a great historical age' that also pleased the Stalinist leadership proved beyond him. In order to rehabilitate his political standing, he began to work on other, non-Ukrainian projects, including *Native Land* (1945), *Michurin*, and *Goodbye, America* (1951).

Banned from Ukraine

Even after Dovzhenko became anathematised in Moscow, he still imagined he could return to the Kiev Film Studio. At the end of February 1944, he learned that its administration had dismissed him from his position as artistic director. Never-theless, he hoped to return to work in Kiev as soon as possible, even in a lesser position.[16]

While Dovzhenko waited for the Cinematography Committee's orders to trans-fer him to Kiev, the NKVD continued to watch him closely. In a report from 12–14 May 1944 a NKVD analyst described Dovzhenko's attitude:

> His morale is now more oppressed than six weeks ago. He is very bitter about the
> writers' meeting in Kiev, which criticised his screenplay. He is especially embittered by
> the talks given by Korniichuk and Bazhan. Dovzhenko's animosity is generally
> directed against Ukrainian writers and the leading party workers, whom he contrasted
> to Russian writers and activists, who he claimed relate to him very sympathetically and
> in a friendly manner … In regard to this a question arose. Should he consider
> returning to Ukraine or should he remain in Moscow, living in Russian culture?
> Analyzing the situation, he does not think that in Ukraine 'they would give him an
> opportunity to recover'.[17]

At the end of 1944, in a review of Dovzhenko's activities, the NKVD noted that the film director

> continues to express nationalistic opinions in a veiled form. Dovzhenko responds in a
> hostile tone to all people who came out against his screenplay, especially against
> Comrade Khrushchev and the leaders of the Ukrainian Writers' Union, who he claims
> gave it a positive review before the Central Committee's decision.[18]

'I am not a politician,' NKVD informants recorded Dovzhenko as saying. I am ready to admit that I can commit mistakes. But why does it happen among us that at the beginning everyone says 'good and beautiful', and then suddenly they react as if it were slander against the Soviet order?[19]

'I do not bear a grudge against Stalin or the members of the Central Committee, who have always been good to me,' the film-maker said in the presence of informants. 'I do bear a grudge against the Ukrainians . . . people who have the audacity to spread malicious lies against me in Stalin's presence after expressing their delight with the screenplay . . .'[20]

It is unclear whether this statement reflects Dovzhenko's true feelings. Perhaps he spoke this way in order to impress the NKVD's informants. Certainly, many writers, cinematographers and party officials in Ukraine felt very cautious after the central party hierarchy's reaction to *Ukraine in Flames* and avoided associating with such a political liability as Dovzhenko. They then joined (some reluctantly, others enthusiastically) the central party in attacking the man whose visions and standards put them in harm's way. By dissociating themselves from him, the Ukrainian intelligentsia hoped to ensure their political and artistic survival.

Rejected both by the Ukrainian literary and political elites and by Stalin and his entourage, Dovzhenko came to a damning conclusion. According to NKVD sources cited in a 29 August 1944 report, he characterised Soviet democracy as 'the greatest lie and hypocrisy which humanity ever knew'.[21] Whether he actually said these words or not, the NKVD placed them in his file. Dovzhenko's recorded statement raised the question not only of his political reliability, but more importantly of his loyalty to the Soviet cause.

By the end of 1944 or the beginning of 1945, the film-maker learned that he could not return to Ukraine and could not participate in the reconstruction of his beloved city or the re-establishment of Ukrainian cinema. On 11 July 1945 he met with Bolshakov, who told him: 'You will work in Moscow. I do not advise you to travel to Ukraine. You do not need to go there.' Dovzhenko recorded that he stared at Bolshakov and thought, 'What's this? Isn't this a covert form of exile?'[22]

Although the Ukrainian political and cultural elites did not want him, the political pariah, to tarnish their reputations, they had no authority to prevent the film-maker from living in Ukraine. The decision to prohibit the most prominent Ukrainian film-maker from returning to his native land must have originated in Moscow, where the central party hierarchy could have overruled all Ukrainian objections, as it had in 1935 when Stalin tapped Dovzhenko to film *Shchors*.

Blocked from resettling in Ukraine, he found employment at Mosfilm as a third-class director. He perceived this demotion as a humiliation and came to hate Mosfilm, calling it 'Maidanek', a reference to the Nazi death camp outside Lublin, which Soviet troops liberated in July 1944.[23] In his 25 November 1945 diary entry, the film-maker wrote:

> Until now I have thought of myself as one of the best film directors. I have become accustomed to this idea, and it has helped me to stay on a high moral level during production. This third-category monthly salary that has been allotted me oppresses me and makes me doubt my abilities.[24]

By demoting Dovzhenko, one of the four major pioneers of Soviet cinematography and a world-famous director, the Soviet authorities questioned his artistic integrity as well as his political reliability. Psychologically, he could not accept this insult. Although he admitted political and artistic mistakes, he felt his creative instincts remained beyond question. As his creative avenues narrowed, the film-maker must have grown sensitive over the issue of his own artistic integrity within the Stalinist order. His demotion to the rank of third-grade director, in light of his complex body of work, made him feel unappreciated and worthless. In words captured by NKVD informants in March 1946, Dovzhenko claimed that the 'human soul can suffer hunger and death of one's close ones, but not humiliation. Why do I need to be degraded?'[25]

For a wide variety of personal and professional reasons, his enemies continued to humble him. In early 1946, according to NKVD sources, Dovzhenko met Alexander Horsky, the main administrator of the Kiev Film Studio, who told him, 'You, Alexander Petrovych, do not exist in Ukraine, you are a nonentity, and it is not intended that you rise again.'[26] This brutal statement, coming from a friend, made Dovzhenko realise that his past contributions would not pave his way home. With the party hierarchy now on their side, Dovzhenko's enemies had gained the upper hand.

In the fall of 1946, Dovzhenko learned of yet another humiliation. The Ukrainian authorities had confiscated his apartment in Kiev. In a letter to his mother and sister, he wrote:

> Some minister was not satisfied with his apartment, so he took mine. You poor, poor Minister, I thought, you have to live in your artist's apartment, anticipating his death.

What a nauseous man! Now I am not a resident of Kiev at all. Ministers in the capital
have very little space![27]

Without a position at the Kiev Film Studio or a Kiev apartment registered in his
name, Dovzhenko had no choice but to accept Moscow as his permanent home.

Isolated from his friends and colleagues in Ukraine, he heard nothing from
them for weeks or months at a time. Sometimes they visited Moscow, but they
did not meet with him – most likely because they feared the security organs. He
took this rejection personally. Feeling dejected, he claimed that in Ukraine 'no one
needs me'.[28] Despite this betrayal, he mourned his ban and hoped to return to
Ukraine, even if only for burial. On 5 November 1945 Dovzhenko wrote: 'I will
die in Moscow without seeing Ukraine. On my deathbed I shall ask Stalin that
my heart be removed from my chest before cremation and buried on my native
soil in Kiev, on a hill overlooking the Dnieper River.'[29]

Bouts of Depression

In addition to the political and artistic barriers he faced, age, exhaustion and heart
troubles slowed Dovzhenko and depressed him. He often felt he had wasted the
best years of his life, that so much he hoped to accomplish would remain unfinished.
These political and creative doubts led to long periods of depression, which interfered with his work. 'Writing half a page is a chain-gang labor for me,' Dovzhenko
wrote in April 1944.

> Sometimes one line drains me. Thousands of thoughts and images crowd together and
> torture me. They filter out of my head through a micron-size opening, and all that I've
> written seems to be a pitiful fraction of what I so passionately wanted to say. Then I
> worry and suffer again from exhaustion.[30]

His writer's block grew especially acute when committees reviewed his projects.[31]
Only in the privacy of his diary could he express his greatest frustration, the diffi-
culty of creating under a political microscope. Ideas swirled in his head and he
desperately tried to capture them on paper, if not on film.

Stalin stood at the centre of Dovzhenko's paralysis. The Ukrainian film-maker
understood that many committees would review his work, but Stalin or members of
his inner circle would make the final decision. They would examine his work in
minute detail. No one, not even those who sought to please Stalin, understood the
party leader's elusive, mercurial standards. The nature of the appropriate, and where
its boundaries began and ended, grew into a complicated and continuously shifting
issue. On 7 February 1948, Dovzhenko wrote: 'I keep thinking that my terrible critic
is standing behind my back examining my every letter and comma with his implaca-
ble eye for treason and undermining. Instead of writing, I suffer.'[32]

In a state of psychological dislocation, he continuously assessed and reassessed his life, especially his profession as a film director. Forced by political circumstances to censor his own creative output and constrained by various physical and material shortcomings, Dovzhenko felt artistically compromised. On 4 July 1945 he wrote:

> In all of my working years, I have not seen a single one of my pictures in a decent theater on a decent screen, printed on good film by qualified technicians. The film theaters are miserable, the screens the size of postage stamps. It never seems to occur to anyone that screens can be large and the effect of the picture quite different – grand and beautiful. The sound is scandalous, and the film quality is disgraceful – dirty and full of reflections. The very thought of seeing one of my pictures makes me sad. The film is always worse than I conceived and made it. This has been one of the misfortunes of my life. I have been a martyr for my work. Not once did I obtain satisfaction or even peace from seeing the results of my immeasurably difficult and complex work. As time goes by I become more and more convinced that the best twenty years of my life have been wasted. What I could have done! [33]

Tempted to judge his career as a film-maker a failure, Dovzhenko now toyed with the idea of becoming a writer, building on the short stories he had written during the war. In comparison to film-making, writing seemed an easier creative medium. As a writer, Dovzhenko did not have to torment himself about the quantity or quality of the film stock given him. He did not have to worry about production costs. Fewer committees would evaluate his work. Stalin would not necessarily act as his final evaluator. He could sit at his desk at home and write, free from the demands of large production crews and the egos of petty administrators. His final written draft would most likely appear in print, without radical revisions. Most importantly, the medium offered greater control over his creativity.[34]

Although writing provided him with an opportunity to satisfy his creative muse with less strain than film-making, Dovzhenko's conflicts with the party hierarchy and with his own internal policeman caused his health to deteriorate, which depressed him even more. His physical state became precarious.[35]

In a 9 November 1946 letter to his mother and his sister, the film-maker complained of pains in his heart and throughout his entire body, forgetfulness, constant weakness and a roar in his head.[36] Worse yet, these physical discomforts exhausted him, preventing him from thinking clearly and from completing his work. On 5 April 1948, Dovzhenko wrote:

> My heart gives me pain, and so often when I get up from the desk after a whole day of work I look back and see how pitifully little I've done. Yet I am as exhausted as if I spent the whole day shifting boulders about.[37]

His political isolation, creative frustration and deteriorating health caused him to reflect on life and his place in it. He expressed more regret than satisfaction. He had not achieved peace with himself or with his world.[38]

His reflections on this sad state of affairs could have included thoughts of suicide. As the noose of the purges tightened around the necks of the political and cultural elites, many of Dovzhenko's closest friends, including the Russian poet Vladimir Mayakovsky, the Ukrainian writer Mykola Khvylovy and the head of the Soviet Ukrainian government Panas Liubchenko, killed themselves in the 1930s. Dovzhenko himself had often threatened to commit suicide before and after Dubovy's arrest in early 1938. He declined to make this final and irrevocable choice, even in the depths of depression following his isolation after January 1944. His personal views on suicide and vengeance help explain his reluctance to take the 'easy way out'.

Lazar Bodyk, Dovzhenko's long-term assistant director, recounted in his memoirs the film-maker's explanation of why in *Earth* the villagers did not kill Khoma the kulak after he murdered the Komsomol hero Vasyl. They chose instead to let Khoma live in ignominy, to wreak vengeance on himself. Dovzhenko asserted that 'to force a person to kill himself is the worst punishment'.[39]

In Dovzhenko's view of the world, making the choice to commit suicide constituted an act of complete self-abnegation, a total betrayal of one's dreams, hopes and illusions. This deed represented an act of complete surrender to one's enemies. Despite his political humiliations, physical exhaustion, illness and creative paralysis, he continued to work on his projects. His output slowed, but he did not stop producing. To continue to develop his talents meant not only to honour himself, but also to honour God.

Return to God

Raised by a family of believers, Dovzhenko retained his faith until the age of seventeen. He claimed that when he entered the Teachers' Institute in Hlukhiv in 1911, he stopped believing in God: 'The college had its own chapel and attendance was absolutely compulsory. There I stopped believing in God, which I admitted at confession to the religion teacher, Father Alexander, the only liberal among all our teachers.'[40] Whether true or not, this statement from Dovzhenko's 1939 autobiography followed the proper Soviet script on how one gained a Communist consciousness.

Between November 1943 and January 1944, he experienced a series of emotional crises. In liberated Kiev, he learned about his father's death, which may have provoked a sense of guilt. He could not attain a sense of closure, as he could not bury him or mourn properly. To make matters worse, upon returning to Moscow on 23 November, he learned about the banning of *Ukraine in Flames*.

When he travelled back to Moscow (in November 1943), his mother, a believer, accompanied him. In the following month he had many conversations with her about the past and about his childhood. Recording his mother's versions of several Ukrainian Christmas carols brought him great pleasure and evoked a sense of nostalgia in him.[41]

His mother's reminiscences most likely jogged his own memories, which highlighted the warmth and love of his early years. From a forty-year perspective, the past enjoyed a unique coherence, a meaning that the present did not. In hindsight, the past represented happiness. Leaving home and abandoning God had brought chaos.

Dovzhenko's conversations with his mother rekindled his belief in God, if not in a systematic theology. On 2 January 1946 he wrote:

> I have begun to pray to God. For thirty-seven years I did not pray to God, and almost never thought about Him. I rejected Him. I myself was God, a man-god. Now I pray to Him. I have at least partly understood my delusion. God is within man. He may or may not exist, but his complete absence would be a great step backwards and downwards. In the future men will come to Him. Not to the priest, of course, or to the church, but to the divine within themselves, to the beautiful, the immortal. Then there will be no oppressive tedium, no wearisome, bestial days.[42]

However theologically unorthodox this passage may appear, it expressed Dovzhenko's search for meaning. God resides within man, and if everyone were to recognise this basic truth, the brutalities of war and personal sufferings would come to an end. Hoping for a better future, he had become a believer in a great power.

Through God, Dovzhenko sought a coherent interpretation of his isolation, suffering, persecution, and deteriorating health. He must have asked himself a variation of Job's most searching questions: 'What strength do I have, that I should hope? And what is my end, that I should prolong my life?' (Job 6:11). Even if his newfound spirituality could not provide answers, it did give him some solace, even as it reaffirmed the centrality of suffering in life. 'I perceive the world as suffering,' Dovzhenko wrote on 7 February 1948. 'I have understood: the dream is to be measured not by the harshness of circumstances, but by the depth of the pain.'[43] His rediscovery of religion could only make it harder for him to live in an anti-religious state.

Raised in the Russian Orthodox tradition, Dovzhenko's return to God acknowledged the mystery of suffering in his own life. Although he may have suffered because of circumstances beyond his control, he sought to make peace with his torment as an integral part of the human condition. He may have found this peace at the end of his life. According to Roberto Manetti, a few months before he died,

Dovzhenko wrote: 'We so much want a beautiful and happy life that we passionately wish for and anticipate a fulfilling season, forgetting that suffering will be with
us for as long as man will be on this earth, as long as he will love and create.'[44]
His psychological and physical pain reminded the film-maker of his own mortality.
Death, moreover, held the promise of resurrection.

'The House' and 'The Dream'

Dovzhenko expressed the tensions he experienced as a film-maker serving two masters, his creative muse and the Stalinist leadership, in two thinly veiled short stories,
'The House' and 'The Dream'. Although he wrote both in September 1945, they
appeared in print only in the early 1960s.[45] Written in an Aesopian style, they represented his frustrations over his censored creativity and over his longing to return
to Ukraine.

Although 'The House' resembles a short story, Dovzhenko actually composed it
as an epic prose poem about the fate of the people who lived in the physical structure.[46] The author lovingly describes a poor, whitewashed and thatched-roof house
similar to the one in which he grew up. Although the small house has no large
rooms, family portraits, or servants, it always gladly receives everyone who enters
its doors.

Over the centuries, the house has many occupants, who welcome others with their
bread, milk and honey, but the hosts remain poor. They never prepare large ban-
quets or entertain their guests with orchestras. No important people ever visit the
impoverished owners, who never attain much happiness. Instead, they experience
heartbreak and sadness. The house witnesses many departures. When opportunities
arise, the occupants' children vacate the hearth. Attracted to foreign places, they
leave and rarely return. In later years, they – who had abandoned their consciences
and neglected the language they spoke in the house – reminisce about the house
and associate it with a happy childhood. In bad times, those who departed return
and remember, however poorly, its language. They feel ashamed. Beyond the house,
the language withers, much like a flower on the road.

'I do not have a house,' Dovzhenko concludes his story. Under the skies, only the
stove stands intact among the ruins. Next to the stove, a widow cries.

Much like the estate in Gabriel Garcia Marquez's *One Hundred Years of Solitude*,
Dovzhenko's house serves as a metaphor for Ukraine's gradual decay. Although the
author did not idealise the Ukrainian past as a 'golden age', he expressed his hope
that Ukraine would regenerate and experience a happier future. After all, the stove
– the house's heart – still remains; nevertheless, as 'The House' testifies, Dovzhenko
recognised that he would never return to Ukraine.

'The Dream' recounts a series of images and emotions that occurred to
Dovzhenko during sleep. He meets God, who heals him of the wounds he had

sustained after expressing concern for his native land, family, himself and his art. Angels pull off his bloody skin and toss it into a fire. They strip him of his talents and tear the tongue from his mouth. The Lord takes the 'burden of the Word', which had become 'the embodiment of falsehood on earth', from him and allows him to choose another vocation. Dovzhenko elects music. He becomes a composer and creates music expressing 'the truth, the whole truth, without sweet, false embellishments, without servility or conniving with aged know-nothings and heartless men of ambition'. His music uplifts everyone with its depiction of the struggle 'to establish a new order on earth'. In his symphony, joy, strength and beauty overcome evil.[47]

In this short story Dovzhenko views his talent for film-making as a curse. Although he imagines that music could better express the truth (which would have come as a surprise to Dmitry Shostakovich, who had his own troubles with Stalin and his lieutenants at this time), he realises at the dream's conclusion that even a different vocation could not bring him home.

Both stories deal with the artist's isolation and suffering as a result of his commitment to his version of the truth, which differed from the party's version. He wanted to satisfy both his creative muse and the Stalinist leadership, but he could not do both simultaneously. As a member of the Ukrainian intelligentsia, he felt a sense of social responsibility to speak his truth despite the seductive siren calls of the Stalinist leadership. Although he often compromised, his sense of social responsibility challenged the inertia produced by his emotional downturns and fuelled his efforts to continue to place his vision on film. He believed his vision represented the truth and thus attained a sense of overwhelming necessity. It needed to survive.

Conclusion

In a letter to Yury Smolych, Dovzhenko wrote on 7 October 1956:

> I am sad, my friend. To write so little in this period, to waste time due to these dogs, busybodies, and conformists. The worst and most horrible thing in cinema is to squander time, waiting for corrections, delays, decisions, planned thematical changes, and simply evil after evil. I must admit to you: I never suffered morally so much as in the last eleven post-war years. Before the war I worked all the time and was happy, because I was born to be active. Nature prepared me to make more than twelve films.[48]

Until his fatal heart attack on 25 November 1956, he experienced long bouts of illness. He felt exhausted most of the time. This fatigue prevented him from fulfilling his desires and ambitions. In the winter of 1955–6, Hryhory Zeldovych, Dovzhenko's former film editor, encountered the film-maker at Mosfilm, where the studio's leadership had convened to discuss a new film by a young director, whom Zeldovych unfortunately did not name. Mosfilm's leaders categorically opposed releasing the film, which they claimed lacked perspective.

Dovzhenko believed otherwise. He came to the studio in order to defend the young director, but instead, he sat outside the conference room with Zeldovych until the review of the young director's film came to an end. Zeldovych grew puzzled as to why his friend did not intervene, but he formulated his own explanation for Dovzhenko's behaviour. 'Only then I understood: his heart hurt ... he did not have the strength to overcome that ... conflict, where his emotions sided with the young director, but his cold reason did not provide enough arguments for his defense.'[49]

In the last decade of his life, Dovzhenko's physical and emotional exhaustion undermined his efforts to transform his ideas into film or print. This politically induced exhaustion became the cross he would bear until his death at the age of sixty-two.

Notes

1. Iurii Smolych, *Rozpovid' pro nespokii* (Kiev, 1968), pp. 169–70.
2. D, p. 32.
3. On the concept of the tsar as 'good father', see Michael Cherniavsky, *Tsar and People: Studies in Russian Myths* (2nd ed., New York, 1969).
4. D, p. 32.
5. Siko Dolidze, 'To, chto dorogo sertsu', *Literaturnaia Gruziia*, vol. 8, no. 10 (1964), p. 89.
6. *PF*, pp. 113–14; *UVOKShch*, p. 276; *Hospody*, p. 258; *ZDUVOShch*, p. 382.
7. *PF*, p. 104; *UVOKShch*, p. 259; *Hospody*, pp. 237–8; *ZDUVOShch*, pp. 361–2.
8. *PF*, p. 149; *UVOKShch*, p. 287; *Hospody*, p. 327; *ZDUVOShch*, p. 453.
9. Ivan Koshelivets', *Oleksandr Dovzhenko: Sproba tvorchoi biohrafii* (Munich, 1980), p. 276.
10. *PF*, p. 121; *UVOKShch*, p. 287; *Hospody*, p. 272; *ZDUVOShch*, p. 396. According to Volodymyr Kubijovyč, ed., *Encyclopedia of Ukraine* (Toronto, 1993), vol. 5, p. 727, 'an estimated 6.8 million Ukrainians were killed' during World War II.
11. Iu. Solntseva, 'O tom, kak snimalsia film ("Povest plammenykh let")', RGALI, 2081/2/261, p. 1; *Storinky*, p. 217.
12. Koshelivets', pp. 277–8; Solntseva, 'O tom', p. 1.
13. *PF*, p. 126; *UVOKShch*, p. 289; *Hospody*, p. 274; *ZDUVOShch*, p. 398. Dmitry A. Polikarpov (1905–65) at this time (1941–55) served as the deputy head of Agitprop; Mikhail Kalatozov (1903–73), a film director, coordinated Soviet feature film production (1945–58). See Borys Lewytzkyj (compiler), *The Soviet Political Elite* (Stanford, CA, 1970), vol. 2, p. 447; Richard Taylor,

Nancy Wood, Julian Graffy and Dina Iordanova, eds, *The BFI Companion to Eastern European and Russian Cinema* (London, 2000), p.119.

14. *Storinky*, p. 218.

15. *PF*, pp. 126–7; *UVOKShch*, p. 291; *Hospody*, pp. 276–7; *ZDUVOShch*, p. 401.

16. *PF*, p. 104; *UVOKShch*, p. 259; *Hospody*, pp. 237–8; *ZDUVOShch*, pp. 361–2.

17. *D*, p. 56.

18. 'Po agenturnym dannym ... Informatsiia Narkoma NKGB V. N. Merkulova Sekretariu TsK VKP(b) A. A. Zhdanovu o politicheskikh nastroeniakh i vyskazyvaniakh sovetskikh pisatelei', *Rodina*, no. 1 (1992), p. 93.

19. 'Po agenturnym dannym', p. 93.

20. 'Po agenturnym dannym', p. 93.

21. *D*, p. 57.

22. *ZDUVOShch*, pp. 379–80.

23. *PF*, p. 146; *UVOKShch*, p. 324; *Hospody*, p. 315; *ZDUVOShch*, p. 440.

24. *PF*, p. 136; *UVOKShch*, p. 308; *Hospody*, p. 296; *ZDUVOShch*, p. 421.

25. *D*, p. 45.

26. *D*, p. 44.

27. TsDA-MLMU, 235/1/182, pp. 1, 3.

28. 'Lyst Dovzhenka O. P. do Stefanyka S. V. (2 October 1956)', TsDA-MLMU, 690/3/10, p. 1.

29. *PF*, p. 126; *UVOKShch*, p. 290; *Hospody*, p. 275; *ZDUVOShch*, p. 399.

30. *PF*, p. 105; *UVOKShch*, p. 260; *Hospody*, p. 239: *ZDUVOShch*, p. 363.

31. *PF*, p. 116; *UVOKShch*, p. 280; *Hospody*, p. 263; *ZDUVOShch*, p. 387.

32. *PF*, p. 115.

33. *PF*, pp. 112–13.

34. *PF*, pp. 127–8; *UVOKShch*, p. 293; *Hospody*, p. 279; *ZDUVOShch*, pp. 403–4.

35. *PF*, p. 138; *UVOKShch*, pp. 313–14; *Hospody*, pp. 302–3; *ZDUVOShch*, p. 428.

36. TsDA-MLMU, 235/1/182, p. 1.

37. *PF*, p. 158; *UVOKShch*, p. 344; *Hospody*, p. 338; *ZDUVOShch*, p. 464.

38. *PF*, p. 165; *UVOKShch*, p. 350; *Hospody*, p. 345; *ZDUVOShch*, pp. 471–2.

39. Lazar Bodyk, *Dzherelom velykoho kino* (Kiev, 1965), p. 72.

40. '1939 Autobiography', p. 10.

41. See *Naspivala maty: Pisennyi svit O. Dovzhenka*, edited and introduced by Vitalii M. Pryhorovs'kyi (Kiev, 1995).

42. *PF*, p. 143; *UVOKShch*, p. 319; *Hospody*, pp. 308–9; *ZDUVOShch*, pp. 434–5.

43. *PF*, p. 155.

44. Roberto Manetti, 'Zaveshchanie poeta', RGALI, 2081/1/1156, p. 14.

45. 'The House' ('Khata') appeared in *Literaturnaia Rossiia*, 8 February 1963; *Prapor*, no. 1 (1964); Oleksandr Dovzhenko, *Tvory v p'iaty tomakh* (Kiev, 1964), vol. 1, pp. 204–6; A. P. Dovzhenko, *Sobranie sochinenii v chetyrekh tomakh* (Moscow, 1968), vol. 3, pp. 511–14; O. Dovzhenko, *Zacharovana Desna; Kinopovisti, opovidannia* (Kiev, 1969), pp. 544–6; O. Dovzhenko, *Tvory v p'iaty tomakh* (Kiev, 1984), vol. 3, pp. 339–41; and O. Dovzhenko, *Kinopovisti, opovidannia* (Kiev, 1986), pp. 661–4. 'The Dream' ('Son') appeared in *Literaturna Ukraina*, 30 June 1963; *Literaturnaia Rossiia*, 11 September 1964; *Tvory v p'iaty tomakh* (Kiev, 1964), vol. 1, pp. 207–9; *Zacharovana Desna*, pp. 547–9; *Tvory v p'iaty tomakh* (Kiev, 1984), vol. 3, pp. 341–3; and *Kinopovisti, opovidannia*, pp. 664–6.

46. Koshelivets', p. 282.

47. *PF*, pp. 121–3; *UVOKShch*, pp. 288–9; *Hospody*, pp. 272–4; *ZDUVOShch*, pp. 396–8.

48. TsDA-MLMU, 169/1/589, p. 10. It is unclear why Dovzhenko counted twelve, not thirteen, films as part of his creative legacy.

49. H. Zel'dovych, 'Uryvky zi spohadiv', Derevianko Archive, p. 13.

10

Cold War Politics

According to the latest estimates, during World War II nearly 8 million Soviet soldiers and up to 20 million civilians died in battle or from hunger, diseases, injuries and other war-related causes.[1] The Germans forcibly drafted nearly 5 million Soviet men and women to work as slave labourers in Germany.[2] Twenty-five million became homeless.[3]

Many Soviet citizens recognised a vast chasm between Communist ideals and the realities of their shattered world during the war. Exposed to Western ways of living, however briefly, many hoped for a less repressive and less ideologically driven postwar regime. 'Now it's time to live!' a Soviet Army major declared on 8 May 1945, Victory-in-Europe Day, in Moscow's Red Square, where thousands of smiling people crowded, eager to congratulate anyone in uniform.[4] His exuberance represented the hopes of the Soviet population after the bloodiest conflict of the twentieth century.

After the end of the war, A. A. Zhdanov, the Leningrad party boss and the ideology chief after Shcherbakov's death in 1945, became the most visible of the party hierarchs to confront a devastated Soviet population hoping for change. By supervising the propaganda campaign for ideological purity and xenophobia in the early postwar years, Zhdanov sought to redirect these energies. The Central Committee's resolution of 14 August 1946, 'On the Journals *Zvezda* and *Leningrad*', and the 4 September 1946 recommendation, 'On the Film *A Great Life*', represented the full flowering of this crusade. The leadership declared an assault on all recent deviations from socialist realism in the arts, literature and cinema, which authorities had barely tolerated between 1941–5.

The August declaration criticised two Leningrad literary journals for publishing works by Mikhail Zoshchenko, a prominent humourist, and by Anna Akhmatova, one of the greatest Russian poets of the twentieth century. The Soviet Writers' Union had expelled both only days before. Zoshchenko had published a story in which a small monkey escapes from the zoo, spends a day observing Soviet life and finds the experience so horrible that he returns with relief to captivity.[5] According to the party's guardians, Zoshchenko depicted Soviet reality in a malicious, 'hooligan-like' manner and accompanied his work with 'anti-Soviet attacks'. They viewed Akhmatova's work, which they derided as 'empty poetry, lacking in moral content, which is alien to our people', as a subtle but more dangerous deviation. Her verse represented 'bourgeois-aristocratic aestheticism' and the decadence of 'art for art's sake'. According to the resolution, the editorial boards of these journals had forgotten that Soviet journals 'cannot be apolitical', a lapse that justified the closure of *Leningrad* and the replacement of *Zvezda*'s entire editorial board.[6]

The decision ended the party's tolerance of art that did not conform readily to the tenets of socialist realism. By identifying itself with a literature of high moral principles (however contrived), heroic attitudes, collectivism and an idealised view of Soviet reality, the party sought to orient literature towards the future, to have it show life 'as it ought to be rather than what it was'.[7]

The second decision condemned the sequel to Leonid Lukov's *A Great Life* (1939), which won a Stalin Prize in 1941. *A Great Life, Part Two* appeared in 1946, but when Stalin previewed the film, he allegedly walked out in anger and banned it.[8]

Subsequently, the Central Committee labelled *A Great Life* 'politically bankrupt' and 'artistically poor'. It claimed that the film did not properly represent the Soviet state's positive role in reconstructing the Donbass mining region after the war. The finding accused Lukov and his scenarist, P. Nilin, of creating the 'false impression' that workers using obsolete technology and old-fashioned backbreaking work, not modern technology, rebuilt the mines.[9] Moreover, the analysis continued, *A Great Life* had intentionally misrepresented workers, engineers and party members as backward and uncultured people with low moral standards who engaged in idle talk and drunkenness. Worst of all, some of the film's central characters had even served in the German police during the occupation! According to the resolution, this film failed to capture the people's high ideals and moral standards on the screen.

The party declaration concluded by criticising Ivan Bolshakov, whose Ministry of Cinematography had also approved Sergei Eisenstein's *Ivan the Terrible, Part Two*, Vsevolod Pudovkin's *Admiral Nakhimov* (1946) and Grigorii Kozintsev's and Leonid Trauberg's *Simple People* (1945). The Central Committee viewed all of these films as 'false and erroneous' and banned them. Only Pudovkin managed to cut the controversial scenes and release an acceptable version in December 1946, which even won him a Stalin Prize the following year.

Although the party harshly criticised these films, the Soviet leaders (even Stalin) failed to tell the directors specifically what kind of films to make, as they themselves did not know. Upon seeing a film, they judged it through very subjective lenses. Either they liked a film, or they did not. They brutally condemned 'failures' and held up 'successful' films as models.[10] Oversight committee after oversight committee delayed the start and the completion of countless films. Each committee feared making a decision the Soviet oligarchs might overturn. Under these circumstances, the number of Soviet feature films produced in the last decade of Stalin's tenure dropped from nineteen in 1945 to a low of nine in 1951.[11] Dovzhenko, along with his colleagues throughout the Soviet film industry, reacted to this zeal with caution.

Although the party criticised the directors whose films 'failed', it allowed them to continue work, hoping that they would learn from these lessons and eventually produce politically acceptable films. Friedrich Ermler's *The Great Turning Point* (1945) and Mikhail Chiaureli's *The Oath* (1946) became the first postwar models. They succeeded, in part, because they raised Stalin's cult of personality to new heights.[12] Ermler's presented a psychological study of a Soviet general who experienced the strain of preparing for battle. As a surrogate for Stalin, General Muravyov demonstrates his acceptance of enormous responsibility and his seriousness in carrying them out.[13] In July 1946 Ermler received a Stalin Prize for his film.

Chiaureli's *The Oath* had a greater impact on Soviet cinematography. Featuring a 'typical' Stalingrad family, the Petrovs, the film included a series of vignettes in which the Petrovs played supporting roles in the great events that transformed the Soviet Union between 1924 and 1945. The Petrovs, in spite of this involvement, do not emerge as the real heroes of the film.

The title refers to Stalin's vow, at Lenin's funeral in January 1924, that the party would remain faithful to the dead leader's teachings. Chiaureli portrayed Stalin not only as Lenin's natural successor, but as a deity of sorts. By deifying Stalin, he created an image of the Soviet leader that other directors attempted to emulate.[14] In the wake of this film, Stalin's 'cult' assumed its greatest dimensions.

As the 1946 resolutions sought to define the contours of Soviet intellectual life, the 'anti-cosmopolitan' campaign of 1948–9 intensified public expressions of xenophobia, anti-Semitism and strident Russian nationalism. Born of the insecurities raised by the war and the beginnings of the Cold War, this drive sought to secure the Soviet home front.

Everything Soviet and/or Russian assumed a position of superiority to everything foreign. Everything 'progressive' in the world originated in Russia. Propagandists claimed that Russians had invented the radio, the light bulb, the airplane, the steam engine and other modern-day conveniences. These exaggerated claims reflected a great deal of apprehension about the potential attraction of foreign, especially Western, ideas and living standards.

Native Land

From 30 January 1944 until Stalin's death nine years later, Dovzhenko did not enjoy the political trust that had characterised his professional life after the success of *Shchors*. Although Stalin and his allies allowed him to work, Dovzhenko disappeared from public view.[15]

Isolated, lonely and frustrated, Dovzhenko sought to win back the political credi-
bility he had lost. He desperately tried to ingratiate himself with potential sponsors,
even to work on films that did not excite him. He displayed a pitiful willingness to
prostitute his talents in order to make movies. Only acts of creation conforming to
his sponsors' political standards would rehabilitate him.

In the post-war period, Dovzhenko worked on two documentaries, *Victory in
Right-Bank Ukraine and the Expulsion of the German Aggressors from Soviet Ukrainian
Territory* and *Native Land*, as well as two feature films, *Michurin* and *Goodbye, America*. He also prepared screenplays and proposals for several other films. Only *Victory
in Right-Bank Ukraine*, *Native Land* and *Michurin* ever reached the screen.

Victory in Right-Bank Ukraine, a sequel to Dovzhenko's *The Battle for Our Soviet
Ukraine*, depicted the Soviet advance from Kiev to the western borders of Ukraine.
Taking documentary footage and inserting captured German material, the film tes-
tified to the inevitability of Soviet victory.

Dovzhenko did not possess complete creative control over these projects. Many
cameramen shot hundreds of reels across many fronts, far from his direct supervision. Thus, the end product may not have reflected what he might have
accomplished had he directed the shooting himself. Of course, Dovzhenko did
select the footage and edit it, as well as write a narrator's text for both documentaries.[16] These efforts provided a start, however humble, to resurrecting his career
from the ashes of *Ukraine in Flames*.

He next turned his attention to projects that did not include Ukraine as a
setting. In the autumn of 1945, he became involved in the production of an
Armenian documentary, *Native Land*, which celebrated the twenty-fifth anniversary of the establishment of the Armenian Soviet Socialist Republic.[17] Dovzhenko
attempted to keep his participation a secret from Bolshakov, who had ordered
him not to work on the film. As a result, although Dovzhenko helped shoot and
edit the film, the credits 'by his own request' listed him only as the author of the
narration.[18]

Following his poetic introduction, 'Armenia. An ancient land ... your fatherland',
he sang Armenia's praises within the context of its tragic history.[19] Beginning in the
seventh century, the Armenians struggled with the Muslims for 300 years. Although
the Armenian state disappeared, the people preserved their Orthodox religion,
architecture, language and culture. Despite Persian and Ottoman occupation, the
Armenians believed in their future rebirth, which occurred in the nineteenth century when tsarist Russia incorporated Eastern Armenia.

The hopes of the nineteenth century turned to tragedy in the twentieth as the
Ottoman massacres during World War I wiped out nearly half of the Armenian
population. Hundreds of thousands more fled Armenia. As Turkish armies threatened an independent Armenia after 1918, only a miracle could have saved the

people. That miracle appeared with 'the Great October Revolution and with Lenin's genius'.[20]

The Red Army proclaimed the establishment of the Armenian Soviet Socialist Republic on 29 November 1920. Over the next twenty-five years under Soviet rule, Armenia thrived economically. In World War II 250,000 Armenians fought gallantly on behalf of the other peoples of the USSR and helped defeat fascism. Under Soviet rule, Armenia, with twenty-five centuries of history, experienced a twenty-five-year renaissance.

Except for one reference, Dovzhenko's text followed the conventional Soviet interpretation of Armenian history. That deviation introduced the Armenian genocide of 1915. The horrors of Maidanek and Auschwitz, he claimed, 'were born on the ancient roads of Armenia'.[21]

Dovzhenko and his Armenian colleagues used archival films from the State Film Archival Institute (Gosfilmofond).[22] Even though he had seen the horrors of war first-hand and served on the Ukrainian War-Crimes Commission, the documentary footage of the 1915 Armenian genocide upset Dovzhenko.[23]

His reference to the mass murder and its connection with the Nazi death camps may have touched on a contentious issue: how to deal with a nation's unique suffering within the Soviet context. Dovzhenko's recognition of the Armenian tragedy not only gave this people a special status, it pronounced their history different from the histories of the other Soviet peoples.

On 23 March 1946 Dovzhenko met with a group of Armenians who thanked him for *Native Land*. They told him that only a master who loved his Fatherland could have made such a film.[24] In response, Dovzhenko wrote in his diary: 'I listen to this high compliment and weep. Yes, I love my country, I love my people, I love them ardently and tenderly as a son or a poet or a citizen can love . . .'[25] He could express his 'Soviet patriotism' publicly, but not his love for Ukraine. *Native Land* may have served as a surrogate for a film on Ukraine, another of the major killing fields of the twentieth century.

Dovzhenko could not present Ukraine's famine of 1932–3 or depict on screen Ukraine's disproportionate casualties in World War II. As a substitute for addressing the horrors that befell his own people, he could discuss the Armenian catastrophe. Of all Dovzhenko's postwar films, *Native Land* brought him the greatest pleasure.

Michurin

While fighting ideological deviations, the party introduced the biographies of prominent, politically acceptable Russians and non-Russians from the past on screen. Adhering to standardised and simplistic formulas, which accented each hero's struggles against political and social constraints (not personal demons), these biographical films stressed that great men, not just class conflict, can radically change the course of history. In conformity to this interpretation, few of the films dealt with workers. At the height of Stalin's cult of personality, they served to create auxiliary mini-cults augmenting Stalin's own. 'One film,' Zhdanov asserted, 'will do the work of many thousands of agitators.'[26]

Unlike films of the 1930s and the war years, which emphasised famous political and military leaders (such as Ivan the Terrible, Peter the Great and Field Marshal Mikhail Kutuzov), the movies produced after 1945 tended to emphasise prominent scientists, intellectuals and members of the creative intelligentsia.[27] Soviet feature films portrayed I. P. Pavlov (the legendary psychologist), N. I. Pirogov (an anatomist), Alexander Popov (the 'inventor' of the radio), N. M. Przhevalsky (a famous geographer) and N. E. Zhukovsky (the 'inventor' of the airplane). In addition to these films celebrating Russian scientists, other historical biographies dealt with famous Russian writers, such as V. G. Belinsky, and prominent Russian composers, including Modest Mussorgsky and Nikolai Rimsky-Korsakov. Mikhail Glinka, the founder of the Russian national music tradition, appeared in two cinematic treatments, one in 1946 and another in 1952.[28] As part of the party's aggressive promotion of Russian legends, heroes and icons after 1945, these motion pictures celebrated those innovators who emerged 'from native Russian folk traditions rather than from European training, traditions, or genres'.[29]

Of the twenty historical biographies filmed and released between 1945 and 1954, only six dealt with non-Russians.[30] The majority of the films depicting acceptable non-Russian heroes, such as the Georgian poet-soldier David Guramilishvili, the Latvian poet and playwright Jan Rainis, the Ukrainian poet Taras Shevchenko and the Kazakh musician Dzhambul, included a russocentric subtext. These men encountered 'progressive' Russians who raised their class consciousness and rekindled the 'age-old friendship' of their peoples with the Russian people.[31] The audiences watching these biographical films most likely perceived them as part of a larger, postwar 'Russian in form, Russian nationalist in content' trend.[32]

Dovzhenko's last film, an idealised screen biography of Russian horticulturalist Ivan Michurin (1855–1935), appeared during this shift towards Russian primacy and at the height of the Lysenko cult. Trofim Lysenko (1898–1976), a Ukrainian agriculturalist, promised a significant increase in agricultural production at a time when the Soviet Union required larger harvests to feed the millions of peasants who had migrated into the cities. After silencing the 'bourgeois specialists' who expressed doubts about the high governmental agricultural quotas, the party hierarchy endorsed Lysenko's pseudoscience. Lysenko, after all, promised to increase agricultural production with a Marxist biology that would 'require nature to submit to Soviet governmental policy'.[33]

An excellent self-promoter, Lysenko cited Marx, Engels and Lenin and claimed that his methods, stressing environment over heredity, conformed to Marxist principles.

His materialist biology denied the existence of genes, emphasising that chromosome theory represented 'reactionary and idealist' views. Lysenko and his followers claimed that only the superstitious church and wealthy capitalists supported genetic theory. By mastering the appropriate Stalinist rhetoric and by conforming to the unspoken assumptions behind Stalin's personality cult, Lysenko gained control of the Soviet scientific community in the summer of 1948, when the Academy of Agricultural Sciences officially endorsed the Lysenko school of Marxist biological sciences.

Although Michurin never openly supported Lysenko, their ideas had much in common. Michurin claimed that humans could speed up evolution by adapting plants to new environments without waiting for nature to take its course. Since his ideas dovetailed with Lysenko's, Soviet leaders systematically built up Michurin's reputation with public ceremonies and awards. After Michurin died in 1935, Lysenko referred to Michurin as a courageous pioneer who paved the way for his own theories, which he labelled 'Michurinism'.

Dovzhenko, an avid naturalist, started work on *Michurin*'s screenplay in early January 1944, after party leaders banned *Ukraine in Flames*. The film-maker needed an ideologically safe subject, one that possessed no 'nationalist tendencies', and Michurin fitted the bill. In his diary entry of 19 January 1944, Dovzhenko wrote that the 'subject doesn't seem to go with my "nationalism"; after all, it's Russian'.[34]

As it appeared in 1948, *Michurin* emphasises a number of episodes in the horticulturalist's life. It opens in the late nineteenth century, when two wealthy Americans visit Michurin's nursery in Kozlov, a small town northeast of Moscow, and offer him work in America. He refuses, choosing instead to serve his own country. Although Russian officials do not support him and the local priest denounces him for 'meddling' in the natural order of things, he carries on. During World War I, he suffers a personal blow with the death of his wife, Alexandra, but the Bolshevik Revolution revives his spirits. As the new Soviet state recognises and supports his research, Michurin's nursery becomes a national showcase. The horticulturalist confronts a final crisis in 1924, when a heavy snowfall threatens his orchards. The trees survive and blossom in the spring. Eleven years later, the Soviet state honours Michurin with a celebration marking his eightieth birthday.

The film's narrative contrasts Michurin's life before and after the Revolution. In the first phase, Michurin experiences a series of denials and hardships. In the second phase, the Soviet state supports and rewards him.

Significantly, though, Michurin's theories do not change from the first half of the film to the second. We do not see him struggle to formulate or refine his ideas. From his first appearance to his last, Michurin possesses the infallible and unwavering wisdom of the 'positive hero'. The Bolshevik Revolution creates an intellectual climate in which Michurin's work thrives. The horticulturalist does not change; the society around him does, thanks to the victory of Communism.[35]

The film concludes with Michurin's state-sponsored eightieth birthday celebration, which compensates him for all the abuse he endured during the first half of the film. He then receives a telegram from Stalin congratulating him. Michurin responds, thanking Stalin for his best wishes and admits that they represent the highest honour of his life. Michurin achieves his success, the film suggests, due to his direct line to the source of all wisdom – the party leadership. In his last film, Dovzhenko finally acknowledged the existence of Joseph Vissarionovich Stalin, if only in several short passages.

Although *Michurin* conformed to Zhdanov's campaign to present positive role models to the Soviet public, Dovzhenko experienced even more trouble with this film than he did with *Shchors*. His work took nearly five years from inception to completion, twenty-six months of which he devoted solely to filming. Six different versions of the screenplay survive in the Dovzhenko archive.[36]

Inviting his old cameraman, the rehabilitated Danylo Demutsky, to work on *Michurin*, Dovzhenko may have imagined that he would create a Russian *Earth*.[37] He probably expected to find a biography of Michurin easier to film than that of Shchors. Little did he know that the postwar Stalinist strait-jacket would bind his creative talents even tighter.

Kornely Zelinsky, Dovzhenko's friend and neighbour at Peredelkino, remembered the director saying, 'I wanted to write a poem about creativity, which attracts conflict, collisions with obstacles. Without this there cannot be creativity.'[38] Influenced by Eisenstein's montage theories based on the pre-Stalinist idea of the dialectic, Dovzhenko envisioned a film emphasising progress through conflict. By the 1930s, however, Stalin had modified these Marxist dialectical laws in order to justify his own theories of progress without conflict.[39] Dovzhenko, once again, failed to synchronise his aesthetic views with Stalin's theoretical revisions. His interpretation of Michurin attracted conflict, but it did not nurture his creativity.

On 28 April 1944 Bolshakov approved Dovzhenko to produce Michurin's biography.[40] The film-maker then continued to hone his screenplay and wrote a play dealing with Michurin's life, *Life in Bloom*, which became the working title for both.

In December 1945 Dovzhenko suffered a minor heart attack after a meeting with three demanding censors. His physical affliction probably represented his internal struggle with Stalinist expectations and his own artistic integrity. How much could he bear to compromise? A good question. He described the censors as 'all cultivated and intelligent people. All three know that they're doing absurd things, and yet they can't help it. They have no minds of their own, no taste, no dignity. How can one even talk about art in these circumstances?' He admitted his fears in his diary: 'I'm scared. Am I no longer an artist? Am I really an invalid? Am I close to death or to being an impoverished cripple? Am I superfluous, unneeded? Living in a realm of film ghouls?'[41] Despite these fears, doubts and illnesses, he continued to work hard.

Dovzhenko planned to start filming *Life in Bloom* on 1 April 1946.[42] He completed the literary treatment and the shooting script on 20 February 1946, and he read a presentable draft of the screenplay at two public meetings in March.[43] The Ministry of Cinematography did not give Mosfilm permission to start production on Dovzhenko's film until 8 July.[44] A revised screenplay appeared in the October–November 1946 issue of the Moscow literary journal *Novyi mir*.

During the winter of 1946–7, Dovzhenko, helped by Solntseva, who served as his assistant director, began to film the winter scenes. After nearly three months of filming, they finished shooting the planned scenes on 13 February 1947.[45] Further production ground to a halt, however. Someone, either at the Ministry of Cinematography or at Mosfilm, had objected to *Life in Bloom*. The reasons for the objection remain unclear, but it delayed the film's production. In a letter to Demutsky dated 10 April 1947, Dovzhenko admitted that he had encountered difficulties with *Life in Bloom*. 'I do not know how I'll complete the film,' he wrote.[46]

Six months later, on 23 August 1947, the Ministry of Cinematography accepted a new version of the final episodes of *Life in Bloom*.[47] On 5 November 1947 Dovzhenko's stage version of *Life in Bloom* premiered in Perm, and then in Leningrad on 7 November, Saratov on 8 November and Rostov-on-the-Don on 11 November.[48]

Although Dovzhenko's play may have met with acceptance on the stage, officials at the Ministry of Cinematography believed that the screenplay needed further revisions. On 18 December 1947 O. Mariamov, the head of the section on screenplays at the Ministry of Cinematography, made additional corrections.[49] On 23 March 1948 the film-maker began to create a second version, which became *Michurin*.[50]

In a diary entry from April 1948, Dovzhenko described his troubles:

> My *Life in Bloom* has been dragging on for several years now … Then when the film had been completed with the utmost effort and it came to life to please even trained snobs, I found myself in some mystical zone where the film was discussed at the artistic council. The minister (Bolshakov) kept running off somewhere with it and demanding new cuts every time he came back.[51]

According to one of Dovzhenko's colleagues, the major problem with the first filmed version of *Michurin* centred on Dovzhenko's failure to reflect 'the main contents of the life of this remarkable Russian transformer of nature'.[52] By portraying Michurin's family life and details of his daily activities, Dovzhenko's film, like Pudovkin's first version of *Admiral Nakhimov*, violated Stalin's interpretation of how film-makers should represent 'great men' in historical films – only in the context of their social activities and not their private lives.[53] Consumed by their missions, 'great men' did not enjoy the luxury of private lives. The public sphere dominated their biographies completely.

Two boys enjoy Michurin's new variety of apples (*Michurin*, 1949)

Stalin's rejection devastated Dovzhenko. For the third time in four years, the authorities had refused one of his projects. He began to fear that he would never produce a new film.

The film-maker desperately wanted to create, even if he had to celebrate Russian socialist realist heroes. During this personal crisis, Dovzhenko found solace from an unlikely source – Zhdanov, who hated Lysenko. After Stalin rejected the first version of *Michurin*, Zhdanov, according to Dovzhenko, 'saved me from asphyxiation. I revived after the meeting with him.'[54] The film-maker claimed that the ideology chief defended the first version, but did not say how or why. He appreciated Zhdanov's defence and took it to heart.[55] Once again, Dovzhenko had sought help from a powerful patron in order to place his vision on the screen.

After extensive revisions, the authorities felt Dovzhenko's second version fitted within the framework of socialist realism. Committees at Mosfilm and at the Ministry of Cinematography then radically revised his work in order to create a smoother, more politically acceptable film, but even they could not perfect it. The Artistic Council of the Ministry of Cinematography pointed out that the new film still did not 'completely show Michurin's role as a brilliant Russian scholar, as the founder of the new progressive orientation in biological science, and as the great transformer of nature'. Nevertheless, the Council finally approved it for release in the autumn of 1948.[56]

At a public screening on 7 December 1948, the audience, which included representatives from the Ministry of Agriculture, collective farms, higher education, elementary and secondary education, the Academy of Sciences, agricultural institutes, film-makers, artists and authors, praised the film highly.[57] According to *Izvestiia*'s critic, Dovzhenko created *Michurin* as a 'genuine and significant work, with the harmonious combination of high idealistic and artistic qualities'.[58] On 1 January 1949 *Michurin* premiered in Moscow, and on 3 January in Kiev.[59]

On 8 April 1949 Dovzhenko and Solntseva received the Stalin Prize, Second Class, for *Michurin*.[60] Although many committees reworked the project, the Soviet Council of Ministers decided to award the prize to Dovzhenko and Solntseva personally. Not surprisingly, official circles then praised the film with enthusiasm. Dovzhenko's friends and colleagues gave the film a more circumspect reception. One of his closest friends, Ostap Vyshnia, wrote that *Michurin* 'as a film, is very interesting, and necessary, but for us, those who value art as ... a factor leading us to Communism, that what was done ... was not quite enough'.[61] Vyshnia, in effect, claimed that the film's political message overwhelmed its artistic possibilities.

Dovzhenko himself gave the film an even more damning evaluation. In a conversation with a colleague at Mosfilm, he said: 'This is someone else's picture, completely not mine. Completely not mine!'[62] Although *Michurin*'s completion may have represented a committee effort and not Dovzhenko's own, his identification with the film resurrected his reputation, blackened by the fiasco of *Ukraine in Flames*.

Goodbye, America

Once Dovzhenko had revived his political honour, he sought to consolidate it by filming a sanitised version of Annabelle Bucar's experiences in the USSR. Making this Cold War adventure would serve Soviet interests and restore, he hoped, his long-lost 'party card'.

On 27 February 1948 Bucar, a thirty-three-year old American, resigned from her job at the US Embassy in Moscow and revealed her thirteen-month secret marriage to Konstantin Lapshin, a baritone at the Moscow Operetta Theatre. In her letter of resignation, she claimed that she 'had acquired a real understanding of the Russians' and condemned the US Embassy policy 'directed against these people'. She called further work there 'incompatible with my present views'. Her abrupt act followed that of her former chief in Moscow, Armond D. Willis, who walked out of the Embassy in April 1947 after criticising American Ambassador Walter Bedell Smith and claiming that US Embassy officials in Moscow were 'Russian haters'.[63]

Bucar's defection shocked the US State Department. Born in Trafford, Pennsylvania, to parents who had immigrated from southeastern Europe, she had appeared in every respect a loyal American. Employed as an assistant information officer on the Russian-language *America* magazine, and on other US Information Agency operations, she proved 'an efficient worker'. State Department officials in Washington claimed that they had no idea she had become dissatisfied.[64]

Why did she defect? Although her father claimed that 'too much education' contributed to her decision, she most certainly responded to more compelling factors.[65] As a single woman, Bucar came to the attention of the Soviet counter-intelligence corps. These officers set up a 'chance' encounter with one of their agents, Konstantin Lapshin. Bucar, in turn, fell in love with him. At the height of their passionate affair, the actor disappeared. Later he sent a note from prison stating, 'Help me, or else I'll die.' She rushed to help Lapshin, who pretended to fear imminent execution. Soviet counter-intelligence officers then blackmailed her.

After she 'saved' Lapshin, she secretly married him and for thirteen months may have passed secret materials to the NKVD. After asking the Soviet government for political asylum, she wrote a book, *The Truth about American Diplomats*, unmasking her American colleagues as spies.[66] Her book became a sensation. In addition to three English-language editions, Bucar's book came out in Russian, Hungarian, Czech, Spanish, Slovak and Bulgarian.[67]

In the spring of 1949, as the Cold War heated up, the Ministry of Cinematography suggested that Dovzhenko create an anti-American film based on Bucar's book, which would follow the model presented by Mikhail Romm's screening of Konstantin Simonov's *The Russian Question* (1947). [68] In Romm's film, Harry Smith, an American journalist, visits the Soviet Union on the orders of his newspaper's owners in order to gather material for a book denouncing the Soviet Union. After seeing the USSR with his own eyes, Smith vows to write the truth about the Russian people. After reading the manuscript, the owners fire Smith, who loses his home and family. Smith, however, continues to speak the truth about the USSR at many 'progressive' public meetings.

Both *The Russian Question* and *The Truth about American Diplomats* represented the US government, the USSR's former ally, as its ideological enemy, driven by its capitalist class to confront the Soviet Union. Despite the reactionary nature of the American ruling circles, some Americans, such as the fictionalised Harry Smith and the real Annabelle Bucar, saw the Soviet environment with their own eyes, had their political consciousness raised, and then challenged their government's lies about the Soviet Union. These works asserted that the American government's anti-Communism did not have the support of the American people.

Although Dovzhenko probably agreed with Bucar's political message, the creation of a cinematic treatment of her book violated Dovzhenko's artistic vision, which emphasised the relationship between man and nature.[69] Despite the fact that Bucar's book did not deal with nature (all of its action took place inside the American Embassy in Moscow), Dovzhenko took the assignment and began to tinker with a screenplay prepared by L. Tubelsky and P. Rizhei in the second half of 1949.

Seeking total control, Dovzhenko claimed that their creative methods and styles differed from his own and fired them.[70] After preparing several drafts of his own screenplay in 1950, he began to film *Goodbye, America*, as he titled his project, in January 1951. Two months later, after one of Mosfilm's administrators learned that the government no longer needed Dovzhenko's film, he turned off the lights in the middle of Dovzhenko's production and told everyone to go home.[71] Twenty-one months of hard work had come to an ignoble end.

At that point, the director had completed nearly half the film. In 1958 Mosfilm placed the scenes Dovzhenko had shot in Gosfilmofond's archives.[72] They remained there in solitary confinement for decades.

After the Soviet Union's collapse, the film historian Rostislav Iurenev restored *Goodbye, America*. He spliced the completed scenes together and added a narrative text in place of those scenes Dovzhenko did not shoot. With the sponsorship of Mosfilm and Gosfilmofond, and financed by the Russian Film Commission (Roskomkino), he premiered the half-fictional, half-documentary *Goodbye, America* at the Berlin Film Festival in March 1996.[73]

The result easily stands out as Dovzhenko's most disappointing film. Conforming to postwar propaganda, xenophobia and Dovzhenko's own anti-Americanism, the crudely made picture tells the story of Anna Bedford (Annabelle Bucar), an employee at the American Embassy in Moscow who becomes disgusted with her colleagues' anti-Communism and embraces the Soviet Union. In the beginning Bedford appears as a patriotic American who sees Russia as a 'mysterious country' with many 'horrible and dangerous people'. During her stay in Moscow, she befriends the Gromov family and comes to realise that the Soviet people pose no danger to America and that the 'Communist threat' represents an invention of the titans of the American military-industrial complex. She comes to this conclusion without any cathartic inner conflict. Dovzhenko's dialogue concentrates on ideology, revealing little of the emotional lives of the film's protagonists or life in the Embassy.

Dovzhenko's American Embassy presents a nest of intrigue, full of capitalist warmongers, spies and rabid anti-Communists. Embassy employees parrot anti-Soviet and anti-Russian clichés. They view the Russians as a horrible people, who, in the words of Anna Bedford's roommate 'eat ice cream on the streets in the winter and are not afraid of death'.[74] When Ambassador Walter Scott, a former general from the Office of Strategic Services (the precursor to the Central Intelligence Agency) arrives, he demands that all Embassy employees become spies. To ensure their political cooperation, he orders electronic surveillance of the Embassy's residential quarters. The Embassy becomes a war bunker, not an outpost of diplomacy.

Interestingly, John Graves, one of the Embassy's intelligence officers, repeats a phrase Counsellor Khurgin told Dovzhenko in Warsaw in 1922. When Bedford first arrives in Moscow, Graves tells her, 'My dear, you are in an embassy. An embassy is a horrible kitchen, where everything should be roasted a little day and night. I am a cook.'[75]

Bedford's friendship with the Gromovs, whom she meets on V-E Day on the Moscow streets, leads her to question her anti-Communist training and to accept them as her new family and the Soviet Union as her true homeland. Through the Gromovs, she meets Yaroslav Voloshyn, a Ukrainian war hero, becoming attracted to him.

After her mother dies, Bedford goes home to Pennsylvania, but cannot find her mother's grave. She learns that two days after the funeral, the government bulldozed the site and built a military airport over it. In Washington DC she attends a McCarthy-like Congressional inquisition of Armand Howard, an Embassy officer who broke down during an important press conference in Moscow and denied the anti-Communist propaganda spread by his own government.

In the screenplay Dovzhenko presents a meeting between Wall Street capitalists and State Department officials. At the meeting James Forrestal, the Secretary of Defence, suddenly commits suicide by leaping from the thirty-eighth floor as the group discusses employing technology to transform the Soviet Union into a desert. Anticipating Stanley Kubrick's *Dr Strangelove or How I Learned to Stop Worrying and Love the Bomb* (1964), Dovzhenko's American capitalists and diplomats come across as cartoonish figures.

If his screenplay appeared politically correct, the restored film tends to undermine this view. Mr Morrow, one of the American Embassy's counsellors and the head intelligence officer, looks and acts like Beria. In one scene, he claims that a blacklist of one million Americans who need to be 'watched' exists in Washington. Morrow then asserts that 'even Presidents need to be observed'.

Although Dovzhenko's true intentions do not clearly emerge from the unfinished film, *Goodbye, America*'s fate denied the director a chance to clarify such ambiguities.

Conclusion

The loss of the authorities' trust led to a decline in Dovzhenko's productivity and in the quality of what little he produced. With the exception of *Native Land*, his postwar films failed to display his unique creative vision. High party officials suspected him of Ukrainian nationalism and of violating the tenets of socialist realism, and many cinematic oversight committees carefully monitored his work. This intense supervision narrowed Dovzhenko's creative options. Constant supervision and second-guessing unnerved him. Censorship induced self-censorship, which generated even more self-doubt, despair and creative paralysis.

Victory in Right-Bank Ukraine, *Native Land*, *Michurin* and *Goodbye, America* represented four very different films with four different agendas, but each film raised the question of personal roots and allegiances. Did one's homeland remain a homeland even if one lived in exile or had been rejected by one's homeland? Should the physical destruction of one's homeland or the massacre of a large number of one's compatriots sever one's emotional ties to it? Can a person ever lose his connection to his homeland?

Dovzhenko answered the first of these questions in the affirmative and the second two in the negative. With the issue of homelands, the film-maker unmistakably attempted to transcend his own isolation far from home. Powerless to return home, he nurtured a hope for a better future.

Notes

1. The numbers vary, but see A. A. Sheviakov, 'Gitlerovskii genotsid na territoriakh SSSR', *Sotsiologicheskie issledovaniia*, no. 12 (1991) and 'Zhertvy sredi mirnogo naseleniia v gody Otechestvennoi voiny', *ibid.*, no. 11 (1992).

2. V. I. Zemskov, 'K voprosu o repatriatsii sovetskikh grazhdan 1944–1951 gody', *Istoriia SSSR*, no. 4 (1990), p. 26.

3. Geoffrey Hosking, *The First Socialist Society: A History of the Soviet Union from Within*, enlarged ed. (Cambridge, MA, 1990), p. 297.

4. Robert C. Tucker, 'V-E Day, Moscow: "Time to Live!"', *New York Times*, 11 May 1985; cited in Hiroaki Kuromiya, *Freedom and Terror in the Donbass: A Ukrainian–Russian Borderland, 1870s–1990s* (New York and Cambridge, 1998), p. 297.

5. Hosking, p. 306.

6. *Kommunisticheskaia partiiia Sovetskogo soiuza v rezoliutsiiakh i resheniiakh s'ezdov, konferentsii i plenumov TsK*, part 3, 7th ed. (Moscow, 1954), pp. 485, 486, 487; and Robert H. McNeal, ed., *Resolutions and Decisions of the Communist Party of the Soviet Union, vol. 3: The Stalin Years: 1929–1953* (Toronto, 1974), p. 241.

7. Hosking, p. 306.

8. See Alla Afinogenova, '"Bol'shaia zhizn" donetskikh shakhterov', *Iskusstvo kino*, no. 9 (1989); cited in Kuromiya, p. 314.

9. 'O kinofil'me "Bol'shaia zhizn"', *Iskusstvo kino*, no. 1 (1947), p. 1.

10. Peter Kenez, *Cinema and Soviet Society, 1917–1953* (Cambridge and New York, 1992), p. 215.

11. Vsesoiuznyi gosudarstvennyi fond kinofil'mov, *Sovetskie khudozhestvennye fil'my: Annotirovannyi katalog* (Moscow, 1961), vol. 2, pp. 346–686; Sergei Zemlianukhin and Miroslava Segida (compilers), *Domashniaia sinemateka: Otechestvennoe kino, 1918–1996* (Moscow, 1996), p. 6.

12. See 'Za vysokuiu ideinost' sovetskogo kinoiskusstva', *Iskusstvo kino*, no. 1 (1947), pp. 5–6.

13. Jay Leyda, *Kino: A History of the Russian and Soviet Film*, 3rd ed. (Princeton, NJ, 1983), p. 392.

14. Kenez, *Cinema and Soviet Society, 1917–1953*, pp. 231–2.

15. Of the thirty-two most prominent Soviet film directors included in the collection of memoirs, *Kak ia stal rezhisserom* (Moscow, 1946), Dovzhenko's memoir and filmography do not appear. This, most likely, was not an oversight.

16. Ivan Koshelivets', *Oleksandr Dovzhenko: Sproba tvorchoi biohrafii* (Munich, 1980), p. 226.

17. *Storinky*, pp. 218, 221.

18. *PF*, pp. 136, 295.

19. Oleksandr Dovzhenko, 'Kraina ridna', in his *Tvory v p'iaty tomakh*, vol. 1 (1964), p. 390.

20. 'Kraina ridna', p. 394.

21. 'Kraina ridna', p. 393.

22. I. Verdiian, 'Strana rodnaia', *Sovetskaia kul'tura*, 6 October 1983.

23. 'Rodnœ imia', *Kommunist* (Yerevan), 18 February 1979.

24. *Storinky*, p. 225.

25. *PF*, p. 145 (censored); *UVOKShch*, p. 323; *Hospody*, p. 314; *ZDUVOShch*, p. 440.

26. Cited in 'Dopovid' pro pidsumky roboty kinematografii URSR za 1950 rik ta zavdannia stvorennia kinofil'miv u 1951 rotsi', TsDAVOVUU, 4733/1/284, p. 34.

27. R. Iurenev, *Aleksandr Dovzhenko* (Moscow, 1959), pp. 111–12.

28. *Sovetskie khudozhestvennye fil'my*, pp. 346–559.

29. David Brandenberger, 'The "Short Course" to Modernity: Stalinist History Textbooks, Mass Culture and the Formation of Popular Russian National Identity, 1934–1956' (unpublished PhD dissertation, Harvard University, 1999), p. 330.

30. *Sovetskie khudozhestvennye fil'my*, pp. 346–559.

31. *Sovetskie khudozhestvennye fil'my*, pp. 367–8, 427–8, 460–1, 467.

32. I am paraphrasing David Brandenberger's turn of phrase. Brandenberger, p. 171.

33. *Service*, p. 136.

34. *PF*, p 102; *UVOKShch*, p. 256; *Hospody*, p. 234; *ZDUVOShch*, p. 358.

35. *Service*, p. 141.

36. See editors' notes in Dovzhenko, *Sobranie sochinenii*, vol. 3, p. 757 (*Service*, p. 179).

37. *Storinky*, p. 226, about Demutsky.

38. K. Zelinskii, 'Chelovek – budushchii', RGALI, 2081/1/1133.

39. Barbara D. Leaming, 'Engineers of Human Souls – The Transition to Socialist

Realism in the Soviet Cinema of the 1930s' (unpublished PhD dissertation, New York University, 1976), pp. 77–8.

40. *PF*, p. 106; *UVOKShch*, p. 261; *Hospody*, p. 240; *ZDUVOShch*, p. 364.

41. *PF*, p. 141; *UVOKShch*, pp. 316–17; *Hospody*, p. 306; *ZDUVOShch*, pp. 431–2.

42. *Storinky*, p. 223.

43. *PF*, pp. 144–5; *UVOKShch*, pp. 322–4; *Hospody*, pp. 312–14; *ZDUVOShch*, pp. 438–40; *Storinky*, pp. 224–5.

44. RGALI, 2081/1/973; cited in *Storinky*, p. 226.

45. *Storinky*, p. 228.

46. Cited in *Storinky*, p. 229.

47. *Storinky*, p. 230.

48. *Storinky*, pp. 230–1.

49. *Storinky*, p. 232.

50. *Storinky*, p. 234.

51. *PF*, p. 158; *UVOKShch*, p. 344; *Hospody*, p. 337; *ZDUVOShch*, pp. 463–4.

52. G. Aleksandrov, 'Vdokhnovennoe iskusstvo', *Sovetskoe iskusstvo*, 10 April 1949.

53. Evgenii Gromov, *Stalin: vlast' i iskusstvo* (Moscow, 1998), p. 217.

54. *PF*, p. 158; *UVOKShch*, p. 344; *Hospody*, pp. 337–8; *ZDUVOShch*, p. 464.

55. A. P. Dovzhenko, 'Svetlyi obraz ego ostanetsia v moem sertse', *Za bol'shevistskii fil'm*, 9 September 1948.

56. RGALI, 2081/1/969, p. 6; RGASPI, 77/132/90, pp. 44–51.

57. *Storinky*, p. 239.

58. Arkadii Perventsev, 'Velikii preobrazovatel'' prirody', *Izvestiia*, 31 December 1948.

59. *Storinky*, p. 240.

60. *Literaturnaia gazeta*, no. 29 (1949); cited in *Storinky*, p. 244.

61. Ostap Vyshnia, 'Dumy moi, dumy moi … ', RGALI, 2081/1/1114, p. 6.

62. Iurii Trankvillitskii, 'Aleksandr Dovzhenko: "Ia ne snial' ni odnoi svoei kartiny"', *Rodina*, no. 11 (1990), p. 57.

63. 'U.S. Embassy Aide Quits in Moscow', *New York Times*, 28 February 1948, p. 3:8.

64. *Ibid.*, p. 3:8.

65. 'Father Disowns Clerk in U.S. Embassy Who Renounced Native Land For Russia', *New York Times*, 29 February 1948, p. 4:2.

66. Mikhail Liubimov, 'V Ukraine', *Komsomol'skaia pravda*, 30 August 1996, p. 14; cited in Aleksandr Rutkovskii, '"Proshchai, Amerika!" Aleksandra Dovzhenko', *Kievskie novosti*, 22 August 1997, p. 8.

67. Annabelle Bucar, *The Truth about American Diplomats* (Moscow, 1949); *The*

Truth about American Diplomats (Moscow, 1951); *The Truth about American Diplomats* (Moscow, 1952); *Pravda ob amerikanskikh diplomatakh* (Moscow, 1949); *Az amerikai diplomatak Igazi Arca* (Budapest, 1949); *Pravda o americkych diplomatech* (Prague, 1949); *La verdad acerca de los diplomaticos norteamericanos* (Moscow, 1949); *Pravda o americkych diplomatoch* (Bratislava, 1949); and *Istinata za amerikanskite diplomati* (Sofia, 1949).

68. O. P. Dovzhenko, *Tvory v p'iaty tomakh* (Kiev, 1966), vol. 5, pp. 366–8.

69. Dovzhenko intertwined his anti-American attitudes with his hatred of Hollywood and the American film industry's dominance of world cinema and with America's low civilian and military losses during World War II. See A. Dovzhenko, 'Alchnye appetity Gollivuda', *Sovetskaia kul'tura*, 24 September 1982 (originally published in the *Biulleten'* of the Moscow House of Cinema, no. 18 [1951]) and *UVOKShch*, pp. 237–8, 254, 260.

70. Dovzhenko, *Tvory*, vol. 5 (1966), pp. 366–8.

71. Iurenev, *Aleksandr Dovzhenko*, p. 133.

72. Vladimir Iurevich Dmitriev, the deputy head of Gosfilmofond, in a talk after the Kiev premiere of *Goodbye, America*, 1 June 1996.

73. Rutkovskii, '"Proshchai, Amerika!" Aleksandra Dovzhenko', p. 8; and Vladimir Dmitriev, 'Eshche raz o Dovzhenko', *Segodnia*, 6 March 1996, p. 10.

74. O. Dovzhenko, 'Proshchai, Ameryko!', in his *Tvory v p'iaty tomakh*, vol. 2 (Kiev, 1984), p. 317.

75. Dovzhenko, 'Proshchai, Ameryko!', p. 313. In Dovzhenko's most detailed autobiography, he wrote: ' "The Embassy is a lousy kitchen", Counselor Khurgin told me, "where everything has to be kept hot at all times of day and night." ' '1939 Autobiography', p. 14.

11

The Thaw

Stalin's death on 5 March 1953 shocked most Soviet citizens. After thirty years of his rule, many people closely identified him with the state and the party, and not just because of his officially generated 'cult of personality'. The majority sincerely considered the end of 'our great leader and teacher, our real father and friend' a sorrowful occasion.[1] Not only Stalinist zealots, but also many of those he repressed, such as Alexander Solzhenitsyn, expressed great loss over his passing, if only for show.[2]

With Stalin's demise, Georgy Malenkov, the deputy general secretary, became the general secretary of the Communist Party as well as the chairman of the Council of Ministers (premier) of the USSR. Many important members of the Presidium of the Central Committee (as the Politburo renamed itself) jockeyed to succeed him.

Lavrenty Beria, the former head of the NKVD and recently ascended Minister of the Interior, became one of Malenkov's closest allies. Most members of the Presidium, especially Nikita Khrushchev, feared the former secret police chief and sought to limit his powers. Despite Khrushchev's efforts, the Malenkov-Beria faction gained fragile control of the Presidium three weeks after Stalin's death. Beria became the First Deputy Chairman of the Council of Ministers, second in rank to Malenkov.

Gaining control of the Presidium did not guarantee total authority. The Malenkov-Beria faction had to establish its authority before the population at large. To win popular support, Beria introduced a number of liberal policies. He rehabilitated those arrested in the so-called 'Doctors' Plot', signalling that the new leadership would no longer tolerate arbitrary police terror.[3]

Beria also began to defend the non-Russians. At the Nineteenth Party Congress (5–14 October 1952), Beria advocated teaching and using native languages, the creation and promotion of party cadres from the local nationalities, and the formation of a 'highly developed system of higher education to ensure the training of national cadres of specialists for all spheres of the economy and culture'.[4] Beria, who had stood out as one of the most important men within Stalin's inner circle, implied that the party's current nationality policy had deviated from the principles laid down by Lenin. In a memorandum to the Central Committee written in May 1953, he called for the promotion of ethnic Ukrainians into the party leadership and the use of the Ukrainian language in conducting official business.[5] The new Minister of the Interior, a Georgian like Stalin, supported a return to the party's indigenisation policy of the 1920s and early 30s.

In response to Beria's report, Moscow's Presidium dismissed L. G. Melnikov, the first secretary of the Communist Party of Ukraine and a Russian, for introducing Russian as the language of instruction in higher education. In his place the Presidium appointed A. I. Kyrychenko, the first Ukrainian to occupy this position since the CP(b)U's founding in 1918. Party officials in Ukraine, Khrushchev's former bailiwick, responded quickly. According to the Ukrainian Canadian ex-Communist John Kolasky, who had extensive contacts in the highest Soviet Ukrainian political circles, 'The ink was not yet dry on Beria's signature when officials in Kiev embarked on a campaign of Ukrainianization. The ministries began to employ Ukrainian in their work. Stenographers and secretaries searched frantically for Ukrainian grammars and dictionaries.'[6]

As Beria accumulated power, Khrushchev sought to block him. The 1953 crisis in the German Democratic Republic provided the opportunity he needed. After East German workers revolted in June, Khrushchev blamed Beria and his moderate reforms. Khrushchev then isolated him within the Presidium and arrested him on 26 June 1953. Before the Soviet authorities announced Beria's arrest on 10 July, Dovzhenko involuntarily became drawn into the political struggle between Beria and Khrushchev. In early July, the Georgian film director Mikhail Chiaureli approached Dovzhenko on Beria's behalf. According to the film-maker:

> Ivan Kozlovsky and I were watching the film *The Jungle* at the Ministry of Culture . . .
> The door opened, and Chiaureli walked in . . . He took me off into the corner. 'Listen,
> Sashko, I have something to tell you', he whispered. 'I have very good news for you. If
> you need . . . to fix yourself up in terms of a job or otherwise in a way that befits your
> stature, whether here in Moscow or in Ukraine, in Kiev, write a brief note to Lavrenty
> Pavlovich [Beria]. Don't put it off. Write 'Dear L. P., I beg you to help me create . . . '
> You understand? He'll do everything he can for you. You understand? You can trust me.
> Remember, it's [me] who's telling you this. You ought to know that he's much more
> kindly disposed to you than he used to be . . .'.[7]

In his diary Dovzhenko admitted feeling shocked by Chiaureli's message. What did it mean? Did Beria, the man who had persecuted Dovzhenko in front of Stalin and other members of the Politburo at that fateful 1944 Kremlin meeting, who had largely engineered the film-maker's subsequent political and artistic isolation, now seek to legitimise his appeal to the non-Russians by turning to Dovzhenko? If so, why did Chiaureli approach the Ukrainian film-maker after Beria's arrest on 26 June 1953, but before the Soviet media announced it two weeks later? Did Beria really send Chiaureli to speak with Dovzhenko, or did Chiaureli engage in provocation?[8] Whatever the truth, Chiaureli played on Dovzhenko's vulnerabilities, especially his desire to return to Ukraine.

Forced to live in Moscow, the Ukrainian director must have felt tempted by Chiaureli's proposal, but fear, uncertainty and pride influenced his decision to reject it. Dovzhenko imagined that Stalin's death would free him, but he did not want to become Beria's client. He passionately hated Beria and most likely experienced great joy over his arrest in June and execution in December 1953. By refusing Chiaureli's offer, the Ukrainian film-maker demonstrated his reliability and loyalty. After the announcement of Beria's arrest, Dovzhenko probably imagined that his fortunes would change.

Other writers, artists and film-makers shared this perspective and sought, however slowly and hesitatingly, to expand the frontiers of the permissible after Stalin's death. They hoped to chip away at socialist realism, if not dismantle it entirely, and tried to carve out a space free from the party's control and its constant emphasis on propaganda. The creative intelligentsia, they claimed, should experiment with more varied forms of expression. Ilya Ehrenburg's *The Thaw*, Vera Panova's *Seasons of the Year*, Nikolai Virta's *The Fall of Pompeii* and Yury Yanovsky's *The Daughter of the Prosecutor* became the most prominent books published in this period. Although these novels criticised corrupt party and government bureaucrats, they did not depart significantly from the guidelines of socialist realism. Nevertheless, their publication aroused hopes that artistic creativity would at last gain freedom from its ideological shackles. Although the 'thaw' developed slowly, the promise of change reinvigorated the creative intelligentsia.

Owing to cinema's high production costs, long lead-time and the conservatism of the film studio administrators, the film-making industry responded at a slower pace than graphic art or literature. As film-makers replaced bureaucrats as studio administrators, they took advantage of the new creative opportunities. Beginning with *Three Men on a Raft* (1954), *Othello* (1955) and *The Forty-First* (1956), Soviet films sought to present problems and dilemmas from a personal, non-ideological point of view. Personal conflict, love, the impact of war, demoralisation, corruption, adultery and other elements of the human condition took centre stage on Soviet screens for the first time in decades. While stereotypes from the socialist realist past remained in the new films, critics urged film-makers to highlight 'individual personality', 'authenticity' and the 'complexity of the era' in their forthcoming films.[9] Further experimentation paved the way for the production of two of the most famous 'thaw' films, Mikhail Kalatozov's *The Cranes are Flying* (1957) and Grigorii Chukhrai's *Ballad of a Soldier* (1959).[10]

By allowing the screening of Italian neo-realist cinema, Soviet authorities added to this creative ferment. Films such as Roberto Rossellini's *Rome Open City* (1945), Vittorio De Sica's *The Bicycle Thief* (1948) and Giusseppe De Santis's *Bitter Rice* (1949) presented visually authentic images of the poverty and social oppression of postwar Italy and depicted ordinary working-class people who struggled to survive. In contrast to Soviet films, Italian neo-realist films included open-ended, not neat and preachy, conclusions. Although these films did not adhere to the socialist realist paradigm honoured in the USSR, authorities hoped that they would show the horrors of life in the West. Offering a visual authenticity rarely seen on Soviet screens, these films raised viewers' expectations and inspired film-makers such as Dovzhenko.[11]

In this brave new world, Dovzhenko expected to gain the freedom to create without interference and, most importantly, to return to Kiev. He slowly reintegrated himself into the Soviet political and creative mainstream. With great fanfare Moscow's writers and film-makers celebrated his sixtieth birthday in January 1955.[12] In spite of this public acknowledgment as the Soviet Union's greatest living film-maker, he never received permission to live permanently in Ukraine.

Dovzhenko's bitter disappointment became evident in his last screenplays, *The Enchanted Desna*, *A Poem about an Inland Sea* and *A Flight to Mars*, which dealt with the themes of family, home and the difficulties of maintaining meaningful communication. Their subtexts, however, dealt with the trauma of his exile in Moscow and his desire to return to Ukraine. The first screenplay concerned itself with his memories of home; the second and third dealt with people coming home.

The Enchanted Desna

After completing *Michurin* in 1948, Dovzhenko hoped to incorporate the ideas, themes and stories he had developed earlier in his notebooks and diaries into a single work that would recount his 'entire life, with great digressions in biography, about my youth, about my family, about nature, to remember all the factors which created and indicated my tastes and delicateness of my perceptions'.[13] The film-maker began to write an early draft of *The Enchanted Desna* in 1942. He finished his last draft in the autumn of 1955.

Instead of recounting his entire life, the published version of *The Enchanted Desna*, which appeared in March 1956, focused on his childhood and youth in Sosnytsia. On the surface, Dovzhenko's autobiography celebrated his affinity for nature, love of family, struggle over life and death and his Ukrainian identity. He painted a loving portrait of his childhood, presenting it as an age of innocence.

Although work on his family's plot of land exhausted him, it provided him with a life-long appreciation of nature. 'We lived in complete harmony with the forces of nature,' Dovzhenko wrote. 'In the winter we froze, in the summer the sun burnt us, in the fall we trod mud, and in the spring we were flooded by water. Those who have not experienced this do not know the happiness and completeness of life.'[14] Respect for the forces of nature brought him peace. This should not be surprising. Although he had no control over nature, he never felt personally betrayed by it (as humans and politics had deceived him).

In Dovzhenko's memoir, his mother's garden took centre stage. Reading his evocative descriptions of cucumbers, pumpkins, potatoes, raspberries, blackcurrants, tobacco, beans, sunflowers, poppies, beets, dills and carrots, the urban reader, who did not have ready access to these fruits and vegetables, must have interpreted the Dovzhenko garden as nothing short of paradise. Not surprisingly, snakes existed at its outer edge.

Family relationships occupied a central role in his memoir. Dovzhenko's emphasis on his family defied Stalin's dictum that the public sphere should dominate private life.

Although he revealed that his mother had troubled relations with her husband and in-laws, *The Enchanted Desna* provided an idealised picture of his family, especially his grandfather. According to the author, his family's patriarch at times looked like St Nicholas and at other times like St Fedosy or even God himself. Dovzhenko's grandfather, who had served as the model for all the grandfathers in his films, combined the worlds of man and nature. He picked mushrooms and berries better than anyone and conversed with animals, with the grasses, with the trees and with every living thing around the family farm. He died, as did the grandfather in *Earth*, by the apple orchard.

Death played a major role in the Dovzhenko family. In *The Enchanted Desna*, the author described his family's greatest tragedy, the deaths of four of his brothers, Lavrin, Serhy, Vasyl and Ivan, who all passed away in a single day from an epidemic during Pentecost in June 1895. In reaction, his father cursed God and threw the priest out of his yard, asserting that he himself would bury his children, much like the father in *Earth*.[15]

Even in death, life remained and reasserted itself. He described his family's religious beliefs and their concurrent adherence to superstition. After describing his mother's icons, he focused on her reprint of the Last Judgment in the main room of their house. The depiction so frightened the household that, according to him, even Pirate, their dog, feared to look at it.

His mother's faith rubbed off on him. In a poetic manner Dovzhenko described stealing and eating carrots from his great-grandmother Marusynia's garden and running away from her as she cursed and chased after him. Until he ate these carrots, Sashko considered himself the most innocent in his family. After eating the 'forbidden fruit' from her 'Garden of Eden', he considered himself a great sinner.[16] In order to gain forgiveness and regain his innocence, he needed to make amends and do good deeds.

The golden age of innocence never returned. Eating the forbidden fruits and vegetables led to young Alexander's eventual departure from the golden garden that had nourished him. He ate, he grew, he matured. He went to school and then left home forever. With hindsight, his past took on an even more golden countenance.

On one of their expeditions, Alexander's paternal grandfather had asserted the superiority of everything in the past. He recalled a time of deeper rivers and lakes, bigger and tastier fish, better mushrooms and berries, thicker forests and grasses, even larger and more dangerous mosquitos.[17] In his memoir, Dovzhenko – now in his latter years himself – repeats his grandfather's claims of fifty years before. Describing the four lakes of his youth, the aging film-maker writes: 'they are no more and never will be again'.[18]

His memories of childhood evinced an intimate sense of his inchoate Ukrainian identity, a concept that neither he nor his family could define with precision.[19] In *The Enchanted Desna*, the author recounts a conversation with his father. One day, after encountering a group of strangers sailing down the Desna River, he asks his father about them. His father replies that they come from far away, from Orlov, and identifies them as Russians. 'But who are we?' young Alexander asks. 'Aren't we Russians?' His father vehemently denies a Russian identity, but he cannot explain the differences between Russians and Ukrainians. Instead, he explains, 'We are simple people. We are *khokhols*, those who make bread. In other words, we are peasants ... They say that we were once Cossacks, but now only the name remains.'[20]

Young Alexander's first day in school exemplified this confusion. Because of his initial shyness, his fears and his inability to understand Russian, the teacher who evaluated Alexander concluded, 'He is not developed.'[21] The teacher assumed the cultural inferiority of his Ukrainian students. He interpreted Russian culture as an advanced, civilising one and the peasant Ukrainian culture (if he identified it as a separate culture at all) as a rural and backward one.

Despite the idealised youth and village of *The Enchanted Desna*, Dovzhenko may have retained mixed emotions about Viuniushche and Sosnytsia. The film-maker visited Sosnytsia for the last time in 1935, when he came from Kiev and moved his parents to the Ukrainian capital, approximately 220 kilometres away.

The circumstances behind this move remain unclear. In the early 1930s the town's collective farm briefly expelled and then reinstated the Dovzhenko family. Perhaps, as the film-maker suspected, the move represented a warning to Dovzhenko to conform to the new Stalinist order.[22] Possibly, the reason for his parents' expulsion had nothing to do with him. Whatever the reasons, Alexander Dovzhenko never returned to his village, not even for a short visit. Instead, he created an idealised version in his memoirs.

In light of his general political isolation and creative restrictions, Dovzhenko's ide-
alisation of his childhood – and specifically his life in Ukraine – appeared to be a
way of coping. But his interpretation of his past also involved a certain amount of
invention.

A Poem about an Inland Sea

Dovzhenko began research for a screenplay he entitled *A Poem about an Inland Sea* in
late August and September 1951, when the authorities allowed him his first extended
stay in Ukraine in eight years. That summer he participated in an expedition to southern
Ukraine and Crimea to observe the construction of the new hydroelectric station on
the lower Dnieper River at Kakhovka, located seventy kilometres from the city of Kherson. Built between 1950 and 1955, the Kakhovka Hydroelectric Dam became one of
the first of the new postwar construction projects. Building on his experience with *Ivan*,
Dovzhenko sought to create a film about a new dam in a new era.

After 1951 the film-maker visited Ukraine once a year for several weeks at a
time.[23] He started to write the screenplay about building this new hydroelectric plant
in May 1952. He completed it on 28 March 1956 and submitted it to Mosfilm for
approval.[24] In July 1956 the Soviet Ministry of Culture approved the screenplay and
assigned its premiere for 1957.[25]

Dovzhenko researching his *A Poem about an Inland Sea* (1950s)

In the screenplay, which drew inspiration from the Italian neo-realist films Dovzhenko had seen in Moscow, the narrator travels down the Dnieper River on a steamship. He is returning to Kakhovka, the village of his birth, for the very last time. A new hydroelectric dam will soon flood the village. Savko Zarudny, the chairman of Kakhovka's collective farm, invites everyone who had left Kakhovka to return for one last farewell party. Many return, some for the first time in decades. Many of these characters represent different aspects of the film-maker himself, at least the qualities Dovzhenko believed he possessed.

General Hnat Fedorchenko, head of the Soviet atomic weapons programme, appears as one of the most prominent returnees. His son Alik accompanies him. His wife plans to join them later. The general represents a 'good' man, while his son and wife (presumably Russian) do not.

Walking to Kakhovka with his son, the general does not recognise his birthplace. Everything appears unfamiliar.

In the village, Fedorchenko meets his old friend Zarudny and his eighty-five-year-old father, Maksym Tarasovych, who always speaks his mind. Modelled on Dovzhenko's cinematic grandfathers, Maksym Tarasovych Fedorchenko asks sharp questions and provides blunt responses. When he meets his grandson, he asks Alik, a university student, what future career he envisions. A prosecutor or judge, the young man replies. 'Ah, you plan to prosecute,' Maksym Tarasovych responds. 'On what basis do you want to prosecute people? Because you do not have any talents?'[26] No one could have overlooked Dovzhenko's anti-Stalinist and anti-Beria barb.

Kravchyna also stands out as a representative of Dovzhenko. A character named Kravchyna recurs in Dovzhenko's works written during World War II, most prominently in the screenplay *Ukraine in Flames*. In *A Poem about an Inland Sea*, the former Sergeant Kravchyna, who had done much 'on behalf of Communism', does not hold a party card (like Dovzhenko). According to *A Poem*'s narrator, Kravchyna's exclusion from the party seems illogical since he 'did not differ with the party program on the main questions. He did not adhere to any isms, no deviations . . . '[27]

Despite the adversity, sufferings, misunderstandings and failures Dovzhenko's protagonists endure, his screenplay celebrates the triumph of life over death. Most of his protagonists lead good, if boring lives. 'What a beautiful world and beautiful life it is,' the narrator thinks to himself. 'And how sad that people rarely feel this way.'[28]

Only hard work and a noble response to life's challenges bring happiness. 'Love the earth!' proclaims Sava Zarudny, another stand-in for Dovzhenko. 'Love to work on the land, because without this there will not be any happiness for us or for our children, not here or on any planet.'[29] As this quote implies, man's transformation of nature constituted another major theme encoded in the screenplay. This change would occur voluntarily, with large doses of patience, not 'by means of brute force'.[30] According to Dovzhenko, the creation of the inland sea symbolised the 'historic fate of our people'.[31] Perhaps the project represented the renewal of Soviet Ukrainian society after the death of Stalin. Following the example of Noah and the flood, the waters of the Dnieper would purge the old society and help create a radiant Communist future.

Dovzhenko's story also possessed a subversive subtext. The inland sea would sweep away the old traditions associated with farming. In place of a close-knit community grounded in the soil, a new industrial society based on electrical energy and mass production would emerge. The waters of the new sea would drown historical landmarks, flooding the islands from which Ukrainian Cossacks launched raids against the Crimean Tartars and the Turks from the fifteenth through to the eighteenth centuries. While the dam represents progress, for Dovzhenko, a descendant of the Cossacks, it comes at a high price.

The Enchanted Desna and *Poem about an Inland Sea* inspired the emergence of the school of Russian village writers, later led by Valentin Rasputin, Vasilii Shukshin and Viktor Astafiev in the 1960s. They valued progress but warned that it came at the expense of traditions and a sense of community. Mourning the passing of the village, where everyone knew each other, these writers claimed that they had lived a more integrated life in the villages of their youth than in the cities. Leaving one's native soil undermined one's spiritual values. These conclusions definitely challenged the socialist realist model of literature.

A Flight to Mars

On 15 June 1954, three years before the Soviet Union launched *Sputnik* and seven years before it launched Lieutenant Colonel Yury Gagarin into space, Dovzhenko wrote an outline for a science-fiction screenplay about the first human flight to Mars. He planned to shoot a film containing 'immense spaces, and time, and movement through the cosmos; a new vision of the world'.[32] He sought to provoke awareness of the 'harmonious, infinite unity of the universe' by juxtaposing the sounds of the Earth with the complete stillness of space.[33]

The treatment contained a simple plot. Three Soviet cosmonauts land on Mars, where they encounter Martians, whose recorded history emerged one and a half million years ago. Because they attained Communism, the Martians have established a civilisation far more advanced than any on Earth.

One of the major accomplishments of the advanced development of the Martians manifests itself in their transcendence of speech. Instead, they 'have been reading each other's minds for millions of years'. In the scenes set on Mars, the 'only sounds will be the comments of the announcer'.[34]

As the cosmonauts deliver a live television broadcast from Mars to Earth, their sound system fails. The television screen transmits images, but 'not a single sound comes through'.[35] Members of the Soviet space crew continue their broadcast, filming their surroundings. The people of the Earth view the Martian landscape and inhabitants on their television screens and experience a thousand-fold expansion of their consciousness. They then conclude that nationalism, wars and conflicts represent 'wretched and monstrous signs of backwardness'.[36]

In the course of this live television broadcast, mankind's greatest technological achievement, the transmission itself breaks down. Over the next seven years no one on Earth hears from the three cosmonauts. Watching the heavens, their families often wonder if they even remain alive.

After seven years of silence, two cosmonauts somehow return to Earth. In an addenda to the screenplay dated September 1956, Dovzhenko wrote that one of the three dies in space. Before their journey to Mars, this cosmonaut did not believe that life existed on other planets. 'The believers reach their goal,' Dovzhenko claimed.[37]

Distance from one's homeland, isolation, alienation and the fragility of meaningful contact between men constituted the unfinished screenplay's major themes. The three cosmonauts become lost in space, surviving on a planet nearly 100 million kilometres from Earth. A vast ocean of cosmic silence divides them from their families and friends. The screenplay represents a metaphor for man's inability to communicate. The vast distance and silence between the men and women on Earth from the Communism on Mars suggest that true Communism represents an extraterrestrial ideal, which the three cosmonauts must divorce themselves from other humans in

Dovzhenko in his study at his Moscow apartment (1956)

order to attain. The film-maker's draft inspires many questions, but in light of its unfinished nature, no certain answers emerge.

Dovzhenko emphasised distance, silence and illusion. The clear evening sky with twinkling stars – however beautiful – represents an optical illusion. The human mind can barely comprehend the vast distance between objects emitting light in the sky. The sharp contrast between what people actually see and what they imagine actually exists in deep space makes them feel small. This sobering and humbling realisation provokes in them, as it did for Dovzhenko, questions dealing with the meaning of life. 'What is our life and death,' the film-maker asked, 'and more accurately, what is being?'[38]

These questions troubled Dovzhenko, especially during the last decade of his life. He often wondered if his life had purpose or meaning. In his last screenplays, he continuously re-evaluated his own life by presenting protagonists voluntarily or involuntarily repeating episodes from his past. Entering his seventh decade and in poor health, Dovzhenko sought to come to terms with his successes and failures. Most distressingly, he never made peace with his involuntary exile in Moscow.

The Desire to Return

After the war ended, the film-maker hoped to return to Ukraine and expressed this desire often to his friends and colleagues.[39] In late August 1952, for example, the

Dovzhenko (right) with his sister's family: Mykola Dudko (his brother-in-law), Polina Petrivna Dovzhenko-Dudko (his sister), Taras Mykolaievych Dudko (nephew in front row) and Alexander Mykolaievych Dudko (nephew) (early 1950s)

film-maker visited his close friend, the writer Yury Yanovsky, and his wife, Tamara. Talking about his work at Kakhovka, Dovzhenko laughed as if in pain and said, 'You cannot even imagine, Yury, how I miss Ukraine.' After this outburst, he spoke for a very long time. A creative person, he said, could not truly develop outside his home-land. 'I would like to live in Ukraine, even if in some hut.'[40]

Whenever he visited his sister and friends in Kiev, he made efforts to return per-manently. He wanted to work in Ukraine, especially at the Kiev Film Studio. Smolych recalled how the film-maker often appealed to the Ukrainian Ministry of Cine-matography and to the studio 'with concrete and realistic proposals for making films. He had brought a screenplay with him, he was not working on other projects, and he was ready to start immediately.'[41] Despite his great expectations, the authorities continuously rejected him. According to Smolych:

> Every time he arrived in Kiev, he sat in my apartment next to the telephone, at times from morning to night, waiting for the promised call from those who would decide the future of his work and his life, the move to Kiev. But there was no call. The telephone would remain silent. At times, something worse would happen. A secretary would call and say that a meeting had been cancelled.[42]

Every trip brought more disappointments. At the end of the summer of 1954, Dovzhenko learned that the head of the CP(b)U's Ideology Department had turned down his request to publish a collection of his Ukrainian-language screenplays in Ukraine.[43] On the occasion of Dovzhenko's last visit to the Ukrainian capital in the summer of 1956, David Kopytsia, the main administrator of the Kiev Film Studio, refused to allow him even to enter its grounds.[44] After this exclusion from the stu-dio he had helped to create, Dovzhenko may have concluded that the post-Stalinist thaw had not yet included him. He would have to step up his fight to return to Ukraine.

He wrote many petitions, including the 10 October 1956 note to the Presidium of the Ukrainian Writers' Union, asking it to help him find living quarters close to Kiev. 'I do not need much space now. All I need is to have a clear view from one window. That I may see on the horizon the Dnieper and the Desna and my Cherni-hiv lands, which have begun to appear so persistently in my dreams.'[45] He did not receive a positive response.

Even after his death, the authorities did not allow Dovzhenko to return to Ukraine. Instead, they buried him at the Novodevichy Monastery in Moscow. The authorities, in effect, enforced his exile even after his death.

Despite claims that local Ukrainian authorities initiated and perpetuated this exile, the men most responsible for his isolation lived in Moscow. Important mem-bers of the Ukrainian elite expected Dovzhenko to return. Even before the thaw in

April 1945, for example, the Ukrainian Politburo's Commission on Culture and Literature met to discuss Dovzhenko's future return. Both Mykola Bazhan, the Minister of Education and Central Committee member who dealt with cultural matters, and M. S. Donskoi, a director at the Kiev Film Studio, anticipated that Dovzhenko would soon come back.[46] But Bolshakov closed the door in July.[47]

Even if the most powerful members of the Ukrainian cultural elite wanted Dovzhenko to return, they could not overturn a decision reached by the highest authorities in Moscow. Neither could Oleksandr Korniichuk (a three-time Stalin Prize winner, a member of the Presidium of the Central Committee of the Communist Party of Ukraine, and the First Deputy Prime Minister), Mykola Bazhan (also a Stalin Prize winner, a Deputy Prime Minister, and a member of the Central Committee), Pavlo Tychyna (a Stalin Prize winner and a member of the party's Central Committee), or Yury Smolych (the head of the executive committee of the Writers' Union of Ukraine). They, the film-maker's long-term associates and colleagues, constituted Soviet Ukraine's political, state and cultural leadership, but they did not have the power to bring Dovzhenko back, even if they wanted to do so.[48] Korniichuk, and perhaps even Bazhan, did not.

Opposition to Dovzhenko's return stemmed not just from political reasons, but professional and personal ones as well. After Dovzhenko began his Kakhovka dam project in 1951, he stopped to visit his sister Polina Petrivna Dovzhenko-Dudko in Kiev at least once a year. When he arrived, she entertained his guests and friends. Many people visited Dovzhenko at her apartment, but few of these visitors represented the film world.[49]

Dovzhenko did not trust the Kievan film-makers. 'I do not need them because they do not like me,' he admitted.

> They do not like me because my creativity somehow comes very easily, but for them it is hard work. They do not like me because I am fanatical in my perseverance and this fanaticism does not appear in everyone ... And finally they do not like me because of my personality ... I did not give peace to my enemies, to people who were dissolute, disorganized externally as well as internally ...[50]

Although Dovzhenko may have exaggerated how easily his creativity emerged and developed, his professionalism, cinematographic standards and vision often did come into conflict with those of his colleagues.

Recounting Dovzhenko's experience shooting his first sound film, *Ivan*, Hryhory Zeldovych called a number of film-makers associated with the Kiev Film Studio narrow-minded professionals who 'could not see beyond their own noses'. For them, Dovzhenko's 'high standards in regard to the quality of sound recordings and to the re-creation of the sounds of nature, voices, and music was not understandable, unnecessary, and untimely'. The Ukrainian film-maker spoke with great dissatisfaction about these people and called them 'the no-nos'. 'No', 'It's impossible!' and 'It can't be done!' constituted their favourite words and phrases.[51] Throughout Dovzhenko's lifetime, he displayed little tolerance for such people – and they responded in kind.

From the perspective of the film-makers in Kiev, Dovzhenko represented a political liability. They most likely remembered the 1930s. Arriving with mandates from Moscow in 1935, he introduced ambitious projects, which often imploded and politically disgraced not only him, but also those who did not possess his network of patrons and protectors. Whatever the reasons, Dovzhenko and Kiev's film-makers did not live on good terms.

According to his sister Polina, the film-maker did not name his enemies, even though he sometimes complained about his shabby treatment. 'Pasha,' he told his sister, 'I did them much good, and even fostered the development of some of them, helped them to write, organized groups for them in Kharkiv and Kiev, and how did they treat me? ... One of the spiritual pygmies did me much harm.'[52] Although Dovzhenko did not reveal the culprit's identity or his malicious acts, he expressed his emotional reactions to these betrayals to his sister. In her unpublished memoir she only described a tiny fraction of her brother's disappointments and frustrations.[53]

If the Ukrainian cultural elite did not have the power to return Dovzhenko to Ukraine, who did?

According to Dovzhenko's diary, three weeks before his death in November 1956, the Ukrainian film-maker spoke with N. Kolmykov, the USSR's Deputy Minister of Culture. Kolmykov agreed with Dovzhenko's idea to return to Ukraine to film *A Poem about an Inland Sea*. According to the film-maker, Kolmykov's support encountered opposition. One powerful 'Ukrainian "uncultural" leader did not agree with me. Neither my petition nor the opinion of the Deputy Minister had any influence on him. Apparently I will never be able to go back to Kiev. Thirteen years of vain hopes ...'[54]

Dovzhenko did not specify the identity of this 'one Ukrainian "uncultural" leader'. Decades later his identity remains unclear. In her brief memoir of her husband's death, Julia Solntseva accused Bazhan and Korniichuk of hastening Dovzhenko's end by preventing him from returning to Ukraine. They also allegedly vetoed his burial in Ukraine.[55]

Solntseva's account does not consider that Kolmykov outranked Bazhan and Korniichuk in the Soviet hierarchy. If Kolmykov could not help Dovzhenko, then Bazhan and Korniichuk certainly could not have blocked Dovzhenko without help from powerful allies in Moscow. Someone higher, most likely Nikita S. Khrushchev, determined Dovzhenko's fate.

Dovzhenko and Khrushchev probably first met in Moscow in the 1930s, after Dovzhenko moved there in 1933, when Khrushchev became Moscow's Second and then First Party Secretary (1932–8).[56] They definitely did meet in Kiev, after Dovzhenko came back in 1935. Both lived in the same neighbourhood (Lypky), Kiev's highest point and the residence of its political and cultural elites.[57] Khrushchev, head of the Ukrainian party from January 1938 until 1949, often met with members of the Ukrainian creative intelligentsia.[58] He and Dovzhenko enjoyed a cordial, if not close, relationship.[59]

During the war, Khrushchev served as a lieutenant-general and a political officer while remaining the head of the Communist Party of Ukraine. Dovzhenko read the *Ukraine in Flames* manuscript to him in August 1943 and claimed that Khrushchev liked it 'very much'.[60]

Khrushchev's appreciation must have encouraged Dovzhenko to believe that the head of the CP(b)U would support and defend him. Under ordinary circumstances, Khrushchev might have protected Dovzhenko's project, but not when Stalin began to raise questions about Dovzhenko and his screenplay. During one of Khrushchev's trips to Moscow in the autumn of 1943, Stalin asked him if he had read the film-maker's screenplay. Khrushchev recalled:

> I said, yes, I had. Actually, I hadn't really sat down and read it, but Dovzhenko himself had read to me during the German offensive of July 1943. Naturally three-fourths of my attention had been taken up by the enemy attack, and I hadn't been able to concentrate on the text of Dovzhenko's work. I explained this to Stalin. He said that I was trying to weasel out of my responsibility for what had happened, and he started a blistering denunciation of Dovzhenko, criticizing him up and down, accusing him of Ukrainian nationalism and all kinds of other sins.[61]

Khrushchev did not defend Dovzhenko at this point or at the fateful January 1944 meeting with Stalin. Dovzhenko, however, protected Khrushchev. When Stalin asked Dovzhenko if he read his screenplay to anyone, the film-maker, to Khrushchev's relief, told Stalin that he had not.[62]

Afterwards, Khrushchev supposedly shook Dovzhenko's hand and thanked him.[63] The film-maker had saved Khrushchev from Stalin's wrath, but this noble action earned him no rewards.

In a conversation the NKVD recorded, Dovzhenko recounted a talk, which took place after the January 1944 meeting, with the Ukrainian party chief:

> Khrushchev not only told me that I let him down with my screenplay, although I read it to him two times, Khrushchev also did more, which horrified and alienated me. In his conversation with me he attempted to create the impression that during my reading of

the screenplay to him I somehow did not read him everything and skipped those parts, which were discovered later to be criminal. He even wanted to convince me that I allegedly simply inserted those scenes after I read the screenplay to him, Hrechukha, Korniets, Korniichuk, Bazhan and others. Khrushchev's behavior shook me to the depths of my soul.[64]

Dovzhenko had every right to feel deceived. According to NKVD reports, the film-maker later claimed that he could not forgive himself for keeping quiet. He should have defended himself more assertively by telling Stalin that Khrushchev and his colleagues had read *Ukraine in Flames* and praised it. 'It's possible that with my chivalrous behavior, I harmed not only myself, but missed the opportunity to show that the entire Ukrainian leadership made a mistake in this matter.'[65] Feeling betrayed, he became very angry. According to NKVD sources, Dovzhenko said:

> I attended two meetings of the Politburo of the Communist Party of Ukraine and the Ukrainian Council of Ministers. I watched the people there and it's a pathetic sight. All the workers of the most important institution in Ukraine possess a low intellect. Khrushchev, for example, only acts and poorly copies Stalin. He does not represent anything on his own. The same with the other peoples' commissars – they are very limited provincial people.[66]

The security organs, commanded by Beria, Khrushchev's most bitter rival within Stalin's inner circle, may have leaked these comments to Khrushchev in order to alienate the film-maker from his former political patrons and to blackmail senior party officials. Having compromised themselves by praising *Ukraine in Flames*, Dovzhenko's former patrons now abandoned him.

After Stalin's death, the new political leadership – contrary to Khrushchev's claims in his memoirs – did not completely rehabilitate Dovzhenko.[67] Although Khrushchev wrote that he considered the film-maker 'an honest, loyal, [and] upright citizen', Stalin's successor did not intervene on Dovzhenko's behalf, not even after his 'secret speech' denouncing Stalin on 25 February 1956.[68] Perhaps he remained resentful over how close Dovzhenko had brought him to disaster. On the other hand, he may have felt unwilling to admit his debt to the film-maker, even to himself.

Whatever Khrushchev's true feelings for Dovzhenko and his actions, the party leader's uncertain political position after Stalin's death persuaded him to keep the film-maker in Moscow. In competing with Malenkov and the old Stalinist guard for the sole leadership of the party, Khrushchev sought to enhance his base of support within the party, relying on those who had served under him in Moscow and Ukraine.[69]

In order to strengthen his patronage network, he gave greater administrative responsibilities to local cadres and tolerated the views of prominently placed Ukrainian intellectuals.[70] His clients in the Ukrainian party organisation, especially those who dealt with cultural matters such as Korniichuk and Bazhan, hated Dovzhenko, who politically endangered them with his *Ukraine in Flames* script. They did not want Dovzhenko to return to Ukraine because they would have assumed all responsibilities for any ideological mistakes the film-maker might make. Khrushchev agreed.

Khrushchev's decision suited Dovzhenko's enemies. Because of professional rivalries and personal animosities, many, if not most, of Kiev's film-makers did not mourn his absence. The most dynamic advocate for a Ukrainian cinematography could not work there or train his own cadres. As a result, after he left Ukraine, the postwar films produced there not only dropped in quality, but often no longer employed the Ukrainian language.[71]

Conclusion

In an effort to come to terms with his own life, Dovzhenko concentrated on his own personal history in *The Enchanted Desna*, *A Poem about an Inland Sea* and *A Flight to Mars*. Beneath the surface of these works, Dovzhenko's nostalgia for his childhood and for his native Ukraine represented homesickness and trauma over his involuntary exile in Moscow. His diary entries reveal constant worry and depression, as well as long struggles with writer's block.

Julia Solntseva at Dovzhenko's funeral bier (November, 1956)

In order to remain true to himself, Dovzhenko had to create, but the creation of honest works entailed certain political ostracism. To deflect political criticism, he had to censor his creative vision. Dovzhenko could continue to create, but not at his own high standards. Most importantly, after January 1944 he had to live far away from the sources of his creativity.

To compensate for the psychological trauma of his exile, Dovzhenko painted an idealised picture of his childhood. If one believes his postwar screenplays, he found peace and solace in the past, in harmony with nature. In his youth, Dovzhenko did not have to compromise, or struggle for survival. He identified leaving his home, family and roots with leaving the Garden of Eden. If his childhood and youth in Sosnytsia symbolised the Garden of Eden, his adulthood under Soviet Communism embodied the inevitable sinfulness of the material world.

Dovzhenko's last works reflect more than just a single man's struggle to understand the meaning of his life. They represent the experiences of millions of Ukrainians who – like Dovzhenko – left their villages for the cities. Decades later these migrants sought to come to terms with the hopes and illusions of their youth and with the failure of the Bolshevik Revolution to live up to its promises.

All childhoods are innocent, but in the Soviet context, writing about one's innocent childhood and not including the 'achievements' of the Soviet experiment represented a vote of no confidence in the Soviet system.

Notes

1. TsDAHOU, 1/24/2743, p. 3.
2. Alexander Solzhenitsyn, *The Gulag Archipelago* (New York, 1978), vol. 3, pp. 421–2. Surrounded by those who wept, Solzhenitsyn recorded his reaction to hearing of Stalin's death: 'My face, trained to meet all occasions, assumed a frown of mournful attention' (p. 421).
3. Amy Knight, *Beria: Stalin's First Lieutenant* (Princeton, NJ, 1993), p. 185.
4. *Pravda*, 9 October 1952, p. 2; cited in Charles Fairbanks, 'National Cadres as a Force in the Soviet System: The Evidence of Beria's Career, 1949–1953', in Jeremy R. Azrael, ed., *Soviet Nationality Policies and Practices* (New York, 1978), pp. 147–8.
5. Knight, p. 188.
6. John Kolasky, *Two Years in Soviet Ukraine* (Toronto, 1970), p. 127.
7. *PF*, pp. 233–4; *UVOKShch*, p. 379; *Hospody*, p. 379; *ZDUVOShch*, p. 506. Khrushchev also reported that Chiaureli approached Dovzhenko on Beria's behalf, and that the Ukrainian film-maker refused to cooperate. See N. S. Khrushchev, *Khrushchev Remembers* (Boston and Toronto, 1970), pp. 340–1.
8. *PF*, p. 234; *UVOKShch*, p. 379; *Hospody*, p. 380; *ZDUVOShch*, p. 506.

9. Josephine Woll, *Real Images: Soviet Cinema and the Thaw* (London and New York, 2000), p. 21.

10. For excellent analyses of film-making during the 'thaw', see Woll, *Real Images*, and Vitalii Troianovskii, *Kinematograf ottepli* (Moscow, 1996).

11. Woll, p. 35. Dovzhenko praised Italian neo-realism. See his 'Progresivnoe kino Italii', *Pravda*, 6 December 1953; reprinted in his *Tvory v p'iaty tomakh* (Kiev, 1965), vol. 4, pp. 129–34, and in his *Tvory v p'iaty tomakh* (Kiev, 1984), vol. 4, pp. 128–33.

12. See '60-letie so dnia rozhdeniia i 30-letie tvorcheskoi deiatel'nosti A. P. Dovzhenko', *Sovetskii film*, no. 5 (1955), part 2; 'Shestdesiat let A. P. Dovzhenko', *Iskusstvo kino*, no. 3 (1955), pp. 109–14.

13. Oleksandr Dovzhenko, *Tvory v p'iaty tomakh*, vol. 5 (Kiev, 1966), pp. 268–9; *Storinky*, p. 234; and *PF*, p. 156.

14. Oleksandr Dovzhenko, 'Zacharovana Desna', *Dnipro*, no. 3 (1956), pp. 59–86. This memoir has since been reprinted many times. I use O. Dovzhenko, 'Zacharovana Desna', in his *Kinopovisti, opovidannia* (Kiev, 1986), pp. 431–72 (abbreviated hereafter as 'ZD').

15. 'ZD', p. 445.

16. 'ZD', p. 439.

17. 'ZD', p. 459.

18. 'ZD', p. 459.

19. '1939 Autobiography', p. 9.

20. 'ZD', p. 460; also cited in *PF*, pp. 198–9.

21. 'ZD', p.470.

22. See Dovzhenko, *Tvory*, vol. 5 (1966), p. 335.

23. Dovzhenko visited Ukraine in September–October 1952, October 1953, September–October 1954, May–early June 1955 and in July 1956. *Storinky*, pp. 258–328.

24. *Storinky*, p. 316.

25. *Storinky*, p. 319.

26. 'Poema pro more', in O. Dovzhenko's *Kinopovisti, opovidannia*, p. 507. Dovzhenko had a very low opinion of Soviet prosecutors, especially those involved in the war. See *UVOKShch*, p. 205; *Hospody*, pp. 173–4; *ZDUVOShch*, p. 296.

27. 'Poema', pp. 543–4.

28. 'Poema', p. 474.

29. 'Poema', p. 559.

30. Regina Dreyer, 'Vzirets' velykoho realizmu', *DIS*, p. 97.

31. A. Dovzhenko, 'Untitled (22. I. 1953)', Autobiography Folder, MDFS.

32. *PF*, p. 240.

33. *PF*, p. 237.
34. *PF*, p. 238.
35. *PF*, p. 238.
36. *PF*, p. 239.
37. *PF*, p. 267.
38. *PF*, p. 239.
39. See, for example, Dovzhenko's diary entries for 30 June 1945, 16 October 1945, 5 November 1945, 30 November 1945, 16 March 1946 and 21 October 1952, in *PF*, *UVOKShch*, *Hospody* and *ZDUVOShch*. Also see V. T. Denisenko, 'Vospominaniia ob A. P. Dovzhenko', RGALI, 2081/1/1121, p. 30; Liubomyr Dmyterko, 'Svitlyi talant', *Ukraina*, no. 24 (December 1956); P. M. Elistratov, 'Krasota zhizni v podvizakh', RGALI, 2081/1/1129, p. 13; and G. A. Mariagin, 'Legendy k biografii Dovzhenko', RGALI, 2081/1/1158, p. 34.
40. Tamara Zhevchenko-Ianovs'ka, 'Spohady pro Iu. I. Ianovs'koho ta O. P. Dovzhenka', TsDA-MLMU, 17/1/199; and T. Ianovs'ka 'Vin skarby tvoryv', RGALI, 2081/1/1210, p. 154.
41. Iurii Smolych, *Rozpovid' pro nespokii* (Kiev, 1968) p. 179.
42. Smolych, pp. 179–80.
43. *Dnipro*, no. 9–10 (1994), p. 72.
44. Interview with Rollan Serhiyenko, Moscow, December 1995. Also see Dovzhenko's diary entry for 7 November 1956: *UVOKShch*, p. 410; *Hospody*, pp. 414–15.
45. F-423, SDM, p. 1; TsDA-MLMU, 690/1/22; MDFS; *PF*, p. 267.
46. TsDAHOU, 1/23/4474, pp. 72, 75.
47. *ZDUVOShch*, pp. 379–80.
48. Andrii Iaremchuk, 'Oleksandr Dovzhenko: "I anhely zderly z mene okryvavlenu shkiru . . .'", *Ukrains'ka kul'tura*, no. 9–10 (1994), p. 6, claimed that Korniichuk, Bazhan, Tychyna and Smolych had the power to allow Dovzhenko to return to Ukraine, but he does not provide any evidence for this assertion.
49. Oleksii Mishurin, 'Polum'iane sertse', in M. Kovalenko and O. Mishurin, *Syn zacharovanoi Desny. Spohady i statti* (Kiev, 1984), p. 267.
50. Quoted in Mishurin, 'Polum'iane sertse', p. 267.
51. H. Zel'dovych, 'Uryvky zi spohadiv', Derevianko Archive, p. 10.
52. Quoted in P. P. Dovzhenko, 'Moi vospominaniia', RGALI, 2081/1/1124, p. 18.
53. Compare P. P. Dovzhenko's unpublished memoir, 'Moi vospominaniia', RGALI, 2081/1/1124, with its published version, Polina Dovzhenko, 'Pro brata', *PZh*, pp. 115–21. The second version is a sanitised variation of the first.

54. *PF*, p. 269; *UVOKShch*, p. 409; *Hospody*, p. 413; *ZDUVOShch*, p. 541.

55. Julia Solntseva, 'S tribuny veka', Derevianko Archive, p. 10.

56. For a brief synopsis of Khrushchev's political career, see A. D. Chernev, *229 kremlevskikh vozhdei* (Moscow, 1996).

57. Iosyp Hirniak, *Spomyny* (New York, 1982), p. 442.

58. V. I. Pryluts'kyi, 'Pershi kroky M. S. Khrushchova v Ukraini: 1938–1939 rr.', in Natsional'na akademiia nauk Ukrainy, Instytut istorii, *M. S. Khrushchov i Ukraina* (Kiev, 1995), p. 36. According to the *Encyclopedia of Ukraine* (Toronto, 1994), vol. 2, p. 495, Khrushchev's tenure as the Ukrainian party boss lasted from 1938 to 1949, 'except for nine months in 1947'.

59. See, for example, Dovzhenko's 5 June 1943 letter to Khrushchev, *Dnipro*, no. 9–10 (1995), p. 60.

60. *PF*, p. 90; *UVOKShch*, p. 221; *Hospody*, p. 191; *ZDUVOShch*, p. 314.

61. *Khrushchev Remembers*, p. 172.

62. See TsDAHOU, 1/70/282.

63. Dovzhenko allegedly told Honchar of this handshake. See Oles' Honchar, 'Koly dumaiesh pro Dovzhenka', *Kul'tura i zhyttia*, 10 September 1994, p. 1.

64. *D*, p. 33.

65. *D*, pp. 43–4.

66. *D*, p. 57.

67. For Khrushchev's claim, see *Khrushchev Remembers*, p. 340.

68. Dovzhenko, according to Khrushchev, 'may have sometimes said things which were unpleasant for the leaders to hear, but it's always better to hear such things from an honest man than from an enemy. You can always talk sense to an honest man if he's wrong, and you can learn from him if he's right.' *Khrushchev Remembers*, p. 341.

69. Martin McCauley, 'Khrushchev as Leader', in M. McCauley, ed., *Khrushchev and Khrushchevism* (Bloomington, IN, 1987), pp. 12–13.

70. Yaroslav Bilinsky, *The Second Soviet Republic: The Ukraine After World War II* (New Brunswick, NJ, 1964), pp. 304–5.

71. *Radians'ka Ukraina*, 1 December 1959.

Conclusion

Because of the Stalinist political elite's interest in movies and their role in mobilising and propagating the proper Soviet mindset, film-makers became and remained a privileged caste within their society, even at the height of the purges. After recognising this group's importance, Soviet authorities employed a carrot-and-stick approach to them, especially to the most prominent.[1] As a whole, film-makers did not experience the arrests, imprisonments and executions, as did the peasants, writers, artists, party members and senior military officers. In addition to the Soviet film industry's senior administrators (such as M. N. Rutsky, Shumiatsky and Dukelsky, shot between 1937 and 1939), only a small number of film directors – including Margarita Chardynina-Barska, Les Kurbas and Faust Lopatynsky – experienced arrest, imprisonment and death.[2]

Despite the small numbers of 'repressed' film-makers, each member of the Soviet film community must have been aware that he or she might be next, Alexander Dovzhenko – most of all. He, who had selected Chardynina-Barska as *Love's Berry*'s leading lady (see p.75), had befriended Kurbas in the early 1920s, and had worked with Lopatynsky on *Vasia the Reformer*, had good reason to fear arrest. The Cheka had arrested him in 1919 as a 'counter-revolutionary'. After his release in early 1920, he joined the ex-Borotbists in creating a Communist Ukrainian culture. After they disappeared during the purges, he had a difficult time mastering socialist realist film-making. He wrote *Ukraine in Flames*, which infuriated Stalin and isolated him for nearly a decade. Often out of sync with the evolving Stalinist system, Dovzhenko desperately wanted to meet the new expectations in order to retain political favour in order to create.

To maintain his fertile output, he compromised politically and artistically at every turn. Doing so, he achieved much in terms of quality, if not quantity.[3] Although Dovzhenko made only thirteen feature-length films, he also wrote numerous screenplays and a few literary works. His early achievements, such as *Zvenyhora*, *Arsenal* and *Earth*, overshadowed his compromises, such as *Michurin*. His masterful integration of man and nature on the screen raised him to the pantheon of the world's first pioneers of cinema. His movies' visual impact created a greater impression on the viewer than his dialogue or his narrative. Tightly woven Ukrainian symbols and images powered his films, especially *Zvenyhora*, *Arsenal*, *Earth* and *Shchors*, which defined Ukrainian cinematography. His film-making techniques, moreover, influenced Andrei Tarkovsky, Sergei Paradzhanov and Yuri Ilienko in the Soviet Union, Jurai Jakubisco in Czechoslovakia and Miklos Jancso in Hungary.[4]

At the end of his life, Dovzhenko completed two screenplays, *The Enchanted Desna* and *A Poem about an Inland Sea*. Both works profoundly impressed Russian and Ukrainian intellectuals who matured after Stalin's death. In Russia, they inspired the Russian village writers. In Ukraine, the journal *Dnipro*'s publication of *The Enchanted Desna* and its republication in book form in 1957, roused the generation of the 1960s (the *shestydesiatnyky*), who challenged the limits of socialist realism there and led the 'second Soviet republic' to independence in 1991.[5]

Paradoxically, the Soviet state simultaneously stifled Dovzhenko's creative vision and established the conditions for much of what he accomplished. Although he had to please review boards at the film studio, the Ministry of Cinematography, Stalin's inner circle and even Stalin himself, the Soviet administrative-command economy freed the film-maker from the demands of the marketplace, which weighed heavily on his counterparts in Europe and in the United States. Dovzhenko did not need to win large audiences, only the approval of those who claimed to know what Stalin and the Stalinist hierarchy wanted. If Dovzhenko's success had depended on the market, he might not have risen as high as he did. His critical success, however, came at great cost to his health, emotional balance and creative powers.

From his beginnings as a film-maker, he defined his mission as the creation of a Ukrainian national cinema equal to those of other countries. In order to achieve his goal, he wanted to produce high quality films reflecting Ukrainian dreams and to forge a common identity for his countrymen at a time when they could not discuss their national identity freely. He felt an overwhelming sense of duty to his compatriots. By grounding his films in the Ukrainian historical memory and by conjuring images taken from folklore and myth, he hoped not only to portray them, but also to speak on their behalf.

With *Zvenyhora*, *Arsenal* and *Earth*, Dovzhenko reached the height of his creative powers. Despite the tensions between what he wanted to film and what the censors allowed him to show, these three films, especially *Earth*, constitute his masterpieces. Reflecting both his own emotional convulsions and the uncertain expectations of an ever-changing punitive state, complex transitions, ambiguities and doubts appear in each of these films. The film-maker raised important questions about the relationship between the old and the new, between honoured tradition and revolutionary innovation, between the countryside and the cities, between life and death and between the people and their soil. Using his Ukrainian and peasant sources as a base, he attempted to connect the tradition-bound Ukrainian national identity to the modernising, Soviet world.

Dovzhenko became a perfectionist, but political circumstances beyond his control checked his efforts to create a 'perfect' work of art. At the height of his creative powers at the end of the 1920s, he began to alienate influential groups that held a monochromic view of the world. Ukrainian intellectuals condemned his harsh criticism of Ukrainian nationalism, as exemplified by the protagonists in *Zvenyhora* and *Arsenal*. Orthodox Communists became critical of Dovzhenko's moral ambivalence with regard to the Revolution and social change, as in *Arsenal* and *Earth*. Although he may have agreed with many of the party's political positions and desperately sought to fit in, his ambition to reflect Ukrainian dreams resisted political simplifications. In the newly emerging Stalinist universe, film-makers – the most important of the 'engineers of human souls' – had to conform to the party's political line, which often shifted mercurially.

Like his colleagues in the first generation of Soviet film-makers – Grigory Kozintsev, Leonid Trauberg, Sergei Eisenstein, Vsevolod Pudovkin and Dziga Vertov – Dovzhenko experienced problems adjusting to Stalinist politics and to socialist realism. As innovators, these film-makers wanted to explore creative avenues in their own ways and at their chosen speed. They resisted ideological strait-jackets and opposed filming Soviet life as a Potemkin village. Unlike his five colleagues, the Ukrainian film-maker could not readily conform to the russocentric model of Soviet nationality politics introduced in the 1930s. Overturning the moderate policies of the 1920s, which had promoted a multi cultural Soviet Union, this new model severely restricted his ability to present on the screen his Ukrainian visions, which fuelled his creative drive.

Following the practices of other Soviet intellectuals, he conformed outwardly while retaining other, private points of view. Despite his private doubts and public compromises, Dovzhenko managed, as did many other prominent Soviet intellectuals, to preserve a part of his personal integrity and retain elements of his moral autonomy.[6]

Throughout his life, Dovzhenko sought to overcome the party's awareness of his past anti-Bolshevik commitments by producing good 'Bolshevik' movies. But he did not succeed. Ironically, his own films and screenplays damaged his reputation with the party. As an artist, he impeded his own efforts at party conformity. He maintained the ideal fantasy – that he could make small compromises, that he could please the party and still adhere to his own set of principles. Almost every time he attempted to compromise his vision, it resurfaced unconsciously, perhaps even consciously, in the details of his work. He found it very difficult, if not impossible, to subordinate his vision and his creativity to the Stalinist slogans of the day. His vision, after all, propelled his creative drive. Without the possibility of expressing even a small aspect of his vision, he could not create.

In reaction to his compromises, Dovzhenko experienced serious physical illnesses and grave psychological doubts. His later films expressed less ambiguity and creativity than his Ukrainian 'trilogy'. Dovzhenko accepted these artistic and political compromises as the price he had to pay, not only to continue his career in cinema, but also to survive.

Even this acceptance, however, contained a spark of spirited rebellion. While his films, especially *Aerograd*, *Shchors* and *Michurin*, outwardly demonstrated his political loyalty, a subversive subtext softens their central, politically approved messages. His 'compromise' films fulfilled the party's requirements, bought him breathing room and encouraged the hope, however slight, of the possibility of more tolerant supervisors in the future. Inasmuch as he claimed to fear exclusion from artistic creation even more than death, he played for time.[7] Dovzhenko compared the prohibition of capturing his visions, dreams and illusions on celluloid or on paper to the deprivation of vital air. Having his avenues of expression blocked and censored, this emotionally volatile artist alternated between the extremes of accommodation and resistance.

He felt traumatised by his isolation after Stalin condemned *Ukraine in Flames*. Although he lost faith in the supreme party leader after January 1944, Dovzhenko sought to win back the political trust he had enjoyed. He desperately wanted to ingratiate himself with anyone (except Beria) who could alleviate his solitude.

Most of all, he wanted to return to Ukraine, but Stalin and his senior colleagues insisted that he stay in the Soviet capital. Exile in Moscow limited the creativity,

Dovzhenko resting during the filming of *Michurin*. Grigory Belov, the actor who plays Michurin, has his make-up applied (*c.* 1948–9)

which Dovzhenko claimed his homeland best nurtured. The film-maker imagined that Stalin's death would clear the way for him to return permanently to Ukraine. Until the end of his life, however, the Soviet authorities refused him permission to do so. Living in Moscow, he could not directly influence Ukrainian cinematography. Soviet leaders rendered impotent the most assertive advocate for Ukrainian national film-making. He died a wounded, but not a broken man.

Dovzhenko definitely did not speak the truth in public after 1919, but how much did he lie? As a spinner of fantastic tales, he juggled the facts more often than he wholly fabricated them. He revised the past in his films. He falsified the Revolution and Civil War (*Zvenyhora*, *Arsenal* and *Shchors*), industrialisation (*Ivan*), collectivisation (*Earth*), historical figures (*Shchors* and *Michurin*) and the Cold War (*Goodbye, America*). He collaborated in the Stalinist transformation of Soviet society, but not completely. Although his films presented a false reality, many included a subtext that moderated their potential political impact. Dovzhenko, for example, did not show the Bolshevik victory in *Arsenal*, the final triumph of collectivisation in *Earth*, or the completion of the construction projects in *Ivan*, *Aerograd* and *A Poem about the Sea*.

Not surprisingly, the master of illusion wove a cloak of myths and wore it in public in order to disguise his true self in an often-treacherous Stalinist world. Conforming to the political demands of the day, other people also invented episodes and ascribed them to Dovzhenko. His second wife, Julia Solntseva, held the role of his gatekeeper and censor for thirty-three years after his death, preserving and expanding the misrepresentations he established.

In addition to Solntseva and Dovzhenko's friends, the Stalinist and post-Stalinist political order also fictionalised the controversial aspects of Dovzhenko's life. Dovzhenko lived in a highly authoritarian society, which nurtured its own set of political myths, especially the image of a classless society without political, cultural, or national conflicts. Stalinist leaders viewed their fantasy as the only existing reality.

Conforming to these beliefs, they viewed film-making, a visual representation of reality, as the most important of the arts. As the Stalinists gained control, they demanded politically orthodox films without nuances or avant-garde experimentation in order to mould a Soviet mass culture in the image and likeness of the radiant Communist future. Films would raise the political consciousness of their viewers and would establish a standard by which audiences could measure their ideological progress. Movies, moreover, would provide a controlled set of shared experiences for the entire multi national Soviet Union. 'Everybody could go into the same dark room – no matter where it happened to be located – and zero in on precisely the same dream,' as one film critic characterised the cinematic foundations of creating loyal citizens in another country.[8]

Although Dovzhenko started his career as a film-maker-entertainer, his three best films – *Zvenyhora*, *Arsenal* and *Earth* – demanded intellectual engagement. He wanted not only to provoke his audiences to think, but also to present Ukrainian dreams on the screen. Most importantly, he hoped to show his version of the Ukrainian, not Soviet, imagined community. After 1930, the Stalinist cultural establishment demanded that Dovzhenko become an entertainer with a Communist perspective.

Like many intellectuals of small nations, Dovzhenko often experienced the anxiety of marginalisation. He sought to speak on behalf of those without a voice, but even those he wished to champion sometimes lacked the ability to understand his vision or identify with his films.

Keenly aware of this problem, he knew that his potential audiences did not possess a strong sense of Ukrainian national identity or confidence in their future as a national group distinct from the Russians. His audiences may have identified themselves as Ukrainians, but this label did not come naturally for most. Living in an 'imperial periphery' of the Soviet Union, a state which itself existed on the outskirts of the world economy and Western civilisation, Dovzhenko's potential audiences did not think about national identity in terms familiar to the intelligentsia.[9] He became one of the few Ukrainian intellectuals, one of the few 'knights of the absurd', who wagered his vocation as a film-maker on the prospect of a Ukraine independent of the Russian and Polish cultures that had dominated it for hundreds of years.

This cause became unpopular, even heretical, during the last two decades of Stalin's reign. In seeking to realise his vision, Dovzhenko risked alienating the state that supported him and the countrymen who nurtured him. Although he may have understood that he had chosen a dangerous course of action on an intellectual level, rejection after rejection challenged his emotional equilibrium. In his diary, he recorded his estrangement on 7 January 1944:

> During moments of my spiritual decline and weakness, I think: why did I kill myself over the fate of the Ukrainian people, why did I weep for them, why do I fear for their future, why do I shout about their difficulties and sufferings? Perhaps they do not exist. Perhaps all that happens around me is a normal, vital, and necessary process of life. Perhaps, my people do not need my intercession, and in fact do not know about it. Am I not a common Don Quixote with contrived and whimsical dreams? In my morbid imagination did I not invent all of these horrors, which I write down in my notebooks and which no one needs? Have I gone mad? Did I not fall into the state of arrogance, into the mania of grandeur and messianism? Did not my morbid reaction against evil not blind me to the good in the life of all people?
>
> Did the horror of the tragedies and destruction not blind my eyes to the greatness of events and to the nobility of the sacrifices and heroism of the Russian and Ukrainian peoples? Am I not a Don Quixote, a petty mourner of the unnecessary? I do not know. Perhaps it is so. Perhaps my *Ukraine in Flames* is a product of Don Quixotism?

Forgive me, my dear world. I'll say one thing in my defense: I never wished anyone harm.[10]

Like Don Quixote's quest, Dovzhenko's self-appointed mission to develop a Ukrainian national cinematography in the Stalinist period remained elusive and unfulfilled. Like the hero of Miguel de Cervantes' novel, Dovzhenko struggled with appearance and reality, madness and sanity, and optimism and pessimism. As an idealist, Dovzhenko believed in the possibility of creating a Ukrainian culture equal to that of the Russian. Perhaps this goal remained a Utopian illusion. But in his demonic commitment to his grand project, he persevered. Even though he remained 'tied up in a sack', unable to escape the consequences of the political choices he made in 1917, he persisted – however inconsistently – in pursuing his vocation as a 'knight of the absurd' to the end of his days. Dovzhenko's arduous journey included many temptations, especially the temptation to believe his own illusions.

He must have often asked himself if he would not find it easier to participate in the much larger and more sophisticated Russo-Soviet culture, rather than to try to raise an underdeveloped nation's cultural standards. To embrace this option, however, would have nullified the very source of his creative drive. At great personal cost, and despite his problems with the authorities, compromises and anxieties of marginalisation, Dovzhenko remained true to his mission.

Notes

1. Even after the public criticism at the First All-Union Conference on Soviet Cinematography in January 1935, Eisenstein received handsome incentives. Since the early 1920s he had lived in a single room in [a] 'collective apartment' but in 1935 he was assigned to a new four-room apartment, and a year later he received a two-story dacha in a Moscow suburb. David Bordwell, *The Cinema of Eisenstein* (Cambridge, MA, 1993), p. 25.

2. A complete list of Soviet film-makers who died during the purges of the 1930s does not exist. Soviet sources are unreliable. Although Western and post-Soviet sources are more reliable, they remain incomplete. Peter Kenez, *Cinema and Soviet Society, 1917–1953* (Cambridge and New York, 1992), pp. 153–4, listed Chardynina-Barska and Kurbas, but not Lopatynsky. In addition to these directors, the Italian communist émigré Gino De-Marki (1902–37) and the Azerbaidzhani Abbas M. Sharifzade (1893–1938) died after the security organs arrested them. See *Kino: entsiklopedicheskii slovar'* (Moscow, 1986); *Bol'shoi entsiklopedicheskii slovar'* (Moscow, 1991); A. Latyshev, 'Poimenno nazvat' ', in L. Kh. Mamotova, ed., *Kino: politika i liudy. 30-e gody* (Moscow, 1995), pp. 157–60; and G. Mar'iamov, *Kremlevskii tsensor: Stalin smotrit kino* (Moscow, 1992), pp. 120–1. I am grateful to Angela

Cannon of the Slavic Reference Service at the University of Illinois' Slavic and East European Library, who kindly shared her assessments of these sources with me.

3. Of the four pioneers of Soviet film-making, Dovzhenko produced almost as many feature films as Eisenstein, but less than Pudovkin or Vertov. See Ephraim Katz, *The Film Encyclopedia*, 3rd ed., revised by Fred Klein and Ronald Dean Nolen (New York, 1998), pp. 390, 418, 1116, 1421.

4. Barbara D. Leaming, 'Engineers of Human Souls – The Transition to Socialist Realism in the Soviet Cinema of the 1930s' (unpublished PhD dissertation, New York University, 1976), p. 192.

5. George S. N. Luckyj, *Literary Politics in the Soviet Ukraine, 1917–1934*, rev. and updated edition (Durham, NC and London, 1990), pp. 247–8.

6. A. Kemp-Welch, *Stalin and the Literary Intelligentsia, 1928–39* (New York, 1991), p. 237.

7. Shimon Peres's remark, 'Political death is more difficult than physical death,' inspired this observation. Ethan Bronner, 'Peres, an Icon of Peace, is Still Awaiting an Assignment,' *New York Times*, 21 August 1999.

8. Geoffrey O'Brien, *The Phantom Empire* (New York, 1993), p. 116; cited in Neal Gabler, *Life the Movie: How Entertainment Conquered Reality* (New York, 1998), p. 57.

9. On Ukraine as an 'imperial periphery' of the USSR, see Roman Szporluk, 'Ukraine: From an Imperial Periphery to a Sovereign State', *Daedalus*, 126, no. 3 (1997), p. 86.

10. Larysa Briukhovets'ka, ' "Chy ne ia zvychainyi Don-kikhot?" ', *Kul'tura i zhyttia*, 11 September 1994, p. 5; *UVOKShch*, p. 251; *Hospody*, pp. 227–8; *ZDUVOShch*, p. 351.

Filmography

Vasia the Reformer (Ukr. and Russ.: *Vasia reformator*), 6 parts, 1603 m., VUFKU (Odessa), 1926.

Love's Berry (Ukr.: *Iahidka kokhannia*; Russ.: *Iagodki liubvi* [alternative titles: *Parikmakherr Zhan Kovbasiuk, Zhenit'ba Kapki*]), 2 parts, 2802 m., VUFKU (Yalta), 1926.

The Diplomatic Pouch (Ukr.: *Portfel' dypkuriera*; Russ.: *Sumka dipkur'era*), 7 parts, 1646 m., VUFKU (Odessa), 1927.

Zvenyhora (Russ.: *Zvenigora*), 6 parts, 1799 m., VUFKU (Odessa), 1927.

Arsenal (Russ.: *Ianvarskoe vosstanie v Kieve v 1918 g.*), 8 parts, 1820 m., VUFKU (Odessa), 1928.

Earth (Ukr. and Russ.: *Zemlia* [alternative title: *Soil*]), 6 parts, 1704 m., VUFKU (Kiev), 1930.

Ivan, 7 parts, 2800 m., Ukrainfilm (Kiev), 1932.

Aerograd (US titles: *Air City* or *Frontier*), 8 reels, 2296 m., Mosfilm (Moscow) and Ukrainfilm (Kiev), 1935.

Shchors, 14 parts, 3844.5 m., Kiev Film Studio, 1939.

Liberation (Ukr.: *Vyzvolennia ukrains'kykh zemel' vid hnitu pol's'kykh paniv i vozziednannia narodiv-brativ v iedynu simiu*; Russ.: *Osvobozhdenie*), 7 parts, 1720 m., Kiev Film Studio, 1940.

The Battle for Our Soviet Ukraine (Ukr.: *Bytva za nashu radians'ku Ukrainu*; Russ.: *Bitva za nashu sovetskuiu Ukrainu*), 7 parts, 2193 m., Central Newsreel Studio and Ukrainian Studio of Documentary Films (Moscow), 1943.

Victory in Right-Bank Ukraine and the Expulsion of the German Aggressors from Soviet Ukrainian Territory (Ukr.: *Peremoha na Pravoberezhnii Ukraini ta vyhnannia nimets'kykh zaharbnykiv za mezhi ukrains'kykh radianns'kykh zemel'*; Russ.: *Pobeda na pravoberezhnoi Ukraine i izgnanie nemetskikh zakhvatchikov za predely ukrains'kikh sovetskikh zemel'*; Eng.: *Ukraine in Flames*), 7 parts, 2020 m., Central Studio of Documentary Films and Ukrainian Studio of Documentary Films (Moscow), 1945.

Michurin, 10 parts, 2730 m., Mosfilm (Moscow), 1948.

Source: Bohdan Nebesio, *Alexander Dovzhenko: A Guide to Published Sources* (Edmonton, Alberta, 1995).

Bibliography

Part One: Unpublished Works

Archives

Central State Archive of Civic
Organisations of Ukraine (Tsentral'nyi
Derzhavnyi arkhiv hromads'kykh
ob'iednan' Ukrainy [TsDAHOU]), Kiev.
f. 1. Central Committee, Communist
Party of Ukraine.
op. 6, d. 29–31, 37, 513, 568, 715, 1083,
2609.
op. 20, d. 2255.
op. 23, d. 67, 84, 86, 94, 125, 396, 447,
448, 450, 451, 685, 725, 858, 2412,
2499, 4474, 4504, 4512.
op. 24, d. 2743, 4255, 4373.
op. 30, d. 15–16, 80, 84, 102, 212, 636.
op. 31, d. 2152.
op. 70, d. 16, 27, 43–4, 52, 60, 64–8, 175,
200, 244, 282, 306, 319, 885.
f. 22. Central Control Commission,
Communist Party of Ukraine. Cadres
Department.
op. 6, d. 4, 100, 239 (1924–5).
op. 7, d. 17 (1930s).
f. 39. Institute of History of the Party,
Central Committee, Communist Party
of Ukraine: Leading Party Activists,
Participants in the Civil War and the
Great Fatherland War.
op. 4, d. 23, 45–6, 77, 93, 95, 97, 116, 121,
131, 142, 192, 193, 237–8.
f. 43. Central Committee, Ukrainian
Party of Socialist Revolutionaries
(UPSR), Ukrainian Communist Party
(Borot'bist) and Local Organisations
(1917–20). op. 1, d. 3, 6, 10, 13, 19, 35,
40, 41, 43–4, 46–7, 50, 51, 54, 56, 77,
82, 85, 88, 96.
f. 57. Collection of Documents Dealing
with the History of the Communist
Party of Ukraine. op. 2, d. 260, 370,
469, 475–6, 490.
f. 263. Security Service of Ukraine.
Extrajudicial Cases of Those
Rehabilitated. op. 1, d. 57017, k 1388
(Danylo Demuts'kyi).

Central State Archive of Film, Photo- and
Phonographic Documents of Ukraine
(Tsentral'nyi Derzhavnyi
kinofotofonoarkhiv Ukrainy), Kiev:
Photographs of A. P. Dovzhenko, his
family, friends and colleagues.

Central State Archive of the Leading
Organs of Government and
Administration of Ukraine (Tsentral'nyi
Derzhavnyi arkhiv vyshchykh orhaniv
vlady ta upravlinnia Ukrainy
[TsDAVOVUU]), Kiev.
f. 1. All-Ukrainian Central Executive
Committee.
op. 8, d. 30, 34.
op. 24, d. 4.
f. 3. Permanent Representation of the
Ukrainian SSR at the Government of

the USSR, Moscow. op. 1, d. 1169.

f. 4. People's Commissariat of Foreign
Affairs of the Ukrainian SSR, City of
Kharkiv. Secretariat.

op. 1, d. 8, 549, 564, 567, 569–70, 597, 667.

op. 2, d. 2, 30, 82, 275–6.

f. 166. People's Commissariat of
Education (Enlightenment).

op. 1, d. 85, 941.

op. 2, d. 74, 263.

op. 3, d. 46–7.

op. 4, d. 180.

op. 5, d. 439.

op. 6, d. 91, 101, 112–13.

op. 7, d. 251–2.

op. 9, d. 784.

op. 10, d. 5, 30.

f. 423. People's Commissariat of Trade,
Ukrainian SSR. op. 4, d. 195.

f. 1238. Ukrainfilm. op. 1, d. 116, 135,
174, 200, 259.

f. 4402. Vlas Iakovlevych Chubar. op. 1,
d. 184, 211, 215, 216.

f. 4605. Main Literary Administration
(Glavlit), Ukrainian SSR.

op. 1, d. 4, 6–7, 11, 16, 20, 26, 32, 38, 44,
49, 53–4, 64.

f. 4669. Dmytro Zakharovych
Manuil's'kyi. op. 1, d. 23, 60.

f. 4733. Administration of
Cinematographic Affairs at the Council
of People's Commissars of the
Ukrainian SSR/Ministry of
Cinematography, Ukrainian SSR.

op. 1, d. 2, 39, 40, 59–61, 68–9, 85–6,
113–15, 120–1, 195–8, 201, 229–31,
233–5, 264–7, 284, 288, 301–10, 326, 328.

f. 5111. Radio and Telegraphic Agency
of Ukraine. op. 1, d. 147, 369, 371, 387,
390, 456, 558, 747.

Central State Archive-Museum of
Literature and Art of Ukraine
(Tsentral'nyi Derzhavnyi arkhiv-muzei
literatury i mystetstva Ukrainy [TsDA-
MLMU]), Kiev.

f. 17. Iurii Ivanovych Ianovs'kyi. op. 1,
d. 199.

f. 22. Andrii Samiilovych Malyshko. op.
3, d. 30.

f. 169. Iurii Korniiovych Smolych. op. 1,
d. 589.

f. 235. Iurii Trokhymovych Tymoshenko
(pseudonym of Heorhii Trokhymovych
Tarapun'ka). op. 1, d. 21, 42, 57, 182.

f. 435. Oleksandr Evdokimovych
Korniichuk. op. 1, d. 670, 697, 701.

f. 535. Mykola Platonovych Bazhan. op.
1, d. 1000.

f. 690. Alexander Petrovych Dovzhenko.

op. 1, d. 16, 22, 23–5, 37, 49.

op. 2, d. 6, 11, 21.

op. 3, d. 1–13.

f. 1196, op. 2. Documents Dealing
with Authors and Artists from the
Archives of the Procuracy, Courts and
KGB Organs of the Ukrainian SSR. d.
2–9, 11–14.

Derev'ianko (Tatiana Timofeevna) Archive,
Kiev.

Solntseva, Julia. S tribuny veka (Memoirs
of A. P. Dovzhenko).

Solntseva, J. Svoi razkaz o tom, kak
delalsia film 'Poema o more'.

Zel'dovych, H. Uryvky zi spohadiv.

Dovzhenko (O. P.) Film Studio Museum
(Muzei kinostudii im. O. P. Dovzhenka
[MDFS]), Kiev.

Dovzhenko's Autobiographies.

Kutsenko, M. V. *Dni i roky O. P. Dovzhenka: Litopys zhyttia i tvorchosti*, first (1974) draft of M. V. Kutsenko's *Storinky zhyttia i tvorchosti O. P. Dovzhenka* (Kiev, 1975).

Langlois, Henri. 'Letter to A. P. Dovzhenko (15 October 1956)'.

Materials prepared for Julia Solntseva's collection of memoirs, *Polum'iane zhyttia: Spohady pro Oleksandra Dovzhenka*, 9 folders.

Materials celebrating A. Dovzhenko's 100th birthday (1994), 2 folders.

Photographs of A. P. Dovzhenko, his colleagues, his friends.

Solntseva, Julia. The Julia Solntseva Archive, 4 unnumbered folders.

Tokarskaia, Nadezhda Petrovna. 'Iz pis'ma k Valentine Mikhailovich Demytskoi', 1 May 1970.

Zel'dovych, H. *'Zemlia' i liudy*.

Dovzhenko (O. P.) Literary-Memorial Museum (Literaturno-memorial'nyi muzei O. P. Dovzhenka [SDM]), Sosnytsia, Chernihiv Oblast.
Auxiliary Materials: A–178, A–196, A–198, A–228, A–266, A–273, A–393.

Dudko (Taras Mykolaivych) Archive, Moscow.
Letters from A. P. Dovzhenko to Barbara Krylova-Dovzhenko; Julia Solntseva's and A. P. Dovzhenko's 1950 marriage certificate

Foreign Policy Archive of the Russian Federation, Historical–Documentary Department (Istoriko-dokumental'nyi

departament Ministerstva inostrannykh del RF [FPARF]), Moscow.
f. People's Commissariat of Foreign Affairs of Ukraine. 1920, op. 5, papka 24, d. 7; 1921, op. 5, papka 25, d. 41.
f. Embassy (Polpred) of the RSFSR in Poland.
1920, op. 1, papka 1, d. 9.
1921, op. 1, papka 2, d. 3.
1922, op. 2, papka 6, d. 5.
1922, op. 21, papka 7, d. 11.
f. Polish Department.
1921, op. 4, papka 7, d. 12, 13, 15.
1921, op. 4, papka 18, d. 189.
1922, op. 5, papka 20, d. 10.

Library of Congress, Manuscript Division, Washington DC
Dmitrii Antonovich Volkogonov Papers.
Reels 2–3. Investigation File, 1918–92.
Reel 3. Ukraine, Sept. 1920–Nov. 1926 Publication of Volodymyr Kyryllovych Vynnychenko's letters, Oct. 1925–March 1926.
Reels 6–7. Lavrentii Pavlovich Beria's alleged criminal activities, July–August 1953.
Reels 7–8. Personal Papers, 1912–95, n.d.
Reels 8–9. Russian Centre for the Preservation and Study of Documents of Modern History, 1887–1992, n.d.
Reels 13–14. People's Commissariat of Nationalities documents, Oct. 1922–Nov. 1923.

Russian State Archive of Film and Photo Documents (Rossiiskii gosudarstvennyi arkhiv kinofotodokumentov), Krasnogorsk, Moscow Oblast.
Photographs of A. P. Dovzhenko, J. I. Solntseva, their friends and colleagues.

Russian State Archive of Socio-Political History (Rossiiskii gosudarstvennyi arkhiv sotsial'no-politicheskoi istorii [RGASPI]), Moscow (before March 1999: Russian Centre for the Preservation and Study of Documents of Modern History [Rossiiskii tsentr khraneniia i izucheniia dokumentov noveishei istorii, RTsKHIDNI].

f. 17, op. 3. Meetings of the Politburo of the Central Committee of the All-Union Communist Party (VKP[b]). d. 3 (1944).

f. 17, op. 26. Dept. of Leading Organs. Information Sector. Communist Party of Ukraine (1926–33). d. 3 (1926).

f. 17, op. 113. Secretariat of the Central Committee of the All-Union Communist Party. d. 844.

f. 17, op. 125. Propaganda and Agitation Administration of the Central Committee of the All-Union Communist Party (1938–45). d. 71, 124, 212–14, 291–3, 372, 467, 638.

f. 17, op. 132. Propaganda and Agitation Department of the Central Committee of the All-Union Communist Party (1948–53). d. 75, 88, 90, 92, 369, 477, 548.

f. 17, op. 133. Literary and Art Dept. of the Central Committee of the All-Union Communist Party and the Central Committee of the Communist Party of the Soviet Union. d. 311, 361, 382–4, 386, 399.

f. 77, op. 1. Andrei Aleksandrovich Zhdanov. d. 671, 698.

f. 88, op. 1. A. S. Shcherbakov. d. 113, 116, 426, 446, 579–80, 603, 810, 965–7, 1051, 1053.

f. 124. All-Union Association of Old Bolsheviks. op. 1, d. 1859 (A. I. Stetskii).

f. 495, op. 18. The Communist International. The Secretariat of the Executive Committee of the Communist International. d. 2, 32–a, 525, 579.

f. 523, op. 1. Dmytro Z. Manuil'skyi. d. 105–6.

Russian State Archive of Literature and Art (Rossiiskii gosudarstvennyi arkhiv literatury i iskusstva [RGALI]), Moscow.

f. 1923, op. 1. Sergei M. Eisenstein. d. 1784.

f. 2081, op. 1. Alexander Petrovych Dovzhenko. d. 136–40, 184, 350, 354–5, 357, 361–4, 367, 369–72, 374–8, 380–5, 388, 389, 391, 394–5, 413–14, 416, 421, 424, 431, 442, 445, 462, 467, 476, 478–9, 482, 484, 503, 507, 522, 526–8, 539, 541, 555, 557–9, 565–7, 570, 577–8, 934–7, 939–45, 947, 949–50, 957, 962–3, 967, 969–70, 973–4, 976, 981, 983, 985, 987, 990, 992, 994, 996–8, 1000–1, 1006, 1008, 1010–12, 1015, 1017, 1019, 1021–2, 1034, 1036, 1045–6, 1093–4, 1095–102, 1104, 1105–9, 1111–19, 1121–4, 1126–31, 1133–98, 1200–13, 1221–2, 1233, 1547, 1590, 1598, 1614, 1625.

f. 2081, op. 2. Alexander Petrovych Dovzhenko. d. 18, 20, 44, 75, 182–4, 186, 191, 202, 210–11, 213, 215–17, 219, 237, 241–2, 261.

f. 2453, op. 2. Moscow Film Studios (Mosfilm). d. 89, 90–1, 353.

f. 2453, op. 3. Mosfilm. d. 917–25; 1781–6.

f. 2453, op. 4. Mosfilm. d. 2872.

f. 2453, op. 5. Mosfilm. d. 656, 1612, 1949.

f. 2456, op. 1. Ministry of Cinematography of the USSR. d. 136, 310.

Shevchenko (T. H.) Institute of Literature at the National Academy of Sciences of Ukraine, Manuscript Division (Vidil rukopysiv Instytutu literatury im. T. Shevchenka pry NAN Ukrainy), Kiev.

f. 75. Soviet Ukrainian Writers. d. 50–2.

f. 116. Iurii Ivanovych Ianovs'kyi. d. 1654–68, 1676–8.

f. 137. Maksym Tadeiovych Ryl's'kyi. d. 4058–60.

f. 139. Volodymyr Sosiura. d. 75.

f. 167. Mykola Platonovych Bazhan. d. 285.

State Archive of the City of Kiev (Derzhavnyi arkhiv mista Kieva [DAMK]), Kiev.

f. 153. Kiev Commercial Institute.

op. 5, d. 2508.

op. 7, d. 2355.

State Archive of the Kiev Oblast (Derzhavnyi arkhiv Kievs'koi oblasti [DAKO]), Kiev.

f. 142. Dept. of Education, Kiev Province. op. 1, d. 317, 488.

f. 768. The Kiev Organisational Committee of the Trade Union of Arts Workers ('Rabis'). op. 1, d. 42.

State Archive of the Zhytomyr Province (Derzhavnyi arkhiv Zhytomyrs'koi oblasti [DAZhO]), Zhytomyr.

f. 1. The Volyn Spiritual Consistory of the City of Zhytomyr, Volyn Province. op. 50, d. 559.

f. R–31. Volyn Province Dept. of Education, City of Zhytomyr. op. 1, d. 15, 42.

f. 1487. Provincial War Commissariat. War Commissariat of the City of Zhytomyr, Volyn Province.

op. 1, d. 15, 26, 36, 37, 46, 203, 333, 395.

op. 2, d. 185, 249.

f. R–1643. Volyn Province Extraordinary Commission, City of Zhytomyr, Volyn Province. op. 2, d. 1.

f. 1820. Volyn Province Revolutionary Tribunal, City of Zhytomyr, Volyn Province. op. 5, d. 10, 12.

State Museum of Theatre, Art and Cinema of Ukraine (Derzhavnyi muzei teatru, mystetstva i kinomystetstva Ukrainy [DMTMKU]), Kiev.

f. 'R' (D. Demuts'kyi Archive), Inventory nos. 7722, 7732, 7738, 7877.

Dissertations and Theses

Brandenberger, David. 'The "Short Course" to Modernity: Stalinist History Textbooks, Mass Culture, and the Formation of Popular Russian National Identity, 1934–1956' (PhD dissertation, Dept. of History, Harvard University, 1999).

Ekeltchik, Serguei [Yekelchyk, Serhy]. 'History, Culture, and Nationhood Under High Stalinism: Soviet Ukraine, 1939–1954' (PhD dissertation, Dept. of History and Classics, University of Alberta, Edmonton, 2000).

Guthier, Steven L. 'The Roots of Popular Ukrainian Nationalism: A Demographic, Social, and Political Study of the Ukrainian Nationality to 1917' (PhD dissertation, Dept. of History, University of Michigan, Ann Arbor, 1990).

Hellbeck, Jochen. 'Laboratories of the Soviet Self: Diaries from the Stalin Era' (PhD dissertation, Dept. of History, Columbia University, 1998).

Leaming, Barbara D. 'Engineers of Human Souls – The Transition to Socialist Realism in the Soviet Cinema of the 1930s' (PhD dissertation, Dept. of Cinema Studies, New York University, 1976).

Nebesio, Bohdan. 'The Silent Films of Alexander Dovzhenko: A Historical Poetics' (PhD dissertation, Dept. of Modern Languages and Comparative Studies, University of Alberta, Edmonton, 1996).

Uzwyshyn, Raymond John. 'Between Ukrainian Cinema and Modernism: Alexander Dovzhenko's Silent Trilogy' (PhD dissertation, Dept. of Cinema Studies, New York University, 2000).

Part Two: Published Works

Abramson, Henry. *A Prayer for the Government: Jews and Ukrainians in Revolutionary Times*. Cambridge, MA, 1999.

——. 'The Scattering of Amalek: A Model for Understanding the Ukrainian–Jewish Conflict', *East European Jewish Affairs*, 24, no. 1 (1994), pp. 39–47.

Aleksandrov, G. V. *Epokha i kino*. Moscow, 1976.

Anderson, Benedict. *Imagined Communities: Reflections on the Origin and Spread of Nationalism*. London, 1983.

Andrew, Christopher M. and Oleg Gordievsky, *The KGB: The Inside Story of Its Foreign Operations from Lenin to Gorbachev*. New York, 1990.

Anninskii, L. A. 'Khrust i iabloko', *KZ*, no. 23 (1994), pp. 167–70.

Aronson, O. V. 'Kinoantropologiia "Zemli"', *KZ*, no. 23 (1994), pp. 141–8.

B. 'Na prosmotrakh "Zemli"', *Kino-front*, 6 April 1930, p. 3.

Babitsky, Paul and John Rimberg. *The Soviet Film Industry*. New York, 1955.

Babyshkin, O. *Oleksander Dovzhenko: Zbirnyk spohadiv i statei pro mytsia*. Kiev, 1959.

Baimut, T. 'Malovidoma storinka z zhyttia O. P. Dovzhenka (1914–1917 rr.)', *Vitchyzna*, no. 10 (1962), pp. 174–5.

——. 'Novye materialy k biografii A. P. Dovzhenko', *Iskusstvo kino*, no. 10 (1959), pp. 149–50.

Barabash, Iurii. 'Natsional'ne ta istorychne: Do problemy natsional'noho kharakteru v tvorchosti O. Dovzhenka', *Prapor*, no. 3 (1960), pp. 102–15.

——. 'V te plamennye gody … Tvorchestvo A. Dovzhenko perioda Velikoi Otechestvennoi voiny', *Znamia*, no. 11 (1965), pp. 231–46.

Bazhan, M. 'Lehendy ta istoriia', *Kino*, no. 21–2 (1928) and *Zhyttia i revoliutsiia*, no. 1 (1928).

——. *O. Dovzhenko. Narys pro mytsia*. Kharkiv, 1930. Republished in: M. Bazhan, *Liudy, knyhy, daty: statti pro literaturu* (Kiev, 1962), pp. 80–103; M. Bazhan, *Liudy, knigi, dati: stat'i o literature* (Moscow, 1968), pp. 5–31; and M. Bazhan, *Tvory v chotyr'oh tomakh, Vol. 3: Spohady* (Kiev, 1985), pp. 77–121.

——. 'Pro "Zvenigoru" ', *Teatr i kino*, no. 31 (14 February 1928).

——. *Razdum'ia i vospominaniia*. Moscow, 1983.

Bazin, André. 'The Stalin Myth in Soviet Cinema', in Bill Nichols, ed., *Movies and Methods: An Anthology* (Berkeley/Los Angeles and London, 1985), vol. 2, pp. 29–40.

Bednyi, Demian. 'Filosofy', *Izvestiia*, 4 April 1930 and *KZ*, no. 23 (1994), pp. 151–62.

——. ' "Kononizatsiia" ili "chto i trebovalos' dokazat" ', *Izvestiia*, 6 April 1930.

Belousov, Iu. A. 'Demyan Bednyi – kritik "Zemli": K biografii fil'ma', *KZ*, no. 23 (1994), pp. 149–50.

Beta. 'Zemlia', *Kino* (M), 5 April 1930, p. 3.

Bettleheim, Bruno. *Surviving and Other Essays*. New York, 1979.

Beumers, Birgit, ed. *Russia on Reels: The Russian Idea in Post-Soviet Cinema*. London and New York, 1999.

Bilas, Ivan H. *Represyvno-karal'na systema v Ukraini, 1917–1953: Suspil'no-politychnyi ta istoryko-pravovyi analiz*. Kiev, 1994. 2 vols.

Bilinsky, Yaroslav. *The Second Soviet Republic: The Ukraine After World War II*. New Brunswick, NJ, 1964.

Bodyk, Lazar Oleksandrovych. *Dzherela velykoho kino. Spohady pro O. P. Dovzhenka*. Kiev, 1965.

Bol'shakov, Ivan. 'Spohady', *Dnipro*, no. 9–10 (1994), pp. 68–70.

Bondarenko, Evhen. 'Zystrichi z Dovzhenkom', *Prapor*, no. 2 (1959), pp. 96–102.

Bordwell, David. *The Cinema of Eisenstein*. Cambridge, MA, 1993.

Borys, Jurij. *The Sovietization of Ukraine, 1917–1923: The Communist Doctrine and Practice of National Self-Determination*, 2nd ed., Edmonton, Alberta, 1980.

Bown, Matthew Cullerne. *Art Under Stalin*. New York, 1991.

Briukhovets'ka, Larysa. ' "Chy ne ia zvychainyi Don-kikhot?" ', *Kul'tura i zhyttia*, 11 September 1994, p. 5.

——. ' "Zvenyhora" i natsional'ne pytannia', *Uriadovyi kur'ier*, 17 September 1994.

Brooks, Jeffrey. 'Russian Cinema and Public Discourse, 1900–1930', *Historical Journal of Film, Radio and Television*, 11, no. 2 (1991), pp. 141–8.

——. *When Russia Learned to Read: Literacy and Popular Literature, 1861–1917*. Princeton, NJ, 1985.

Bucar, Annabelle. *Pravda ob amerikanskikh diplomatakh*. Moscow, 1949; trans. as *The Truth About American Diplomats*. Moscow, 1952.

Buriachkivs'kyi Oleh. ' "Zvenyhora" O. Dovzhenka: istoriosofiia Ukrainy', in V. H. Horpenko and O. S. Musiienko, eds., *Zmina paradyhmy: Zbirnyk naukovykh prats'* (Kiev, 1995), p. 22–52.

Carynnyk, Marco, ed. 'Alexander Dovzhenko's 1939 Autobiography', *Journal of Ukrainian Studies*, 19, no. 1 (Summer 1994), pp. 5–27.

——. 'Na pozharyshchakh velykoi materi-vdovytsi', *Novyny kinoekrana*, no. 9 (1990), pp. 2–3; no. 10 (1990), pp. 4–5.

Cherevatenko, Leonid. 'Dovzhenko, iakyi poperedu', *Kiev*, no. 10 (1986), pp. 137–45.

——. 'Z Dovzenkovoho lystyvannia', *Dnipro*, no. 1–2 (1997).

——. and Anatolii Lemysh. 'Dovzhenko v pritsele VChK-OGPU-NKVD-KGB: K stoletiia so dnia rozhdeniia A. P. Dovzhenko', *Kievskie vedomostie*, 3 September 1994.

Cherikover, I. *Antisemitizm i pogromy na Ukraine, 1917–1918*. Berlin, 1923.

Chernev, A. D. *229 kremlevskikh vozhdei*. Moscow, 1996.

Clark, Katerina. *Petersburg: Crucible of Cultural Revolution*. Cambridge, MA, 1995.

——. *The Soviet Novel: History as Ritual*, 1st ed. Chicago, 1981.

Cohen, Louis Harris. *The Cultural–Political Traditions and Developments of the Soviet Cinema, 1917–1972*. New York, 1974.

Conquest, Robert. *Harvest of Sorrow: Soviet Collectivization and the Terror-Famine*. London and New York, 1986.

Craig, Gordon A. *Germany, 1866–1945*. New York, 1978.

D. ' "Zemlia" v ARRKe', *Kino* (M), 5 April 1930, p. 3.

Dalrymple, Dana. 'The Soviet Famine of 1932–1934', *Soviet Studies*, 15, no. 3 (1964), pp. 250–84.

Davies, R. W., M. B. Tauger and S. G. Wheatcroft. 'Stalin, Grain Stocks, and the Famine of 1932–1933', *Slavic Review*, 54, no. 3 (1995), pp. 642–57.

'Demuts'kyi Danylo Porfyrovych', *Dnipro*, no. 6 (1991), p. 196.

Derev'ianko, Tatiana and Inna Zolotoverkhova. 'Dovzhenko smiietsia, zasterihaie, nahaduie', *Uriadovyi kur'ier*, no. 16 (31 January 1995), p. 7.

Deslav, Evhen. 'Dovzhenko i Stalin', *Kul'tura i zhyttia*, 11 September 1993, p. 5.

Dmitriev, Vladimir Iurevich. 'Eshche raz o Dovzhenko', *Segodnia*, 6 March 1996, p. 10.

Dolidze, Siko. 'To, chto dorogo sertsu', *Literaturnaia Gruziia*, vol. 8, no. 10 (1964), pp. 88–90.

'Dovzhenko A. P. (obituary)', *Pravda Ukrainy*, 27 November 1956 and *Sovetskaia kul'tura*, 27 November 1956.

——. 'Alchnye appetity Gollivuda', *Sovetskaia kul'tura*, 24 September 1982.

——. 'Delat' bol'she', *Vecherniaia Moskva*, 10 January 1935.

——. 'Ia poterpel bol'shoi uron v zhizni', *Iskusstvo kino*, no. 9 (1990), pp. 120–4.

——. 'Iazykom myslei', *Kino*, 22 April 1934.

——. *Izbrannoe: Sbornik stsenariev, rasskazov, statei*. Moscow, 1957.

——. 'Na prieme u tovarishcha Stalina. Beseda s rezhisserom A. Dovzhenko', *Vecherniaia Moskva*, 26 May 1935.

——. 'Pochemu "Ivan"?', *Kino*, 24 November 1932, p. 2.

——. *Sobranie sochinenii v chetyrekh tomakh*. Compiled by Julia Solntseva. Moscow, 1966–9. 4 vols.

——. 'Svetlyi obraz ego ostanetsia v moem sertse', *Za bol'shevistskii fil'm*, 9 September 1948.

——. 'Tianet menia vpered. Neopublikovannoe pismo A. P. Dovzhenko', *Pravda Ukrainy*, 7 February 1971.

——. 'Uchitel' i drug khudozhnika', *Iskusstvo kino*, no. 10 (1937), pp. 15–16.

——. *The Poet as Filmmaker: Selected Writings*. Edited and translated by Marco Carynnyk. Cambridge, MA, 1973.

Dovzhenko, O. 'Interviu', *Kul'tura i zhyttia*, 10 March 1985 and *Dnipro*, no. 3–4 (1996), pp. 92– 4 (first appeared in *Arbeiterbühne und Film*, July 1930).

——. 'Neopublikovani lysty Oleksandra Dovzhenka', *Dnipro*, no. 9–10 (1994), pp. 26–37.

——. '"Ty moie iedyne sviato": Nevidomi lysty Oleksandra Dovzhenka' (with an introduction by Irina Grashchenkova), *Kinoteatr*, no. 3 (1996), pp. 30–4.

——. *Aforyzmy. Krylati vyrazy. Tvorchi rozdumy. Skilka dumok vysokykh*. Edited, with an introduction, by M. Kovalenko and O. Pidsukha. Kiev, 1968.

——. *Bachyty zavzhdy zori: statti, vystypy, promovy*. Edited by O. K. Babyshkin. Kiev, 1979.

——. *'Hospody, poshly meni syly': Kinopovisti, opovidannia, shchodennyk*. Edited by Roman Korohods'kyi. Kharkiv, 1994.

——. *Kinopovisti, opovidannia*. Kiev, 1986.

——. *Tvory v p'iaty tomakh*. Kiev, 1964–6. 5 vols.

——. *Tvory v p'iaty tomakh*. Edited by Julia Solntseva. Kiev, 1983–4. 5 vols.

——. *Zacharovana Desna/Ukraina v ohni/ Shchodennyk*. Kiev, 1995.

Dziuba, Ivan. 'Cherez moie zhyttia', *Kul'tura i zhyttia*, no. 30 (24 July 1996).

Eisenstein, Sergei. 'The Birth of an Artist', in his *Notes of a Film Director*. NY, 1970.

——. *Film Forum: Essays in Film Theory*. New York, 1977.

——. 'Montazh attraktsionov', *LEF*, no. 3 (1923), pp. 70–5.

——. *Selected Works*. Edited by Richard Taylor. London and Bloomington, IN, 1988–96. 4 vols.

Eklof, Ben. *Russian Peasant Schools: Officialdom, Village Culture, and Popular Pedagogy, 1861–1914*. Berkeley, CA, and London, 1986.

Eley, Geoff. 'Remapping the Nation: War, Revolutionary Upheaval, and State Formation in Eastern Europe, 1914–1923', in Peter J. Potichnyj and Howard Aster, eds, *Ukrainian–Jewish Relations in Historical Perspective* (Edmonton, Alberta, 1988), pp. 205–46.

Encyclopedia of Ukraine. Edited by Volodymyr Kubijovyč. Toronto, 1984–93. 5 vols.

Engelstein, Laura and Stephanie Sandler, eds. *Self and Story in Russian History*. Ithaca, NY and London, 2000.

Fairbanks, Charles. 'National Cadres as a Force in the Soviet System: The Evidence of Beria's Career, 1949–1953', in Jeremy R. Azrael, ed., *Soviet Nationality Policies and Practices* (New York, 1978), pp. 144–86.

'Father Disowns Clerk in U.S. Embassy Who Renounced Native Land for Russia', *New York Times*, 29 February 1948, p. 4:2.

Fedyshyn, Oleh S. *Germany's Drive to the East and the Ukrainian Revolution, 1917–1918*. New Brunswick, NJ, 1971.

Fesenko, Oleksandr. 'Iak tvoryvsia mif pro "ukrains'koho Chapaeva"', *Literaturna Ukraina*, 17 August 1989, p. 17.

Festinger, Leon. *Extending Psychological Frontiers: Selected Works of Leon Festinger*, edited by Stanley Schachter and Michael Gazzaniga. New York, 1989.

Figes, Orlando. *A People's Tragedy: The Russian Revolution, 1891–1924*. New York, 1998.

Fitzpatrick, Sheila. *The Cultural Front:
Power and Culture in Revolutionary
Russia*. Ithaca, NY, 1992.
——. *Everyday Stalinism: Ordinary Life in
Extraordinary Times: Soviet Russia in the
1930s*. New York, 1999.
——. 'Intelligentsia and Power.
Client–Patron Relations in Stalin's
Russia', in Manfred Hildermeier and
Elisabeth Muller-Luckner, eds,
*Stalinismus vor dem Zweiten Weltkrieg.
Neue Wege der Forschung/Stalinism Before
the Second World War. New Avenues for
Research* (Munich, 1998).
——. ed. *Stalinism: New Directions*.
London and New York, 2000.
——, Alexander Rabinowitch and Richard
Stites, eds. *Russia in the Era of NEP*.
Bloomington, IN, 1991.
Fleishman, Lazar. *Boris Pasternak: The Poet
and His Politics*. Cambridge, MA, 1990.
Fromm, Erich. *Escape from Freedom*. New
York, 1969.
Gabler, Neal. *Life the Movie: How Entertainment
Conquered Reality*. New York, 1998.
Garros, Veronique, Natalia Korenevskaya
and Thomas Lahusen, eds. *Intimacy and
Terror: Soviet Diaries of the 1930s*. New
York, 1995.
Gellner, Ernest. *Thought and Change*.
Chicago, 1965.
——. *Nations and Nationalism*. Ithaca, NY,
1983.
Gerasimov, Sergei. *Zhizn', fil'my, spory:
Stranitsy avtobiografii o moiei professii:
polemika, portrety dlia molodykh i o
molodykh*. Moscow, 1971.
Gitelman, Zvi, ed. *Bitter Legacy: Confronting
the Holocaust in the USSR*. Bloomington,
IN, 1997.

Goldman, Wendy E. *Women, the State and
Revolution: Soviet Family Policy and
Social Life, 1917–1936*. Cambridge and
New York, 1993.
Gomery, Douglas. *Movie History: A Survey*.
Belmont, CA, 1991.
Goodwin, James. *Eisenstein, Cinema, and
History*. Urbana, IL and Chicago, 1993.
Grabowicz, Oksana. 'Kolonial'na
spadshchyna v s'ohodnishnii Ukraini:
Kil'ka kliuchovykh pytan' ', *Arka*, no. 1
(1994), pp. 14–17.
Graffy, Julian. 'Cinema', in Catriona Kelly
and David Shepherd, eds, *Russian
Cultural Studies: An Introduction* (New
York, 1998), pp. 165–91.
Graziosi, Andrea. *Bol'sheviki i krest'iane na
Ukraine, 1918–1919 gody*. Moscow, 1997.
——. *The Great Soviet Peasant War:
Bolsheviks and Peasants, 1917–1933*.
Cambridge, MA, 1996.
Gromov, Evgenii. *Stalin: vlast' i iskusstvo*.
Moscow, 1998.
Grossman-Roshchin, V. 'Malenkoe ili
bol'shoe?', *Kino* (M), 26 November
1932, p. 2.
Groys, Boris. *The Total Art of Stalinism:
Avant-Garde, Aesthetic Dictatorship and
Beyond*. Princeton, NJ, 1992.
Halfin, Igal. 'From Darkness to Light:
Student Communist Autobiography
During NEP', *Jahrbücher für Geschichte
Osteuropas*, 45, no. 2 (1997),
pp. 210–36.
Haraszati, Miklos. *The Velvet Prison: Artists
Under State Socialism*. New York, 1987.
Haslam, Jonathan. *The Soviet Union and the
Threat from the East, 1933–1941:
Moscow, Tokyo, and the Prelude to the
Pacific War*. Pittsburgh, 1992.

Heifetz, Elias. *The Slaughter of the Jews in the Ukraine in 1919*. New York, 1921.

Hellbeck, Jochen. 'Fashioning the Stalinist Soul: The Diary of Stepan Podlubnyi (1931–1939)', *Jahrbücher für Geschichte Osteuropas*, 44, no. 3 (1996), pp. 344–73.

Higson, Andrew. 'The Concept of National Cinema', *Screen*, 30, no. 4 (1989), pp. 36–46.

Hjort, Mette and Scott MacKenzie, eds. *Cinema and Nation*. London and New York, 2000.

'Hniv narodu', *Radians'ka Ukraina*, 22 December 1953, p. 3 (a reprint of *Pravda*'s lead editorial, 20 December 1953).

Hoffer, Eric. *The True Believer: Thoughts on the Nature of Mass Movements*. New York, 1951.

Honchar, Oles'. 'Koly dumaiesh pro Dovzhenka', *Kul'tura i zhyttia*, 10 September 1994, pp. 1–2.

Horpenko, V. H. and O. S. Musiienko, eds. *Zmina paradyhmy: Zbirnyk naukovykh prats', Chastyna 1*. Kiev, 1995.

Hosking, Geoffrey. *The First Socialist Society: A History of the Soviet Union from Within*. Enlarged ed. Cambridge, MA, 1990.

Hryshchenko, Oleksandr Savych. *Z berehiv zacharovanoi Desny*. Kiev, 1964.

Hunczak, Taras, edn. *The Ukraine, 1917–1921: A Study in Revolution*. Cambridge, MA, 1977.

Iakimovich, A. K. 'Dovzhenko i novaia "pervobytnost"', *KZ*, no. 23 (1994), pp. 137–41.

Iankovskii, M. 'Zemlia', *Kino-front*, 6 April 1930, p. 2.

Ianovs'kyi, Iurii. 'Hollivud na berezi Chornoho moria', in his *Tvory v p'iaty tomakh*, vol. 5 (Kiev, 1983).

Iaremchuk, Andrii. 'Oleksandr Dovzhenko: "I anhely zderly z mene okryvavlenu shkiru …" (Notatky pro te, chomu velykii kinorezhyser ne zniav fil'mu pro polit liudyny na Mars', *Ukrains'ka kul'tura*, no. 9–10 (1994), pp. 1, 4–8.

'Iedyna komunistychna partiia', *Borot'ba*, 21 March 1920, p. 1.

Il'ienko, Ivan. 'Zastupyvsia za narod svii … kinopovist' Oleksandra Dovzhenka "Ukraina v ohni" – vyklyk totalitaryzmu', *Uriadovyi kur'ier*, 28 May 1994, p. 9.

'Iubilei klassika kinematografisty vstretiat pochtitel'nym molchaniem', *Kommersant-daily*, 10 September 1994.

Iurenev, R. N. *Aleksandr Dovzhenko*. Moscow, 1959.

Iutkevich, S. 'Puti razvitiia', *Kino* (M), 26 November 1932, p. 2.

K., H. 'Materialy k voprosu o zemel'noi politike na Ukraine', *Ukrainskii kommunist*, no. 1 (November 1919), pp. 7–18.

Kak ia stal rezhisserom. Moscow, 1946.

Kappeler, Andreas. 'The Ukrainians of the Russian Empire, 1860–1914', in A. Kappeler, ed., *The Formation of National Elites: Comparative Studies on Governments and Non-Dominant Ethnic Groups in Europe, 1850–1940* (Aldershot and New York, 1992), vol. 6.

Keep, John L. H. *The Russian Revolution: A Study in Mass Mobilization*. New York, 1976.

Kemp-Welch, A. *Stalin and the Literary Intelligentsia, 1928–39*. New York, 1991.

Kenez, Peter. *The Birth of the Propaganda State: Soviet Methods of Mass Mobilization, 1917–1929*. Cambridge and New York, 1985.

——. 'Black and White: The War on Film', in Richard Stites, ed., *Culture and Entertainment in Wartime Russia*. Bloomington, IN, 1995.

——. *Cinema and Soviet Society, 1917–1953*. Cambridge and New York, 1992.

Kepley, Vance, Jr. *In the Service of the State: The Cinema of Alexander Dovzhenko*. Madison, WI, 1986.

Kheryshev, N. S. *Komandarm Dubovoi*. Kiev, 1986.

Khmurnyi, Vasyl. 'Arsenal', *Dnipro*, no. 9–10 (1994), pp. 52–5.

——. 'Zvenyhora', *Dnipro*, no. 9–10 (1994), pp. 51–2.

Khrushchev, N. S. *Khrushchev Remembers*. With an introduction by Edward Crankshaw. Boston, 1970.

——. 'Secret Speech of Khrushchev Concerning the "Cult of the Individual", Delivered at the Twentieth Congress of the Communist Party of the Soviet Union, 25 February 1956', Columbia University, Russian Institute, *The Anti-Stalin Campaign and International Communism: A Selection of Documents* (New York, 1956), pp. 1–89.

'Kino v konteksti ukrains'koi kul'tury', *Kiev*, no. 5 (1988), pp. 116–24.

Klering, Hans. 'Spohady pro nezabutnie', *Na ekranakh Ukrainy*, no. 45 (8 November 1986), p. 4.

Knight, Amy. *Beria: Stalin's First Lieutenant*. Princeton, NJ, 1993.

Kokhno, L. *Danylo Porfyrovych Demuts'kyi*. Kiev, 1965.

Kolasky, John. *Education in Soviet Ukraine: A Study in Discrimination and Russification*. Toronto, 1968.

——. *Two Years in Soviet Ukraine: A Canadian's Personal Account of Russian Oppression and the Growing Opposition*. Toronto, 1970.

Kondakova, I. A., compiler. *Otkrytyi arkhiv: Spravochnik opublikovannykh dokumentov po istorii Rossii XX veka iz gosudarstvennykh i semeinykh arkhivov (po otechestvennoi zhurnal'noi periodike i al'manakham). 1985–1996*. 2nd rev. ed., Moscow, 1999.

Kononenko, Natalie O. *Ukrainian Minstrels: 'and the blind shall sing'*. Armonk, NY, 1998.

Kopelev, Lev. *The Education of a True Believer*. New York, 1978.

Korniichuk, O. 'Natsional'ne pytannia v ukrains'kii kinematografii', *Radians'ke mystetstvo* (Kiev), no. 13–14 (1931), pp. 14–15.

Korniichuk, O. and Iv. Iurchenko, 'Rozhromyty natsionalizm v kinematohrafii', *Komunist* (Kharkiv), 30 December 1933, p. 2.

Korohods'kyi, Roman. '"... Budem robyty i budem maty ..."' (Industrial'na doba u filosofs'komu i khudozhnomu osmyslenni, abo Real'na tsina odniei utopii)', *Prosvita*, August 1994, p. 3.

——. 'Dovzhenko v poloni: natsional'na porazka i bil'shovyts'ka "Nauka peremahaty"', *Kur'ier kryvbasu*, no. 67–8 (1996), pp. 67–83.

——. *Dovzhenko v poloni: Rozvidky ta esei pro Maistra*. Kiev, 2000.

——. 'Naistarodavnisha zav'iaz: pryroda-liudyna-mystetstvo', *Pryroda i liudyna*, vyp. 3 (1970), pp. 126–33.

——. 'Neiubileine (Do 100-richchia vid dnia narodzhennia O. P. Dovzhenka)', *Kul'tura*, no. 140 (10 September 1994).

——. 'Shkitsyk do portretu Dovzhenka vidomoho i nevidomoho', *Knyzhnyk*, no. 2 (1991), pp. 9–13.

——. 'Velyka tsytata, abo liubovni lysty polenenoho', *Suchasnist*, no. 1 (1999), pp. 129–49 and no. 2 (1999), pp. 108–22.

——. ed. 'Visimnadtsat' lystiv pro kokhannia: Oleksandr Dovzhenko – Oleni Chernovii', *Kul'tura i zhyttia*, no. 48 (27 November 1996), p. 3; and no. 49 (4 December 1996), p. 3.

——. 'Zadushenyi holos: Shkits po portreta vidomoho i nevidomoho Dovzhenka', *Slovo*, no. 12 (June) 1991.

Koshelivets', Ivan. *Oleksandr Dovzhenko: Sproba tvorchoi biohrafii*. Munich, 1980.

——. 'Pro zatemneni mistia v biohrafii Oleksandra Dovzhenka', *Dnipro*, no. 9–10 (1994), pp. 2–25.

——. *Rozmovy v dorozi do sebe*. Munich, 1985.

Kosmins'kyi, P. 'Donos sviatoho ottsia', *Molod' Ukrainy*, 7 September 1983, p. 2.

Kostiuk, Hryhorii. *Okaianni roky: Vid Luk'ianivs'koi tiurmy do Vorkuts'koi trahedii (1935–1940 rr.)*. Toronto, 1978.

——. *Stalinist Terror in the Ukraine: A Study of the Decade of Mass Terror (1929–1939)*. New York, 1960.

Kot, Serhii, compiler. 'Neopublikovani avtohrafy Oleksandra Dovzhenka', *Dnipro*, no. 9–10 (1994), pp. 73–7.

Koval', M. V. 'Sprava Oleksandra Dovzhenka (Do 100-richchia z dnia narodzhennia', *Ukrains'kyi istorychnyi zhurnal*, no. 4 (1994), pp. 108–20.

Koval', Vitalii. ' "I ni odyn holos z Ukrainy": Rekviiem moskovs'koi katorhy Oleksandra Dovzhenka', *Dnipro*, no. 6 (1991), pp. 92–107.

Kovalenko, Mykhailo and Oleksii Mishurin. *Syn zacharovanoi Desny. Spohady i statti*. Kiev, 1984.

Koval'ska, Nina. 'Do istorii dyplomatychnykh vidnosyn URSR', *Vsesvit*, no. 5 (1988), pp. 159–61.

Kozlov, L. 'Eisenshtein i Dovzhenko', *Voprosy kinoiskusstva*, no. 9 (1966), pp. 308–12.

Kozlovskii, Ivan. *Muzyka – radost' i bol' moia: Stat'i, interv'iu, vospominaniia*. Moscow, 1992.

Krawchenko, Bohdan. *Social Change and National Consciousness in Twentieth Century Ukraine*. New York, 1985.

Kubijovič, Volodymyr, ed. *Encyclopedia of Ukraine: Map and Gazetteer*. Toronto, 1984.

Kuran, Timur. *Private Truths, Public Lies: The Social Consequences of Preference Falsification*. Cambridge, MA and London, 1995.

Kurin, Viacheslav. 'Velych i trahediia heniia', *Komunist*, no. 25 (1994), p. 4.

Kuromiya, Hiroaki. *Freedom and Terror in the Donbass: A Ukrainian–Russian Borderland, 1870s–1990s*. New York and Cambridge, 1998.

Kutsenko, Mykola. ' "Duzhe sumuiu za Ukrainoiu" ', *Slovo i chas*, no. 9–10 (1994), pp. 20–6.

——. 'Spovid' pro trahichne kokhannia',
   Vitchyzna, no. 4 (1991), pp. 181–94.
——. *Storinky zhyttia i tvorchosti O. P.
   Dovzhenka*. Kiev, 1975.
——. ' "Sumlinnia moie chyste pered
   narodom" ', *Visti z Ukrainy*, no. 32
   (April 1989).
Kuziakina, Natalia. 'Oleksandr Dovzhenko
   i Les' Kurbas', *Ukrains'kyi teatr*, no. 6
   (1989), pp. 8–11.
Kuznetsova, Anna. *Narodnyi artist: Stranitsy
   zhizni i tvorchestva I. S. Kozlovskogo*.
   Moscow, 1964.
Lasunskii, Oleg. *Volshebnoe zertsalo*.
   Voronezh, 1981.
Lav'iuk, D. and V. Makarenko. 'Semen
   Tarasovych – Did O. Dovzhenka',
   Chervonyi prapor, 22 August 1959.
Lavrinenko, Iurii, ed. *Rozstriliane
   vidrodzhennia*. Paris, 1959.
Lawton, Anna, ed. *The Red Screen: Politics,
   Society, and Art in Soviet Cinema*.
   London and New York, 1991.
Levin, E. 'Piat dnei v 49-m', *Iskusstvo kino*,
   no. 1 (1990), pp. 93–9; no. 2 (1990),
   pp. 93–101; and no. 3 (1990),
   pp. 77–89.
Lewin, Moshe. *The Making of the Soviet
   System: Essays in the Social History of
   Interwar Russia*. New York, 1985.
Lewytzkyj, Borys, compiler. *The Soviet
   Political Elite*. Stanford, CA, 1970.
   2 vols.
——. *The Stalinist Terror in the Thirties:
   Documentation from the Soviet Press*.
   Stanford, CA, 1974.
Leyda, Jay. *Kino: A History of the Russian
   and Soviet Film*, 3rd ed. Princeton, NJ,
   1983.
Liber, George O. 'Adapting to the Stalinist

Order: Alexander Dovzhenko's
   Psychological Journey, 1933–1953',
   Europe-Asia Studies, 53, no. 7 (2001),
   pp. 1097–1116.
——. 'Commemorating Stalin's Cinematic
   Invention', *Kyiv Post*, 1 April 1999.
——. 'Death, Birth Order, and Alexander
   Dovzhenko's Cinematic Visions',
   KINEMA, no. 13 (Spring 2000),
   pp. 57–74.
——. 'Dovzhenko, Stalin, and the (Re)
   Creation of *Shchors*', *Harvard Ukrainian
   Studies*, 21, no. 3–4 (1997), pp. 271–86.
——. *Soviet Nationality Policy, Urban
   Growth, and Identity Change in the
   Ukrainian SSR, 1923–1934*. Cambridge
   and New York, 1992.
——. ' "Till Death Do You Part": Varvara
   Krylova, Yuliya Solntseva, and
   Oleksandr Dovzhenko's Muse',
   *Australian Slavonic and East European
   Studies*, 14, nos. 1–2 (2000), pp. 75–97.
Liehm, Mira and Antonin J. Liehm. *The
   Most Important Art: Eastern European
   Film After 1945*. Berkeley, CA and
   London, 1977.
Listov, V. S. ' "Chisteishii moveton".
   Kommentarii k stikhotvoreniiu Demyana
   Bednogo "Filosofy" ', *KZ*, no. 23
   (1994), pp. 162–6.
——. 'Nazvanie kazhdoi kartiny
   utverzhdaetsia komissiei orgbiuro', *KZ*,
   no. 31 (1996), pp. 108–30.
Luckyj, George S. N. *Literary Politics in the
   Soviet Ukraine, 1917–1934*. New York,
   1956.
Mace, James E. *Communism and the
   Dilemmas of National Liberation:
   National Communism in Soviet Ukraine,
   1918–1933*. Cambridge, MA, 1983.

——. 'Famine and Nationalism in Soviet Ukraine', *Problems of Communism*, no. 33, May–June 1984, pp. 37–50.

——. 'The Famine of 1932–1933: A Watershed in the History of Soviet Nationality Policy', in Henry R. Huttenbach, ed., *Soviet Nationality Policies: Ruling Ethnic Groups in the USSR* (London, 1990), pp. 177–205.

McNeal, Robert, ed. *Resolutions and Decisions of the Communist Party of the Soviet Union, vol. 3: The Stalin Years: 1929–1953*. Toronto, 1974.

Magocsi, Paul Robert. *A History of Ukraine*. Seattle, WA, 1996.

Majstrenko, Ivan (Ivan). *Borot'bism: A Chapter in the History of Ukrainian Communism*. New York, 1954.

——. *Istoriia moho pokolinnia: Spohady uchasnyka revoliutsiinykh podii v Ukraini*. Edmonton, Alberta, 1985.

Mamatova, L. Kh. ed. *Kino: politika i liudy. 30-e gody*. Moscow, 1995.

Manukhin, Vl. 'Vokrug "Zemli" (Na obshchestvenno-diskussionnykh prosmotrakh)', *Kino* (M), 31 March 1930.

Margolit, E. Ia. 'Postroenie sotsializma ekrannymi sredstvami', *KZ*, no 23 (1994), pp. 107–11.

——. and Viacheslav Shmyrov. *Iz'iatoe kino (1923–1954)*. Moscow, 1995.

Mar'iamov, A. *Dovzhenko*. Moscow, 1968.

——. 'Razbeg', *Iskusstvo kino*, no. 9 (1964), pp. 21–35.

Mar'iamov, G. *Kremlevskii tsensor: Stalin smotrit kino*. Moscow, 1992.

Martych, Iukhym. 'Kukhol' Dovzhenka', in his *Zustrichi bez proshchan': Biohrafichni rozpovidi* (Kiev, 1970), pp. 161–200.

Mashchenko, Mykola. 'Oleksandr Dovzhenko', *Kul'tura i zhyttia*, 23 April 1997, p. 3.

Masokha, Petro. 'Dovzhenko ta ioho aktory', *Prapor*, no. 9 (1974), pp. 90–4.

——. 'Zakokhanyi u prekrasne: Spohady pro O. P. Dovzhenko', *Dnipro*, no. 9 (1964), pp. 128–31.

Mast, Gerald. *A Short History of the Movies*. Indianapolis, 1975.

Maximenkov, Leonid, ed. 'Stalin's Meeting with a Delegation of Ukrainian Writers on 12 February 1929', *Harvard Ukrainian Studies*, 17, no. 3–4 (1992), pp. 361–431.

Medvedev, Roy. *Let History Judge: The Origins and Consequences of Stalinism*. Rev. and exp. ed., New York, 1989.

Merridale, Catherine. 'The Collective Mind: Trauma and Shell-Shock in Twentieth Century Russia', *Journal of Contemporary History*, 35, no. 1 (2000), pp. 39–55.

——. *Night of Stone: Death and Memory in Twentieth-Century Russia*. New York, 2001.

Mikhalkovich, V. I. 'Naturfilosofia "Zemli"', *KZ*, no. 23 (1994), pp. 111–22.

Milgram, Stanley. *Obedience to Authority: An Experimental View*. New York, 1974.

Milosz, Czeslaw. *The Captive Mind*. New York, 1990.

Mitchinson, Paul. 'The Shostakovich Variations', *Lingua Franca*, May/June 2000, pp. 46–54.

Mol'nar, Mykhailo. 'Z Cheko-slovats'kykh zustrichei Oleksandra Dovzhenka', *Slovo i chas*, no. 8 (1995), pp. 38–45.

Montagu, Ivor. 'Dovzhenko: Poet of Life Eternal', *Sight and Sound*, 27, no. 1 (1957), pp. 44–8.

Motzkin, Leo, ed. *The Pogroms in the Ukraine under the Ukrainian Governments, 1917–1920*. London, 1927.

Muratov, Oleksandr. 'Spomyn pro Dovzhenka', *Dnipro*, no. 9–10 (1994), pp. 58–64.

Narysy istorii ukrains'koi intelihentsii (persha polovyna XX st.). U 3-kh knyhakh. Kiev, 1994, 3 vols.

Naspivala maty: Pisennyi svit O. Dovzhenka. Edited and introduced by Vitalii M. Pryhorovs'kyi. Kiev, 1995.

'Natsionalizatsiia kinematohrafiv', *Borot'ba*, 30 March 1920, p. 2.

Nazarenko, Ia. 'Dovzhenko i Sosnyts'kyi teatr', *Radians'kyi patriot* (Sosnytsia), 24 May 1966, p. 4.

——. 'Ego shkol'nye gody', *Raduga*, no. 9 (1964), pp. 141–52.

——. 'K sol'ntsu, k schast'iu!', *Znamia*, no. 7 (1965), pp. 133–41.

Nebesio, Bohdan Y. 'A Compromise with Literature?: Making Sense of Intertitles in the Silent Films of Alexander Dovzhenko', *Canadian Review of Comparative Literature*, September 1996, pp. 679–700.

——. Y. *Alexander Dovzhenko: A Guide to Published Sources*. Edmonton, Alberta, 1995.

Neilsen, Asta. *Die schweigende Muse*. Berlin, 1977.

Nesterovich, Olga. 'Dovzhenko na tribune', in Soiuz kinematografistov SSSR, kommissiia veteranov, *Zhizn' v kino: Veterany o sebe i svoikh tovaryshchakh* (Moscow, 1986), vyp. 3, pp. 228–37.

——. 'Zapiski redaktora', in O. Nesterovich, compiler, *Zhizn' v kino: Veterany o sebe i svoikh tovarishchakh* (Moscow,1971), vyp. 1, pp. 274–92.

'Nikolai Shchors – legenda i real'nost'', *Iskusstvo kino*, no. 9 (1990).

'O kinofil'me "Bol'shaia zhizn"', *Iskusstvo kino*, no. 1 (1947), p. 1.

Ol'khovyi, B. S., ed. *Puti kino: Pervoe Vsesoiuznoe partiinoe soveshchanie po kinematografii*. Moscow, 1929.

Onyshchenko, Olena. 'Try symvolichni trylohii', *Kul'tura i zhyttia*, 20 August 1994.

Ostrovskii, G. 'Dovzhenko v Odesse', *Znamia kommunizma* (Odessa), 2 August 1964.

Ostrovs'kyi, Heorhii. 'Pratsia O. P. Dovzhenka na Odes'kii kinofabrytsi (1926–1929)', *Literaturna Odessa*, no. 17–18 (1957), pp. 248–57.

Pamiatnaia knizhka Volinskoi gubernii na 1917 god'. Zhitomir, 1916.

Panch, Pavlo. *Vidlitaiut' zhuravli: etiudy*. Kiev, 1973.

Panchuk, M. and V. Kotyhorenko, 'Natsional'ni aspekty destalinizatsii rezhymu', in Natsional'na akademiia nauk Ukrainy, Institut istorii Ukrainy, *Pochatok destalinizatsii v Ukraini* (Kiev, 1997).

Pasolini, Pier Paolo. 'The Cinema of Poetry', in Bill Nichols, ed., *Movies and Methods: An Anthology* (Berkeley/Los Angeles and London, 1985), vol. 1, pp. 542–58.

Pazhitnikova, L. I. and Iu. I. Solntseva, eds. *Dovzhenko v vospominaniiakh sovremennikov*. Moscow, 1982.

'Pered chistkoi', *Kino* (Moscow), 10 May 1930, p. 1.

Perez, Gilberto. 'All in the Foreground: A Study of Dovzhenko's *Earth*', *Hudson Review*, 28, no. 1 (1975), pp. 68–86.

——. *The Material Ghost: Films and Their Medium*. Baltimore and London, 1998.

'Pervoe Vsesoiuznoe soveshchanie tvorcheskikh rabotnikov sovetskoi kinematografii', in E. Zil'ber, ed., *Za bol'shoe kinoiskusstvo* (Moscow, 1935).

Pervyi Vsesoiuznyi s'ezd sovetskikh pisatelei 1934: Stenograficheskii otchet. Moscow, 1934; reprint: Moscow, 1990.

Piatnitskii, V. K., compiler. *Golofa: Po materialam arkhivno-sledstvennogo dela no. 603 na Sokolovu-Piatnitskuiu Iu. I.* St Petersburg, 1993.

Pidsukha, Oleksandr. 'Dlia bil'shoi iasnosti', *Literaturna Ukraina*, 21 June 1990, p. 4.

——. 'Provisnyk', *Kiev*, no. 9 (1989), pp. 102–7.

Pipes, Richard. *A Concise History of the Russian Revolution*. New York, 1995.

——. *The Formation of the Soviet Union: Communism and Nationalism, 1917–1923*. Rev. ed., Cambridge, MA, 1997.

Plachynda, Serhii, ed. *Dovzhenko i svit: Tvorchist' O. P. Dovzhenka v kontektsi svitovoi kul'tury*. Kiev, 1984.

——. *Oleksandr Dovzhenko: Zhyttia i tvorchist*. Kiev, 1964.

'Plenym Spilky radians'kykh pys'mennykiv Ukrainy', *Literatura i mystetstvo*, 8 July 1944, p. 1.

'Po agenturnym dannym ... Informatsiia Narkoma NKGB V. N. Merkulova Sekretariu TsK VKP(b) A. A. Zhdanovu o politicheskikh nastroeniiakh i vyskazyvaniiakh sovetskikh pisatelei', *Rodina*, no. 1 (1992).

Pohrebins'kyi, M. B. 'Do naukovoho zhyttiepysu O. Dovzhenka', *Radians'ke literaturoznavstvo*, no. 8 (1971), pp. 77–8.

'Pokhorony A. P. Dovzhenko', *Sovetskaia kul'tura*, 29 November 1956.

Polianovskii, Georgii. *Ivan Semenovich Kozlovskii*. Moscow and Leningrad, 1945.

Popyk, Viacheslav, ed. 'Pid sofitamy sekretnykh sluzhb', *Z arkhiviv VUChK-HPU-NKVD-KHB*, no. 1–2 (1995), pp. 235–80.

——. 'Pid sofitamy VChK-DPU-NKVS-NKDB-KDB: Dokumental'na dopovid' za materialamy arkhivnoi spravy-formuliaru na Dovzhenka Oleksandra Petrovycha', *Dnipro*, no. 9–10 (1995), pp. 21–60.

'Posetiteli kremlevskogo kabineta I. V. Stalina: Zhurnaly (tetradi) zapisi lits, priniatykh pervym gensekom, 1924–1953', *Istoricheskii arkiv*, no. 6 (1994); nos 2, 3, 4, 5–6 (1995); nos 2, 3, 4, 5 (1996); no. 4 (1998).

'Postanova TsK Ukrains'koi komunistychnoi partii (borot'bistiv) pro likvidatsiieiu partii', *Borot'ba*, 31 March 1920, p. 1.

Povolotskaia, I. 'Nash uchitel'', *Voprosy kinoiskusstva*, no. 9 (1966), pp. 317–19.

'Priem v Kremle v chest' komanduiushchykh voiskami Krasnoi Armii', *Izvestiia*, 25 May 1945, p. 1.

Pryhorovs'kyi, Vitalii. 'Dovzhenko i Stalin', *Komsomol's'kyi hart* (Chernihiv), 4 June 1988, pp. 6–7.

——. ' "Ia komunistom buv, ie i bydy": Do istorii z partkvitkom Oleksandra Dovzhenka', *Komunist*, no. 23 (August 1994).

——. 'Koly narodyvsia Dovzhenko', *Prapor*, no. 5 (1972), pp. 100–1.

——. 'Oleksandr Dovzhenko – pedahoh', *Zhovten'*, no. 9 (1974), pp. 124–8.

——. 'Pershyi uchytel' ', *Komsomol's'kyi hart*, 1 March 1977, p. 3.

——. 'Tarasovychka: Pro matir O. P. Dovzhenka', *Desnians'ka pravda*, 19 July 1994, p. 3.

——. ' "Unykaty riznochytan" (Deiaki utochnennia do biohrafii O. P. Dovzhenka)', *Ukrains'ka mova i literatura v shkoli*, no. 8 (1979).

——. ' "Zahynuv vid holody": Z notatok pro bat'ka O. P. Dovzhenka', *Ukraina moloda*, 9 September 1994.

Pryluts'kyi, V. I. 'Pershi kroky M. S. Khrushchova v Ukraini: 1938–1939 rr.', in Natsional'na akademiia nauk Ukrainy, Instytut istorii, *M. S. Khrushchov i Ukraina* (Kiev, 1995).

Pudovkin, Vsevolod. 'Liniia ogromnogo soprotivlenniia', *Kino* (M), 26 November 1932, p. 2.

——. ' "Ochen' ser'eznyi vopros – unichtozhenie rezhisserov" ', *Iskusstvo kino*, no. 12 (1991), pp. 141–9.

Rabinovich, V. L. 'Vsegda – na pervoi stranitse', *KZ*, no. 23 (1994), pp. 122–9.

Rachuk, I. 'Esteticheskie vzgliady Aleksandra Dovzhenko', *Baikal*, no. 1 (1962).

Rassweiler, Anne D. *The Generation of Power: The History of Dneprostroi*. New York and Oxford, 1988.

Reshetar, John S., Jr. *The Ukrainian Revolution, 1917–1921: A Study in Nationalism*. Princeton, NJ, 1952.

Rimberg, John David. *The Motion Picture in the Soviet Union: 1918–1952*. New York, 1973.

Robin, Regine. *Socialist Realism: An Impossible Aesthetic*. Stanford, CA, 1992.

'Rodnoe imia', *Kommunist* (Yerevan), 18 February 1979.

Romanivs'ka, Maria. 'Daleka hasha kinoiunist' ', *Vitchyzna*, no. 11 (1969), pp. 152–9.

Romm, Mikhail. *Ustnye rasskazy*. Moscow, 1989.

Rosefielde, Steven. 'Excess Colletivization Deaths, 1929–1933: New Demographic Evidence', *Slavic Review*, 43, no. 1 (1984), pp. 83–8.

Rotha, Paul. *The Film Till Now: A Survey of World Cinema*. 3rd ed. London, 1967.

Rothbaum, Fred, John R. Weisz and Samuel S. Snyder. 'Changing the World and Changing the Self: The Two-Process Model of Perceived Control', *Journal of Personality and Social Psychology*, 42, no. 1 (1982), pp. 5–37.

Ruane, Christine. *Gender, Class, and the Professionalization of Russian City Teachers, 1860–1914*. Pittsburgh, 1994.

Rubenstein, Joshua. *Tangled Loyalties: The Life and Times of Ilya Ehrenburg*. Tuscaloosa, AL, 1999.

Rutkovskii, Aleksandr. 'Grad nebesnyi Aleksandra Dovzhenko', *Zerkalo nedeli* (Kiev), 9 December 1995, p. 14.

——. ' "Proshchai, Amerika!" Aleksandra Dovzhenko', *Kievskie novosti*, 22 August 1997, p. 8.

Rybalka, Oleksandr, ed. ' "Moia trahediia iak khudozhnyka poliahaie v tomu …" ', *Starozhytnosti* (Kiev), no. 13–14 (1993), pp. 24–8.

Ryl's'kyi [Rylsky], Bohdan. 'Vbyla nenavist' i zlo', *Literaturna Ukraina*, 4 January 1990, p. 3.

Ryl's'kyi [Rylsky], Maksym. 'Slovo o Dovzhenko', *Sovetskoe kino*, 29 August 1964.

Samoilov, Evgenii. 'Ee svet: k iubileiu Iu. I. Solntsevoi', *Sovetskii ekran*, no. 17 (1986), pp. 18–19.

Saunders, David. 'What Makes a Nation a Nation? Ukrainians since 1600', *Ethnic Studies*, vol. 10 (1993), pp. 101–24.

Savčenko, Fedir. *The Suppression of Ukrainian Activities in 1876*. Munich, 1970.

Savyts'kyi, Roman, Jr. 'Pomiry "Zemli" O. Dovzhenka', *Suchasnist'*, no. 7–8 (1975).

Schlegel, Hans-Joachim. 'Berlin i Germaniia Aleksandra Dovzhenko', *KZ*, no. 31 (1996).

Shapoval, Iurii Ivanovych. 'Oleksandr Šumskyj: The Last 13 Years of His Life', *Jahrbücher für Geschichte Osteuropas*, 42, Heft 1 (1994), pp. 64–76.

——. '"On Ukrainian Separatism": A GPU Circular of 1926', *Harvard Ukrainian Studies*, 18, no. 3/4 (1994), pp. 275–302.

——, Volodymyr Prystaiko and Vadim Zolotar'ov. *ChK-HPU-NKVD v Ukraini: osoby, fakty, dokumenty*. Kiev, 1997.

'Shcherbakov A. S. (obituary)', *Pravda*, 11 May 1945, p. 1.

Shengelaia, N. 'Fil'ma obrazov i idei', *Kino*, 26 November 1932, p. 2.

'Shest'desiat let A. P. Dovzhenko', *Iskusstvo kino*, no. 3 (1955), pp. 109–14.

Shkandrij, Myroslav. *Modernists, Marxists, and the Nation: The Ukrainian Literary Discussion of the 1920s*. Edmonton, Alberta, 1992.

Shklovskii, V. 'O netoroplivosti i neskhodstve udach', *Voprosy kinoiskusstva*, no. 9 (1966), pp. 291–4.

Shumiatskii, B. Z. ' "Ochen' sil'no i kul'turno skomponovannaia veshch …": O chem dumal i govoril tov. Stalin pri prosmotre otechestvennykh kinofil'mov', *Rodina*, no. 9 (1995), pp. 89–92.

Shvachko, Oleksii F. '"Dozvol'te zniaty fil'm"', *Druh chytacha* (Kiev), 9 September 1969, pp. 5–6.

—— *Rozpovidi pro suchasnykiv*. Kiev, 1983.

Siegelbaum, Lewis H. *Soviet State and Society Between Revolutions*. New York, 1992.

—— and Andrei Sokolov, eds, *Stalinism as a Way of Life: A Narrative in Documents*. New Haven and London, 2000.

Silnitsky, Frantisek. 'Lenin i Borot'bisty', *Novyi zhurnal*, no. 118 (1975), pp. 228–35.

—— *Natsional'na politika KPSS v period ot 1917 po 1922 god*. Munich, 1978.

'60-letie so dnia rozhdeniia i 30-letie tvorcheskoi deiatel'nosti A. P. Dovzhenko', *Sovetskii film*, no. 5 (1955), p. 2.

Skliarova, M. A. 'Dvi zustrichi: Rozpovid pershoi aktrysy iaku znimav velykyi mytets' ', *Kul'tura i zhyttia*, 27 August 1989, p. 3.

Skuratovskii, Vadim. 'Vgliad na mir s vysota Absoliuta', *Vseukrainskie vedomosti*, 10 September 1994, pp. 8–9.

Smolych, Iurii. *Rozpovid' pro nespokii*. Kiev, 1968.

Sokolov, Ippolit. 'Zemlia', *Kino* (M), 10 April 1930, pp. 4–5.

Solntseva, Iuliia. 'Poslednii den' Aleksandra Dovzhenko', *Dnipro*, no. 9–10 (1994), pp. 78–93.

Solntseva, Iu. I. and L. M. Novychenko, eds. *Polum'iane zhyttia: Spohady pro Oleksandra Dovzhenka*. Kiev, 1973.

Solov'ev, V. 'My uchilis' u Dovzhenko', *Voprosy kinoiskusstva*, no. 9 (1966), pp. 312–17.

Soroka, Ivan. 'Hohol' u Sosnytsi', *Dnipro*, no. 5 (1964), pp. 129–31.

Sosiura, Volodymyr. *Tretia rota: roman*. 2nd ed., Kiev, 1997.

'Sostavy orgbiuro Tsentral'nogo komiteta Kommunisticheskoi partii', *Politicheskoe obrazovanie*, no. 14 (1988), pp. 88–90.

'*Spilka Vyzvolennia Ukrainy*'. *Stenohrafichnyi zvit sudovoho protsesu*. Kharkiv, 1931. 2 vols.

[Stalin, I. V.?] 'Ob antileninskikh oshibkakh i natsionalisticheskikh izvrashcheniiakh v kinopovesti Dovzhenko "Ukraina v ogne"', *Iskusstvo kino*, no. 4 (1990), pp. 84–96.

'Stalin i kino', *Iskusstvo kino*, no. 3 (1993), pp. 100–2.

Stepanyshyn, Borys. 'Triumf i kaskad trahedii: Do 100-richchia z dnia narodzhennia O. Dovzhenka', *Kul'tura i zhyttia*, no. 29 (13 August 1994).

Stephan, John J. *The Russian Far East: A History*. Stanford, CA, 1994.

Stokes, Gale. 'Cognition and the Function of Nationalism', *Journal of Interdisciplinary History*, 4, no. 4 (1974), pp. 543–70.

Strauss, Leo. *Persecution and the Art of Writing*. Chicago and London, 1988.

Stroeva, A. 'Hliadach vymahaie', *Radians'ka Ukraina*, 1 December 1959, p. 3.

Subtelny, Orest. *Ukraine: A History*. Toronto and Buffalo, 1991.

Sudaplatov, Pavel and Anatoli Sudaplatov. *Special Tasks: The Memoirs of an Unwanted Witness – A Soviet Spymaster*. Boston and New York, 1994.

Suny, Ronald Grigor. *The Soviet Experiment: Russia, the USSR, and the Successor States*. New York and Oxford, 1998.

Svashenko, Semen. 'Khudozhnyk, grazhdanin, chelovek', *Sovetskii ekran*, no. 17 (1964).

——. 'Kliuch k chelovecheskoi dushe', *Sovetskii ekran*, no. 17 (1964), p. 12.

——. 'Priglashenie', in Olga Nesterovich, compiler, *Zhizn' v kino: Veterany o sebe i svoikh tovarishchakh* (Moscow, 1971), vyp. 1, pp. 352–63.

Sydorenko, O. I. and D. V. Tabachnyk. *Represovane 'vidrodzhennia'*. Kiev, 1993.

Szporluk, Roman. *Communism and Nationalism: Karl Marx versus Friedrich List*. New York and Oxford, 1988.

——. *Russia, Ukraine, and the Breakup of the Soviet Union*. Stanford, CA, 2000.

——. 'Ukraine: From an Imperial Periphery to a Sovereign State', *Daedalus*, 126, no. 3 (1997), pp. 85–119.

Taran, F. T. 'Z pytan' pro fil'm "Ivan" O. Dovzhenka', *Kino* (K), no. 19–20 (1932).

Tarasenko, B. N. and G. M. Kapel'gorodskaia, eds. *Uroki Aleksandra Dovzhenko: Sbornik statei*. Kiev, 1982.

Taubman, William, Sergei Khrushchev and Abbot Gleason, eds. *Nikita Khrushchev*. New Haven and London, 2000.

Tauger, Mark B. 'The 1932 Harvest and the Famine of 1933', *Slavic Review*, 50, no. 1 (1991), pp. 70–89.

Taylor, Richard. *Film Propaganda: Soviet Russia and Nazi Germany*. London and New York, 1998.

——. and Ian Christie, eds. *Inside the Film Factory: New Approaches to Russian and Soviet Cinema*. London and New York, 1991.

——. *The Film Factory: Russian and Soviet Cinema in Documents 1896–1939*. Cambridge, MA, 1988.

———. and Derek Spring, eds. *Stalinism and Soviet Cinema*. London and New York, 1993.

———. Nancy Wood, Julian Graffy and Dina Iordanova, eds. *The BFI Companion to Eastern European and Russian Cinema*. London, 2000.

Taylor, Shelley E. *Positive Illusions: Creative Self-Deception and the Healthy Mind*. New York, 1989.

Tertz, Abram [Andrei Siniavsky]. *The Trial Begins and On Socialist Realism*. New York, 1960.

'III komunistychnyi Internatsional pro borotbistiv', *Borot'ba*, 3 March 1920, p. 1.

Thompson, Kristin. 'Government Policies and Practical Necessities in the Soviet Cinema of the 1920s', in Anna Lawton, ed., *The Red Screen: Politics, Society, and Art in Soviet Cinema* (London and New York, 1992), pp. 19–41.

———. '*Ivan the Terrible* and Stalinist Russia: A Reexamination', *Cinema Journal* (1977), pp. 30–43.

Thurston, Robert. *Life and Terror in Stalin's Russia, 1934–1941*. New Haven and London, 1996.

Tolchenova, N. *Iuliia Solntseva*. Moscow, 1979.

Trankvillitskii, Iurii. 'Aleksandr Dovzhenko: "Ia ne snial' ni odnoi svoei kartiny"', *Rodina*, no. 11 (1990), pp. 56–7.

Troianovskii, Vitalii. *Kinematograf ottepli*. Moscow, 1996.

Troinitskii, N. A., ed. *Pervaia Vseobshchaia perepis' naseleniia Rossiiskoi imperii, 1897 g.* St Petersburg, 1902–1905. Vols 8, 13, 16, 32, 33, 41, 46, 47, 48.

Troshin, A. S. ' "Zemlia" i my. Priglashenie k razgovoru', *KZ*, no. 23 (1994), pp. 103–7.

Trymbach, Serhii. 'Dovzhenko: Chervone i chorne', *Kul'tura i zhyttia*, no. 36–7 (11 September 1993), p. 5.

———. 'Dovzhenko i Khvylovyi', *Dnipro*, no. 9–10 (1994), pp. 45–9.

———. ' "Ia khochu zhyty na Vkraini": Do 100–richchia z dnia narodzhennia O. P. Dovzhenka', *Kul'tura i zhyttia*, no. 24 (July 9, 1994).

———. 'Kinorezhisser, pisatel', publitsist: 10 cent.–100 let so dnia rozhdeniia A. P. Dovzhenko', *Donbass*, 9 September 1994.

———. 'Pochva i sud'ba', *Iskusstvo kino*, no. 12 (1994), pp. 106–8.

———. ' "Roztlinna zemlia" Oleksandra Dovzhenka', *Kul'tura i zhyttia*, no. 30 (24 July 1996).

———. ' "Zvenigora", "Arsenal", "Zemlia": Obraz messii', *KZ*, 23 (9 July 1994), pp. 129–37.

Tsivian, Yuri. *Early Cinema in Russia and Its Cultural Reception*. London and New York, 1994; Chicago, 1998.

———. *Testimoni silenziosi: film rusi, 1908–1919*. Pordenone, Italy, 1989.

TsSU SSSR, otdel perepisi. *Vsesoiuznaia perepis' naseleniia 1926 goda*. Moscow, 1929–31. Vols 11, 12, 13, 28, 29, 30.

Tsybul'nyk, Sulamif. 'Pershi uroky', *Dnipro*, no. 9–10 (1994), pp. 63–7.

Turchyk, S. 'Dushevnoi krasy liudyna', *Za radians'kyi film*, 28 January 1958.

Turovskaya, Maya. 'The Tastes of Soviet Moviegoers During the 1930s', in Thomas Lahusen with Gene Kuperman, eds, *Late Soviet Culture: From Perestroika to Novostroika* (Durham, NC and London, 1993), pp. 95–107.

Tymoshenko, Borys, compiler. *Druhyi zumovyi pokid: Lystopadovyi reid/Bazar*. Kiev, 1995.

'U.K.P. (b) znykla – khai zhyve komunizm', *Borot'ba*, 31 March 1920, p. 1.

Ukraine: A Concise Encyclopedia. Toronto, 1963. 2 vols.

'Ukrainskii "Chapaev"', *Pravda*, 5 March 1935, p. 6.

Ukraintsi: Skhidna diaspora: Atlas. Kiev, 1993.

'U.S. Embassy Aide Quits in Moscow', *New York Times*, 28 February 1948, p. 3:8.

'V itoge disputov', *Kino-front*, 11 April 1930, p. 2.

Vaisfel'd, Illia. 'Shche pro nevycherpnoho Dovzhenka', *Novyny kinoekrana*, no. 9 (1988), pp. 4–5.

Valuiev, Iurii. 'Oleksandr Dovzhenko: "Oi, zemle ridna, maty moia i moia pechal'. Pryimy mene khoch mertvoho"', *Visti z Ukrainy*, no. 6 (1994), p. 10.

'Velikii russkii narod', *Pravda*, 26 May 1945.

'Velykomy rosiis'komu narodovi', *Literaturna hazeta*, 4 July 1945, p. 1.

Verdiian, I. 'Strana rodnaia', *Sovetskaia kul'tura*, 6 October 1983.

Vertov, Dziga. 'Avtobiografiia', *Iskusstvo kino*, no. 11 (1987), pp. 45–8.

——. 'Kinoki. Perevorot', *LEF*, no. 3 (1923), pp. 135–43.

Veryha, Vasyl'. *Lystopadovyi reid*. Kiev, 1995.

Vinhranovs'kyi, Mykola. 'Holos talantu, muzhnosti i liubovi', *Holos Ukrainy*, 10 September 1994, p. 8.

——. 'Rik z Dovzhenkom', *Kul'tura i zhyttia*, 27 August 1994, p. 3.

Vishnevskii, Vsevolod. *Stat'i, dnevniki, pis'ma o literature i iskusstve*. Moscow, 1961.

Volyns'kyi, Kost'. 'Dovha tin' "Kremlivs'koho rozp'iattia"', *Literaturna Ukraina*, 16 April 1992, p. 5.

Vovchyk-Blakytna, Lidiia. 'Tovarysh Vasyl' i Sashko', *Vitchyzna*, no. 1 (1984), pp. 163–5.

Vsesoiuznyi gosudarstvennyi fond kinofil'mov. *Sovetskie khudozhestvennye fil'my: Annotirovanyi katalog*. Moscow, 1961. 2 vols.

Walker, Barbara. 'On Reading Soviet Memoirs: A History of the "Contemporaries" Genre as an Institution of Russian Intelligentsia Culture from the 1790s to the 1970s', *Russian Review*, 59, no. 2 (2000), pp. 327–52.

Wandycz, Piotr. *Polish–Soviet Relations, 1917–1921*. Cambridge, MA, 1969.

Weiner, Amir. 'The Making of a Dominant Myth: The Second World War and the Construction of Political Identities within the Soviet Polity', *Russian Review*, 55, no. 3 (1996), pp. 638–60.

Weisz, John R., Fred M. Rothbaum and Thomas C. Blackburn. 'Standing Out and Standing In: The Psychology of Control in America and Japan', *American Psychologist* (September 1984), pp. 955–69.

Woll, Josephine. *Real Images: Soviet Cinema and the Thaw*. London and New York, 2000.

Youngblood, Denise. *Movies for the Masses: Popular Cinema and Soviet Society in the 1920s*. Cambridge and New York, 1992.

——. *Soviet Cinema in the Silent Era, 1918–1935*. Ann Arbor, MI, 1985.

——. *The Magic Mirror: Moviemaking in Russia, 1908–1918*. Madison, WI, 1999.

'... Z poroha smerti ...': Pys'mennyky
   Ukrainy – zhertvy stalins'kykh represii.
   Kiev, 1991.
'Za vysoku bil'shovyts'ku ideinist' v
   literature i mystetstvi', Literatura i
   mystetstvo (Kiev), 21 March 1944, p. 1.
Zahrebel'nyi, Pavlo. Nelozhnymy ustamy:
   Statti, ese, portrety. Kiev, 1981.
Zasenko, Oleksa. Dorohi moi suchasnyky.
   Kiev, 1983.
Zemlianukhin, Sergei and Miroslava
   Segida, compilers. Domashnaia
   sinemateka: Otechestvennoe kino,
   1918–1996. Moscow, 1996.
Zemskov, V. I. 'K voprosu o repatriatsii
   sovetskikh grazhdan 1944–1951 gody',
   Istoriia SSSR, no. 4 (1990).
Zhukova, Alla. 'Chas poshukiv (Nove pro

pochatok tvorchoi roboty O. Dovzhenka
   v kino)', Dnipro, no. 9–10 (1994),
   pp. 56–7.
Zhulyns'kyi, Mykola. 'Pechal' dyshi i
   sviatist' bosonosnoho dytynstva', Holos
   Ukrainy, 14 September 1994, pp. 4–5.
Zhurov, Heorhii Viktorovych. Kievs'ka
   kinostudiia imeni O. Dovzhenka: Narys.
   Kiev, 1962.
———. 'Oleksandr Dovzhenko – dyplomat',
   Vsesvit, no. 5 (1988), pp. 159–61.
'Zhyttia partii', Borot'ba, 31 March 1920,
   p. 2.
Zolotoverkhova, I. I. Ukrains'kyi radians'kyi
   kinoplakat 20–30-kh rokiv. Kiev, 1983.
———. and H. Konovalov. Dovzhenko –
   khudozhnyk. Kiev, 1968.

Index

Films and other works indexed by title are by Dovzhenko unless otherwise indicated; italicised page numbers denote illustrations; those in bold indicate detailed analysis; *n* = endnote (indexed only for background information, not citations)